3-23-60

PIONEER
PEASANT COLONIZATION
IN CEYLON

PIONEER
PEASANT COLONIZATION
IN CEYLON

A STUDY IN ASIAN AGRARIAN PROBLEMS

BY

B. H. FARMER

Fellow of St. John's College, Cambridge and
University Lecturer in Geography

WITH A FOREWORD BY

LORD SOULBURY

Issued under the auspices of the
Royal Institute of International Affairs

OXFORD UNIVERSITY PRESS

LONDON NEW YORK TORONTO

1957

Oxford University Press, Amen House, London E.C.4

GLASGOW NEW YORK TORONTO MELBOURNE WELLINGTON
BOMBAY CALCUTTA MADRAS KARACHI
CAPE TOWN IBADAN NAIROBI ACCRA SINGAPORE

PRINTED IN GREAT BRITAIN
AT THE UNIVERSITY PRESS, OXFORD
BY CHARLES BATEY, PRINTER TO THE UNIVERSITY

FOREWORD

S o far as can be foreseen, the economic and social future of the people of Ceylon will depend primarily upon the development of agriculture, and the production of food—mainly rice—to meet the needs of, and provide employment for, a rapidly increasing population. Moreover, the present heavy importations of rice are a serious strain upon the country's reserve of foreign exchange, and might create a very grave problem in the event of a setback to the principal sources of export, the tea, rubber, and coconut plantations. Some three hundred years ago the retiring Dutch Governor of Ceylon, Ryckloff van Goens, pressed his successor to encourage agriculture, 'in order to do without foreign rice, which consumes most of the money of the inhabitants'. The position is much the same today.

The obvious solution is, of course, to open up more land for cultivation and to apply better methods to the land already culti-vated. Another Dutch Governor wrote a hundred years later: 'If only the Singalese could be induced similarly as in Java and else-where to plant the paddy [rice] instead of only sowing it, they would appreciably contribute to making Ceylon richer in grain.' A large number of Ceylonese cultivators have not yet followed that good advice.

For the past twenty years and more the Government of Ceylon has been strenuously endeavouring to bring more land into use by colonizing, i.e. settling landless peasants upon the undeveloped portion of the island known as the Dry Zone. That area comprises the major part of five of the nine provinces of Ceylon and amounts to about two-thirds of the land surface of the country. Readers of Mr. Farmer's book will appreciate the immense difficulties that have beset this undertaking.

My first sight of the Dry Zone was in January 1945 when I was the Chairman of a Commission on the constitutional reform of Ceylon, and I can still recollect my feelings of astonishment, in-deed almost of horror, at the sudden transition a few miles north of

Kandy from lush and luxurious vegetation to what seemed to be a limitless expanse of arid scrub and secondary jungle. I was at that time on my way to visit the rock fortress of Sigiriya and the ruined cities of Anuradhapura and Polonnaruwa, places which I visited on various occasions later on when I was Governor-General of Ceylon. I wondered then, and I still wonder, what brought about the ruin and abandonment of those cities—vast aggregations of palaces, temples, and dwellings—and of the great reservoirs or tanks, which provided the irrigation required to produce food for a far larger population than exists in that area today.

My guess—and in the absence of records, it can only be a guess —is that the principal factor was malaria. The building of Anuradhapura and Polonnaruwa, the erection of a palace on the summit of the rock of Sigiriya, the construction of tanks thousands of acres in extent, presuppose hardy, virile, healthy, and well-nourished inhabitants, very different from their modern descendants. It may be that as a consequence of successive invasions from South India during the Middle Ages, the irrigation system was destroyed, and resultant swamps caused malaria to become endemic and the population diseased and debilitated. Historians have cited malaria as one of the reasons for the decline of the Roman Empire. At any rate, malaria has for centuries been the scourge of the Dry Zone, and, as Mr. Farmer indicates, has constituted the main obstacle to successful reclamation and colonization of that region.

Mercifully, the advent of DDT towards the close of the last world war has completely changed the situation. Malaria is no longer the menace that it was, and the prospect of developing the Dry Zone is now infinitely better than a decade ago.

It is therefore not unreasonable to hope that what man was once able to do in that Zone, he will be able to do again. But time presses. The civilization that reached its zenith in the reign of the great King Parakramabahu (A.D. 1153–86) had taken over a thousand years to develop. But at the present rate of increase the population of Ceylon will have doubled in two decades. How will it then be fed? If the Dry Zone is to play its part, Ceylon has only a few years in which to repair the ravages of centuries. No one can read Mr. Farmer's brilliant and exhaustive study of the Dry Zone problem without being impressed by its difficulty, gravity, and urgency. The authorities responsible for the programme of colonization will find that Mr. Farmer has given most careful and suggestive consideration to almost every aspect of the task that confronts them. His book will be a very important factor in the saving of time and the avoidance of past errors, and is likely to be the standard work on the subject for many years to come. I am very glad to have had the opportunity of contributing this foreword to it.

SOULBURY

PREFACE

THIS book is primarily about the efforts which the Government of Ceylon has made in recent years to encourage the settlement, in the largely derelict Dry Zone of the Island, of Ceylonese peasants hailing from other and more crowded regions, or from land-hungry villages in settled parts of the Dry Zone. This process of peasant settlement is known in Ceylon, as in the Punjab and elsewhere, as 'colonization', and the specially organized reception area is known as a 'colony'. It will help to avoid ambiguity if I state at the outset that the words 'colonization' and 'colony' will accordingly be used in this book in the connotation which they have in the Dry Zone of Ceylon; and will not, except where it is required by the context, refer to the immigration into Ceylon of people from outside, or to spontaneous movements within the country, or to the political control of the country by an alien power.

The colonization schemes of Ceylon are a noteworthy achievement and hold great promise for the future; they are the result, as this book will try to show, of the efforts of many able hands and minds to overcome truly formidable difficulties. If this book can do anything to make Ceylon's efforts in this direction more widely known, it will have achieved one of its purposes.

The book will not, however, be merely descriptive, still less will it be an uncritical advertisement. The oldest of the colonization schemes in the Dry Zone of Ceylon have only been in operation for some twenty-odd years, and it is not surprising that the colonies as a whole involve many problems whose solutions have not yet been found. This book will therefore be not only a record of achievements, but also a discussion of problems. These problems will, quite naturally, be those which are encountered when the attempt is made to apply current government policies; but the question will be raised whether the problems are then altogether correctly formulated and whether the aims of colonization need redefinition.

Although this book is concerned primarily with experiments in peasant colonization in Ceylon, there will be frequent references to conditions elsewhere and, in particular, to schemes in other countries which are comparable, in one way or another, with the colonies of the Dry Zone. These references will, I hope, have some practical value to Ceylon, where inevitably there is some tendency to insularity of outlook (though I do not overlook the many ways in which ideas have been interchanged between Ceylon and other countries). It is hoped, too, that the comparative nature of the treatment will enhance the interest of the book to those concerned with colonization and settlement elsewhere; from their point of view it may be seen as a case history which contrasts sharply, I hope, with the vague generalizations about Asia and the tropics which are all too current. Possibly the book will interest a still wider circle of readers, those who feel concern over the general problems of living standards in South and South East Asia and in other so-called 'underdeveloped' areas, and over the impact of Western ideas, capital, and technology on Eastern peasant societies.

No attempt will be made, however, to write a full account of colonization in any other territory. There are one or two studies which have been freely drawn on;[1] but by and large material on colonization under conditions comparable to those in Ceylon is scanty and incomplete and does not answer the questions I learnt to ask in Ceylon. Nothing short of field-work in each of the countries concerned would serve to elicit the whole story, and field-work of this sort is assuredly highly desirable.

A book like this might have been arranged in many different ways, and might have had many different points of emphasis; for example, it could have been written solely as the story of the evolution of a policy; or as a study in which the general economic problems of Ceylon were in the forefront and in which the colonies were examined purely in relation to them; or, with a dash of romanticism, as the epic of the peaceful reconquest of their ancestral homeland, the *Rāja Rata* (the King's Country), by the heirs of an ancient and splendid civilization. But I am a geographer by training and profession, and my method bears the imprint of my discipline. In particular, I recognize two kinds of problems susceptible of geographical analysis; problems in 'pure' geography (e.g. the reasons for the individuality of a region) and problems in 'applied' geography (e.g. the reasons for the particular difficulties which beset human activity in a specific regional setting,

---

[1] e.g. K. J. Pelzer, *Pioneer Settlement in the Asiatic Tropics* (New York, Amer. Geog. Soc., 1945), which deals with colonization in Indonesia and the Philippines only.

and consequential practical recommendations). And I look for the answers to both kinds of problem in the action and interaction of a complex of forces, some natural and physical, like climate, soil, and water-supply, some created by man, like techniques of land use, agrarian organization, and social structure. In this book Part I is introductory; it introduces the Dry Zone of Ceylon, the scene of peasant colonization, as a region characterized by past glory and recent difficulty, and attempts to analyse its physical, economic, and social character. (This part of the book might almost be considered an essay in 'pure' geography were it not that it was written with an eye on what would later be said about the practical problems of peasant colonization.) Also in Part I is an introduction to the Wet Zone of Ceylon as a region with an agrarian situation to which an answer or at any rate a partial answer has been sought in Dry Zone colonization. Part II is frankly historical, and describes the evolution of a policy of peasant colonization. Part III, the bulk of the work, is an essay in the application of geographical method which casts its net wide, and seeks under a number of headings the reasons for the successes and failures, the achievements and difficulties of Dry Zone colonization as it is today. It deals with a whole host of interacting forces and situations, and concludes with an assessment of the contribution of peasant colonization to the solution of Ceylon's population problem, and with suggestions for future action and research.

The book, then, is conceived geographically, not only because of its concern with the land as a setting for policy but also because its method of analysis, its ecological approach, involves the study of many different categories of factors in the same way as do problems in 'pure' geography. But I hope that the book is more than an academic study in human geography, and that it will have some practical utility, contributing something to a fuller understanding of Asian agrarian problems in general and of the agrarian problems of Ceylon in particular.

I am well aware that in trying to analyse conditions in the Dry Zone colonies in terms of a wide range of factors, and at the same time, incidentally, to interest a wide range of readers, I touch on much which lies outside my competence. I ask the indulgence of my fellow geographers, some of whom may consider that I have well over-stepped the bounds of our study, and of the specialist who sees his subject maltreated. I am only too conscious of unevenness of treatment and of the danger of solecisms. I am conscious, too, that I may have been too eclectic, and, in seeking to draw in concepts from disparate fields, may have tried to reconcile the irreconcilable. But there is also the opposite danger, of lack of synthesis, particularly as the writing has been spread over a considerable period, during which my own ideas and methods have changed. Of all these faults I am certainly aware.

The method by which the actual research was done may be of some interest. There is a great deal of material about colonization scattered through the pages of Ceylon government publications, and this book aims to gather at least some of them under convenient and, I hope, significant headings. The material and the subject are such, however, that no coherent account, still less a critical analysis designed to serve practical ends, can be constructed without work in the field. Accordingly, having previously had my appetite whetted by a war-time posting, I visited Ceylon from June to December 1951, and spent as much time as possible in a systematic study of the colonies. A pilot survey of Nachchaduwa and nearby colonies gave a method of attack which was used with necessary local modification in other schemes. All the colonies in operation in 1951 were visited, many on several occasions; but although this statement might seem to imply study in great detail, in point of fact much longer would have to be spent to extract the full flavour of each colony, and my study cannot claim to be more than an ecological reconnaissance. In addition to work in the field, I had the privilege of working on unpublished material at government offices, and of many valuable discussions with Ministers, officials, colonists, and others.

The book itself has been an unconscionably long time in the writing, for ever since I returned to Cambridge from Ceylon in January 1952 there has been a heavy burden of teaching and administration which could not conscientiously be shifted on to colleagues to make room for authorship. I am most grateful to Chatham House, and in particular to its Research Secretary, Miss Margaret Cleeve, O.B.E., for calmly and patiently bearing with each successive postponement of completion date. Delay has had its compensations, however, for I have been able to take into the reckoning a number of changes of policy and a number of important events which have taken place since December 1951, though, clearly, I have not been able to see their imprint in the field.

Something should perhaps be said about the problem of transliterating Sinhalese and Tamil words. For place-names I have followed, for general convenience, the excellent one-inch maps of the Ceylon Survey Department, even though they sometimes transgress current canons of orthography. For other words, I have sought the guidance of Dr. E. R. Leach (for Sinhalese words) and of Mr. M. Y. Banks (for Tamil words), though I have been stubborn enough not always to accept their advice. I am very grateful to both of them. In some cases in which there is a familiar but incorrect transliteration of a word, I have shown it as well.

A few words in this Preface should, perhaps, be specially addressed to the Ceylon reader. In this study I have attempted to be fair, and to be critical, in the best and most constructive sense of the word, in my analysis of the ways in which government policy appears to act on the colonies. You may feel that in doing this I have stressed problems rather than achievements, and that the romance of the reoccupation of *Rāja Rata* has been lost in the process. This may well be true. But there are not lacking those who will tell you that all is well in the colonies, and abler pens than mine can portray the romance. I stress difficulties and problems because I believe that good can come from free discussion of them. My only fear is that I may inadvertently have provided ammunition for ill-informed and purely destructive critics. If any such are tempted to take any of my statements out of their context, I ask them very earnestly to think again, and above all to take my arguments, and those I quote, as a whole. I have tried to arrive at balanced conclusions and to be objective. I cannot, of course, claim to be completely objective, for, amongst other things, I am a Westerner writing about the East from a standpoint which I adopt because of the intellectual climate in which I was brought up and in which I still live. There may, then, be things that I have misunderstood; but at least I have no axe to grind in Ceylon affairs. If my wish for my book is that it will, outside Ceylon, deepen interest in Ceylon affairs, then I hope that in Ceylon it will, if only by its defects and omissions, draw attention to matters on which research is needed.

One other thing ought to be said for Ceylonese ears. When this book was very nearly finished, I was invited by your Government to serve on a Commission to investigate land policy. I should like to make it quite clear that the book was finished before I sat as a Commissioner, and that in consequence no evidence that came my way as a Commissioner finds a place in this book (though I have used the opportunity of a further visit to Ceylon to correct one or two errors of fact); nor is our Report necessarily foreshadowed.

Finally, my thanks are due to those persons and organizations who made this work possible. I could not have undertaken work in Ceylon but for generous grants from the Royal Institute of International Affairs, the Leverhulme Trustees, and the Royal Geographical Society; and but for leave of absence from my College and University. The amount of help, encouragement, and hospitality which I received in Ceylon, from Ministers, civil servants, F.A.O. experts, field officers of various departments, and from colonists, peasants, and other private individuals, makes it quite impossible to mention all these persons by name. Indeed, Ceylonese help began far from Ceylon, with the High Commissioner and his staff in London and with Ceylonese students and visitors at Cambridge.

I am indebted to the Surveyor-General, Ceylon, for permission to reproduce Maps 7, 8, and 12 (which are based on the maps of his Department); to the Royal Geographical Society for permission to reprint Plates 3, 5, 6, 19, and 22 (which have already appeared in the *Geographical Journal*); and to Messrs. George Philip and Son for permission to publish Map 4.

I wish also to thank a number of people who very kindly agreed to comment upon portions of my manuscript: Mr. W. T. I. Alagaratnam, Mr. S. F. Amerasinghe, Mr. R. L. Brohier, Mr. D. B. Ellepola, Mr. D. T. E. A. de Fonseka, Mr. A. T. Grove, Mr. N. U. Jayawardena, Dr. A. W. R. Joachim, Mr. K. Kanagasundram, Dr. E. R. Leach, Mr. S. A. Pakeman, Mr. M. Rajendra, Mr. C. T. Smith, Mr. M. Srikhanta, Professor J. A. Steers, and Mr. S. J. Tambiah. Although, wherever possible, I gave effect to their comments, the opinions finally expressed are, of course, my own. I am also very grateful to the Gal Oya Development Board for permission to quote from certain of their memoranda. The burden of typing and retyping the manuscript has been nobly undertaken by Miss J. M. Swann and Miss M. J. Clark, of the Cambridge Department of Geography, and by my wife (who also helped with the index). I gratefully record the help and encouragement which, at all stages, I have received from the Research

Secretary and the Staff at Chatham House, particularly from Miss Hermia Oliver, who skilfully prepared the manuscript for the press and cheerfully shouldered extra burdens created by my absence from England. And, last but by no means least, I am greatly indebted to Lord Soulbury for writing a Foreword.

B. H. FARMER

Colombo, Ceylon
1 June 1956

CONTENTS

TABLES

MAPS

ILLUSTRATIONS

(*All photographs by the author*)

ABBREVIATIONS[1]

Admin. Reports: Agriculture	*Administration Reports of the Director of Agriculture.*
Admin. Reports: Co-operative Societies	*Administration Reports on the Working of Co-operative Societies.*
Admin. Reports: Eastern Province	*Administration Reports of the Government Agent, Eastern Province.*
Admin. Reports: Forests	*Administration Reports of the Conservator of Forests.*
Admin. Reports: Medical	*Administration Reports of the Director of Medical and Sanitary Services.*
Admin. Reports: North-Central Province	*Administration Reports of the Government Agent, North-Central Province.*
Admin. Reports: Rural Development	*Administration Reports of the Director of Rural Development.*
ARDLD	*Administration Reports of the Director of Land Development.*
ARLC	*Administration Reports of the Land Commissioner.*
B.O.P.	Blocking-out Plan.
C.A.P.S.	Co-operative Agricultural Production and Sales.
Census of Ceylon, 1946	Dept. of Census and Statistics, *Census of Ceylon, 1946*: vol. i, pt. 1, *General Report*, by A. G. Ranasinha; pt. 2, *Statistical Digest*.
Cmd. 3132 and RCAI, iii	Royal Commission on Agriculture in India, *Report*, Cmd. 3132 (1928) and *Minutes of Evidence*, vol. iii.
Cook	E. K. Cook, *A Geography of Ceylon*; revised by K. Kularatnam under the title *Ceylon: its Geography, its Resources and its People*. Madras, Macmillan, 1951.
Co-operative Societies in Burma	*Reports on the Working of Co-operative Societies in Burma*. Rangoon, Supt. of Govt. Printing, 1915–41.
CUCL	*Report of the Committee on Utilization of Crown Lands*, S.P. 3 of 1953.
DSC	*Debates of the State Council of Ceylon.*
D.R.O.	Divisional Revenue Officer.
Economic and Social Development	Ceylon, Ministry of Finance, *Economic and Social Development of Ceylon, 1926–50; a Survey*. Ceylon, Govt. Press, 1951.

[1] This list does not include commonly used abbreviations of periodicals.

Fisher and Steel	C. A. Fisher and R. W. Steel, eds., *Geographical Essays on British Tropical Lands*. London, Philip, 1956.
Food Supply Committee	*Report of the Committee appointed to consider what measures should be adopted to make Ceylon self-supporting in regard to its Food Supply*, S.P. 2 of 1920.
GODB	Gal Oya Development Board.
Ievers	R. W. Ievers, *Manual of the North-Central Province of Ceylon*. Colombo, Govt. Printer, 1899.
INCIDI, *Rural Development*	Institut International des Civilisations Différentes, *Programmes and Plans for Rural Development in Tropical and Sub-Tropical Countries; Record of the 28th Session held in The Hague in September 1953*.
IPR	Institute of Pacific Relations.
KPC	*Report of the Kandyan Peasantry Commission*, S.P. 18 of 1951.
Land Reform	UN, Dept. of Econ. Affairs, *Land Reform*, New York, 1951.
LC	*Final Report of the Land Commission*, S.P. 18 of 1929.
L.D.O.	Land Development Ordinance, No. 19 of 1935.
Minneriya Irrigation Scheme Committee	Report of the Committee appointed to work out a Plan for the Development of Lands under the Minneriya Irrigation Scheme in the North-Central Province, S.P. 14 of 1932.
Prelim. Rep. Econ. Survey Rural Ceylon	*Preliminary Report on the Economic Survey of Rural Ceylon, 1950*, S.P. 11 of 1951.
RCAI, iii	See Cmd. 3132.
Tarai and Bhabar Report	*Report of the Tarai and Bhabar Development Committee* (Allahabad, Supt. of Printing, 1947).
SL	*Report on Survey of Landlessness*, S.P. 13 of 1952.
S.P.	(Ceylon) Sessional Paper (all published by the Govt. Press, Colombo).
Spate	O. H. K. Spate, *India and Pakistan*. London, Methuen, 1952.
Tennent	James Emerson Tennent, *Ceylon*. London, Longmans, 1859.
Unemployment Census	'Unemployment Census', *Ceylon Government Gazette*, no. 10083, 11 March 1951.
V.E.	Village Expansion.
Village Survey: Chilaw	'Report on the Economic Survey of Five Villages in Chilaw District', Min. of Labour, Industry and Commerce, *Bulletin*, no. 7, 1937.

Village Survey: Galle	'Report on the Economic Survey of Nine Villages in Galle District', ibid., no. 11, 1949.
Village Survey: Hambantota	'Report on the Economic Survey of Five Villages in Hambantota District', ibid., no. 13, 1949.
Village Survey: Kalutara	'Report on the Economic Survey of Five Villages in Kalutara District', ibid., no. 6, 1937.
Village Survey: Rayigam	'Report on the Economic Survey of Seven Villages in Rayigam Korale of Kalutara District', ibid., no. 5, 1937.
Village Survey: Kurunegala	'Report on the Economic Survey of Kurunegala District', ibid., no. 10, 1949.
Village Survey: Matale	'Report on the Economic Survey of Six Villages in the Matale District', ibid., no. 9, 1940.
Village Survey: Matara	'Report on the Economic Survey of Six Villages in Matara District', ibid., no. 12, 1949.
Village Survey: Puttalam	'Report on the Economic Survey of Five Villages in Puttalam District', ibid., no. 8, 1939.
Ward	*Speeches and Minutes of the late Sir Henry George Ward.* Colombo, Govt. Printer, 1864.
WBR	International Bank of Reconstruction and Development (World Bank), *The Economic Development of Ceylon.* Reference *outside* brackets is to edition published at Baltimore, 1953, by the Johns Hopkins Press; reference *inside* brackets is to edition published at Colombo, 1952, by Ceylon Government Press.

NOTE

'Co-operative', 'Co-operation', refer to the officially sponsored Co-operative movement; the corresponding words spelt without a capital initial letter refer to more general cases of the combination of individuals into groups for various purposes.

PART ONE

GEOGRAPHICAL INTRODUCTION

1

Introduction to the Dry Zone

The Dry Zone Defined

THE peasant colonization schemes whose achievements and problems form the subject of this book all lie within the distinctive and fascinating region familiarly known in Ceylon as the 'Dry Zone'; and colonization will, except where otherwise indicated, mean 'Dry Zone colonization'. There is, in fact, only one major peasant colonization scheme outside the Dry Zone; this is in the broken, hilly region of Pasdun Korale East (inland from the west coast town of Kalutara), is very much *sui generis*, because of the terrain in which it is set, and cannot readily be fitted into the pattern of this study; it will, however, receive occasional mention.[1] There are also a few tiny colonies in Galle, Matara, and Kegalla Districts.[2]

The whole Dry Zone occupies about 70 per cent. of the land area of Ceylon. If one draws two lines from the Kandyan town of Matale, one west to the west coast near Chilaw and the other south to the south coast at Tangalla, then, roughly speaking, the Dry Zone covers the whole island north and east of these lines (see Map 2 for these and other place-names). The Zone thus crudely defined includes, however, parts of the hill country in the centre of the island, notably the delightful Uva Basin around Badulla; this 'dry' hill country covers a relatively small area (some 700 square miles) but has its own features and problems, and is not the scene of peasant colonization, which is confined to the lowlands below the 1,000-foot contour. It is therefore to the *lowland* Dry Zone, north and east of the two lines from Matale but below the 1,000-foot contour, that the term 'Dry Zone' will refer throughout this book. This lowland Dry Zone covers over two-thirds of the land area of the island (see Map 1).

---

[1] See the *First Report of the Pasdun Korale East Colonization Scheme*, S.P. 37 of 1930, and *ARLC* from 1931 onwards.

[2] The hierarchy of administrative units in Ceylon is, in descending order, Province, District, and Divisional Revenue Officer's (D.R.O.'s) Division.

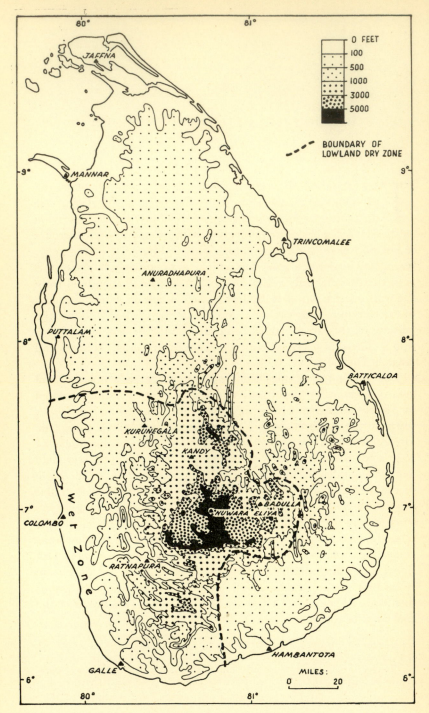

O FEET
100
500
1000
3000
5000

BOUNDARY OF
LOWLAND DRY ZONE

JAFFNA

MANNAR

TRINCOMALEE

ANURADHAPURA

PUTTALAM

BATTICALOA

KURUNEGALA

KANDY

COLOMBO

Wet Zone

NUWARA ELIYA

BADULLA

RATNAPURA

HAMBANTOTA

GALLE

MILES:
0   20

MAP 1. Ceylon: Relief.

Similarly, the 'Wet Zone' may be defined, very roughly, as the south-west quadrant of the island, lying between the two lines from Matale; it too has its lowland and upland segments.

The boundaries of the Dry Zone here adopted are, of course, very rough and ready. Many attempts have been made to define them more precisely, for example in terms of the 75-inch annual isohyet (see Map 3), or of the 20-inch isohyet for the five south-west monsoon months. The latter line approximates more closely to the boundary of the Dry Zone as visible on the ground. Theoretically, P. G. Cooray's definition of the Zone as the area where soil moisture falls below wilting-point for at least two months in the average year is even better;[1] but, although the method used by Cooray may eventually have wide practical applications and, with work on similar lines, serves to draw attention to some of the climatic handicaps of the Dry Zone, lack of observed values makes the drawing of his line something of an academic exercise.[2] Indeed, the same might be said of any attempt to define the Dry Zone precisely in terms of isopleths of climatic values.

The important point, at least from the practical point of view of the present study, is that the Dry Zone is a most distinctive region sharply distinguished from the Wet Zone; it will be the main function of the two following chapters to analyse the reasons for its distinctiveness, especially in their practical implications.

Although there is marked internal differentiation within the Dry Zone, this is nowhere as sharp or, indeed, as spectacular as the almost literally sudden change from Wet Zone to Dry Zone which strikes even the most unobservant traveller as he moves north from Chilaw on the coast road from Colombo to Puttalam, or north-east from Kurunegala on the way from Colombo to Trincomalee, or, perhaps most suddenly of all, immediately east of Tangalla on the south coast of the island.[3] A similar sharp change is also encountered surprisingly close to the hill capital of Kandy, which epitomizes the popular conception of a verdant beauty spot in the humid tropics. Everywhere the transition from Wet Zone to Dry Zone takes the form of a change from dense settlement and a mainly cultivated landscape to sparse settlement set in great tracts

[1] P. G. Cooray, 'Effective Rainfall and Moisture Zones in Ceylon', *Bull. Cey. Geog. Soc.*, vol. iii (1948–9), pp. 39–42.
[2] See, for example, B. H. Farmer, 'Rainfall and Water Supply in the Dry Zone of Ceylon', in Fisher and Steel.
[3] See Cook, pp. 315–50, and Farmer, 'Ceylon', in Spate.

of jungle, or less often in the scrub or poor grass to which man has reduced the jungle. During the Dry Zone's dry season (from May to September) the contrast is emphasized by a difference in colour between the greens of the Wet Zone and the browns or brown-greens of the Dry Zone; the latter are shown up rather than mitigated by the tender light green of the young paddy in the occasional villages or colonies.

The General Desolation of the Dry Zone in Modern Times

When Portuguese, Dutch, and British travellers first visited the Dry Zone there were only two sizable areas with anything approaching a high density of population. The first of these was the Jaffna region in the far north, peopled by Ceylon Tamils (descendants of immigrants who long ago had come over from South India and, probably, displaced an earlier Sinhalese population; *recent* Tamil immigrants, mainly estate workers, are known in Ceylon as 'Indian Tamils'). The Dutch made Jaffna a principal port and fortress. Already, in their day, the Jaffna Peninsula and Islands were so densely settled that there was talk of moving people to the Wanni, the jungle-covered region immediately south of the lagoon that separates the Peninsula from the mainland. Thus among points which a Governor-General and Council of India instructed the Governor of Ceylon to observe were these:

That measures should be taken to bring about an increase in the population of the Wannias, situated between Manaar and Pooneryn, which is at present scantily peopled.

That this object may be attained if some of the superfluous population of Jaffnapatam were diverted to the lands of Pooneryn. Orders must be issued in course of time with this object.

That some wells and tanks must be made in this district, as these would greatly improve the fertility of the soil, and tend to the relief of Jaffnapatam, which is thickly populated. On account of the fertility of the soil, the affection of the people for the place of their birth, and their long residence there, they cannot easily be moved, though the lands do not yield a sufficiency to provide for them all.[1]

The schemes of the Dutch came to nought, however, and the accounts of later travellers testify that the densely settled Peninsula

---

[1] *Instructions from the Governor-General and Council of India to the Governor of Ceylon, 1656 to 1665*, trans. Sophia Peters (Colombo, Govt. Printer, 1908), p. 12.

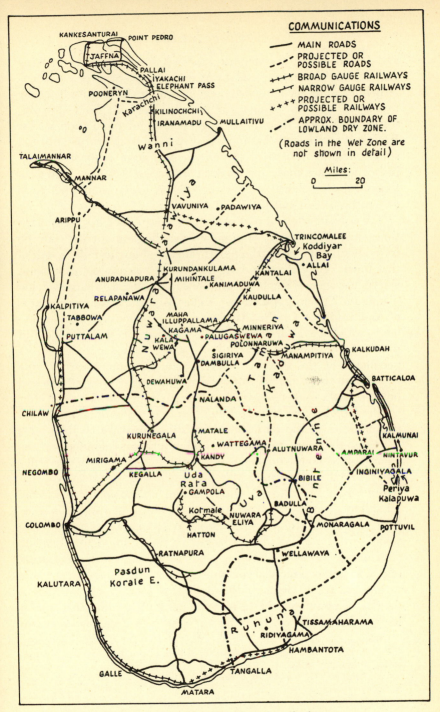

COMMUNICATIONS

———	MAIN ROADS
- - - -	PROJECTED OR POSSIBLE ROADS
+++++	BROAD GAUGE RAILWAYS
+++++	NARROW GAUGE RAILWAYS
× × × ×	PROJECTED OR POSSIBLE RAILWAYS
—·—·—	APPROX. BOUNDARY OF LOWLAND DRY ZONE.

(Roads in the Wet Zone are not shown in detail)

Miles:
0   20

KANKESANTURAI   POINT PEDRO
JAFFNA
PALLAI
IYAKACHI
ELEPHANT PASS
POONERYN
Karachchi
KILINOCHCHI
IRANAMADU
MULLAITIVU
TALAIMANNAR
Wanni
MANNAR
Kalawiya
ARIPPU
VAVUNIYA   PADAWIYA
TRINCOMALEE
Koddiyar Bay
KURUNDANKULAMA   KANTALAI   ALLAI
ANURADHAPURA   MIHINTALE
RELAPANAWA   KANIMADUWA
Nuwara   KAUDULLA
KALPITIYA
TABBOWA   MAHA
ILLUPPALLAMA   MINNERIYA
PUTTALAM   KAGAMA
KALA   PALUGASWEWA
WEWA   POLONNARUWA
SIGIRIYA   MANAMPITIYA
DAMBULLA   Tamankaduwa   KALKUDAH
DEWAHUWA
NALANDA   BATTICALOA
CHILAW
MATALE   Bintenne
KURUNEGALA   WATTEGAMA
MIRIGAMA   ALUTNUWARA   KALMUNAI
KANDY   AMPARAI   NINTAVUR
NEGOMBO   KEGALLA   INGINIYAGALA
Uda   BIBILE   Periya
Rata   Kalapuwa
GAMPOLA
COLOMBO   Kotmale   Uva
NUWARA   BADULLA
ELIYA
HATTON   MONARAGALA   POTTUVIL
RATNAPURA   WELLAWAYA
KALUTARA   Pasdun
Korale E.
Ruhuna   TISSAMAHARAMA
RIDIYAGAMA
HAMBANTOTA
GALLE   TANGALLA
MATARA

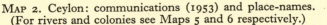

MAP 2. Ceylon: communications (1953) and place-names.
(For rivers and colonies see Maps 5 and 6 respectively.)

and Islands have, throughout modern times, stood in striking contrast to the emptiness of the Wanni. Tennent gives a particularly interesting account of the region as it was in the middle of the nineteenth century.[1] Census returns are available from 1871 onwards, and show that the average density of population in the Peninsula and Islands has increased steadily from 651 persons per square mile in 1871 to 1,151 per square mile in 1946. Densities, in fact, approach those of crowded parts of the Wet Zone, and even those of the hopelessly overcrowded deltaic lowlands of other parts of Southern Asia and the Far East.

The only other major part of the Dry Zone which has, in modern times, had a fair density of population is the strip of coast running from about 20 miles north of Batticaloa to about 40 miles south of that town. Here a sandy bar, Tennent's 'narrow embankment', shields a system of lagoons from the sea and carries a large Ceylon Tamil and 'Moor' population.[2] (The 'Moors' are the descendants of Arab traders.) On the island side of the lagoons are deltaic lowlands which have long carried a great tract of paddy fields and provided the staple food required by the coastal population. A peculiarity is the sparsity of permanent settlement west of the lagoons; the great majority of cultivators live in coastal villages and only cross the lagoons to work seasonally in the fields.

The Dutch at one time had high hopes of exploiting the evident potentialities of the Batticaloa District; a canal which they built increased the paddy revenue fourfold, but the unwillingness of the Company to invest further capital inhibited greater things still.[3] Early British writers were also impressed with the relative prosperity here. 'The villages', said Pridham, '. . . are populous and the inhabitants contented and industrious.' The same assiduous compiler says of Batticaloa town, 'The development of its agricultural wealth will . . . eventually place it in the position to which its advantages entitle it.'[4] Tennent found not only extensive areas of paddy, but commercial coconut estates on the sand-bars.[5]

The coastal divisions of the Batticaloa District had in 1871 a density of population of 54 persons per square mile; this was in itself higher than the density for any other Dry Zone region except

---

[1] Tennent, ii. 517–50. [2] Ibid., p. 456.
[3] P. E. Pieris, *Ceylon and the Hollanders*, 3rd ed. (Colombo, Colombo Apothecaries, 1947), pp. 98–99.
[4] C. Pridham, *Ceylon and its Dependencies* (London, T. & W. Boone, 1849), ii. 562–3. [5] Tennent, ii. 454–62.

Jaffna, but the density on the coastal sand-bars was over 300 per square mile if one assumes that, as in 1931, 80 per cent. of the people lived on them. There were about 550 and 640 persons per square mile on the sand-bars in 1931 and 1946 respectively. Densities have increased steadily from census to census; this has been due almost entirely to natural increase, and has been quite uncharacteristic of the Dry Zone as a whole. The Batticaloa District was, in fact, one of the few regions of the Dry Zone in which the restoration of ancient irrigation works from the 1870's onwards was responsible for a marked increase in the cultivated area and in peasant population.[1]

The topographers of the Dutch and early British periods found only occasional densely populated spots in the Dry Zone outside the Jaffna and Batticaloa regions; these were nearly always forts or trading stations. Their activity served only to emphasize, by contrast, the desolation around them. 'No other than commercial motives could have led to the formation of populous towns in the midst of arid wastes', said Tennent with the example of Mannar before him:[2] and Mannar had, in fact, been a seaport and fortress used successively by Arabs, Portuguese, and Dutch in their efforts to control the passage through the straits between Mannar Island and the mainland of Ceylon; these were in those days a favourite route between the Arabian Sea and Bay of Bengal, so that Mannar then had some of the functions later assumed by Trincomalee. Trincomalee itself was (and still is) likewise a foreign body set down in a wilderness, though behind it thick jungle replaces the thorny, sandy wastes of Mannar. And there were a handful of smaller places, such as Puttalam, famous for its salterns and notorious for its insalubrity;[3] and Koddiyar, on the south side of the bay outside Trincomalee, a considerable port in Dutch days and the scene of that encounter between the frigate *Anne* and a Kandyan *dissawe* (disāva) which led to Robert Knox's enforced sojourn in the Kandyan kingdom (his account of his experiences may well have been read by Defoe and contributed to *Robinson Crusoe*).[4]

[1] See also below, pp. 105–6.
[2] Tennent, ii. 556.
[3] A. Oswald Brodie, 'On the Manufacture of Salt in the Chilaw and Puttalam Districts', *J.R. As. Soc.* (Cey. Br.), no. 3 (1847), pp. 99–108; and 'Notes on the Climate and Salubrity of Puttalam', ibid., pp. 163–74.
[4] Robert Knox, *An Historical Relation of the Island of Ceylon* (London,

Outside the Jaffna Peninsula and Islands and the Batticaloa Coast, and outside a few outposts like Mannar, authors, apart from those writing very recently, unite in painting a picture of desolation and decay. There are, however, relatively few accounts of the interior, apart from Knox's, before the British conquest of the Kandyan kingdom in 1815. Knox gives a number of indications of the emptiness of at least part of the Dry Zone. He determined to escape from the metropolitan highlands of Kandy 'to the northward, that part of the country being least inhabited';[1] and, describing his intended route north of Anuradhapura, says, 'it is two days journey farther through a desolate wilderness before there are any inhabitants'.[2] Dutch comments on the Wanni have already been mentioned.

From the accounts of mid-nineteenth-century British travellers it is clear, however, that, although there was ruin and decay everywhere, there were still local differences in density of population. Thus the ancient division of Nuwarakalawiya, centred on Anuradhapura, was found to contain numerous, jungle-encircled villages grouped mainly around small irrigation tanks and cultivating paddy and *chena* crops.[3] (A *chena* is a patch in the jungle cultivated by the method of shifting cultivation; see below, pp. 47–50. *Chena* is an anglicization of the Sinhalese *hēna*.) Most of the villages were Sinhalese, but there were also some Moors, and, in the north, marching with the Wanni, Tamils. The whole countryside, with its isolated, village-centred patches of cultivation, must have presented much the appearance of medieval England; and, indeed, it wears much the same aspect today, except where there have been colonization schemes or other modern settlements.

Everywhere in Nuwarakalawiya travellers found the ruins of an ancient civilization and of the irrigation works which had formed its material basis: great works, consisting of large tanks and long, cleverly engineered channels, very different from the tiny village tanks which served the miserable surviving population. There are

Richard Chiswell, 1681), and E. F. C. Ludowyk, ed., *Robert Knox in the Kandyan Kingdom* (London, OUP, 1948).

[1] Ludowyk, *Robert Knox*, p. 42.

[2] Ibid., p. 47.

[3] See, for example, Tennent, ii. 602–25; J. Forbes, *Eleven Years in Ceylon* (London, Richard Bentley, 1840), pp. 202–48 and 277–390; and Brodie, 'Topographical and Statistical Account of Nuwarakalawiya', *J.R. As. Soc.* (Cey. Br.), vol. iii (1856–8), pp. 150–79.

many good descriptions of the decayed scene; thus Tennent wrote
of Anuradhapura, the ancient capital:

Here the air is heavy and unwholesome, vegetation is rank, and
malaria broods over the waters as they escape from the broken tanks;
one of which, Abaya-weva, is the oldest in Ceylon. The solitary city
has shrunk into a few scattered huts that scarcely merit the designation
of a village.[1]

Nuwarakalawiya had a population density of only about 21 per
square mile in its 2,800 square miles of territory, according to the
1871 census, although the figure may be too low owing to difficulties of enumeration.[2] Even this figure was higher than for any other
large Dry Zone region, except for the regions of relatively dense
population already discussed and for certain areas bordering on the
Wet Zone. The density had only risen to 29 persons per square
mile by 1931. The small increases which had been recorded in
most decennial periods were due to immigration rather than to
natural increase, and often the local population lost ground. Even
before the 1871 census, observers had commented on the fact that
this was a region of great difficulty. Thus, as early as 1833, Skinner
had pointed out that the population was rapidly decreasing owing
to disease and drought.[3] Matters were made worse by the ill-
advised abolition by the British of the ancient custom of *rājakāriya*
(the performance of a service, such as the repair of irrigation works,
in return for land tenure) and of the village council, or *gansabhā*.
In the absence of these, village communities lacked both the
means and the authority to tend their irrigation works. In the
period 1931–46 population density in Nuwarakalawiya increased,
on the other hand, from 29 to 42 per square mile; colonization
policy and other ameliorating influences were bearing fruit.[4]

The atmosphere of desolation and decay hung even heavier over
most of the remaining regions of the nineteenth-century Dry Zone
than it did over Nuwarakalawiya; Table 1 shows what low densities were recorded for them at the first modern census, compared
with the mean density for the whole island, and also how small,

[1] Tennent, ii. 611. See also R. L. Brohier, *Ancient Irrigation Works in Ceylon*
(Colombo, Ceylon Govt. Press, 1934–5).
[2] Here taken, for convenience, to comprise the three modern *Palātas* of
Nuwaragam, Kalagam, and Hurulu.
[3] Thomas Skinner, *Fifty Years in Ceylon* (London, W. H. Allen, 1891).
Skinner was Commissioner of Public Works and a great road-maker.
[4] There has been a further spectacular increase since 1946.

relatively speaking, were subsequent increases of population in most
of them. The unhealthiness of Puttalam has already found comment; the somewhat higher density for its district, and the growth
in it, is mainly to be accounted for in terms of the somewhat ill-
advised extension of commercial coconut cultivation northward
from the Wet Zone. The wastes of Mannar have also been men-

TABLE I

*Population of Certain Regions in the Dry Zone, 1871,
1931, and 1946*

	Population (density per sq. mile in parentheses)		
	1871	*1931*	*1946*
Puttalam Coast . .	24,551 (29)	35,087 (39)	42,669 (47)
Mannar Coast and Island .	21,063 (21)	25,137 (26)	31,471 (32)
Trincomalee Coast . .	19,449 (19)	37,492*(36)	68,635* (67)
Ruhuna	38,418 (13)	81,900 (28)	118,887 (41)
Bintenne. . . .	32,204 (19)	39,043 (23)	43,592 (25)
Wanni	28,753 (14)	32,413 (16)	36,115 (18)
Tamankaduwa. . .	4,770 (4)	7,907 (7)	12,902 (17)
Ceylon Total . . .	2,400,380 (95)	5,306,871 (210)	6,657,339 (26)

* Increase since previous census mainly due to influx into Trincomalee town.
Sources: G. S. Williams, *Census of the Island of Ceylon, 1871*, vol. i (Colombo,
  Govt. Printer, 1873); L. J. D. Turner, *Report on the Census of Ceylon,
  1931*, vol. i (Colombo, Statistics Office, 1931); and *Census of Ceylon, 1946*,
  vol. i, pt. 1.

tioned. In the mid-nineteenth century Baker ('Baker of the Nile')
wrote of this area: 'Nothing can exceed the desolation of the coast.
. . . For many miles the shore is a barren waste of low sandy ground,
covered for the most part with scrubby thorny jungle, diversified
by glades of stunted herbage.'[1] Later in the century the region had
a singularly bad bill of health, even for the Dry Zone, and maternal
mortality was high; in fact, a decrease in population was recorded
in three out of the six decades between 1871 and 1931.

Similarly, the immediate hinterland of Trincomalee struck early
visitors as almost completely empty. John Davy found only one
solitary field beneath the great tank of Kantalai, and called the
country 'almost desert'.[2] It remained so, in spite of spasmodic

[1] S. W. Baker, *Eight Years' Wanderings in Ceylon* (London, Longmans, 1855),
p. 363.
[2] John Davy, *An Account of the Interior of Ceylon* (London, Longmans, 1821),
p. 392.

growth in Trincomalee town. Ruhuna is the traditional name for the south-east coast region; here there were many ancient works, but, in the early nineteenth-century settlement was almost entirely confined to the western part of the coastal lowlands, between Tangalla and Hambantota. Farther east settlement thinned out, and Tissamaharama, with its mighty decayed works, was still a 'desolate wilderness' in 1871.[1] Farther east still, Panawa Pattu, an area of 470 square miles, had only fourteen villages and 700 people in the 1830's.[2] The nineteenth-century restorations of irrigation works did, however, attract people in fair numbers into the stretch between the Wet Zone boundary and Tissamaharama.

There remain three other regions: Bintenne, roughly the region between the east coast and the hills, which has throughout the modern period had a very bad reputation for poverty and disease (but, it should be noted, had fewer signs of former prosperity than elsewhere):[3] the Wanni of the north which preserved its deserted aspect all through the period under review; and Tamankaduwa, where decay was more striking in the nineteenth century than anywhere else. Here was a region abounding in great ancient works like the tanks of Minneriya, Giritale, and Parakrama Samudra, with their intricate connecting channels, and containing also the ruins of Polonnaruwa, capital after the abandonment of Anuradhapura, and other signs of former greatness such as the exquisite and moving Watadāge at Medirigiriya;[4] yet it carried only four persons per square mile at the census of 1871. This was, it is true, but little lower than the density in many other parts of the Dry Zone whose tabulated mean densities are in any case inflated by the populations of towns and coastal settlements which are essentially alien elements. What is striking, however, is that such a low density should prevail over a region of some 1,190 square miles,

[1] From the diary of T. Steele, quoted by E. B. Denham, *Ceylon at the Census of 1911* (Colombo, Govt. Printer, 1912), p. 88.

[2] From Casie Chitty's *Gazetteer*, quoted by Denham, pp. 90–91.

[3] Bintenne is here used as a *nom de pays*. The name will be found on the modern map in the northern part only of the region here visualized, being restricted to two administrative Divisions, one in Batticaloa District and the other in Badulla District. But it is traditionally applied as far as the Wet Zone boundary near Ratnapura, e.g. in C. H. Collins, 'The Archaeology of the Sabaragamuwa Bintenne', *J.R. As. Soc.* (Cey. Br.), vol. xxxii (1932), pp. 158–84.

[4] This is figured on the current (May 1956) Ceylon 1-rupee stamp. Medirigiriya is about 3½ miles north of the northernmost point of the modern Minneriya Colony.

full of signs of ancient occupation. Brohier has given a good account of the desolation in nineteenth-century Tamankaduwa, quoting from a series of travellers' accounts.[1] Everywhere the forest reigned, except where there were grassy clearings (*damanas*).[2] 'Man', says Brohier, 'had almost entirely deserted these woods and given them up undisputed to wild animals such as the elephant, buffalo and deer.'[3] And in Tamankaduwa the mere restoration of tanks as carried out up to 1932 had an effect on settlement quite incommensurate with the magnitude of the work. Tamankaduwa has only really revived in the last twenty years.

The Ancient Dry Zone

All over this generally desolate Dry Zone lay the concrete evidence of an ancient civilization in the shape of ruined cities, decayed irrigation works, and inscriptions (see Plates 1 and 2); there is also a certain amount of documentary evidence, which of necessity has to be used with caution;[4] and the peasantry preserve innumerable fascinating legends of the 'Golden Age'. For a general survey of the period the reader is referred to one of the excellent histories which have appeared;[5] all that will be attempted here is to discuss the aspects most relevant to this study, namely the distribution and density of settlements in ancient Ceylon, and the reasons for the decay of the Dry Zone in subsequent centuries.

The early Sinhalese seem to have come by sea from North India, and at first to have settled in two main areas; the first, which they reached from the north-west coast, was around Anuradhapura, and became the nucleus of the Rāja Rata, 'the king's country'. The other was in the south-east, Ruhuna. Thence settlement seems to have spread in the last few centuries B.C. into other parts of the Dry Zone, although some areas may have remained sparsely peopled or even empty for the whole of, or for parts of, the ancient period. More research is needed on this point. It is certain, however, that for a long time settlement on any large scale avoided alike the Wet

[1] R. L. Brohier, *The Tamankaduwa District and the Elahera-Minneriya Canal* (Colombo, Govt. Press, 1941), pp. 8–13.

[2] See below, p. 32; see also Plate 3.

[3] *Tamankaduwa District*, p. 9.

[4] For example, the *Mahāvaṃsa*, see trans. by W. Geiger, rev. ed. (Colombo, Govt. Information Dept., 1950).

[5] For example, G. C. Mendis, *The Early History of Ceylon*, 3rd ed. (Calcutta, Y.M.C.A., 1938), and H. W. Codrington, *A Short History of Ceylon*, rev. ed. (London, Macmillan, 1939).

Zone and the Hills. Probably the early Sinhalese found the Dry Zone jungle easier to clear than the thick rain forest which then mantled the wetter parts of the island; possibly also they found in the Dry Zone a region analogous to the part of India from which they came and to which their techniques of agriculture and irrigation were adapted.

From very early times the Sinhalese were rice-growers (though it also seems clear that *chena* cultivation was also practised in ancient times); and rice cultivation under Dry Zone conditions demanded irrigation works. Some tanks still extant are very old indeed, but many of the larger and more spectacular tanks and *elas* (channels) were built after the fourth century A.D. and even after 1017, when, with increasing pressure from India, the capital was shifted from Anuradhapura to Polonnaruwa. There is firm evidence of a high degree of technological skill.

As time went on and pressure from India increased there was increasing activity in the Wet Zone and in the Hills. Finally, there came, after about A.D. 1235, a confused period of invasion and war. The glory of ancient Ceylon departed; the north of the Dry Zone, together with the east and north-west coasts, was left to the Tamils, and the rest became derelict, or supported only the ancestors of the miserable peasantry to be described by the European topographers.

It is not surprising that, with the magnificent ruins of great cities before them, popular imagination conceives of ancient Ceylon in general, and its Dry Zone in particular, as having had a very large population, much larger than at present.[1] It is also inevitable that both the glories and the population tend to be exaggerated by that backward-looking romanticism which is characteristic of nationalist movements, especially those which, as in Ceylon, are affected by the malaise of a people who have been under alien rule and subjected to the heavy cultural impact of the West. Unfortunately, the impression that ancient Ceylon had a very large population is reinforced by a reading of certain ancient documents, which have been too often accepted at something approaching their face value. Yet, as E. B. Denham said, 'In no particular is ancient history more inaccurate than in its statements about population';[2] and exaggeration of numbers is inevitable as stories pass down by word of mouth

---

[1] For a brief discussion see Brohier, *Land, Maps and Surveys*, vol. i (Colombo, Govt. Press, 1950), p. xix.

[2] *Ceylon at the Census of 1911*, pp. 8–9.

through people whose main aim is to extol the heroes of old, and thus to attribute to them impossibly large armies, cities, and numbers of subjects. Thus one manuscript, mentioned by Denham, credits ancient Ceylon with a total population of 70½ million (ten times the present population);[1] and Anuradhapura with 900,000 buildings in four main streets alone! Such figures are so obviously exaggerated as to be absurd; the reader will be even more convinced of their absurdity after reading the chapters which will follow, and realizing how limited are the physical resources of the Dry Zone.

More sober estimates (which vary from 5 to 17 million, through the figure of 10 million adopted by Sir Ponnambalam Arunachalam) are also apt to be too large rather than too small;[2] most of them have been based on such evidence as the number and magnitude of irrigation works (on the unjustified assumption that all works in a catchment operated together); or on the area covered by ancient cities like Anuradhapura (a very false clue, since such cities hardly had urban functions as we know them today; rather were they the seat of the Court and its attendants, and the centres of religious pilgrimage, apt to have far more buildings and cover a far larger area per 1,000 of the population than a modern, commercial city). Altogether, it is quite impossible to estimate the past numbers or distribution of the Dry Zone's population. But it is important to give the lie to estimates which are grossly exaggerated. If such receive credence, as they unfortunately do, they engender false optimism about the carrying capacity of the Dry Zone, and hence about the present population problem of Ceylon; and encourage the view that there is no urgency in the vital questions of land use and conservation which will be discussed later in this book.

Whatever the truth about the ancient population of the Dry Zone, however, it was certainly greater than the modern population. What caused the decline? There has been considerable controversy over this question, although most authorities blame, directly or indirectly, the Tamil invasions and the internal dissensions of the confused period after A.D. 1235.[3] Probably the depopulation of the Dry Zone is not to be ascribed to any one cause such as these

---

[1] *Ceylon at the Census of 1911*, p. 9.
[2] See *The Census of Ceylon, 1901* (Colombo, Govt. Printer, 1902), p. 1.
[3] See, for example, the discussion in Brohier, *Ancient Irrigation Works*, vol. i, pt. 1, pp. 1–2.

1. SIGIRIYA: LION'S CLAWS
One of the carvings on the remarkable Sigiriya Rock

2. ANURADHAPURA: KING'S BATH
Beneath Tissa Wewa

3. *DAMANA* AT MANAMPITIYA, TAMANKADUWA
Savana, probably man-made

4. JUNGLE ON POTTUVIL–WELLAWAYA ROAD
Deceptively verdant

invasions and dissensions (as some have maintained), but rather to a combination of factors. Thus there must inevitably have been a breakdown of the organized government necessary to the mainten- ance of major irrigation works, together with the death or flight to the Hills of a substantial part of the peasantry. There is evidence, too, that malaria either arrived for the first time, or became more virulent.[1] And there may have been deliberate destruction, although it is not necessary to invoke this, since under Dry Zone conditions *bunds* are soon breached and channels choked with weeds and silt by natural agency, given a few years' neglect. (Some breaches, such as that at Padawiya, may well have occurred long before the period of general decay, and have been due to the building of *bunds* on insecure foundations which the ancient engineers, for all their skill, could not have discovered in advance of construction.)

It is also possible that, locally at least, other causes of depopula- tion have been at work. It is fashionable to attribute the decay of ancient civilizations to soil erosion, and prophets of the current creed have not been lacking in Ceylon. Thus H. I. S. Thirlaway has maintained that the decay of tanks, brought about by soil erosion and consequent silting, was the cause and not the effect of the collapse in the Dry Zone.[2] Serious silting of tanks there undoub- tedly was, and it will be seen that in many areas the problem is serious today.[3] But the fact remains that there has not been a single tank which, when its breaches have been restored, has failed to function because of silting. On the other hand, *local* depopulation may have occurred because of the exhaustion of particular areas of soil (e.g. the *damanas* of the east, see p. 32).

It is also clear that in some parts of the Dry Zone the finishing touches to the process of decay and depopulation were added fairly recently. Thus the great tank at Kaudulla in Tamankaduwa seems only to have breached about 1680;[4] according to Tennent the final ruin of the Wanni was the result of conflict between the local people and Europeans (Dutch and British),[5] and a great deal of destruction was caused by the British in areas bordering on the Hills during the suppression of the Kandyan rebellion of 1817.[6]

---

[1] See p. 21 for a fuller discussion.
[2] H. I. S. Thirlaway, 'Ruhuna and Soil Conservation', *Loris J.* (Colombo), vol. iii (1945), pp. 1–5.   [3] See below, pp. 191–4.
[4] Brohier, *Tamankaduwa District*, p. 8.
[5] Tennent, ii. 508–16.
[6] Davy, *Account of the Interior of Ceylon*, pp. 330–1.

The Arrested Revival of the Dry Zone

The Dry Zone of Ceylon is thus a region which was the scene of an ancient civilization and the home of a considerable population, although it is quite impossible and, indeed, highly dangerous to attempt an estimate of the numbers. For various reasons the region fell into decay, and, as will be apparent from what has been said, most parts of it have only revived very slowly during the period, since the 1870's, in which attempts have been made to rebuild ancient irrigation works and to carry out other measures of restoration. Only in favoured areas, such as the hinterland of Batticaloa, or those parts of Ruhuna adjacent to the Wet Zone, did an appreciable increase in settlement density follow these attempts, at least until the modern colonization of the last two decades. And, as Map 11 shows, the Dry Zone today, in spite of this new colonization, remains that rare phenomenon in Southern Asia, a region which makes up two-thirds of a country but is sparsely peopled.[1]

The sparsity of population in the Dry Zone owes something to Palk Strait which insulates it from India; and, as will be shown in Chapters 5 and 6, the slow resettlement of the Dry Zone was due in part to an inadequate government policy, although care must be taken not to rush into a harsh judgement, and past policies must be seen against the background of the political philosophies, economic conditions, and technical skills current at the time of their formulation. But the continuing absence of dense population also owed much to the repellent nature of the physical environment and the weakness of the autochthonous people. The next two chapters will analyse these factors more fully.

---

[1] The population map published in *WBR* contains grave inaccuracies; in particular, it shows far too high a population in the Wanni, in Tamankaduwa and the area thence to Batticaloa, and in the area immediately west of the Batticaloa lagoon. See *WBR*, facing p. 8 (vol. i, facing p. 4).

2

Dry Zone Problems set by Nature

I N this chapter the natural causes which make the Dry Zone a
difficult region, both for its indigenous peasantry and for immigrant colonists, are discussed more fully. They are set out in the
order of the apparent importance of their adverse effect on human
settlement. Malaria is considered first, then climate (particularly
drought as the cause of famine), water-supply (surface and underground), the jungle, and the soil. A concluding section will sketch
regional differences within the Dry Zone, and draw comparisons
with other Asian regions.

Malaria

Modern work on malaria in Ceylon has shown that the disease
was, until the coming of adequate control measures, hyperendemic
almost throughout the Dry Zone, except for the fortunate Jaffna
Peninsula; in the Wet Zone, however, it only occurred in occasional
epidemics.[1] There can be no doubt that the hyperendemicity of
malaria was a major depressing factor in the Dry Zone. As has been
seen, the nineteenth-century writers unite in describing the Dry
Zone as disease-ridden; and the worst disease was malaria. Census
report after census report ascribes high death-rates to it. Thus it is
blamed for the fact that there was a large apparent excess of deaths
over births in the Mannar District in the period 1911–21 (12,409
recorded deaths, 9,251 recorded births).[2] Mortality was particularly
high among children. Leonard Woolf records the harrowing tale
of a child of five at Andarawewa, in Hambantota District, in 1911;

---

[1] See, in particular, H. F. Carter and others, *Report on Malaria and Anophe-
line Mosquitoes in Ceylon*, S.P. 7 of 1927; *The Ceylon Malaria Epidemic, 1934–5*,
S.P. 22 of 1935; C. A. Gill, *Report on the Malaria Epidemic in Ceylon 1934–5*,
S.P. 23 of 1935; C. L. Dunn, *Malaria in Ceylon* (London, Baillière, Tindall &
Cox, 1936); K. J. Rustomjee, *Observations upon the Epidemiology of Malaria in
Ceylon*, S.P. 24 of 1944; S. Rajendram and S. H. Jayewickreme, 'Malaria in
Ceylon', *Ind. J. of Malariology*, vol. v (1951), pp. 1–124; and *Admin. Reports:
Medical*.

[2] L. J. B. Turner, *Report on the Census of Ceylon, 1921*, vol. i, pt. 2 (Colombo,
Govt. Press, 1924), pp. 116–22.

the child was 'a pallid yellow colour, absolutely skin and bones, but his belly about three times the size of the rest of his body. His uncle ... gave him quinine "the *maha* before this" ... probably he will die; most of our families are dying.'[1]

In addition to its effect on the death-rate and on the ability of the Dry Zone population to maintain itself, malaria induced mental and physical inefficiency in its victims. The incidence of fever was unfortunately highest during the rainy season, especially from early December to mid-February, just when the stricken cultivators should have been busy with their *Maha*, or main paddy crop, and with their *chenas*. It is not surprising that general debility and seasonal fever helped, with other factors, to produce low crop yields and low nutritional standards; these in turn, and coupled with debility, made the peasantry a ready prey for other diseases (such as smallpox) and generally incapable of improving their lot. Pierre Gourou wrote: 'Undoubtedly, malaria is largely responsible for the poor health, small numbers, absence of enthusiasm for work, stationary demographic character, and backwardness of tropical peoples.'[2] His generalization is well borne out by the experience of the Dry Zone of Ceylon. The Dry Zone, indeed, rivalled other notoriously malarial regions, like the Terai at the foot of the Himalayas.[3]

Although many species of anopheline mosquito occur in Ceylon, only one, *Anopheles culicifacies*, has ever been found to be an important vector of malaria. This species spends its larval stage in shallow, more or less stagnant water. The dry season reduces most Dry Zone rivers to a chain of pools and these, quite apart from irrigation works, active or derelict, form an ideal breeding-ground. In the Wet Zone, on the other hand, the streams are normally perennial and any larvae which may find their way into them are soon swept away; it is only when, as in 1934–5, an abnormal drought reduces Wet Zone rivers to Dry Zone proportions that the mosquitoes breed in great numbers and a malaria epidemic ensues. (The low incidence of malaria in the Jaffna Peninsula is probably due to the absence of surface water on its limestone terrain.)

[1] From Leonard Woolf's MS. diary as Assistant Government Agent, Hambantota, for 13 Jan. 1911 (quoted by kind permission of its author); Leonard Woolf's novel, *A Village in the Jungle* (London, Arnold, 1913, and New Phoenix Library, 1951), also gives a very good impression of conditions in the south-east forty years ago.

[2] Gourou, *The Tropical World*, trans. E. D. Laborde (London, Longmans, 1953), p. 8.   [3] See *Tarai and Bhabar Report*, pp. 8–9.

It is doubtful whether malaria was endemic in the ancient Dry Zone; there appear to be no certain references to it in the texts, and such accounts as there are of plagues and pestilences seem to be more suggestive of some epidemic fever, and not of endemic malaria. There is, for example, the passage in the *Rāja Ratnacari* which reads: '. . . on account of a pestilential fever, which became general throughout the island, more dreadful than the plague which broke out in our own Budhu's time, in the city called Wisawla Maha Nuwara, all flesh began to die'.[1] And as L. Nicholls pointed out, it is inconceivable that the ancient cities of Ceylon could have been built by a people in the inert, febrile state of their nineteenth-century descendants.[2] On the other hand, it is not now as fashionable as it was when Nicholls wrote to attribute the waning of any civilization to malaria, and, as has been hinted already, malaria may well have been one factor only, albeit an important one, in the complex circumstances which led to the decay of ancient Ceylon.

The power of the grip which malaria has had on the Dry Zone is in no way better demonstrated than by the complete transformation which came about when this grip was relaxed; this was due to the introduction in 1945 of spraying with DDT.[3] Earlier efforts at control had concentrated mainly on anti-larval measures, but the reader will realize the virtual futility of this approach in a region where most rivers and many artificial sheets of water are potential breeding-grounds. The scheme now operated with such success involves the spraying of the interior of houses all over the Dry Zone at intervals, and is carried out efficiently and thoroughly. It is, of course, expensive; for the three years 1947–9 the annual average cost was slightly under 3 million rupees. But this, if allowance is made for the changed value of money, is only a small fraction of the 10 million rupees per annum which Nicholls estimated would be the cost of eradication by the methods which were used in Panama.[4] The cost, in fact, works out at only about 65 cents

[1] *The Mahāvansi, the Rājā-Ratnācari and the Rājā-vali*, trans. E. Upham (London, Parbury, Allen, 1833), ii. 3.

[2] L. Nicholls, 'Malaria and the Lost Cities of Ceylon', *Ind. Med. Gaz.*, vol. lvi (1921), pp. 121–30. See also T. W. Tyssul Jones, 'Malaria and the Ancient Cities of Ceylon', *Ind. J. of Malariology*, vol. v (1951), pp. 125–34.

[3] There is an excellent account of the scheme in the Dept. of Information's *Ceylon: the Health of the Nation* (Colombo, 1950); for more detail see *Admin. Reports: Medical*, and Rajendram and Jayewickreme, in *Ind. J. of Malariology*, vol. v, pp. 1–124.

[4] Nicholls in *Ind. Med. Gaz.*, vol. lvi, pp. 121–30.

(about 6*d*.) per head of the population protected per annum, for the years 1947–9.

The transformation which has been effected in the Dry Zone in general, and in its colonization schemes in particular, is truly spectacular. The author was fortunate enough to visit the Zone in 1943–4, before DDT was sprayed, and again in 1951, and can testify that the claims made by the authorities, which might at first sight seem exaggerated, are in reality not so.[1] The colonization schemes themselves furnish some of the best evidence available; this will be discussed in Chapter 11. But more general statistics are also eloquent. In the formerly malarial districts crude death-rates had come down from 35 or 40 per thousand to between 9 and 17 per thousand in 1950.[2] And the $2\frac{1}{2}$ to 3 million malarial cases which used annually to be diagnosed in government hospitals had by 1949 been reduced to 727,769.

Provided that success does not engender carelessness, that DDT supplies can be maintained, and that no DDT-resistant strain of *Anopheles culicifacies* is bred, it can be said with confidence that malaria need no longer be a serious deterrent to Dry Zone settlement. Success has, however, created two new problems. One is demographic, the other takes the form of an optimism about the Dry Zone, falsely based because its victims imagine that, with malaria suppressed, all is now plain sailing. Malaria may long have been the dominant problem, but there remain many more to be solved before the Dry Zone can be completely conquered.

Climate, especially Rainfall

Apart from narrow coastal strips in the Mannar and Hambantota Districts, most of the Dry Zone receives a mean annual rainfall of from 50 to 75 inches (see Map 3) and much of Bintenne receives between 75 and 100 inches. To the reader used to temperate or even to sub-tropical conditions, these amounts might well seem more than adequate, and, were he to visit the Dry Zone, he would consider his impression confirmed by the apparent luxuriance of much of its jungle. A leader-writer in *The Times* wrote of Ceylon: 'She enjoys many natural advantages in a good climate, fertile soils and

[1] A third visit, in 1955–6, revealed a conquest so complete that periodical spraying everywhere had been replaced by *ad hoc* work where hospital returns suggested a potential danger.

[2] *Report of the Registrar-General of Ceylon on Vital Statistics for 1950* (Colombo, Govt. Press, 1952), p. 21.

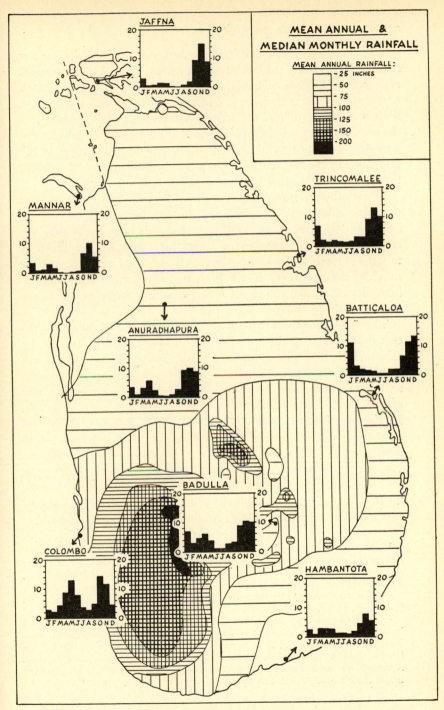

MAP 3. Ceylon: rainfall (isohyets and shading on the map indicate mean annual rainfall: diagrams indicate median monthly rainfall).

other natural resources, and in the industry of her inhabitants; but like many relatively undeveloped countries she lacks large capital resources.'[1] Ceylon certainly lacks capital, but capital is not all that she lacks; in particular, the Dry Zone cannot be said 'to have a good climate' (or for that matter intrinsically 'fertile soils'). It shares with many other tropical regions the difficulties inherent in a markedly seasonal rainfall, difficulties which are enhanced in the Dry Zone by the fact that drought comes at the hottest and windiest time of the year, so that loss by evaporation is very high.

The south-west monsoon wind passes over the Dry Zone without dropping any appreciable rain, and, indeed, becomes a desiccating agent, like the *föhn* of the Alps, as it descends from the hills to the eastern plain. The months of June, July, and August are thus months of rarely interrupted drought all over the Dry Zone, and for much of the time there is 'the blowing', the period dominated by high, drying winds, called *yal hulunga* by the Sinhalese peasantry and *kăchchān* by the east-coast Tamil.[2]

The wet season in the Dry Zone comes with the so-called 'north-east monsoon' of about November to January; the winds, and the rains which they bring, are uncertain, and in particular are apt occasionally to arrive late.[3] But normally a large proportion of the annual rainfall falls in the three north-east monsoon months: over 40 per cent. everywhere, and as much as 60 per cent. at Jaffna. In the two inter-monsoon periods (roughly February–May and September–October), there may be rains due to depressions and to local convectional circulations, but at most places these rains are variable and unreliable. Rains in the period before the south-west monsoon (i.e. before the dry season) are sometimes spoken of as the 'little monsoon'; and, occasionally, during a year with a weak north-east monsoon, represent a high proportion of the year's rainfall.

[1] *The Times*, 1 Aug. 1950. Opposition members of Parliament in Ceylon have also been apt to castigate the Government for what they claim to be a poor standard of achievement in the light of deceptive mean annual rainfall figures (see, for example, Ceylon, House of Representatives, *Debates*, vol. x, pp. 971, 1227).

[2] See H. Jameson, 'The Batticaloa *Kachchan*', *Q.J.R. Met. Soc.*, vol. lxvii (1941), pp. 55–56.

[3] While this book was being written in 1952 this letter arrived from a friend in Ceylon: 'The north-east monsoon this year has been a failure so far as Nuwara Kalawiya is concerned. . . . As a result, most village tanks are empty and the level of water in the major tanks has not increased since the end of September. Although we are in the middle of December, no cultivation has been started under these tanks.' The failure of 1955–6 was even worse.

Variability of rainfall is a phenomenon to be reckoned with in any assessment of the Dry Zone problem.[1] One or two years of heavy rainfall may so inflate the mean for a twenty-year period that it gives a very exaggerated impression of the rainfall that may be expected. The mean July rainfall at Anuradhapura for the period 1906-45 was 1·33 inches, but in half the years the rainfall was less than 0·28 inches, and in two-thirds of the years was less than the mean. A run of 'deficit' years (i.e. years in which rainfall is less than the mean) is thus only to be expected, and is not a sign of a worsening climate, as has sometimes been claimed.[2]

Many false judgements about the Dry Zone have been based on a quite understandable failure to appreciate the danger of mean monthly values of rainfall; the median values plotted on the diagrams in Map 3 give a far more accurate picture of rainfall expectancy. (If one arranges twenty years, say, of rainfalls for a given month at a given station in order of size, then the middle member of the column is the median. Clearly, in half the years rainfall has been less than the median, and in half the years greater than the median, so that the median represents 'mean expectation' of rainfall.)

Such of the Dry Zone peasant's difficulties as are due to the vagaries of the rainfall are increased by the fact that it is apt to fluctuate, especially at certain seasons, about the critical level which is 'effective'; effective rainfall may be defined as that which is just enough to keep soil moisture above wilting-point, and thus to keep shallow-rooted plants alive.[3] It is not possible, with existing data, to determine accurately the amount of rainfall necessary for effectiveness at Dry Zone stations, but it is possible for certain stations to make an estimate based on climatic figures, and then to compute the approximate percentage of years in which, at each month and each station, rainfall is effective. The result is shown in Map 4.[4]

The basis of the calculation finds some support in what is now known of evaporation rates in the Dry Zone; these are astonishingly

[1] For a fuller discussion see Farmer, 'Rainfall and Water Supply in the Dry Zone of Ceylon', in Fisher and Steel, and references there quoted.

[2] See, for example, the popular beliefs discussed in 'Report on the Devastated Coconut Areas in the Puttalam District', *Cey. Coconut Q.*, vol. ii (1951), pp. 128–30.

[3] For a fuller discussion of the concept of effective rainfall and its application to the Dry Zone, see Farmer, in Fisher and Steel.

[4] Based on a map in ibid. by kind permission of Messrs. George Philip & Son.

high in the dry season (in the region of half an inch daily from a free water surface at Maha Illuppallama) because of high temperatures, strong winds, and low relative humidity.[1] High temperatures here appear in the guise of an enemy, but it must not be forgotten that it is these temperatures, and the high intake of solar energy which they betoken, which constitute one of the Dry Zone's greatest assets, approaching as they do the optimum for the growth of rice.

It may be seen from Map 4 that rainfall is generally effective throughout the Dry Zone in the wet season, when, in fact, water-logging is common, but there are occasional months of ineffective-ness which may spell disaster to *chena* crops; and to say that rainfall is 'effective' is far from saying that it is adequate for a thirsty crop like rice. In the dry season, on the other hand, rainfall is nearly always ineffective; annual plants wilt and die, and the apparently luxuriant natural vegetation survives only because of its deep roots, deciduous habit, small leaves, or other adaptation. In the inter-monsoon periods there is a chance of effective rainfall which varies with the station from 50:50 to about 70:30, a tantalizing state of affairs for the cultivator.

The Dry Zone of Ceylon is thus a difficult region for unirrigated annual crops, and, indeed, an impossible one in some seasons and in some years; it is also a difficult region for perennial crops not adapted to drought and for pasture. Quite apart from the fact that theirs was a rice-based culture, it is not surprising that the ancient Sinhalese practised irrigation. Indeed, R. W. Ievers, who knew the Dry Zone well, went so far as to say, 'It may broadly be stated that without artificial irrigation and storage of water human exis-tence in the North-Central Province would be impossible.'[2] It is admittedly often possible in the *Maha* season to grow rain-fed paddy, but a crop can only be assured by irrigation. A *Yala*, or 'little', cultivation (i.e. one in the dry season) can only be attempted if irrigation is available, and the same applies to the *Mäda* (*Meda*) harvest sometimes taken between the *Maha* and *Yala* seasons.

And it is not surprising that, as in other countries of variable rainfall, famine has not been infrequent, and government relief measures have often been necessary. It is also clear that drought

---

[1] The author is indebted to Mr. E. F. L. Abeyaratne, Agricultural Research Officer at Maha Illuppallama, for these figures and for the benefit of valuable discussions.

[2] Ievers, p. 133. For ancient irrigation generally, see Brohier, *Ancient Irriga-tion Works.*

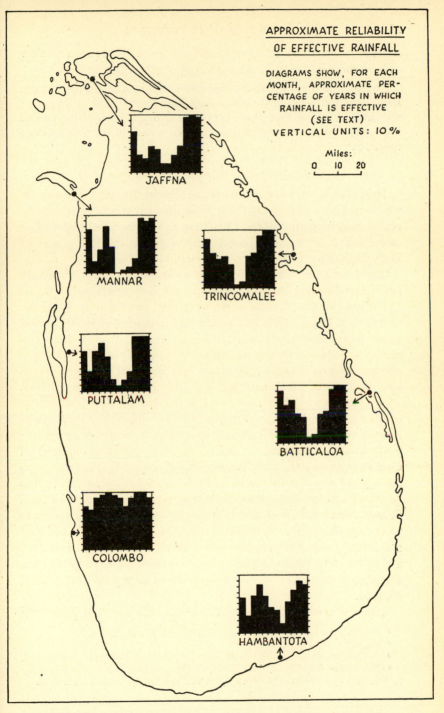

MAP 4. Ceylon: Approximate Reliability of Effective Rainfall.

and famine were not unknown in ancient times. There are a number
of references in the ancient texts; to quote the *Rāja Ratnacari*:

And in those days the four chief castes filled the island with wealth
and riches, by means of their cows and buffaloes; but while they were
thus living in abundance, there happened such a drought that a famine
followed as grievous as the famine which happened in our own Budhu's
time. . . .[1]

Water-Supply, Surface and Underground

Irrigation is not only an insurance against drought, it is also, as
will be seen,[2] a mitigator of soil difficulties. But it is important to
realize that irrigation in the Dry Zone cannot be as widespread or
as reliable as in more favoured regions, because of the nature of
both the surface and underground water-supplies.

The Dry Zone is watered for the most part by short, relatively
small radial streams which rise within the Zone itself and thus feel
to the full the effects of its seasonal rainfall (see Map 5). Thus the
Gal Oya at Inginiyagala had a mean daily discharge in the period
1939–46 of about 3,000 cusec. in December but of only about 100
cusec. in August;[3] and many streams cease to flow at all in the dry
season.[4] Clearly there is little scope here for great perennial canals
like those of the Punjab. Irrigation direct from rivers can in most
places function in *Maha* only; and, as in Madras, storage tanks are
of necessity the commonest types of work. Moreover, because of
rainfall variability, yields of catchments vary greatly from year to
year; in the years 1939–46 the mean daily discharge of the Gal
Oya at Inginiyagala varied from under 1,200 cusec. to some 5,000
cusec., and *actual* daily discharges from under 200 cusec. to 35,000
cusec. There are thus years of greatly reduced cultivation or total
failure on the one hand, and of flood siltation and great damage to
works on the other. It becomes difficult to say what is the safe
maximum cultivable area beneath a given tank if water resources
are to be fully utilized. Most modern engineers have played for
safety, but the waste of water in years of heavy rainfall is then
colossal.

There are one or two major streams, such as the Mahaweli

[1] *The Mahávansi, the Rájá-Ratnácari and the Rájávali*, ii. 8–9.
[2] See below, p. 46.
[3] 1 cusec. is a measure of the flow of water equal to 1 cubic foot per second.
[4] The author is indebted to the Ceylon Irrigation Department and especially
to Mr. Shirley J. Bocks, Hydrologist, for access to gaugings and other data.

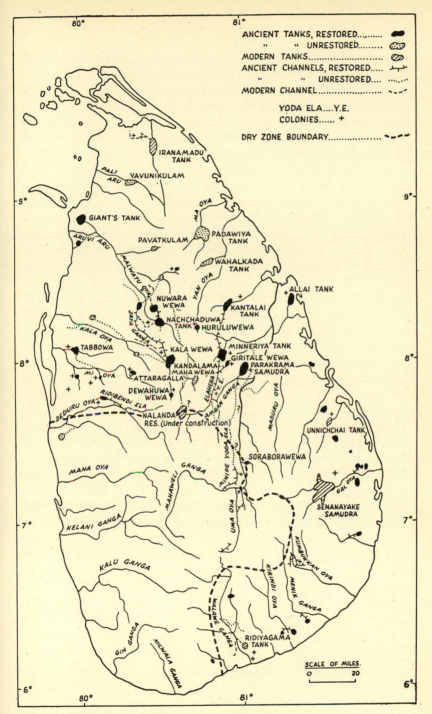

ANCIENT TANKS, RESTORED..............

"   "   UNRESTORED..........

MODERN TANKS...........................

ANCIENT CHANNELS, RESTORED.....

"   "   UNRESTORED.....

MODERN CHANNEL......................

YODA ELA....Y.E.

COLONIES...... +

DRY ZONE BOUNDARY...................

IRANAMADU TANK

VAVUNIKULAM

PALI ARU

GIANT'S TANK

ARUVI ARU

MA OYA

PAVATKULAM

PADAWIYA TANK

MALWATU OYA

WAHALKADA TANK

YAN OYA

NUWARA WEWA

ALLAI TANK

KANTALAI TANK

NACHCHADUWA TANK

HURULUWEWA

JAYA GANGA

KALA OYA

TABBOWA

KALA WEWA

MINNERIYA TANK

GIRITALE WEWA

KANDALAMA

MAHA WEWA

PARAKRAMA SAMUDRA

ATTARAGALLA

MI OYA

ELAHERA

AMBAN GANGA

MADURU OYA

DEWAHUWA WEWA

DEDURU OYA

RIDIBENDI ELA

NALANDA RES. (Under construction)

MINIPE YODA ELA

Y.E.

UNNICHCHAI TANK

MAHA OYA

SORABORAWEWA

MAHAWELI GANGA

UMA OYA

SENANAYAKE SAMUDRA

GAL OYA

KELANI GANGA

KALU GANGA

KUMBUKKAN OYA

GIN GANGA

NILWALA GANGA

WALAWE GANGA

KIRINDI OYA

MENIK GANGA

RIDIYAGAMA TANK

SCALE OF MILES.

0   20

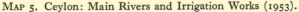

MAP 5. Ceylon: Main Rivers and Irrigation Works (1953).

Ganga and its tributary the Amban Ganga, which rise in the Wet Zone and have a perennial flow, though they are still subject to great seasonal fluctuation. But, though a small-scale map may suggest that much of the Dry Zone is a dead level plain, there is sufficient relief to hinder the tapping of these rivers, and this is especially true of the Mahaweli Ganga; only in its lowermost reaches does it become deltaic and approach the conditions which have, in Madras, enabled such good use to be made of the Cauvery.

In the limestone country of the Jaffna Peninsula, water supplied by the rains is stored naturally underground and may be tapped by shallow wells.[1] Unfortunately these conditions are not widely reproduced in the rest of the Dry Zone. There are a few stretches of permeable coastal sand, and a belt in the north-west where there are water-bearing sedimentary rocks, but the whole of the rest of the Dry Zone is floored with crystalline rocks, virtually impervious except for rare and irregular joints.[2] Over this rock is a variable layer, from 0 feet to about 40 feet thick, made of decomposed rock, subsoil, and soil; this layer does hold some water, but quantities are small even when it is saturated during the rains, and in the dry season underground water appears to dwindle away, except where the water-table is preserved by an adjacent tank, channel, or stream. (More research is, however, needed, on the exact behaviour of the water-table.)[3] There is, therefore, little hope of supplementing tank irrigation by well irrigation, except in a small way in places where the water-table is artificially preserved. An investigation was made in 1906 of the water-levels of wells in the Vavuniya District and the conclusion was reached that there were good supplies of underground water; but the author discovered that almost all of the wells observed were situated under the *bund* of a tank, i.e. where the water-table was artificially maintained by the tank.[4]

This shortage of underground water clearly means that the Dry

[1] S. Mahadeva, 'The Hydrology of Jaffna', *Trans. Eng. Assoc. Cey.* (1938), pp. 131–56.

[2] See espec. L. J. D. Fernando, 'The Geology and Mineral Resources of Ceylon', *Bull. Imp. Inst.*, vol. xlvi (1948), pp. 303–25, and C. H. L. Sirimanne, 'In Search of Water', *Bull. Cey. Geog. Soc.*, vol. iv (1949), pp. 6–11.

[3] See, however, *Water Supply Investigations, Hambantota District and North-Western Province*, S.P. 30 of 1929, pp. 37–38; also *Admin. Report: Agriculture*, 1952, pp. 37–38.

[4] The author was able to study the file containing the results of this investigation by courtesy of the then Surveyor-General of Ceylon, Mr. G. B. King.

Zone must rely almost entirely on surface supplies for irrigation, with all the waste by evaporation that that implies; it also means that the supply of water for domestic purposes presents a serious problem.

The Jungle

Much of the lowland Dry Zone, outside the areas of permanent cultivation, is covered with high forest of mixed evergreen and deciduous composition.[1] Probably this forest is, like tropical forests in general, secondary, owing its character to human interference and especially to shifting cultivation.[2] At first sight the jungle, with its deceptive luxuriance, might appear to be a severe obstacle to settlement; and it is true that colonization schemes encounter labour problems in clearing it.[3] But the Dry Zone peasant, unworried by costs, has a perfectly good technique of jungle clearing, even though his Wet Zone and Up-country cousin have to be taught the tricks of the trade. It is not particularly difficult to fell jungle and to burn it at the close of the dry season, as is done annually by thousands of *chena* cultivators. The existence of jungle has certainly never been a limiting factor in settlement as has malaria or water shortage. (The same might, in fact, be said of many tropical lands.)

On the other hand, the jungle harbours wild beasts; and elephants, wild boar, and monkeys can be terribly destructive of crops, especially in exposed *chenas* or on the long frontiers of ribbon-like colonization schemes.[4] The time and energy spent in watching crops by night, together with the sheer loss of food supplies, is certainly a debit item to be laid at the door of the jungle. And the Dry Zone villager, with his own peculiar blend of Animism, Hinduism, and Buddhism, peoples the jungle with creatures even more terrible than the wild fauna, and propitiates his deities in order to obtain protection from jungle enemies both natural and supernatural.

One further point may be mentioned here, though it will be developed more fully in Chapter 11. In the eastern Dry Zone,

---

[1] See espec. C. H. Holmes, 'The Climate and Vegetation of the Dry Zone of Ceylon', *Bull. Cey. Geog. Soc.*, vols. v–vi (1951), pp. 145–53, and *The Grass, Fern and Savannah Lands of Ceylon* (Oxford, Imp. Forestry Inst., 1951).

[2] Gourou, *Tropical World*, p. 13.

[3] See Chapter 10.

[4] See Chapter 9.

especially east of the Mahaweli Ganga, jungle clearings tend to be invaded by grasses, especially that universal scourge of the tropics, *Imperata cylindrica*, or *illuk* in Sinhalese, and if, as usually happens, there is periodical burning, the forest cannot re-establish itself, and *damana*, or poor savannah, results.[1] The effect on the soil is adverse, it is extremely hard to eradicate *illuk* for cultivation, and, altogether, *damana* has far more limitations for the settler than the forest.

General Problems of the Soil

The soil, like the jungle, cannot be directly blamed for the failure of the Dry Zone to attract population; except, that is, for such areas as the *damanas* of the east. In the Dry Zone as a whole the peasant is perfectly capable, with the indigenous techniques to be described in the next chapter, of utilizing the soils which he encounters, though, as will become apparent, his methods are not beyond reproach and tend, with increasing population, to become positively dangerous.

It is nevertheless vital to realize that the soils of the Dry Zone, like so many other tropical soils, are not for the most part rich in plant nutrients, at least in comparison with the average temperate soils.[2] The myth of the bursting fertility of tropical soils dies hard, and, like false ideas on the climate of the Dry Zone, owes a great deal to the deceptive luxuriance of the forest. This luxuriance is primarily due to sunlight and temperature; but the same factors ensure, through their encouragement of termites and bacteria, the rapid and unceasing decomposition of dead animal and vegetable matter, so that even in virgin jungle soils there is little of the humus which gives many temperate soils their favourable properties, while fields cleared for cultivation are exposed to even higher temperatures and soon lose the little humus stored in them. There is also the point that tropical rains, acting at high temperatures, leach away soluble nutrients far more rapidly than under temperate conditions. All this applies, with more or less force, to the great majority of tropical soils, and would not be laboured here were it

[1] See Holmes, *Grass, Fern and Savannah Lands*, pp. 66–70; and, for the general problem of *Imperata cylindrica* see Imp. Agric. Bureaux, *Imperata cylindrica, Taxonomy, Distribution, Economic Significance and Control* (Oxford and Aberystwyth, 1944).

[2] There is an excellent summary of the difficulties associated with tropical soils in Gourou, *Tropical World*, pp. 13–24.

5. PALUGASWEWA: *YĀYA*
Typical paddy tract in a Nuvarakalawiya village, harvest-time

6. KANIMADUWA: *GANGODA*
Typical village enclosure in Nuvarakalawiya

7. *CHENA* NEAR MONARAGALA

8. JAFFNA LANDSCAPE NEAR PALLAI
Showing palmyras and dry fields (July)

not for constant reminders that the relatively low fertility of the tropics is still insufficiently realized. The immediate relevance to the study of the Dry Zone is that, quite apart from other factors, its soils are such that the supportable population is not as great as is sometimes imagined. Moreover, the ease with which fertility is lost means that there is always the possibility of disaster if dry cultivation is practised; the particular relevance of this point to the colonies will be discussed in Chapter 12. Irrigated cultivation of paddy is another matter, for it is a method of mitigating some at least of the natural soil difficulties; this point will be taken up in more detail in the next chapter.[1]

Three other points remain to be made. The first is a consequence of the geological make-up of the Dry Zone.[2] Everywhere in the Zone there is a tendency towards laterization (i.e. a tendency for soils to lose elements like calcium, potassium, and silicon by chemical action and to accumulate an undue proportion of iron and aluminium hydroxides), although, it should be noted, nowhere has the process gone as far as in the Wet Zone; so that, although most Dry Zone soils are poor in phosphorus, lime, organic matter, and replaceable bases, they are richer in bases than are Wet Zone soils.

Now, the tendency towards laterization is resisted in regions built of such materials as alluvium, basic lava, or limestone, where rock composition or physiography, or both, serve to prevent leaching, or to ensure replenishment of substances which *are* leached. But the Dry Zone has few such areas. Floored mainly by ancient, acid, crystalline rocks, its soils are generally at the mercy of its climate; and consist mainly of loams varying in consistency from very sandy to quite heavy, and with the red colour and relative infertility which are associated with soils derived from crystalline rocks under tropical conditions. The fortunate exceptional areas include the Jaffna Peninsula, whose limestones carry, in parts, red loams of *terra rossa* type and of considerable fertility; and such regions as the Mahaweli Ganga delta and the lowlands west of the Batticaloa lagoon, which bear good alluvial soils.

Secondly, it is clear that the catena concept as developed in East

[1] See p. 46 below.
[2] Much work remains to be done on Dry Zone soils, but see A. W. R. Joachim, 'A Review of Progress in the Study of Soils in Ceylon', *Proc. 1st Ann. Sess. Cey. Assoc. Sci.*, pt. 3 (1945), pp. 21–30, and a series of papers by Joachim, S. Kandiah, and D. G. Pandittesekere, *Trop. Agriculturist*, vols. lxxxiv (1935)–xcviii (1942).

B 5559 D

Africa is applicable to many parts of the Dry Zone;[1] in other words, there is a tendency for there to be on hill-tops and watersheds a marked zone of leaching and of the washing-out of fine particles, and a grading down-hill into a zone which receives the material washed down the slopes. The valley floors thus often have soils which are relatively rich in humus, clay particles, and nutrients. Since by their position they are frequently irrigable, they constitute a real asset to the Dry Zone, especially since paddy cultivation is, wherever it can be practised, in a very real sense the key to the use of tropical soils.[2]

Thirdly, quite apart from their tendency to lose fertility, Dry Zone soils are all too prone to suffer loss by erosion where there is sufficient slope; and, although a small-scale map may give a different impression, that is unfortunately almost everywhere, even in the apparently flat country of the Wanni north of Vavuniya. There are a number of factors which together produce this state of affairs. Thus soils generally lack cohesion, and especially is this true of the sandier soils of Gal Oya and the east. Again, at the close of the dry season the soil surface is baked hard and the first heavy rains run off, eroding as they go, instead of sinking in; later, the soil becomes saturated, with the same result. And, as in the tropics generally, very heavy falls of rain are a commonplace; thus at Maha Illuppallama in December 1951 1 inch of rain fell in 20 minutes and 3 inches in 97 minutes in a storm which was carefully observed.[3] Such heavy rain not only has a direct erosive effect; it also increases the compaction of the soil and thus aids run-off. Thus in the storm already quoted, 60 lb. pressure was necessary to enable a sharp instrument to penetrate 2 inches into the soil, whereas before the storm it penetrated with a pressure almost too small to be measured.[4]

The Dry Zone Environment: A Summary and Some Comparisons

The Dry Zone of Ceylon is thus a region in which human settlement has been, and to a considerable extent still is, hampered by a number of adverse natural circumstances. Everywhere, except in the Jaffna Peninsula, malaria was endemic until the very recent

[1] See G. W. Robinson, *Soils*, 3rd ed. (London, Murby, 1949), p. 508, and works there cited. [2] See below, p. 46.
[3] One inch of rain fell in 8 minutes at the same place in 1955.
[4] The author is indebted to Mr. E. F. L. Abeyaratne for these data.

introduction of spraying with DDT. Everywhere, there are still the hazards of seasonal drought and of variability of rainfall. In the general absence of adequate underground water, the only natural insurance against these hazards is a surface water-supply which is limited and not without its attendant difficulties; only in Jaffna and in a few lesser areas is well irrigation on a large scale at all feasible. And almost everywhere the jungle and its animals, and the poverty and ephemeral tendencies of the soil, add to the problems, recognized or unrecognized, of the settlement of the Dry Zone. 1128038

The Jaffna Peninsula emerges from this scrutiny as a region of exceptional possibilities which contrasts strongly with the rest of the Dry Zone; with its underground water, absence of malaria, and patches of relatively fertile *terra rossa*, it is not surprising that it has long supported a dense population. It is only fair to add, however, in anticipation of a fuller discussion in the next chapter, that the Peninsula owes much, too, to the technical skill and industry of its Tamil inhabitants; and it must also be noted that trade and other activities supplement the yield of the soil. It would also be wrong to give an impression of abounding natural fertility; much of Jaffna is sandy or rocky and naturally dry and barren, and its possibilities, though exceptional, are only realized by dint of much skill and labour.

Clearly, too, the Batticaloa Coast, with its alluvial immediate hinterland, has potentialities, as the Dutch realized. But for the rest of the Dry Zone the drawbacks which have been discussed have served to discourage settlement and depress living standards; and one must repeat the warning that, even if malaria is conquered, the other problems remain. If problems have been stressed at the expense of assets, it is because of the conviction that a check on excessive optimism is needed, particularly in discussions of colonization. Assets, of course, there are: wide, unsettled spaces, ample sunlight and high temperatures to encourage plant growth, and the soil properties of the *deniyas*, the relatively fertile and often irrigable valley bottoms.

It will also be apparent that the Dry Zone, even outside such exceptional areas as Jaffna and the Batticaloa Coast, is a region of very considerable variety. Relief varies from the very broken country on the fringe of the Hills to the deceptively gentle slopes of the Wanni; there are variations in amount and seasonal incidence of rainfall; the sandy soils of Gal Oya differ greatly from the red loams of Nuwarakalawiya.[1] Attempts to settle the Dry Zone must take account of these differences and, in fact, of differences which are even more local in their range; because of the soil catena and also because of ground-water conditions, methods of cultivation which will serve at the top of a slope may not serve at the bottom. If what Edward H. Graham called the 'natural principles of land use' are to be put into operation, careful surveys of local potentialities are clearly called for, and all available land must be put in paddy.[2]

It is useful to bear in mind the fact that there are other regions in Asia and elsewhere with one or more of the characteristics which contribute to the personality and problems of the Dry Zone; experience in them is clearly relevant to the study of the region. One need not labour the point that malaria is, or at least has been until recently, an almost universal scourge in the tropics. Again, many regions, especially tropical and sub-tropical ones, suffer from a dry season in which high temperatures, and often strong winds, lead to rapid evaporation and to desiccation. Thus Burma has its own 'Dry Zone', covering some 38,000 square miles; most of it has a mean annual rainfall of less than 30 inches. And a marked dry season is, of course, characteristic of almost all of the Indian sub-continent and of Eastern Java and the Lesser Sunda Islands. Again, it has been seen that the rainfall of the Dry Zone is subject to considerable variability; but the author has shown elsewhere that, in terms of a statistical index of variability much used in rainfall study, the rainfall of the Dry Zone as a whole is no more variable than is normal in the great monsoon region of which it forms a part, and is less variable than that in some of the truly arid parts of India.[3] (The Dry Zone of Burma also suffers from great variability.) It must be remembered, however, that Dry Zone rainfall has an unfortunate tendency, at certain seasons, to oscillate about a value critical to the cultivator of dry crops.

The jungle and its wild animals are, moreover, hazards facing any would-be pioneer in an unsettled tropical area; and tropical

[1] For schemes of regional subdivision of the Dry Zone, see Cook, pp. 315–34, and Farmer, 'Ceylon', in Spate, pp. 777–82.

[2] E. H. Graham, *Natural Principles of Land Use* (New York, OUP, 1944).

[3] The index used is the semi-interquartile range as a percentage of the median monthly rainfall; see Farmer, 'Rainfall and Water Supply in the Dry Zone of Ceylon', in Fisher and Steel.

rain forests, like those of Sumatra, present greater problems than the relatively thin tropophilous forest of the Dry Zone of Ceylon. The insidious problems of tropical soils—insidious because concealed, generally unrecognized, and apparently belied by the natural vegetation—are problems which afflict most tropical areas, although the Dry Zone is unlucky in its almost completely crystalline rock floor, and in its absence of fertilizing agencies, such as great alluvial plains and active volcanoes.

The Dry Zone of Ceylon has, therefore, no monopoly of trouble, and the claims of its present-day conquerors should be all the more modest in consequence. Many other regions have gone into decay, and J. W. Russell's report on the Terai might well have been written of the Dry Zone a few years ago:

> Life in most of our Tarai villages is one of continual struggle for existence, against the depredations of wild animals, the rank and vigorous vegetation, the enervating climate, malaria, bad drinking water, high death rate and infant mortality, low birth rate, bad communications and lack of ordinary amenities.[1]

Yet in these Terai jungles are the ruins of its 'epic age', for there was a well-populated kingdom here in the thirteenth century.[2]

But a superficial resemblance between the Dry Zone and other regions should not be allowed to conceal the fact that the Dry Zone has a combination of natural characteristics and problems which cause peculiar difficulty. That this is indeed so is well demonstrated by a comparison between the Dry Zone and the region, of all regions, which would appear to have most in common with it, namely Tamil Nad, the part of Madras State just across Palk Strait. Geologically, Ceylon is but a detached portion of Southern India, and the climatic régime of the Dry Zone is analogous to that of Tamil Nad, although mean annual rainfalls are lower in the latter (only over 50 inches in a narrow coastal strip, and below 30 inches in places) and although there is at most stations, in terms of mean figures, a little more rain in the dry season and somewhat less in the wet season than at Ceylon stations.[3]

Tamil Nad, like the Dry Zone, is malarial.[4] And, like the Dry

---

[1] *Tarai and Bhabar Report*, App. 1, p. 59.   [2] Ibid., p. 49.
[3] The author is indebted to his wife for preliminary work on rainfall data. For a modern general account of Tamil Nad, see Spate, pp. 693–742.
[4] RCAI, iii. 474–5, 498, and 505.

Zone, it suffers from variable rainfall. This has usually been the immediate cause of the recurrent and disastrous famines which have visited it, especially in the drier areas;[1] at the time of writing, there has been failure of rain in four successive years, and yet again there is famine. (Disequilibrium between population and resources is, of course, the underlying cause of famine.) As in the Dry Zone of Ceylon, tank irrigation is in many areas the characteristic defence of the peasant against drought. Many of the tracts of Tamil Nad have red soils akin to those of the Dry Zone and presenting the same general problems.

Clearly, then, Tamil Nad has many points of resemblance to the Dry Zone of Ceylon. Yet a population map will show that, even away from the towns, it is densely settled; everywhere the rural density exceeds 250 per square mile, and often it exceeds 500. These facts are sometimes used by Indian visitors to Ceylon as proof that the Tamil has a far greater mastery than the Dry Zone Sinhalese of the general environment which they share. That there is a certain amount of technical superiority cannot be denied;[2] and it is also true that the Tamil is, in brief but superficial terms, more industrious. But it is also all too clear that there is in Tamil Nad, in relation to physical resources and current techniques of land use, considerable pressure of population on marginal land, so that population densities give an exaggerated measure of the ability of the Tamils to derive a living from their country. By contrast, much of the Dry Zone is not fully settled, though there is locally incipient over-population in relation to current land-use techniques.[3] These questions of technique, industry, and over-population will be considered more fully in the next chapter.

Meanwhile it is important, while the physical resources of the Dry Zone are still fresh in the mind of the reader, to draw attention to the fact that, in spite of many similarities between the two neighbours, Tamil Nad has certain important physical resources which are denied to the Dry Zone. There are wide stretches of alluvium (e.g. in the Cauvery delta). Elsewhere, not all soils are red and relatively infertile; there are, especially between Madura and Tinnevelly, tracts of *regur*, akin to black cotton soil, and more

[1] *Report of the Indian Famine Commission*, Cs. 2591 and 2735 (1880); *Papers regarding the Famine and Relief Operations in India*, C. 8302 (1897) and Cs. 8388, 8504, 8660, 8737, 8739, 8812, and 8823 (1898).
[2] See pp. 52–56.	[3] See below, pp. 65–66.

fertile and more retentive of water than anything in the Dry Zone. And even the red soils are often richer in nutrients than Dry Zone soils, because they are derived from *basic* crystalline rocks under a drier climate. But the chief difference lies in water resources, both surface and underground. Tamil Nad is crossed by great rivers like the Cauvery, which now irrigates more than a million acres; the contrast with the short, unreliable Dry Zone rivers is obvious. And there are far more opportunities for well construction. The alluvium, deltaic and coastal, which covers such wide areas is an aquifer, as are also the sedimentary rocks which cover a large proportion of the region—large, at any rate, when compared with the ratio between Jaffna and the rest of the Dry Zone. There seems, if anything, to be under-exploitation of these underground water resources.[1]

In fact, only the crystalline, red-soil areas of Tamil Nad away from great rivers are truly comparable to the Dry Zone of Ceylon. Even there, the soil differences already noted prevail; gentler slopes and a lower rainfall intensity reduce the danger of soil erosion; and there appear to be superior underground water resources. The Dry Zone of Ceylon cannot be expected, by reason of its poorer resources, ever to have the same density of rural population as Tamil Nad, given a common standard of land-use technology and of living. Even if one thinks in terms of a density in the latter sufficiently reduced to provide an adequate nutritional standard and to remove the threat of land exhaustion, then such a density would still be greater than the maximum possible in the Dry Zone. To realize this is a salutary lesson for Ceylonese optimists, and for Indian visitors who consider the only reason for the backwardness of the Dry Zone to be the backwardness of its people. There is, however, some substance in their criticism of Dry Zone land-use technology; the grounds of such criticism will emerge in the next chapter.

[1] A. V. Williamson, 'Indigenous Irrigation Works in Peninsular India', *Geog. Rev.*, vol. xxi (1931), pp. 613–26.

3

Economic and Social Conditions in the Dry Zone

As has already been hinted, the picture of the Dry Zone of Ceylon as a problem area is not complete without some reference to economic and social matters and, in particular, to indigenous systems of land use. To say that these help to constitute a problem is not to condemn them out of hand as outmoded or pernicious; for many local practices are found, on investigation, to be nicely adjusted to the hazards of the local physical environment. Certain problems of the Dry Zone are, moreover, not indigenous, but due to government policy (or lack of it), and also to that neglect of the Dry Zone by commercial interests which was the counterpart of their concentration of effort on the Wet Zone and the Hills, particularly the latter with their possibilities for plantation agriculture.

A review of land use and other economic features in the Dry Zone is particularly relevant to the study of peasant colonization. In the first place, it will serve to demonstrate traditional adaptations to the physical environment which, emphasizing as they do the potentialities and limitations of the region, are clearly likely to have lessons for the peasant colonist. In the second place, the colonization schemes are set, for the most part, not in completely empty country, but cheek by jowl with existing villages; relations with these villages form an important aspect of colonization.[1] In the third place, many colonists are drawn from the Dry Zone itself. It may at first sight seem strange that there is any need to settle peasants who have around them at least the appearance of plentiful land; but, quite apart from the need to give land to those displaced from their holdings by irrigation works or colonization schemes, the present chapter will show that there is, strange as it may seem, landlessness and a prevalence of under-sized holdings in parts of the Dry Zone, and it is important to discuss means by which the intensity of these possible qualifications for places in the colonies

[1] See below, pp. 308–10.

may be assessed. Lastly, this chapter touches on a number of considerations which bear on the general problem of future land use, and on the special problem of the availability of land for future large, irrigated colonization schemes.

Sources

Much that is included in this chapter and the following one is necessarily tentative because of the lack of published material and, indeed, of basic factual knowledge about many of the subjects which will have to be discussed. Thus, while the excellent one-inch-to-one-mile topographical map of Ceylon gives land-use information which is not available on the great majority of the world's national maps, it has many obvious limitations. Since its sheets have been compiled and revised at various times, they give a view of the situation which is not simultaneous over the whole country and which cannot, for example, give a true version of the areas under *chena* at any one time; the map also cannot give any reliable indication of the relation of land use to such physical features as the soil catena, and cannot show the size of family holdings and their degree of fragmentation. Data on some of these points are available as a result of the 1946 Census of Agriculture.[1] But there is a very real need in Ceylon for a comprehensive land-use survey, both to reveal the present state of affairs and to discover land potential as a basis for future planning. This need was recognized by the mission of the International Bank for Reconstruction and Development (the World Bank) which visited Ceylon in 1951, but it is a need which it will not be easy to satisfy.[2]

Again, some invaluable work was done between 1936 and 1948 on the economies of sample villages;[3] but, as has been pointed out, 'the operations were too much extended in time and too little extended in space to afford a picture of the rural sector of the Island as a whole',[4] and it is doubtful whether the results are accurate. The defects of these surveys were to some extent remedied when in 1950–1 work was done on one village in each of the D.R.O.'s

---

[1] See *Cey. Govt. Gaz.*, nos. 9575, 9596, 9612, 9632, 9668, 9682, 9693, 9758, 9764 (1946–7), and *Census of Ceylon, 1946*, vol. i.

[2] *WBR*, pp. 28 and 365–9 and (i. 18 and ii. 157–60). See also *CUCL*, espec. pp. 12–16 and 68.

[3] Published as *Bulletins of the Ministry of Labour, Industry and Commerce*, nos. 5–14 (Colombo, Govt. Press, 1937–48).

[4] *Prelim. Rep. Econ. Survey, Rural Ceylon*, p. 6.

Divisions of the island. At the time of writing only a preliminary report, and data about landlessness, are available.[1] Data on the economy of the peasantry are also available in other scattered contemporary sources, for example in the Report of the Kandyan Peasantry Commission;[2] in the Administration Reports of various government departments;[3] and in other places which will find mention in due course; but very much remains to be done.

One of the greatest gaps in our knowledge of the Ceylonese peasantry concerns its social structure and mental attitudes. Both social and psychological considerations are inextricably woven into the fabric of economic life, and in many aspects of the present study lack of fundamental knowledge of these factors will be a severe handicap, both in the interpretation of current economic and social phenomena and in the suggestion of means whereby defects and abuses in the present state of affairs may be remedied. The only scholarly comprehensive works which discuss the indigenous societies of Ceylon are mainly interested in institutions from the legal point of view;[4] and, as the writer of one of them remarks, 'It is perhaps to be regretted that anthropologists, who have interested themselves in Ceylon, should have confined their researches to the primitive Veddas, paying little attention to the modern Ceylonese.'[5] This was written in 1921, but is still broadly true today; for very little has been done in the meantime. True, the late Miss Elsie Cook included some of the results of her original surveys in her admirable human geography of Ceylon;[6] but much more remained unpublished and, indeed, incomplete at the time of her death.[7] More recently a certain amount of sociological reconnaissance has been done;[8] and there will be occasion to draw atten-

[1] *Prelim. Rep. Econ. Survey, Rural Ceylon* and *SL*.   [2] *KPC*.

[3] For example, the *Admin. Reports* of the Government Agents and Assistant Government Agents and of the Director of Rural Development.

[4] e.g. F. A. Hayley, *A Treatise on the Laws and Customs of the Sinhalese* (Colombo, Govt. Press, 1921); and H. W. Tambiah, *The Laws and Customs of the Tamils of Jaffna* (Colombo, Times of Ceylon Press [1951]), and *The Laws and Customs of the Tamils of Ceylon* (Colombo, Tamil Cultural Soc., 1954).

[5] Hayley, p. 153.

[6] E. K. Cook, *A Geography of Ceylon* (Madras, Macmillan, 1931), revised by K. Kularatnam under the title *Ceylon: its Geography, its Resources and its People* (Madras, Macmillan, 1951).

[7] The author wishes to record his debt to the late Mrs. P. de S. Kularatne for the opportunity of studying material left by Miss Cook.

[8] See, for example, Bryce Ryan, 'Socio-Cultural Regions of Ceylon', *Rur. Soc.*, vol. xv (1950), pp. 3–19, and 'The Ceylonese Village and the New Value

tion to a few other pieces of work in this chapter and the next. But an enormous amount of basic research remains to be done in this field and it is gratifying to record that it is now being entered by local scholars as well as others from Cambridge and elsewhere. Among the reasons for the neglect of such vital inquiries in the past is the fact that the tradition of indigenous learning was mainly literary and philosophical, and that what was grafted on this by early colonial civil servants nurtured in the Western classical tradition was an interest in similar aspects of Western learning, together with an interest in history aroused by the sight of so many splendid memorials of an ancient civilization superficially reminiscent of those of Greece and Rome. Thus there has been a spate of books by British writers and by Western-educated Ceylonese on Buddhism and Buddhist texts, on epigraphy, and on ancient history, but relatively few on important aspects of natural history, geography, rural economics, and sociology; further, the importance of these subjects is still insufficiently realized.

This chapter and the next have had to rely on the sparse information which is available, supplemented by such observations as the author was able to make incidentally to field study of the colonization schemes; but these chapters are all the more necessary because of the absence of comprehensive accounts.

The Dry Zone Economy and Society

As might be expected, the Dry Zone economy is primarily agricultural and rural; only at wide intervals are there urban centres of any size, and, as has already been remarked, many of these have functions which are largely independent of their physical hinterlands. The Dry Zone villages still attempt to a surprisingly large extent to be self-sufficient in staple foodstuffs (except in years of drought and shortage) and buy relatively little from outside. But, except in remoter regions, such as those parts of Bintenne which are away from main roads, most of the Dry Zone has fallen under the spell of a money economy, so that some proportion at least of local production is sold, and journeys are made to market centres so that purchases may be made.

The Dry Zone village is also, characteristically, self-contained institutionally; but pilgrimages have always been made to Buddhist

System', ibid., vol. xvii (1952), pp. 9–28, and *Caste in Modern Ceylon* (New Brunswick, Rutgers. Univ. Press, 1953).

and Hindu shrines (it is impressive to motor out of Anuradhapura on a *poya* day and see villagers walking in to the sacred city from places 30 or 40 miles away); and in the last few years contacts of many villages with the outside world have multiplied because of a growing habit of making protracted pilgrimages in a vehicle which is, by courtesy, a bus, but in reality a ramshackle ex-Army truck or van.

Very little of this is true of Jaffna, however, which, in its market-orientated economy as in its density of population, resembles the Wet Zone rather than the rest of the Dry Zone. And, indeed, there are considerable regional variations both social and economic, in the latter. Thus Miss Cook, in discussing settlement types and (in an elementary way, perforce) land use, distinguished the tank villages of Nuwarakalawiya and the Wanni from those of Tamankaduwa, Ruhuna, and Bintenne (making the point that in the last-named there were far fewer tanks than in the other regions); and all of these from the villages of the Trincomalee Bay and Batticaloa alluvium, of Giants' Tank, of the coconut areas of Puttalam and elsewhere, of the long coastal stretches, and of Jaffna.[1]

Again, Bryce Ryan recognized a number of 'socio-cultural regions' in the Dry Zone: Jaffna, the Northern Wanni, and Mannar, the North-Central Dry Zone Jungle, the East Coast, and the Eastern Dry Zone Jungle (the latter approximating to the region which, in the present work, has been called 'Bintenne').[2] It is not proposed here to discuss the basis for these divisions (indeed, more work will need to be done before they can be accurately delimited), and in general it will suffice to treat the economy and society of the Nuwarakalawiya–Wanni area as the Dry Zone norm, and to make brief reference to significant local departures from that norm. But the fact that there *are* local differences must be stressed very strongly: it is a valid criticism of Ceylon's colonization policy that it has been applied with too little regard for, and sometimes apparently in ignorance of, local human conditions.

The relevant components in the human geography of the Dry Zone will now be discussed under three main headings: land use, other features of the economy, and the society. The first of these is most relevant and will be discussed at greatest length.[3]

[1] See Cook, pp. 279–310, and espec. fig. 97, p. 295.
[2] Ryan, in *Rur. Soc.*, vol. xv, pp. 3–19.
[3] See Farmer, 'Problems of Land Use in the Dry Zone of Ceylon', *Geog. J.*, vol. cxx (1954), pp. 21–33.

Land Use in the Dry Zone: Nuwarakalawiya and Wanni

Agriculture in Nuwarakalawiya–Wanni is characterized by a threefold system of land use: there are (1) irrigated paddy fields, (2) village gardens, and (3) *chenas*, or patches under shifting cultivation in the jungle (see Plates 5, 6, and 7).[1] Such a threefold system can, of course, be matched in many other parts of Southern Asia. Thus Java has its *sawah*, or paddy fields, its gardens, and its *tegalan*, or unirrigated 'high land' cultivation.[2] ('High land' will throughout this work be used in the sense of land above the reach of irrigation.)

The *yāya*, or paddy tract, is normally irrigated from a village tank by customary techniques well adapted to the needs of the environment, and part at least is held under traditional tenures, each landholder possessing holdings in different parts of the *yāya* and having obligations to the whole body of landholders. Considerably more water is, however, used for the irrigation of the growing crops than is strictly necessary. The peasant is also often criticized for waiting until his tank is full before starting *Maha* (north-east monsoon) cultivation, thus wasting the direct effect of early rains which occur often enough to permit preliminary cultivation without irrigation. But this practice is in reality, like so many apparently ill-based indigenous customs, a sensible reaction to local circumstance; for if, encouraged by early rains, the peasant cultivates before his tank is full, he stands to lose both effort and seed if later rains fail. Another wise custom, and one that conserves water, is that of *bethma*, practised during *Yala* (south-west monsoon) cultivation, when there is often only enough water to irrigate part of the *yāya*. It would then be wasteful if each peasant cultivated an appropriate part of each of his holdings in the *yāya*, since the entire system of field channels would be in use and loss by seepage and evaporation at a maximum. Effort is therefore concentrated on a compact block adjacent to the tank, each villager cultivating the holdings which he has in that block.

In the Dry Zone *yāya*, techniques of cultivation are in general inefficient, and much effort is being directed to their improvement. Traditionally, the peasant cultivates with simple wooden

---

[1] The author is greatly indebted to Dr. E. R. Leach for discussions on practices in a Nuwarakalawiya village.

[2] K. J. Pelzer, *Pioneer Settlement in the Asiatic Tropics* (New York, Amer. Geog. Soc., 1945), pp. 44–77.

implements, or by 'mudding' (i.e. by driving pairs of buffaloes round and round the flooded fields; see Plate 19); he has no real system of manuring or rotations, though cattle are grazed on fallow fields; and, generally, poor seed is used, and is sown broadcast, the higher-yielding method of transplanting being rarely practised. It is not surprising that yields are lower than they need be, although it is unfair, in view of soil and other conditions, to compare these yields in Ceylon with those in other countries and to lay the whole of the blame on the peasant.[1]

It cannot be doubted that paddy is ecologically the best crop for all irrigable areas of suitable soil. The field *bunds* retain soil as well as water; and paddy, unlike other annual crops, tends to give economic yields for all time on tropical land without manuring, for reasons which are not wholly understood but which include the regular addition of organic matter by the ploughing in of weeds, the decelerated decay of organic matter under waterlogged conditions and at lower temperatures than prevail in dry-cultivated soil, the inflow of soil and nutrients in irrigation water and down high land slopes, and the activity of nitrogen-fixing algae.[2] Paddy cultivation, in fact, to some extent builds its own soil and mitigates some at least of the difficulties of natural tropical soils. Quite apart from the traditional importance of rice as an article of diet, it is not surprising that it is the ownership of paddy land, as distinct from high land, which often carries social prestige; this is a cultural consideration which has to be borne in mind in discussing colonization schemes *without* paddy land.[3]

The second element in the land-use pattern is the *watte* (garden) in the *gangoda*, or 'village place', containing closely packed houses and neat, thatched *bissas* (baskets on stilts for rice storage) in tiny, fenced compounds. Around the compound lies that familiar Asian feature, the wild garden of trees, vegetables, and other plants, in part self-sown and sometimes mistaken for jungle by Europeans, who in any case usually long to 'tidy up' its apparent confusion.

[1] Such a comparison is made, for example, by S. D. Bailey, *Ceylon* (London, Hutchinson's University Library, 1952), p. 155. The fact that the Ceylon yields which he quotes are gross under-estimates makes comparison even more risky. Bailey's table also lumps together countries growing the *japonica* varieties of rice with those (such as Ceylon) growing the *indica* varieties; the former give two to three times the yield of the latter, other things being equal.

[2] For the advantages of tropical rice cultivation, see Gourou, *Tropical World*, p. 100, and R. L. Pendleton, 'Agricultural and Forestry Potentialities of the Tropics', *Agronomy J.*, vol. xlii (1950), p. 120.   [3] See Chapter 17.

But the very approximation to jungle is in itself a wise measure, well suited to protect the soil from the effects of sun and rain; it has, in fact, been argued that tree cultivation is the ideal method of using high land in the tropics.[1] It must be stressed, however, that the *gangoda* represents a very special type of Dry Zone high land, in whose subsoil the water-table is usually preserved by proximity to a tank. Only a few *gangoda* trees, such as the mango (*Mangifera indica*), are naturally adapted to the Dry Zone. Others, such as the dominant coconut (*Cocos nucifera*) and the jak (*Artocarpus integrifolia*) are really Wet Zone trees, and are only able to grow because of the artificial soil moisture conditions.

Wells are frequently sunk in *gangodas* to tap the water beneath, but are hardly ever used for irrigation as they are in similar situations in South India.[2] Here, possibly, is a hint for an intensification of village garden cultivation.

Around the *yāya* and *gangoda* of the villages of Nuwarakalawiya and the Wanni there stretches the jungle, used, like the very comparable waste around the medieval English village, as a source of timber, game, and wild vegetable products, and as 'pasture' for village cattle when they are not grazing on fallow fields. 'Pasture' is something of a euphemism for the poor grasses, secondary scrub, and jungle normally encountered by village cattle, and as in many Asian countries, there are frequently too many animals. As in the colonization schemes,[3] the problem of pasture is a difficult one.[4]

More important than these uses of jungle is the practice of *chena* cultivation. The general routine of felling and burning jungle in the dry season, broadcast sowing on lightly hoed soil at the beginning of the wet season, and abandonment after two or three years has much in common with that customary in other parts of Asia and in Africa. But shifting cultivation in Ceylon is interesting, though not unique, because it is practised by a peasantry which undertakes *permanent* methods of cultivation in its paddy fields and gardens.[5]

---

[1] Pendleton, in *Agronomy J.*, vol. xlii, p. 122.
[2] See below, p. 53.   [3] See Chapter 12, pp. 256–8.
[4] See the *Report of the Communal Pastures Committee*, S.P. 27 of 1925 which is, however, inconclusive and altogether not a very satisfactory document.
[5] The same applies to shifting cultivation in Korea, Siam, and Indo-China; see Hoon K. Lee, *Land Utilization and Rural Economy in Korea* (London, OUP for IPR, 1936), p. 107; and W. R. C. Paul 'Roving Agriculture and the Problems of Dry Farming', *Trop. Agriculturist*, vol. cv (1949), pp. 4–14.

On the *Maha chena* are grown, in mixed cultivation, such cereals as maize and *kurakkan* (*Eleusine coracana*, the coarse or finger millet, the *ragi* of India), crops such as manioc (*Manihot utilissima* —cassava) and plantains (*Musa* spp.), and vegetables such as pumpkins, tomatoes, and chillies. *Elvī* (dry or hill paddy) may be grown in waterlogged situations. A crop of gingelly (*Sesamum indicum*, sesame) may be taken during the 'little monsoon', though the danger of ineffective rainfall is considerable. In fact *Maha chenas* may also fail through drought, though when cereals fail (as they did in 1952–3), vegetables may do well; the spreading of the risk is, in fact, the essential aim of the system of mixed cultivation.

The abandonment of *chenas* is enforced by weeds rather than by decreased fertility, and is usually followed in Nuwarakalawiya by a plant succession from weeds through scrub and secondary jungle to relatively high jungle.[1] The peasant has a term for each of the various stages in regeneration, and is aware of the insufficiency of the short period of regeneration (e.g. seven years) enforced by a growing population.

It cannot be doubted that *chena* cultivation dates from ancient times, and that under the physiographic and demographic conditions which have prevailed since then in most parts of Nuwarakalawiya and the Wanni it has enabled high land to be used for very many centuries without impairing the soil; it has also in some places enabled a sparse population to survive the dereliction of their tanks and *yāyas*. It has been shown that under the system practised in these regions *chena* cultivation depends almost entirely on nitrogen and nutrients made available by the burning of the jungle, soil reserves remaining largely untapped and in any case being readily restored after five to ten years of regeneration. Weed cover not only forces abandonment before much damage is done, but serves also to protect the soil from sun and rain. Material which is eroded cannot in any case proceed very far before it is checked by weeds or stumps or by the ambient jungle.[2] It is still customary in Ceylon to condemn *chena* cultivation as primitive and pernicious, but, as will be shown later in this book, it is by no means certain that an alternative method has yet been developed which will enable annual food crops to be grown in perpetuity on

[1] A. W. R. Joachim and S. Kandiah, 'The Effect of Shifting (*Chena*) Cultivation and Subsequent Regeneration on Soil Composition and Structure', *Trop. Agriculturist*, vol. civ (1948), pp. 3–11.   [2] Ibid.

Dry Zone high land.[1] Critics of the *chena* would be well advised to stay their hand till such an alternative method has become established.[2]

Work in the field shows, however, that *chenas* are extremely dangerous on steep slopes or on easily erodible soils; there irreparable damage may be done in one season. And, as in other parts of the world, the system becomes truly pernicious if population density increases so much that time for regeneration becomes too short. This stage appears to have been reached in a number of areas, for instance, immediately to the west of Kala Wewa (Map 2), and again at various points on the Anuradhapura–Kurunegala road. It would be useful, clearly, if one knew what the critical density was. There is, however, little to be gained by following some workers[3] and quoting the figure of 50 per square kilometre (130 per square mile) evaluated by van Beukering in Indonesia:[4] for there shifting cultivators are entirely dependent on their *ladangs* (jungle patches), whereas in Nuwarakalawiya the normal villager has also his paddy and his village garden. To judge by the Kala Wewa area, the critical density is about 200–250 per square mile; but further field research is needed.

Chena cultivation is one of a number of non-intensive ways of using high land which are to be found in various parts of Monsoon Asia, especially where high land, in the Ceylon sense, is also upland, in the general sense.[5] In China and elsewhere the comparative neglect of such land is, at least in part, a reflection of the stress which society puts on vegetable as distinct from animal foodstuffs, since some high land at least could be used as managed pasture if animals were more highly valued. The Sinhalese, too, are vegetarians, and have made no attempt to develop intensive pastoralism; this is, from one standpoint, just as well, in view of the disastrous results of efforts to provide pasture by burning the coarse grasses which invade *chenas* in parts of the Dry Zone.[6] In fact, whatever be the truth about the possibilities for more intensive use of high

---

[1] See below, pp. 342–8.   [2] See also *CUCL*.
[3] e.g. D. Rhind, *Some Aspects of Rotational Agriculture in Ceylon* (unpublished), quoted *CUCL*, p. 18.
[4] See Pelzer, *Pioneer Settlement*, pp. 23–24, quoting J. A. van Beukering, *Het Ladangsvraagstuk* (unpublished typescript, 1940).
[5] Gourou and others, in IPR, *The Development of Upland Areas in the Far East* (New York, 1949 and 1951); also Gourou, *L'Utilisation du sol en Indochine française* (Paris, Hartmann, 1940), p. 7.   [6] See p. 32.

land elsewhere in Asia, work in the field in the Dry Zone soon drives home the point that the *chena* system is a wise concession to the nature of the region, and in particular to the difficulty of growing annual crops in perpetuity where periodical soil regeneration is essential because of erodible soils, significant slopes, high temperatures, and seasonally heavy rainfall; and to the difficulty, in view of the behaviour of soil moisture, of establishing on true high land ecologically sound and economically useful tree crops such as are grown in the *gangoda*.

Land Use in the Remaining Regions of the Dry Zone

The most striking deviation from the 'normal' Dry Zone land-use pattern as found in Nuwarakalawiya–Wanni is that in the Jaffna Peninsula; it is related to the distinctive physical conditions which prevail there, but also owes much to a technical skill and an attitude to work which are rarely found elsewhere in Ceylon. The technology and powers of application of the Jaffna Tamil are very reminiscent of the best agricultural customs to be found amongst the Tamils of South India.[1] In particular, the Jaffna cultivator rivals the Coimbatore *ryot* in his careful attention to organic manuring; cattle and sheep are folded on the fields, leaves of trees are used as green manure, and every scrap of vegetable matter is returned to the soil.[2] And well irrigation, made possible by the water-bearing qualities of the limestone, is almost universal in the Peninsula.

Jaffna has its own threefold system of land use. Paddy is cultivated in areas of grey loam soils, but it is almost entirely rain fed in this land where there is no surface water for irrigation. The more fertile red soils mentioned in the previous chapter are mainly under a careful, well-irrigated garden cultivation of tobacco, chillies, and vegetables; a Jaffna garden is a delight to the European eye. And the 'high land' areas of bare limestone, thin soil, or sand are variously given over to millets, palmyra, and waste (there are also commercial coconut estates in the south-western part of the Peninsula). Of the three elements in the land-use pattern, the paddy and the gardens are very intensively cultivated; and, bearing

[1] See below, pp. 52–56.
[2] For an excellent account of the agriculture of Jaffna see S. F. de Silva, *A Regional Geography of Ceylon* (Colombo, Colombo Apothecaries, 1954), pp. 241–56.

in mind physical factors and the skill and industry of the Jaffnese, one begins to appreciate why the Peninsula can support such a dense population. (In most years, however, it is a net importer of food.)

In the Tamil areas of the east coast, another variant of the Dry Zone pattern is to be found. Most of the people live in crowded settlements on the coastal sand-bar, surrounded by gardens of coconut and other trees, as in the *gangoda*, though here there is no preservation of the water-table by irrigation works; the trees depend instead on the natural water in the sands, and are apt to suffer from drought. The same applies to commercial coconut plantations. The paddy lands are distinctive; they lie, not adjacent to the villages, but farther inland, across the lagoons and creeks which separate the coastal bar from the mainland. Here are some of the largest tracts of paddy land in the island, mainly visited by cultivators during the cultivation season only. There are similar wide alluvial paddy lands and sandy coconut groves in the Mannar region, though there some of the people live among gardens in *gangoda*-like situations, and there is no *chena*. There is commercial coconut cultivation here and at Puttalam.

In much of the Bintenne region, between the marginal scarps of the central highlands and the eastern and south-eastern coastal strips, there are few tanks, and hence relatively little paddy and *gangoda* garden. A sparse population lives almost entirely on *chena* cultivation, perpetuating a pattern common elsewhere in the Dry Zone before village tanks were restored; and it is here that abandoned *chenas* tend to be invaded by *illuk* (*Imperata cylindrica*), with disastrous results on the ecological situation.[1] Bintenne does appear, however, especially in the vicinity of Bibile, to be better suited than other Dry Zone regions to the high land cultivation of such tree crops as citrus, possibly because of the higher rainfall.

Finally, mention must be made of land use in areas settled by individual initiative in the days before the beginning of the systematic, government-aided colonization which forms the main theme of this book.[2] Such areas include most of the lands under Kala Wewa and under the group of tanks at Tissamaharama, and those along the lower Walawe Ganga. Here, in general and in modified form, the familiar threefold pattern emerges. Paddy land tends, in these wide irrigated tracts, to dominate the landscape to a greater

---

[1] See above, p. 32.   [2] See Chapters 5 and 6.

extent than in the villages of Nuwarakalawiya. But there are many patches of garden in *gangoda*-like situations near tanks or channels, or in unirrigable tracts among the paddy; and *chena* is often practised on surrounding high land. Perhaps in these major schemes the landscape of ancient Ceylon is being reconstituted.

Land Use in Tamil Nad; a Comparative Sketch

The previous chapter has shown that Tamil Nad has a climate closely analogous to that of the Dry Zone, and, where the bed rock is crystalline, at least an approximation to the soil and ground-water conditions to be met in Nuwarakalawiya and the Wanni; it was also hinted, in a review of the physical factors behind Tamil Nad's comparatively great population density, that differences between Tamil Nad and the Dry Zone were also a matter of techniques and attitudes. These techniques and attitudes will now be reviewed, with special, but not exclusive reference to the crystalline, red-soil areas which, of all Tamil Nad, approximate most closely to the Dry Zone of Ceylon.

At the time of writing the author had had no opportunity of studying the region in the field, and the remarks which follow are necessarily tentative; they are based on some acquaintance with the region from the air, and on study of maps and literature.[1] Unfortunately, the Survey of India one-inch map does not carry land-use information comparable with that carried by its Ceylon counterpart, and very little of the literature adopts the criteria of this chapter, either in classifying land or in assessing the suitability of current practice as a method of conserving land resources for perpetual use. The Royal Commission on Agriculture in India did, however, point out that there were three types of villages in Madras, villages with wet lands, villages with 'superior dry lands' (predominantly gardens irrigated by means of wells), and villages with 'inferior dry lands'.[2] Here, clearly, are the counterparts of the familiar *yāya*, *gangoda*, and true high land of the Dry Zone of Ceylon, but in separate villages rather than combined in the same village, and with well irrigation in the *gangoda* and permanent cultivation rather than *chena* on the 'inferior dry lands'.

[1] See espec. the *Madras Agric. J.*, the *J. of the Madras Geog. Assoc.*, and the *Indian Geog. J.* (Madras). See also G. Slater, *Southern India* (London, Allen & Unwin, 1936); E. Simkins, 'The Coast Plains of South India', *Econ. Geog.*, vol. ix (1933), pp. 19–50 and 136–59; and *Final Report of the All India Soil Survey Scheme*, pp. 21–22 and 87–111.   [2] RCAI, iii. 59.

One is immediately struck, in fact, with the many similarities between land use in Tamil Nad on the one hand, and that in Nuwarakalawiya and the Wanni on the other (almost certainly the techniques of the two regions have a common origin, though the Tamil claim to have invented irrigation and wet rice cultivation would be hotly disputed by the Sinhalese, and no doubt by other Asian peoples).[1] In the crystalline country especially, many Tamil villages are built, like Dry Zone villages, on land of *gangoda* character, though, as might be expected from the Royal Commission's classification, not all have paddy tracts. But there is a much greater density of tanks and of villages than in the Dry Zone, especially in the Madura–Ramnad 'tank country'.[2] In some areas it seems that every tiny valley has been dammed to form a tank, and the total effect must be to tend to preserve the water-table over wide areas. Possibly the ancient Dry Zone had a comparable density of tanks; certainly one is constantly coming across small *bunds* in the jungle.

The possibility of tapping underground water has been far more fully seized upon by the Tamils than by the Dry Zone Sinhalese; and the wells are widely used for irrigation. About a quarter of the wells in Madras are in wet land under government irrigation works, and are used to supplement such works. The rest are *ayahat* wells, i.e. they are in land assessed as dry for revenue purposes, the criterion being that the well should be more than 100 yards from a government irrigation work.[3] But most *ayahat* wells appear not to be in true high land, but to benefit from perennial rivers, or from government works *more* than 100 yards away; others are in valley bottoms occupied by small streams which are seasonally dry, but where doubtless the water-table is more constant than in the interfluves. In other words, a great many wells are in a position hydrologically comparable to that of the Sinhalese *gangoda*. A field investigation in the crystalline regions of Tamil Nad would be very rewarding, and might suggest ways in which wells could be sunk in the Dry Zone. But there is nothing to indicate that the Tamils have solved on a large scale the problem of bringing water to true high land; as in the Dry Zone, natural conditions are against this.

---

[1] Cmd. 3117, p. 231.   [2] Spate, pp. 731–2.
[3] *Report of the Indian Irrigation Commission, 1901–3*, pt. 2, Cd. 1852 (1903), p. 123.

The preservation of the water-table by means of tanks and the use of wells for irrigation introduce the possibility of more intensive cultivation, especially of land in a *gangoda* position, than that which characterizes the half-wild 'garden' around the Nuwarakalawiya village. But the possibilities are only realized because of the great assiduity of the Tamil *ryot*, which reaches a peak in the irrigated gardens of Coimbatore.[1] In such gardens, vegetables are grown on a most intensive system which involves the use of manures, composted wastes, and rotations. Whether the qualities of the Tamil are due to some virtue of his culture (as Ceylon Tamils are apt to aver when they look at their easy-going Sinhalese compatriots), or whether they are a response to the needs of a high population density, the fact remains that these qualities must be counted among the factors which distinguish Tamil Nad from Nuwarakalawiya and the Wanni.

But one of the most striking points of difference lies in the far more intensive use which is made of true high land in Tamil Nad. It is true that there are very few villages on such land (presumably such as there are fall into the Royal Commission's third class). And it is also true that there are, especially in inland regions, considerable areas under jungle, reserved forest, scrub, and grassland: in other words, uncultivated high land. But a great deal of high land is characterized by permanent cultivation. In places there are groves of permanent tree crops adapted to drought, for example palmyras (*Borassus flabellifer*) and cashew trees (*Anacardium occidentale*). Far more commonly, high land is under annual crops, such as millets, cotton, groundnuts, and oilseeds. Having regard to what has been said about the difficulties of permanent high land cultivation in the Dry Zone of Ceylon, what factors enable the Tamils of South India apparently to succeed? Gentler slopes and lower rainfall may reduce the danger of soil erosion. Well irrigation is occasionally used, though naturally wells in true high land are generally small and uncertain.[2] More important are methods of maintaining fertility. Cow dung, leaf-mould, and tank silt are used, and regular ploughing practised. On the other hand, it is clear that techniques are far from perfect. Sir William Denison remarked on the 'continuous cropping, the deficiency of manure, and its consumption as fuel, the defective implements, the

[1] Spate, p. 714.
[2] *Report of Indian Irrigation Commission*, pt. 4, Cd. 1854 (1903), pp. 115–17.

lack of trees' as long ago as 1863.[1] The Royal Commission of 1928 stressed the need for research into high land cultivation,[2] and stated that it was the dry farmer who, of all Tamil *ryots*, needed most assistance.[3] And, as in peninsular India generally, erosion is not regarded by the peasant as a serious danger, and contour *bunds* and similar devices are seldom used.[4]

Signs are not lacking that permanent high land cultivation in Tamil Nad has been pushed by pressure of population into areas where, with the techniques in use, it is dangerous. Much of the country has, from the air, a dry, burnt-up appearance probably indicative of human interference with the ecological equilibrium of Nature; and there is much useless scrub. In some places a gravelly, lateritic crust, a sure sign of erosion, forms the present surface.[5] Severe erosion is further suggested by the existence of tanks containing far more silt than is usual in the jungle-girt tanks of the Dry Zone of Ceylon.

Experiments at Sholapur, in the Bombay Deccan, while not carried out in conditions exactly representing those to be found in Tamil Nad, give a vivid impression of the dangers of permanent cultivation of high land; no less than 43·99 tons of soil per acre were lost under a single crop of *jowar* (*Andropogon sorghum*, sorghum, the *chōlăm* of the Tamils).[6] Again, in experiments at the Dry Farming Station at Hazari, in the 'Ceded Districts' of Madras, plots of *regur* with a gradient of no more than 1 in 80 lost 6·6, 9·9, and 7·4 tons of soil per acre by sheet erosion under rainfalls of 9·2, 15·7, and 8·4 inches respectively.[7] Clearly, since the Tamils do not in general practise systematic conservation, the danger of erosion is very great except on very gentle slopes or under light rainfall.

To sum up, evidence from Tamil Nad suggests that there is some substance in the charge that lack of technique and of assiduity are factors in the present backwardness of at least some parts of the Dry Zone and, in particular, in its relatively easy-going methods of land use. Wells for the intensive irrigation of existing

[1] Cmd. 3132, p. 22. [2] RCAI, iii. 154.
[3] Ibid., p. 173.
[4] N. V. Kanitkar, *Dry Farming in India* (Delhi, Imp. Council of Agric. Research, 1944), pp. 29–31. [5] Spate, p. 731.
[6] Kanitkar, *Dry Farming in India*, p. 138 (43·99 tons per acre is about 2½ lb. per sq. ft.).
[7] A. Subba Rao, 'Soil Erosion by Surface Run-off', *Madras Agric. J.*, vol. xxviii (1940), pp. 272–5.

gangoda gardens; the construction or restoration of a multitude of small tanks to preserve the water-table and thus to create further possibilities for *gangoda* cultivation, for wells, and for high land tree cultivation; the growing on high land of drought-adapted tree crops like palmyra and cashew; and the preoccupation with the job in hand which is characteristic particularly of the Coimbatore *ryot*; all of these may either have immediate application or be worthy of experiment in Nuwarakalawiya and the Wanni. But under the physiographic and climatic conditions which prevail in these Dry Zone regions permanent high land cultivation of annual crops on the Tamil Nad model appears to be a far more hazardous affair. It is not without its dangers even on the gentler slopes of Tamil Nad. It seems very likely that it has been pressure of population, rather than the discovery of a superior and foolproof technique, which has forced the Tamil on to the high land. And the evident degradation of much of the countryside, together with the frequency of distress and famine, show all too clearly what may happen to the Dry Zone given excessive population, insufficient research, and an inadequate technique of land use.

Land Tenure in the Dry Zone

Something has already been said of the landlessness and under-sized holdings to be found in the Dry Zone of Ceylon. It is now proposed to discuss these and other modern land-tenure problems a little more fully. Most attention will be paid to paddy land, which is fundamental to the village economy (except in parts of Jaffna, in the poor *chena* villages of Bintenne, and in other exceptional regions); and the individual and the village community stand or fall in prosperity and in social esteem according to their holding of paddy. It also happens that most of the scanty and confused data concern paddy land. The topics to be discussed are dictated partly by the nature of the Dry Zone land-tenure problem, but partly also by the availability of statistics. They are: (1) the tenurial system under which paddy 'holdings' are cultivated, a holding being a plot of land worked as a unit (one cultivator may work several such units and one owner may possess several holdings cultivated by various persons); (2) the ownership of paddy land, particularly the distribution of units of ownership of various sizes and the incidence of landlordism; (3) the distribution of very small holdings; (4) gardens and *chenas*; (5) the incidence of absolute landlessness. The whole discussion will perhaps not so much clarify the agrarian situation as show how, with existing data, it is very difficult to arrive at a simple index to indicate the pressure of population on land.

   1. *Tenurial systems.* Tables 2 and 3 show the tenure of paddy holdings according to the 1946 Census of Agriculture, and relate to Revenue Districts which lie wholly or mainly in the Dry Zone.[1] It should be explained that an *ande* tenant is one who holds his land by métayage paying a fixed proportion of his crop (usually one-half) to the landowner; that a *tattumāru* owner is one who owns a piece of land jointly with other parties, each co-owner cultivating for one year in turn; and that the final column of each table includes cultivators who are hired labourers, usufructuary mortgagees (who had obtained possession of mortgaged land and enjoy its

TABLE 2

Tenure of Paddy Holdings, Dry Zone Districts, 1946

District	Total no. of holdings	Percentage of holdings cultivated by				
		Owner	Lessee	Ande tenant	Tattu-māru owner	Others
Anuradhapura	126,630	76·3	1·7	16·2	3·5	2·2
Vavuniya .	8,258	73·2	12·9	11·4	0·2	2·1
Jaffna . .	57,484	88·1	9·5	0·1	0·2	2·2
Batticaloa .	17,291	61·8	21·2	0·1	2·7	·14·1
Trincomalee .	4,737	66·0	25·2	4·6	1·1	2·9
Mannar. .	9,044	78·8	17·5	0·2	1·5	2·0
Puttalam .	7,833	74·7	4·5	14·1	5·5	1·4
Hambantota .	10,362	55·7	5·8	28·0	5·3	5·1
Ceylon Total .	771,908	60·8	3·6	25·8	6·8	2·9

Source: Census of Ceylon, 1946, vol i, pt. 2.

produce in lieu of interest), holders of land under colonization and other schemes subject to the Land Development Ordinance,[2] and cultivators who perform services (e.g. tom-tom beating) at temples or to hereditary landlords in lieu of rent.

   It will be gathered that land tenure in Ceylon is a matter of some complexity; it represents the impact of Western ideas and of a

   [1] Cf. data for other Asian countries in *Land Reform*, pp. 53 and 55.
   [2] See below, pp. 159–60.

modern economy on an already involved system of tenure whose
origins still cause controversy.[1] According to some authorities
there are, as elsewhere in the East and in Africa, signs of an ancient

TABLE 3

Tenure of Paddy Holdings by Area, Dry Zone Districts, 1946

District	Total area of holdings (acres)	Percentage of area cultivated by				
		Owner	Lessee	Ande tenant	Tattu-māru owner	Others
Anuradhapura	95,876	69·8	5·1	17·3	2·5	5·0
Vavuniya .	22,644	70·3	17·2	9·3	0·3	2·8
Jaffna . .	52,881	77·5	17·2	0·3	0·2	4·8
Batticaloa .	119,170	59·2	24·3	0·3	2·6	13·7
Trincomalee .	21,592	64·2	32·1	0·9	1·0	1·8
Mannar. .	23,356	74·3	21·3	0·1	0·8	3·5
Puttalam .	7,983	62·6	12·4	15·8	6·8	2·4
Hambantota .	38,417	46·8	11·7	32·5	3·2	5·7
Ceylon Total .	899,970	55·2	9·1	23·6	6·5	5·2

Source: Census of Ceylon, 1946, vol. i, pt. 2.

communal system of land tenure under which lands were held and
administered by the village society, or at least by the joint family;[2]
on this view the customs concerning rights over *chena* land[3] are
survivals of such communal tenure. It is possible that until
Western influence made itself felt there was no concept of absolute
ownership of land, but only of proprietorship, often under service
tenures. The idea of ownership is now only too well established,
and litigation over land is a national disease; but the Land Development Ordinance is sometimes claimed to restore the concept
of proprietorship, leaving ultimate ownership with the Crown.[4]
Proposals for co-operative cultivation, similarly, may be seen in

[1] See Hayley, *Laws and Customs of Sinhalese*, espec. pp. 165–6 and 222–8;
Codrington, *Ancient Land Tenure and Revenue in Ceylon* (Colombo, Govt. Press,
1938); Brohier, *Land, Maps and Surveys*, i. 1–31; Tambiah, *Tamils of Jaffna* and
Tamils of Ceylon; also C. K. Meek, *Land Law and Custom in the Colonies*
(London, OUP, 1946), pp. 57–61. See also J. de Lanerolle, 'An Examination of
Codrington's Work on Ancient Land Tenure and Revenue in Ceylon', *J.R. As.
Soc.* (Cey. Br.), vol. xxxiv (1938), pp. 199–230.
[2] Hayley, *Laws and Customs of Sinhalese*, pp. 165–6 and 222, and Codrington,
Ancient Land Tenure, p. 3; cf. *Land Reform*, pp. 27–33.
[3] See below, p. 64.   [4] See below, pp. 159–60.

some lights as a revival of an old, communal order.[1] But in all these matters it is all too easy for the modern administrator to see his imposed solution of tenurial problems as a restoration of tradition.

Tables 2 and 3 may now largely be left to speak for themselves, but a few comments may perhaps be made. In the first place, it will be clear that everywhere in the Dry Zone the majority of the holdings are in the hands of owner-cultivators, especially in intensively cultivated Jaffna and in Nuwarakalawiya–Wanni (or, at least, in Anuradhapura and Vavuniya Districts).[2] The lowest figures for ownership by cultivators are in the east coast districts (Batticaloa and Trincomalee) where over 20 per cent. of the holdings are leased to peasant cultivators, and in the Puttalam District and, lowest of all, in Hambantota District, where much land under major irrigation works is largely let out on *ande* or worked by hired labour. *Tattumāru* tenure is nowhere very significant, land not owned by the cultivator being held either by lessees or on *ande* tenure. Other systems are in no district very important, though in colonization schemes tenure under the Land Development Ordinance is in force, and though particular villages are apt to be dominated by service tenure, which was thought by the Kandyan Peasantry Commission to have undesirable consequences under modern conditions.[3] The Commission also drew attention to the oft-quoted disadvantages of the *ande* system, especially the insecurity of tenure, and the lack of incentive to increased production if the landlord is to reap half of the increase.[4] (Security of tenure and other improved conditions should theoretically result if the Paddy Lands Act, No. 1 of 1953, is widely applied.) But *ande* tenure is nevertheless strongly reinforced by traditions deeply rooted in the social system. Nowhere in the Dry Zone, it should be stressed, are there great estates worked by hired labourers, as in Egypt and other countries, or Zamindars, as in India.[5]

[1] See below, p. 370, and compare with the ideal, co-operative village of the Indian planners, *The First Five Year Plan* (Delhi, Manager of Publications, 1951), pp. 100–2.

[2] The proportion of owner-cultivators appears to have risen in the last thirty years; cf. *Agricultural Wages and Earnings of Primary Producers in Ceylon*, S.P. 2 of 1950, p. 11.

[3] *KPC*, pp. 107–9.   [4] Ibid., pp. 109–10.

[5] Doreen Warriner, *Land and Poverty in the Middle East* (London, RIIA, 1948), pp. 14 and 36; *Land Reform*, pp. 9–10 and 51–54; A. K. S. Lambton, *Landlord and Peasant in Persia* (London, OUP for RIIA, 1953), espec. pp. 259–74.

That is not to say, however, that landlordism is absent from the Dry Zone. Although Tables 2 and 3 clearly mark out most of the Dry Zone as an area where peasant proprietorship is the rule, the reader will probably have noted the discrepancy between corresponding figures in the two tables. Cultivation by the owner in all cases accounts for a smaller percentage of the paddy *area* than of the number of paddy *holdings*, indicating that, on the whole, it is the smaller holdings which are owned by the cultivator, and the somewhat larger ones which are leased or rented out.

TABLE 4

Ownership of Dry Zone Paddy Land, 1946

District	Percentage of owners of paddy land owning total areas in acres of									
	<2	2<3	3<4	4<5	5<10	10<15	15<20	20<30	30<50	>50
Anuradhapura	41·1	17·9	12·6	13·7	8·5	3·5	1·2	1·1	0·4	0·1
Vavuniya .	21·3	17·7	12·4	13·6	21·8	7·9	2·5	1·5	0·8	0·3
Jaffna . .	80·9	10·9	3·7	2·2	1·4	0·4	0·1	0·2	0·1	0·1
Batticaloa .	6·1	4·9	6·2	6·9	27·7	18·4	14·6	11·5	2·9	0·9
Trincomalee .	18·7	18·2	16·5	13·4	17·6	6·9	4·8	1·2	2·1	0·5
Mannar. .	20·8	18·9	15·7	14·6	16·1	6·5	3·3	2·0	1·1	0·7
Puttalam .	52·8	28·7	7·8	4·8	4·9	0·5	0·3	0·3	0·2	..
Hambantota .	13·3	21·2	16·2	15·4	12·8	7·7	6·4	3·3	2·8	0·9
Ceylon . .	71·2	13·3	6·1	4·0	2·9	1·3	0·6	0·4	0·2	0·1

Source: Investigation carried out by the Internal Purchase Scheme, 1946, and quoted in *SL*.

2. *Ownership of paddy land.* What is known of ownership of paddy land, as distinct from tenure of holdings, is summed up in Table 4. Unfortunately, data for Anuradhapura and Batticaloa Districts are defective, rough estimates only being available for the Divisions of Tamankaduwa (Anuradhapura District) and Kalmunai (Batticaloa District).[1]

Table 4 confirms that the ownership of land in great estates is not characteristic of the Dry Zone; nowhere do more than 1 per cent. of the owners of paddy land own more than 50 acres, or more than 3 per cent. own more than 30 acres. On the other hand, it will be clear that in the Batticaloa District in particular a high proportion of owners possess areas of paddy which are large by Ceylon standards; nearly half of them own more than 10 acres (compared with under 3 per cent. owning a similar extent in Ceylon as a whole) and over three-quarters of them more than 5 acres.

[1] *SL*, pp. 31–38.

These relatively high figures, taken with the high percentage of holdings cultivated by lessees (Table 2), show how important a figure the landlord is on the Batticaloa coastal alluvium. There is also some tendency towards the ownership of large areas in the Vavuniya, Trincomalee, Mannar, and Hambantota Districts; in the two last named this is associated with the grant of fairly large blocks under restored irrigation works.[1] On the other hand, it will be clear that a very high proportion of Jaffna's paddy landowners possess very small extents: 80 per cent. of them under 2 acres, and over 90 per cent. of them under 3 acres. The same is true, in a lesser degree, of Anuradhapura and Puttalam Districts.

3. *Very small holdings.* The size of a holding becomes particularly important at the lower end of the scale, though a high incidence of very small 'holdings' is not a clear index of pressure on land because of the definition adopted.[2] Table 5 sums up the distribution of paddy holdings of less than 5 acres.

TABLE 5

Paddy Holdings of less than 5 Acres, by Number and Area,
Dry Zone Districts, 1946

District	Percentage of holdings with an area (in acres) of				Percentage of acreage in holdings of (acres)			
	$<\frac{1}{2}$	$\frac{1}{2}<1$	$1<2$	$2<5$	$<\frac{1}{2}$	$\frac{1}{2}<1$	$1<2$	$2<5$
Anuradhapura .	41·0	33·2	17·4	6·8	11·8	23·4	25·3	23·2
Vavuniya . .	2·9	14·2	25·6	42·5	0·3	3·0	11·2	43·6
Jaffna . .	45·7	29·8	15·2	7·2	12·7	20·6	20·3	21·2
Batticaloa .	0·9	1·3	8·1	37·2	0·0	0·1	1·5	16·7
Trincomalee .	3·6	13·5	16·5	35·2	0·2	1·7	4·3	23·0
Mannar . .	11·8	14·7	25·2	34·4	1·0	3·3	12·1	38·2
Puttalam . .	34·7	34·1	16·9	11·6	8·1	18·1	18·7	29·7
Hambantota .	9·6	16·0	21·8	31·7	0·6	2·6	7·4	26·5
Ceylon . .	31·4	32·8	21·1	11·2	6·4	16·4	21·6	25·7

Source: Census of Ceylon, 1946, vol. i, pt. 2.

The table brings into sharp contrast the state of affairs in Batticaloa District on the one hand, and in Jaffna, Anuradhapura, and Puttalam Districts on the other. There is clearly a relatively low number of very small paddy holdings in Batticaloa District, where, in fact, some 80 per cent. of the paddy land is in holdings of over

[1] See below, pp. 105–6.   [2] See above, p. 56.

5 acres and some 50 per cent. in holdings of over 10 acres.[1] These figures might be taken as an indication that, since the peasant is not forced to cultivate a very small holding, there is no great pressure of population on land; and that, given the prevalence of land-lordism, land reform may be required rather than the colonization of a surplus population. But the figures do not tell the whole story. In point of fact, there *is* pressure of population on land, and in consequence the landlords are able to procure *ande* tenants and lessees on terms more unfavourable to the cultivator than any-where else in the country. Whereas in many other areas the land-lord gives the cultivator seed and buffaloes, and shares the harvest on a 50:50 basis, in Batticaloa the landlord recovers advances for seed, buffalo hire, and harvesting expenses with 50 per cent. interest, and even then takes two-thirds of the harvest. Moreover, there is also a considerable volume of migratory seasonal labour which leaves the east coast for as far afield as Mannar and Vavuniya Districts.

But a very different state of affairs prevails in Jaffna, Anuradha-pura, and Puttalam Districts, where there is a high percentage of very small paddy holdings. The presence of Jaffna in this group of districts need occasion no surprise, for not only is it outstanding for its small peasant proprietors, but it is also a region where centuries of settlement and pressure of population might be ex-pected to have led to cultivation in very small units.

But Anuradhapura and Puttalam Districts have a percentage of very small paddy holdings which may appear astonishingly high if one thinks of them as regions of sparse population, as a 'pioneer fringe' with plenty of land to spare. Their proportions of holdings of under half an acre approach the very high figures for the con-gested Up-country districts:[2] and the average paddy holding in Anuradhapura District has been quoted as 0.76 acres.[3] The reasons for this state of affairs deserve detailed field investigation; but it may be suggested (1) that many village tanks are irrigating as large a *yāya* as they can, given present techniques of irrigation and in particular the absence of supplemental well irrigation, so that

---

[1] See *Census of Ceylon, 1946*, vol. i, pt. 2, table 70, pp. 393–4.

[2] Cf. Table 12, p. 87.

[3] *SL*, p. 28. It is possible that the statistics exaggerate the proportion of very small holdings by taking no account of some or all of the many holdings which have in the last fifteen years or so been alienated in units of over an acre under the Land Development Ordinance (see below, pp. 159–60).

holdings have been subdivided instead of waste being reclaimed; (2) that, until the recent operation of village expansion schemes,[1] it has not been easy for the villager legally to reclaim Crown waste; (3) that the villager has tended to stay in his home village where, *inter alia*, his wealthier relatives have an obligation to let him land on *ande*; (4) that the sensible custom of distributing an individual's parcels of land between tracts at different distances from water-supply results in a 'holding' much smaller than the total area that he owns or cultivates.

The remaining districts clearly take up positions intermediate between the two contrasting extremes which have been discussed; nothing further need be said about them here.

To what extent is the general problem of very small holdings due, as so frequently elsewhere, to subdivision of older holdings between several heirs? Unfortunately no coherent information is available on this problem. In the absence of any custom of primogeniture, inherited holdings do tend to become subdivided;[2] but the working of holdings in several, apparently fragmented parcels is, on the other hand, not only the traditional solution to the problem of 'fair shares' of water but also not necessarily uneconomic given present techniques of cultivation.

4. *Gardens and* chena. It may be asked at this stage whether the small extents per owner and the tiny holdings which are beginning to emerge as the main agrarian problems of paddy cultivation in many parts of the Dry Zone, and in particular in Nuwarakalawiya, are not in effect counterbalanced by the existence of the two other classes of land which were defined earlier in this chapter; namely *gangoda* garden and *chena*.

The Census of Agriculture of 1946 does not enumerate *gangoda* gardens as such. But most of them are probably included in the category 'town and village gardens', which are defined as 'a holding of 1 acre and less with any form of cultivation, usually forming the compound of a dwelling house'.[3] There were 120,104 such gardens in the Dry Zone districts (including Jaffna), roughly one for every five persons (though not by any means all of them were cultivated).[4] The cultivated gardens covered 30,848 acres, and their average size varied from about one-seventh of an acre in the

---

[1] See below, pp. 174–5.   [2] See Meek, *Land Law and Custom*, p. 58.
[3] *Census of Ceylon, 1946*, vol. i, pt. 2, Introduction (unpaginated).
[4] Ibid., pp. 386–7.

Mannar District to half an acre in the Hambantota District. The average size in Anuradhapura District, the home of the *gangoda*, was about one-quarter of an acre. These gardens thus make a by no means inconsiderable contribution to the land-use pattern of the Dry Zone, though one must bear in mind their generally unkempt and unirrigated condition. There are no data on the tenure of these gardens; many are held by individual or joint owners in association with paddy land. The Census also recognized a category of 'small holding', 'a holding of less than 20 acres and more than 1 acre on which there exists any cultivated agricultural products' (*sic*; in point of fact paddy lands and *chena* were excluded from this category).[1] Many such were cultivated with commercial crops (e.g. the coconuts of the Puttalam and Batticaloa coastal areas) but some must be large *gangoda* gardens, or high land plots cultivated permanently.

Jaffna District, as might be expected, has a large area of gardens; actually there were 127,060 gardens, with 25,220 cultivated acres, in 1946;[2] no comprehensive data on tenure are available, but many of these gardens are known to be in individual ownership. There were also 10,739 acres of 'small holdings' in the Jaffna District.

As for *chena*, little needs to be said. According to the 1946 Census of Agriculture, there were in that year 16,992 *chenas* in the Dry Zone districts, with a cultivated acreage of 13,122 and an uncultivated of 19,529; but all of these figures may be under-estimates. The average size of *chenas* varied from district to district, but pressure on potential *chena* land is better measured by the study of ecology than by study of statistics, since in two areas with equal availability of land there may be quite different numbers and sizes of *chenas* owing to differing customs and differing possibilities for alternative methods of cultivation. While, as has been stressed already, there are areas where population is pressing on available high land, this is today mainly a matter of sheer physical shortage of land rather than of land tenure. Traditional custom is certainly no bar to the cultivation of *chena*.[3] In many Dry Zone villages a man may still occupy a *chena* so long as he cultivates it, after which, as it reverts to jungle, he has no claim to it.[4] There

---

[1] *Census of Ceylon, 1946*, vol. i, pt. 2, Introduction (unpaginated).
[2] Ibid., pp. 386–7.
[3] See *First Interim Report of the Land Commission*, S.P. 2 of 1928, p. 18.
[4] This was the state of affairs in 1848 as reported by Ievers, pp. 115–16. See

are also 'private' *chenas*, only too often involving the reprehensible use of high land in perpetuity; but they have on the whole little effect on the availability of land. Government action has, however, done something to modify ancient custom. The Crown Lands Encroachments Ordinance, No. 12 of 1840, under which all apparently 'waste' land, including *chena*, was declared Crown property, did not have in the Dry Zone the disastrous effect which it had Up-country, where much Crown land was alienated to estate owners and village rights to *chena* thus destroyed;[1] but in other ways policy towards *chena* cultivation, though variable, was generally hostile and control strict. Occasional voices did, however, venture the opinion that 'the outcry against *chenas* can be overdone', and that villages needed them for their very existence.[2] Today things are easier. Each village has an area (largely traditional) within which *chena* may be practised; the headman merely prepares and posts a list of *chenas* authorized in his villages, and reports his list to his D.R.O.; but illicit *chenas*, and penalties incurred by their cultivation, are still common.

5. *Landlessness*. One final aspect of the problem in the Dry Zone needs mention; it concerns landlessness and its meaning and significance. Clearly the fact that a high proportion of the peasantry are without holdings of their own is of more significance in a region of small holdings dominated by peasant proprietorship than in a region of landlords and of traditional *ande*, or in one of large holdings needing wage labour, and there is every reason to beware of crude figures which merely show numbers of 'landless' peasants. Table 6 is, however, given for what it is worth; and with the further warning that it is based on sampling only (actually on a survey of one village from each D.R.O.'s Division).

The only districts which call for comment are Anuradhapura, Vavuniya, Jaffna, and Puttalam. The remainder have either relatively low figures, or have high or fairly high percentages at least partly explicable in terms of the prevalence of tenancy. The four districts named, however, all have holdings dominated by the peasant proprietor, and all have figures approaching or exceeding the Ceylon average. There seems to be some reason, then, for considering these districts as afflicted by a form of landlessness which

---

also Codrington, *Ancient Land Tenure*, espec. p. 4; and, for private *chenas*, Brohier, *Land, Maps and Surveys*, pp. 7–8 and 13.

[1] See below, pp. 90–91.   [2] Leonard Woolf's MS. Diary.

does in part represent a disequilibrium between land and population, though one must always bear in mind the traditional nature of *ande*. In three of these districts (Anuradhapura, Jaffna, and Puttalam) there are also many small extents in individual ownership. In Nuwarakalawiya and the Jaffna Peninsula, in fact, the

TABLE 6

Estimated Percentage of Dry Zone Agricultural Families who were Landless, 1946

District	Percentage	District	Percentage
Anuradhapura . .	21·9	Mannar . . .	11·1
Vavuniya . . .	25·6	Puttalam . . .	27·2
Jaffna	31·7	Hambantota . .	34·0
Batticaloa . . .	57·8		
Trincomalee . . .	20·0	Ceylon Average . .	26·3

Source: SL.

Dry Zone is anything but the typical pioneer land of large farms and land in plenty. Limited by physical geography and by traditional land-use and land-tenure practices, these regions have in fact many of the characteristics of 'old' Asian territories, with some of the signs of pressure of population on resources. That this is indeed so is a very important point to bear in mind in any discussion of peasant colonization in the Dry Zone of Ceylon; particularly as so many colonies are located in and around Nuwarakalawiya. Clearly, only new land-use techniques can colonize these regions, and clearly, too, Nuwarakalawiya and Jaffna themselves call for relief of population pressure, though whether so insistently as the Wet Zone regions will become more clear in the next chapter. But there seems no great case, on the evidence at present available, for the selection of colonists from most other parts of the Dry Zone except from particularly afflicted villages and from depressed parts of the unique Batticaloa District.[1] But, as was said at the outset, it is not easy to assess the need of any one region for relief. Much more information is required.

[1] There are local black spots; thus the Bintenne Division of Uva Province has 36·2 per cent. of its families landless (*KPC*, p. 95).

Income, Poverty, and Debt in the Rural Dry Zone

It has already been pointed out that, in the absence of a full report on the 1950 Economic Survey of Rural Ceylon, facts about rural economics can only be pieced together from scattered sources. It seems important, however, to attempt a sketch of the economic status of the Dry Zone peasantry, if only to complete a picture of the region in which colonization schemes are set and from which, for reasons which should now be apparent, they obtain some of their colonists. It is not easy to do this with a firm hand when basic data have been derived from different places at different times, and it is in any case hard to interpret statistics of income for a largely or partly self-sufficient peasant community. Incomes must inevitably be expressed in money terms, if there is to be a standard for comparison; but a false idea of the part played by money in the economy is thus conveyed to the Western reader, and the reality behind the figures all too often escapes him.[1]

The generalizations which follow appear, however, to be valid, provided that it is borne in mind that there is great regional variation, and that the Jaffna Peninsula constitutes an exception to most Dry Zone rules.

In the first place, the Dry Zone village suffers, like so many peasant villages in the East, from bitter poverty. It is true that its largely subsistence economy is more resilient to economic shock than the far more market-oriented village economy of the Wet Zone, which tends to have the weakness of the external economy of Ceylon as a whole in being tied all too firmly to world prices for the three primary commodities which make up over 90 per cent. of Ceylon's exports, namely tea, rubber, and coconuts; and it suffers severely in times of depression like those of the 1930's.[2] The Dry Zone village, on the other hand, normally produces little of these fickle sources of income, unless it be in the coconut groves of Puttalam, Jaffna, or Batticaloa. It is also true that, with malaria virtually conquered, one of the major factors tending to depress the Dry Zone economy has nearly disappeared. But the Dry Zone village still all too often lies at the mercy of drought. Even areas

---

[1] For a general discussion, though mainly in an East European context, see Warriner, *Economics of Peasant Farming* (London, OUP, 1939).

[2] For a recent general review of the problem of Ceylon and other primary producers in a similar position, see UN, Dept. of Econ. Affairs, *Instability in Export Markets of Under-Developed Countries* (New York, 1952).

fed by major irrigation works may sometimes suffer; while this chapter was being written a letter came describing the government relief works which had become necessary because of the failure of Kala Wewa.[1] What has been said in this chapter on peasant technology, land shortage, and land tenure will supply further reasons for poverty and bring much of the Dry Zone into line, in the mind of the reader, with other so-called 'under-developed' countries. There is the further point that many Dry Zone villages are far from good roads or railways; so long as villages remain in the subsistence state this fact does not affect their income, though it does clearly affect them in other ways, e.g. in their accessibility to relief in time of famine. But lack of communications is a very real handicap when, with the coming of a money economy, villages seek to sell some of their produce in an outside market. One may not agree with the sweeping statement of the Kandyan Peasantry Commission that 'the most potent factor retarding the development of the Dry Zone is the absence of communications.'[2] But it is generally true that the poorest villages are the most remote.

How poor, then, were, and are, these Dry Zone villages? The question is not an easy one to answer. The pre-war Economic Surveys collected data concerning incomes and concerning degree of self-sufficiency in foodstuffs, but only for a few Dry Zone villages (4 in Puttalam District, 1 in Matale District, 10 in Kurunegala District, and 3 in Hambantota District).[3] Much fascinating information is provided by these reports, but it is unfortunate that there is no comparable information for the type area of Anuradhapura or for Jaffna. The detailed results of the 1950 Survey are awaited with great interest. The pre-war Surveys revealed, for their limited range of villages, mean gross monthly earnings, in cash and kind, and including home production expressed in cash value, varying from only Rs. 4.28 (about 6s. 5d.) per family in a very poor village in Puttalam District to Rs. 31.57 (about £2. 7s. 4d.). In most villages the majority of gross earnings were worth less

[1] Mar. 1953; I am indebted for this letter, for much other help, and for many fruitful discussions, to Mr. M. Rajendra, C.C.S.

[2] *KPC*, p. 4.

[3] Published in the following numbers of *Min. of Labour, Industry and Commerce Bull.*: no. 8 (1939), Puttalam District; no. 9 (1940), Matale District; no. 10 (1949), Kurenegala District; no. 13 (1949), Hambantota District; referred to as *Village Survey: Puttalam*, &c.

than Rs. 15 per family per month, with a median for *all* villages in the region of Rs. 12 per month (about 18*s.*). These incomes are clearly very low, although matters were no worse than in many another Eastern peasant community, and, in fact, better than in most; direct comparisons of figures are apt to be misleading, but perhaps one may quote Miss Warriner's figure of 60 piastres (13*s.*) per month for the pre-war Egyptian fellah family.[1]

The Surveys even found a number of villages which were far from self-supporting in basic foodstuffs, and the surveyors commented on 'the paradox of a peasant economy which is unable even to produce its own food requirements, not to speak of creating a surplus'.[2] It is indeed something of a mystery how such villages managed to survive.

It is not surprising that the Dry Zone peasant, like the peasant of most Eastern regions overtaken by a money economy, was very heavily indebted. That this was true over almost the whole Dry Zone in the 1930's is shown by the evidence submitted to the Ceylon Banking Commission;[3] and more precise data is available for the villages covered by the Economic Surveys. In the Survey villages, more than 50 per cent. of the families, and sometimes over 80 per cent., were in debt, to the tune of as much as Rs. 200. Most loans were not, as so often in India, for cultivation expenses, or for ritual and ceremonial purposes, but for the purchase of provisions and household goods.[4] The money-lender was usually a local *boutique*-keeper or landowner. In the case of the latter at any rate it is important to realize that indebtedness may merely be one element in a system of reciprocal social obligations; in that case the picture is not as black as it looks to European eyes. The evidence given to the Banking Commission also showed how often land has been mortgaged, and how in many cases mortgages had been foreclosed. How far this process, together with the sale of land for debt or under civil writs, has helped to produce landlessness, can only be guessed;[5] they may well have been potent factors,

[1] Warriner, *Land and Poverty*, pp. 38–39.
[2] *Village Survey: Puttalam*, p. 10.
[3] Ceylon Banking Commission, vol. i, *Report*, and vol. ii, *Memoranda and Evidence*, S.P.s 22 and 23 of 1934.
[4] Cf. Sir Malcom Darling, *The Punjab Peasant*, 4th ed. (London, OUP, 1947); also Sir Edward Blunt, ed., *Social Service in India* (London, HMSO, 1939), espec. pp. 107–11.
[5] For a suggestion about the influence of sale under civil writs see L. B. Clarence, 'Ceylon', *Scot. Geog. Mag.*, vol. xiii (1897), pp. 169–88.

but, again, it must be recognized that mortgage (*ukas*) is a recognized traditional procedure and not necessarily a sign of degradation.

Almost certainly the general economic situation in the Dry Zone has improved since the pre-war years, though just how far the improvement has gone it is not easy to say. The control of malaria, improved medical services and a greater readiness to use those services, government interest in food production and in the peasant, and the growth of rural development societies and of Co-operatives and motor transport have all contributed to this somewhat happier state of affairs. There is no need to discuss these factors here since they have all also affected the colonization schemes, and will find their proper place in subsequent chapters. Colonization schemes have themselves contributed substantially to a revival in the region in which they are set; not only have they given a higher standard of living to Dry Zone peasants who have been fortunate enough to obtain allotments in them, they have also been the scene of experiments in Dry Zone agriculture, and, perhaps most important of all, have, with the help of DDT, dispelled finally the Dry Zone bogey, the feeling that the Dry Zone was dangerous, deadly, and incapable of being improved.

There are unfortunately few statistics with which one can measure the improvement in the Dry Zone since pre-war days. But it is said that in Hambantota and Puttalam Districts at least the percentage of family expenditure spent on food has declined considerably, from 82 to 73 per cent. in the former and from 77 to 70 per cent. in the latter.[1] This presumably indicates that there is more money to spend on other items. Probably many Dry Zone villages have also shared in the rise in incomes and fall in indebtedness which appears to be characteristic of Ceylon as a whole;[2] though that there are still many black spots (e.g. Bintenne) is obvious in the field, and there is always the menace of drought. In fact there is no room for easy optimism about the condition of the Dry Zone peasantry; and the contrast in living standards between colonization scheme and *purāna* (ancient) village is a fruitful source of friction and jealousy.[3]

---

[1] *Prelim. Rep. Econ. Survey Rural Ceylon*, p. 12. The calculation, of course, includes an estimate of the cash value of home production consumed at home; it must also be remembered that food has been subsidized in recent years.

[2] Ibid., pp. 10–13.

[3] See Chapter 15, p. 308.

Some Features of the Dry Zone Social System

At the risk of extending an already long chapter, it seems desirable to include some account of the social system of the Dry Zone village. For the Dry Zone peasant is not merely an economic unit, owning paddy and cultivating *chena* and possessing (or lacking) an income; he is not merely an individual, although it is pleasant to recall many hospitable and entertaining friends among the peasantry; he is also a social creature, and it is impossible to understand his reaction to colonization schemes, or many of the problems which beset these schemes, without knowing something of his village society and its values. Some discussion of the social system may also help the Westerner, unused to peasant attitudes, to avoid making the fatal mistake of measuring Ceylon economics with a Western yardstick. The sketch which follows will mainly have reference to Sinhalese areas, partly because of present availability of data (although, as was pointed out on page 42, these are sadly lacking everywhere), partly because of the preponderance of Sinhalese in colonization schemes.[1]

It is important to realize, in the first place, that, as in many oriental societies, the village community is the social group. Although now much affected by outside influences, the Dry Zone Sinhalese village functions as a unit, being largely made up of related families who are closely bound together and to the village by ties of kinship, custom, and religion. This strong social cohesion often finds expression in a marked spirit of co-operation; the practice of *bethma*[2] is one result of this, as is the habit of pooling resources for mudding, ploughing, harvesting, and so on; irrigation works are still to some extent tended by the 'united unpaid labour of the landowners'.[3] The village is, or was, largely self-sufficient institutionally, though not necessarily in terms of modern, imposed institutions like co-operative societies, clubs, and political bodies.[4] It was traditionally ruled by a *gansabhā* (*gamsa-*

---

[1] Mr. M. Y. Banks is at present preparing a study on Jaffna Tamil society, especially in relation to the social problems of the Iranamadu colonies, under the auspices of Chatham House.

[2] See above, p. 45.

[3] An early Government Agent, North-Central Province, quoted by Ievers, p. 74.

[4] It is in terms of these imposed institutions that 'villages have shown no traces of any active collective life' (*Village Survey: Puttalam*, p. 20).

baya), or village council; the modern 'village committee' is in fact a resuscitated and modified *gansabhā*.[1] The village has its own largely traditional boundaries.

The peasant is very much concerned to preserve the status of his family, and to serve its interests, above all to maintain its land. Lack of land, especially of paddy land, is an economic and social disability. In some villages even the sale of paddy may involve loss of status.[2] With these attitudes to land and its produce goes the honouring of agricultural work, provided that it is not done for hire; as Robert Knox put it:

husbandry is the great employment of the country. In this the best men labour. Nor is it held any disgrace for men of the greatest quality to do any work either at home or in the field, if it be for themselves; but to work for hire with them is reckoned for great shame.[3]

That this healthy attitude to work on the land is not shared by English-educated, urban Ceylonese (or apparently, by the sons of the present generation of cultivators), is one of the most unfortunate results of Western impact.[4]

Family solidarity is very strong. Support by the family is an insurance against ill health, old age, or personal disaster. For the same reason, there is in the *purāna* (ancient) village no such thing as unemployment, only under-employment; an individual, back from work in the town, merely joins the family group, each of whom applies less labour to the same land in consequence, or obtains land on *ande*.

Although Buddhist, and hence technically classless, Sinhalese society is in fact stratified according to caste; but the divisions are neither so numerous nor so rigid as in Hindu society.[5] A general notion of the stratification as it was fifty years ago may be obtained from Table 7, which shows the number of villages of each caste in the North-Central Province when R. W. Ievers wrote in 1899; the general picture remains the same today. The castes are arranged

---

[1] See *The Village Communities Ordinance*, No. 9 of 1924, cap. 198, as amended (Colombo, Govt. Press, 1946). Irrigation is administered by an elected *vel vidāne*, or irrigation headman.

[2] H. E. Peries, 'Agrarian Problems of Ceylon', *Public Admin.*, vol. xviii (1940), p. 275.   [3] Ludowyk, *Robert Knox*, p. 155.

[4] For a discussion of this point see D. S. Senanayake, *Agriculture and Patriotism* (Colombo, Lake House Press, 1935), p. 71.

[5] Since this section was written Ryan's *Caste in Modern Ceylon* has appeared. See espec. ch. 10, pp. 239–60.

TABLE 7

Number of Villages of Each Caste in the North-Central Province of the 1890's

Caste	No. of villages
1. Goyigama (cultivators) . . .	618
Karāwe (fishers)	5
Tamil karāwe (fishers) . . .	7
Veddahs	25
Vidanela	3
2. Guruwas or pusaries . . .	4
Waggai or kammalai (from India by own tradition)	12
Blacksmiths (navandanna) . .	53
Potters	16
Moors	108
Moorish barbers	1
Tamils	8
Dhobies (washermen) . . .	65
3. Madinno or toddy-drawers (durawe) .	2
Chalias	2
Willi durai ⎫ Probably slaves or low-	⎧ 7
Batgam durai ⎪ caste followers of	⎪ 30
Panna durai ⎬ chiefs; now mainly in	⎨ 1
Tamil durai ⎭ temple villages .	⎩ 1
Kandāyo (jaggery caste) . . .	23
Tom-tom beaters	69
Kaffirs	1
4. Mixed caste villages	8

Source: Ievers, pp. 91–92.

in the table with the highest at the top. It should be noted that the cultivators (*goyiyas* or *goyigama*) take precedence over all other castes in the table, though they themselves yield pride of place to the descendants of the ancient aristocracy, the *vannikura*, the equivalent of the Kandyan *bandāras*, who do not appear in the table since they do not live in separate villages. It will also be noted that a number of the 'castes' are in reality communal groups (Tamils of various castes, Moors, Veddahs, &c.); their place in the table is according to a Sinhalese rating, and is not necessarily their own idea of their status. Indeed, there is dispute about the number and status of castes among the Sinhalese themselves.

One of the most interesting points about caste in the Sinhalese

Dry Zone (and a point which has practical repercussions in colonies) is that almost all of the villages consist of people of a single caste; this contrasts strongly with the mixed-caste villages of India or, for that matter, of Jaffna or much of the Wet Zone. Moreover, whereas in India the castes are still to a large extent occupational groups inside the village community, in these Sinhalese villages every man is first and foremost a cultivator whatever his caste; only a few castes (e.g. dhobies and tom-tom beaters) devote much time to their craft. In ancient times each low-caste group was given land in return for the performance of services for one or more *goyiya* villages, but the system is breaking down, at least on the economic plane (for ritual functions remain). Indeed, the sharpness of caste distinctions is today becoming even more blurred; but caste can still cause trouble in colonization schemes[1] and elsewhere.

Not much need be said about caste in Hindu Jaffna. It in general follows the familiar lines of Hindu society, and even transects Christian communities, but is more secular than in India.

One point only will be made about religion (although clearly there is much that might be said about the Hinduism of the Tamils and the Hinayana Buddhism of the Sinhalese): the Buddhism of the Dry Zone villager cannot be understood in terms of the lofty Buddhist philosophy which, chiefly, has attracted the attention of Western scholars.[2] Investigation of the real religious attitudes of the Sinhalese peasantry is greatly needed; but it is abundantly clear that their Buddhism is strongly tinged with Hinduism (many are the altars to Ganesh and to other deities) and also with primitive animism, so that the jungle is peopled with devils and other supernatural creatures more terrible than the material hazards of tangled thicket, wild animals, and disease. This has been a strong element in the 'fear of the wild-wood' which in turn has been part of the Dry Zone bogey. Religious customs and ceremonies again enter into every aspect of daily life, notably into rice cultivation,

---

[1] See Chapter 15, pp. 301–3.
[2] There is great need for a comprehensive work on popular Buddhism comparable to L. S. S. O'Malley, *Popular Hinduism* (Cambridge Univ. Press, 1935). See, however, O. Pertold, 'The Ceremonial Dances of the Sinhalese: an Enquiry into . . . Folk Religion', *Archiv orientální* [Prague], vol. ii (1930), pp. 108–37, 201–54, and 385–426; and R. Pieris, 'The Brodie Papers on Sinhalese Folk Religion', *Univ. of Cey. Rev.*, vol. xi (1953), pp. 110–28.

which thus tends to have ritual significance as well as economic and social importance.[1]

Finally, it must be realized that the ideal village unit, seemingly immemorial, with its strong family ties, attachment to the land, and principles of co-operation, is a phenomenon now subject to rapid change under the pressure of outside forces. Only in the low-caste villages and in villages remote from roads are many of the old customs preserved. Almost everywhere caste is breaking down; villagers are becoming more mobile and less attached to the old village; money values creep in; and Low-country Sinhalese and other alien elements have come not only into the colonies and the roadside, ribbon-like bazaars but also into many *purāna* villages.[2] Nevertheless, no economic research project or development scheme in the Dry Zone can afford to ignore the strong social forces which operate in Sinhalese (and, for that matter, in Tamil) society; and it is unfortunate that social factors have, relative to other considerations, been neglected in research and in practice.[3]

Unemployment and Under-Employment

This chapter has been deliberately confined almost entirely to rural conditions since it is the state of affairs in the village which is most relevant to the subject of this book. But there is, of course, urban life in the Dry Zone, especially in the Jaffna Peninsula; there, and elsewhere, important sections of the population live by trade (especially with India) and by manufacturing; and the towns have their own problems, especially that of unemployment. Thus there were 989 and 790 urban unemployed in Jaffna and Trincomalee respectively in October 1949.[4] But the problem of urban unemployment is outside the scope of this book, except that it is to a certain extent a product of a drift from overcrowded rural areas, and that it can provide a pool of mobile labour for development projects, even though many urban unemployed are obviously unsuitable material for colonists.

[1] See, for example, Ievers, 'Customs and Ceremonies connected with Rice Cultivation', *J.R. As. Soc.* (Cey. Br.), vol. vi (1880), pp. 46–52; a series of papers on the same subject by H. C. P. Bell, ibid., vol. viii (1883), pp. 44–93; vol. xviii (1884), pp. 398–442; and vol. iv (1889), pp. 167–71; and P. E. Pieris, 'Some Political Conventions and Social Customs of the Sinhalese', *Univ. of Cey. Rev.*, vol. iii (1943), pp. 1–10.

[2] For examples of changing attitudes see Ryan, 'The Ceylonese Village and the New Value System', *Rur. Soc.*, vol. xvii (1952), pp. 9–28.

[3] See Chapter 14. [4] *Unemployment Census*, pp. 240–51.

The 1949 Unemployment Census also gave figures for 'rural unemployment' which are quoted, for what they are worth, in Table 8. It would appear from the table that some 70 per cent. of 'rural unemployment' is concentrated in the Jaffna District; conditions are actually worst in the islands to the west of the Jaffna Peninsula. But in the Dry Zone as a whole 'rural unemployment'

TABLE 8

Rural Unemployment in Dry Zone Districts, October 1946

District	Unemployed	
	Male	*Female*
Anuradhapura	350	29
Vavuniya.	70	3
Jaffna	4,259	332
Batticaloa	716	46
Trincomalee	92	2
Mannar	105	6
Puttalam	60	6
Hambantota	41	9
Total	5,693	433

Note: Figures for Hambantota District *exclude* Giruwa Pattu West, which is in the Wet Zone.

Source: Unemployment Census, pp. 240–51.

gives no clue to the incidence of economic difficulties; it is rather an index of departure from the peasant norm. For, as has already been explained, peasant societies tend to conceal unemployment within the family or village group, and to be under-employed rather than unemployed.[1] The concept of peasant under-employment has been considerably clarified of late;[2] and if it were possible to measure the difference between the effort actually expended by labour and the maximum effort of which it is capable, then one would possess for any given region a useful single index of rural overcrowding and hence of its claims, in comparison with other regions, to allotments in colonization schemes designed to relieve

[1] For similar social reasons, chronic under-employment may coexist in an area with acute lack of wage-labour, e.g. *Admin. Report: Agriculture*, 1952, p. 9.
[2] See, for example, Chiang Hsieh, 'Underemployment in Asia', *Int. Lab. Rev.*, vol. lxv (1952), pp. 703–25 and vol. lxvi (1952), pp. 30–39 and M. L. Dantwala, 'Notes on Some Aspects of Rural Unemployment', *Ind. J. Agric. Econ.*, vol. viii (1953), pp. 19–32.

such overcrowding. But, quite apart from the almost complete lack in Ceylon and elsewhere of field investigations of under-employment, there are many other difficulties.[1] Under-employment may be 'disguised' (if the labour force appears to be fully occupied, but if in fact a proportion of it could be released by relatively simple changes in organization within the existing technological and institutional framework); or 'potential' (if labour could be released by more fundamental changes).[2] Moreover, economists tend to think of under-employment only in economic terms, and to forget that seasonal under-employment may fulfil a social function; for instance, peasants may be so fully engaged in the cultivation season, working harder than many Western workers, that a period of apparent idleness may be necessary for religious observances, festivities, and other occasions, which, quite apart from their intrinsic merit, are amongst the bonds of society. Maximum utilization of labour would then only weaken these bonds. However, with these reservations, one may express the hope that research on under-employment will be carried on;[3] meanwhile, the need for colonization and other forms of relief can only be expressed inexactly in other and more confusing terms.

In a wider and more general sense, 'under-employment' is the persistent theme of this chapter. Clearly, much Dry Zone land, for lack of population or capital or policy, or because of the recent dominance of malaria, is not employed usefully at all; other land is only used by a system of shifting cultivation which, while admirably adapted to physical conditions, is out of tune with the times; while even paddy land and village garden, limited as is their distribution and excellent as local usage is by ecological standards, could be used far more efficiently, possibly by borrowing some, but by no means all, of the techniques practised in Tamil Nad. Again, techniques of land use, local systems of tenure and social organization, and population pressure conspire to produce a state of under-employment of labour, with attendant poverty and distress. Colonization schemes may be regarded as efforts to rectify under-employment, both of land and of labour.

---

[1] It was reported in Dec. 1951 that the ILO was to send a team to Ceylon to make field inquiries into under-employment. See *Ceylon Daily News*, 6 Dec. 1951.
[2] Chiang Hsieh, in *Int. Lab. Rev.*, vol. lxv, pp. 709–13.
[3] For a preliminary study see E. M. Wijenaike, 'The Problem of Under-employment in Ceylon', *Cey. Lab. Gaz.*, vol. iii (1952), pp. 3–15.

4

Some Economic and Social Problems of the Rural Wet Zone

For the sake of simplicity in this book the 'Wet Zone' of Ceylon will be taken to include not only the Lowland Wet Zone and the Wet Zone Hills, but also the 'dry' hill country of Uva,[1] for the latter shares many economic and social characteristics with the Wet Zone proper.

The greater Wet Zone thus defined is, like Malaya or Java, a classic area for the study of a dual economy; there is an indigenous peasant economy, with ancient roots, originally concerned with subsistence but now much modified; and there is an introduced estate or plantation economy, of recent origin, depending almost entirely, in its early days, at any rate, on immigrant Indian labour, concerned with the production of a few staple commodities for export, and supplying the mainstay of the island's external economy. It cannot be too strongly stressed that the two elements have always been distinct, and that although the stronger, plantation element has greatly influenced the weaker, peasant element, they remain distinct today. In many Kandyan valleys the valley floor belongs to a peasant community whose agronomy, economy, society, and habits of thought are completely different from those of the European planter and his Indian Tamil labour who occupy the upper slopes and the hill-tops. Because the economy has this dual character, it is most misleading to lump the Ceylon estates with the Latin American *latifundia* and to say that 'in Ceylon . . . the agrarian structure is dominated by large estates'.[2] Quite apart from the fact that there are very few estates at all in the Dry Zone, the estates of the Wet Zone do not directly enter into the peasant 'agrarian structure', since they do not own the land which the peasant cultivates; they have, however, a potent influence on the peasant in other ways, as this chapter will endeavour to show.

Since this chapter is concerned with part of the background of peasant colonization, and since it is the peasant element in the dual

<hr />

[1] See above, p. 3. [2] *Land Reform*, p. 18.

economy which alone contributes colonists, very little will be said about the estates *per se*, as distinct from the estates in relation to the peasant. Similarly, little will be said about conditions in Wet Zone towns, although these contain some 87 per cent. of the urban population of the island;[1] like the estates, towns are a result of Western impact; and they do not at present contribute colonists, except those who have worked as labourers in the preparation of colonies.[2]

In concentrating mainly on the peasant element in the Wet Zone economy, attention will be primarily directed to economic and social conditions and, in particular, to land hunger and other phenomena for which relief has been sought through colonization and other schemes. Land-use customs need not be given much space. They have some relevance, since the emigrant colonist tends to carry them with him to the Dry Zone; but there need be no discussion of the wisdom of these customs in relation to physical conditions, such as that which occupied much of the last chapter, for such a discussion would clearly have little relevance to the problem of land use in Dry Zone colonies.

The General Situation in the Wet Zone

The essential difference between the physical conditions in the Dry Zone and those in the Wet Zone is that over most of the latter, excluding Uva, there is no marked dry season; the amount of rainfall and its distribution between the seasons varies from station to station within the Wet Zone (see Map 3) but the irrigation of paddy is in general only a matter of tapping some local perennial stream, and elaborate storage systems are unnecessary. And high land cultivation can normally go on without hindrance from drought; coconut palms and other tree crops can be grown almost everywhere that soil and temperature conditions are suitable. High land, in fact, behaves like Dry Zone *gangoda*, and there is nothing to correspond to the drought-stricken 'true high land' of the Dry Zone. Only in the topmost Kandyan villages does 'high land' become a problem; coconuts, for instance, grow only very poorly above 3,500 feet.

Most parts of upland Uva provide exceptions to what has just

[1] It is, of course, very hard to define an 'urban population' in a country like Ceylon; see *Census of Ceylon, 1946*, vol. i, pt. 1, pp. 73–74.
[2] See below, p. 205.

been said, for in them there is marked seasonal drought, made all
the worse by high wind, and some Dry Zone land-use problems
begin to appear.

Over the whole of the Wet Zone, there is, as in the Dry Zone,
a tendency for soil to accumulate in valley bottoms at the expense
of the hill slopes. Such valley bottoms, watered by natural streams
and by run-off and seepage from the slopes above, are known as
deniyas, and are ideal for paddy (see Plate 11). Up-country, however, the natural water-supply to *deniyas* tends to be interfered
with by the tea estates which now occupy the higher ground. In
the lowland Wet Zone, the area between successive *deniyas* consists of low, rounded lateritic hills, infertile, subject to erosion,
and best left under tree crops. Up-country, soil conditions are
more complicated and there is much bare rock.[1]

The Wet Zone of Ceylon bears a strong physical resemblance
to the Malabar Coast of India;[2] and some resemblance to the west
coast of Malaya.[3]

Everywhere in the Wet Zone outside the towns and the estates
the society is still essentially a peasant one, clearly derived from
the same origin as Dry Zone Sinhalese society; and many of the
remoter Kandyan villages bear a strong resemblance to the *purāna*
villages of Nuwarakalawiya. But the different physical environment permits fuller use of high land, so that, with the absence of
any mandatory site for the village as clearly defined as the *gangoda*,
a denser and more dispersed settlement pattern is permitted. And
the concentration of the Sinhalese population in the Wet Zone
(following decay in the Dry Zone) has, together with the forceful
impact of Western political control and economic interest, been
responsible for many other changes. Today the Wet Zone (apart
from some Kandyan areas) has a close network of communications, a dense pattern of settlement (largely in scattered villages
along roads), an economy in which money and labour for hire play
a large part, and a society which, while retaining many recog-
nizable features of the old order, has clearly been very much

[1] See Joachim in *Proc. 1st Ann. Sess. Cey. Assoc. Sci.*, pt. 3 (1945), pp. 21–30.
'Up-country' is a useful term, a literal translation of the Sinhalese *Uda Rata*.
[2] See Spate, pp. 616–35; C. Daryll Forde, *Habitat, Economy and Society*
(London, Methuen, 1934), pp. 260–84; and A. Mayer, *Land and Society in
Malabar* (Bombay, OUP, 1952).
[3] See, for example, E. H. G. Dobby, *Southeast Asia* (Univ. of London Press,
[1950]), espec. pp. 87–104.

9. SCENE NEAR KURUNEGALA

Typical Wet Zone cultivation of paddy in valley-bottom and coconut on 'high land'

10. SCENE NEAR BADULLA

Up-country terraced paddy and steep 'high land' garden

11. THE DUAL ECONOMY OF THE HILLS
Terraced village paddy and tea estate near Gampola

12. *ANICUT* FOR RIDIBENDI ELA
River nearly dry (August) and silt piled up behind anicut (weir)

modified; and, above all, from the point of view of this study, a crowded rural population, tending to suffer from landlessness and economic distress.

Comments on sources given in Chapter 3 (pp. 41–43) apply, in general, to the Wet Zone as well. There are, however, a greater number of available Economic Surveys;[1] the Report of the Kandyan Peasantry Commission is invaluable, though contentious in parts; and much may be gleaned from the Reports of the Government Agents.[2]

Peasant Land Use in the Wet Zone[3]

In many parts of the Wet Zone today it is possible to discern a threefold pattern of peasant land use similar to, and probably derived from, that of the Dry Zone; in *deniyas*, or, in the Hills, in laboriously constructed terraces, there is paddy; on unirrigable high land one may see gardens (*watte*) containing coconut, areca-nut, plantains, the kitul palm (*Caryota urens*, a useful source of *jaggery* sugar), and other trees and vegetables, very like the gardens in the Dry Zone *gangoda*; and there are some *chenas*. But there are many obvious adaptations of the system to the physical and social environment of the Wet Zone. Thus the spectacular rice terraces of Kandyan villages represent not only an adaptation to steep slopes, but also, in many places at any rate, a response to population pressure; and the wide distribution of high land gardens is a clear result of a less inhibiting set of climatic and hydrological conditions. Again, use of forest for *chena* and pasture is relatively rare, for there are few stretches of virgin jungle in this densely settled and commercially exploited region. Only rare villages retain their 'village waste': for example, the remote Uva village of Ella on whose steep hill-sides there are zones of pasture on the unproductive, windswept upper slopes, of dry, *chena*-like cultivation on middle slopes, and of gardens and terraced paddy on lower slopes;[4] something like this must have been characteristic in the Kandyan country before the days of the Crown Lands

[1] *Village Surveys: Rayigam Korale, Kalutara, Chilaw, Matale, Kurunegala, Galle,* and *Matara.*

[2] See, for example, the *Admin. Reports of the Govt. Agents and Assistant Govt. Agents for 1950* (Colombo, Govt. Press, 1951).

[3] See Plates 9–11.

[4] R. Wikkramatileke, 'Ella Village', *Econ. Geog.,* vol. xxviii (1952), pp. 355–63, espec. p. 358.

Encroachments Ordinance and of the alienation of hill slopes to planters.[1]

Other modifications of the early land-use system have followed the spread of a money economy. Most peasants now have at least a few cash crops; and there are in the Wet Zone all stages of peasant commercialism from the growing of a few vines of pepper in village gardens to the use for coconuts of almost all land, even land fit for paddy, which characterizes parts of the Negombo–Kurunegala–Chilaw 'Coconut Belt'.[2] And the great estates, practising the virtual monoculture of tea, rubber, or coconuts, are a still more alien element in the Sinhalese scene.

Peasant agriculture in the Wet Zone is, for the most part, characterized by similar low technical standards to those which prevail in the Dry Zone. Better methods are, however, practised in parts of the Kandyan country, notably in some of the villages between Kegalla and Kandy. Here one may see paddy being transplanted.[3] But in these same hills there is dry cultivation on dangerously steep and unterraced slopes, which may in part at least be a result of pressure of population on the land.

Peasant Land Tenure in the Wet Zone

1. *Tenurial systems.* Tables 9 and 10 show the tenure of paddy holdings in districts lying wholly or mainly in the Wet Zone (1946). It will be appreciated from the foregoing paragraphs that paddy land does not now hold in the Wet Zone quite the pre-eminence which it holds in the Dry Zone; but it is nevertheless important to the peasant economically and as a sign of social standing. The terminology of the tables has already been explained.[4] The dominant position of the owner-cultivator will be apparent; but it will also be noticed that he is responsible for a smaller percentage of both holdings and area than in most Dry Zone districts.[5] There is a corresponding increase in the prevalence of other forms of tenure. Locally, service tenure is important.[6] High percentages under *ande* tenancies (especially Up-country and in the southern District

---

[1] See below, pp. 90–91.

[2] Farmer, 'Ceylon', in Spate, pp. 771–2.

[3] W. Molegoda, 'Paddy Cultivation in Kandy', *Trop. Agriculturist*, vol. xcix (1943), pp. 152–6.   [4] See above, pp. 56–57.

[5] Cf. Tables 2 and 3, pp. 57 and 58.

[6] See, for example, *KPC*, pp. 237–8, 301, 346.

of Matara) will be noted, and also the relatively large proportion of *tattumāru* owners in the Ratnapura and Kegalla Districts.

TABLE 9

Tenure of Paddy Holdings, Wet Zone Districts, 1946

District	Total no. of holdings	Percentage of holdings cultivated by				
		Owner	Lessee	Ande tenant	Tattu-māru owner	Others
Low Country						
Colombo . .	68,097	66·2	0·6	28·7	3·2	2·1
Kalutara . .	30,790	58·8	3·3	21·2	14·4	2·2
Galle . . .	32,884	65·0	9·9	13·8	7·8	3·5
Matara . .	27,655	44·2	4·0	44·2	4·2	3·0
Chilaw . .	10,584	60·9	1·1	27·0	9·3	1·9
Kurunegala .	118,149	54·8	0·5	28·4	9·7	6·5
Up-country						
Kandy . .	67,025	53·2	2·0	42·8	1·0	1·1
Matale .	38,642	53·6	1·2	42·3	1·8	1·1
Nuwara Eliya .	25,462	61·2	2·1	34·8	1·0	0·8
Badulla . .	44,950	56·2	3·7	35·7	3·0	1·6
Ratnapura . .	31,778	21·7	3·2	48·7	25·3	0·9
Kegalla . .	34,253	34·1	1·1	27·8	35·7	1·0

Note: For explanation of terms see Chapter 3, p. 57.
   Source: Census of Ceylon, 1946, vol. i, pt. 2.

2. *Ownership of paddy land.* Table 11 shows the percentage of the owners of paddy land who possess extents of various sizes, and may be compared with Table 4, which tabulates comparable statistics for the Dry Zone. The tabulation of the Wet Zone districts by geographical regions brings out the fact that these districts fall into three groups. In the first place, there are the south-western lowland districts of Colombo, Kalutara, Galle, and Matara, in all of which over 70 per cent. of the paddy landowners possess less than 2 acres each, and in all of which there are very few owners of medium and large areas. In the second place, there are the Up-country, Kandyan districts; here there is an even more striking concentration in areas of under 2 acres, and there are very few owners of medium or large extent. The situation is often even worse than the table suggests; thus in the Kotmale Division nearly one-fifth of the peasant families possess less than a quarter of an

acre each.[1] In the third place, the Districts of Kurunegala and Chilaw have fewer owners of very small amounts and rather more owners of medium-sized amounts of 3–10 acres; these districts

TABLE 10

Tenure of Paddy Holdings by Area, Wet Zone Districts, 1946

District	Total area of holdings (acres)	Percentage of area cultivated by				
		Owner	Lessee	Ande tenant	Tattu-māru owner	Others
Low Country						
Colombo . .	62,567	58·9	0·8	34·6	3·4	2·2
Kalutara . .	46,132	52·7	4·0	23·5	16·6	3·1
Galle . . .	48,992	61·2	12·8	14·9	7·3	3·9
Matara . .	48,789	37·8	4·1	51·3	3·5	3·1
Chilaw . .	14,336	53·7	2·7	34·9	4·6	3·8
Kurunegala .	125,348	47·3	0·7	29·3	11·7	11·1
Up-country						
Kandy . .	39,731	47·7	3·6	45·9	0·8	2·0
Matale . .	21,292	47·2	1·7	47·2	1·5	2·3
Nuwara Eliya .	16,646	56·1	2·2	40·2	0·9	0·8
Badulla .	33,747	51·3	6·5	35·3	3·7	3·3
Ratnapura .	33,541	19·2	3·3	50·2	26·0	1·3
Kegalla . .	26,929	30·4	1·2	31·8	35·6	1·1

Source and Notes: As for Table 9.

begin to approach the state of affairs in Anuradhapura District (cf. Table 4).

It is very clear that, by and large, there is a far higher percentage of owners of very small amounts of paddy land in the Wet Zone than in the Dry Zone. It must be stressed straight away that 'agrarian reform', in the sense of the redistribution to peasant owners of land at present held in large amounts, is no answer to the Wet Zone paddy land problem, whatever view may be held about the evils of landlordism. Ceylon in this respect contrasts strongly with such countries as Egypt. In Egypt 94·2 per cent. of the owners held amounts of under 5 feddans in 1947 (1 feddan = 1·038 acres) and only 0·4 per cent. of owners held over 50 feddans;[2] super-ficially, these figures bear a strong resemblance to those of Table 11. But whereas in Egypt the first category, of small owners, held

[1] *KPC*, pp. 95 and 316. [2] *Land Reform*, p. 9.

only 33·5 per cent. of the area, and the second category, of large
owners, held 36·8 per cent. of the area, in the Wet Zone it is probable that over 80 per cent. of the paddy land is owned in units of
under 5 acres, and under 5 per cent. in units of over 50 acres;
indeed, Table 11 makes it clear that in some districts no land at

TABLE 11

Ownership of Wet Zone Paddy Land, 1946

District	Percentage of owners of paddy land owning total areas in acres of									
	<2	2<3	3<4	4<5	5<10	10<15	15<20	20<30	30<50	>50
Low Country										
Colombo	71·8	18·8	5·0	2·7	1·2	0·4	0·1	0·1	0·0	0·0
Kalutara	70·2	19·8	5·5	2·2	1·1	0·5	0·3	0·2	0·1	0·0
Galle	75·2	11·4	5·5	3·7	2·5	0·7	0·2	0·1	0·0	0·0
Matara	70·8	12·0	7·0	4·9	3·2	1·2	0·4	0·3	0·1	0·1
Chilaw	64·8	14·2	7·1	4·8	6·2	1·8	1·0	0·3	0·2	0·1
Kurunegala	63·8	18·8	10·0	4·7	1·7	0·7	0·2	0·1	0·0	0·0
Up-country										
Kandy	91·0	5·3	1·8	1·1	0·6	0·2	0·1	0·0	0·0	0·0
Matale	82·5	10·8	2·9	2·0	1·2	0·3	0·1	0·1	0·0	0·0
Nuwara Eliya	84·0	6·2	4·1	2·4	2·0	0·5	0·5	0·2	0·1	..
Badulla	88·7	6·0	2·9	1·0	0·7	0·3	0·2	0·1	0·1	0·0
Ratnapura	82·4	8·7	3·7	2·2	1·6	0·8	0·1	0·1	0·0	0·0
Kegalla	78·0	10·4	4·8	2·9	1·8	1·1	0·8	0·0	0·0	..
Ceylon	71·2	13·3	6·1	4·0	2·9	1·3	0·6	0·4	0·2	0·1

Source: Investigation carried out by the Internal Purchase Scheme, 1946, and quoted in *SL*.

all is owned in units of over 50 acres. (Unfortunately no data are
available on the area actually owned by each category of owner
shown in Table 11; but it is fairly easy, from the source of the
table, which gives the number of owners in each category, and
from an assumption about the mean size of unit held under each
category, to arrive at estimates of the kind which have just been
quoted.) The marked incidence of *ande* tenure in the Wet Zone
is, in fact, not the result of the existence of great estates of paddy
land which are let out to small tenants, but of the letting of relatively small amounts, or even of very small amounts, by hereditary
landowners; some of these are no doubt honouring the traditional
obligation to lease land to kinsmen and friends, but others have
left their ancestral village for the towns, or are engaged in more
lucrative occupations than agriculture. It frequently happens, too,
that *boutique*-keepers or others have foreclosed on small parcels of
mortgaged land and hence joined the ranks of *ande* landlords. In

the Kandyan districts Indian Tamils who have acted as money-lenders appear to be acquiring a great deal of land. Indeed, it was a far more frequent complaint to the Kandyan Peasantry Commissioners that village land was passing into the ownership of outsiders than that it was held by the hereditary Kandyan aristocracy (the *'bandāras'*, see p. 73).[1] *Ande* tenure is ancient;[2] but its very high incidence today is felt by Kandyans to be a symptom of a deep-seated malaise. Here is a peasantry whose chief mark of status is the possession of paddy land either owning very small amounts of land or reduced in some cases to selling ancestral holdings and to cultivating the land of another. (And what is true of the Kandyan regions is true, *mutatis mutandis*, of the congested Low Country districts.)

3. *Very small holdings.* It is clearly a concomitant of the ownership of paddy land in very small parcels, of the leasing of some of these parcels in still smaller parcels, and of other factors such as cultivation in scattered blocks and the need for terracing, that the holdings in which the land is actually cultivated shall be very tiny indeed. That this is indeed so is borne out by the data tabulated in Table 12 (which may be compared with Table 5, for the Dry Zone). It will be clear that very small holdings are particularly numerous in the Kandyan districts. In fact, the mean size of paddy holding in the Kandy, Matale, Nuwara Eliya, and Badulla Districts are respectively 0·59, 0·55, 0·65, and 0·75 acres;[3] in Ella village, already mentioned, 80 per cent. of the holdings are between 0·5 and 1·0 acres.[4] Holdings are not quite so small, though still small enough, in the Low Country, where the mean sizes of paddy holdings vary from 0·92 acres in Colombo District (the same as for the Jaffna District) to 1·76 acres in Matara District. The position, is of course, aggravated by joint ownership, whether under *tattumāru* (the extent of which may be gauged from Tables 8 and 9) or under the contemporaneous form of joint tenure, under which, as in parts of Kurunegala District, the co-owners cultivate jointly and share the produce each

---

[1] e.g. *KPC*, pp. 258, 275, 346 (but *bandāras* were on the Commission, Indians were not). For the view that the villagers originally owned their holdings, even in villages granted by the king to an aristocrat, see de Lanerolle, in *J.R. As. Soc.* (Cey. Br.), vol. xxxiv, pp. 203–6. See also, espec. for Sabaragamuwa, R. E. Lewis, 'Rural Economy of the Sinhalese', ibid., vol. iv (1848–9), pp. 27–52.

[2] Brohier, *Land, Maps and Surveys*, i. 6.

[3] *SL*, p. 28.

[4] Wikkramatileke, in *Econ. Geog.*, vol. xxviii, i. 357.

season.[1] No comprehensive data are available on the extent of the latter practice, which is not revealed in the tables. However, paddy land is in some places (but rarely Up-country) a subsidiary means

TABLE 12

Paddy Holdings of less than 5 Acres, by Number and Area; Wet Zone Districts, 1946

District	Percentage of holdings with extent in acres of				Percentage of acreage in holdings of (acres)			
	$<\frac{1}{2}$	$\frac{1}{2}<1$	$1<2$	$2<5$	$<\frac{1}{2}$	$\frac{1}{2}<1$	$1<2$	$2<5$
Low Country								
Colombo . .	32·8	35·2	22·6	8·1	8·7	23·4	30·0	22·5
Kalutara . .	16·4	28·5	30·7	19·6	2·6	11·0	24·4	35·3
Galle . .	19·5	29·4	28·9	17·4	3·2	12·1	23·8	32·0
Matara . .	14·8	22·6	29·4	29·1	2·4	8·1	21·8	46·8
Chilaw . .	28·8	25·0	28·8	14·9	4·8	11·6	27·2	30·3
Kurunegala .	22·2	37·4	25·6	12·6	5·0	20·3	28·6	30·0
Up-country								
Kandy . .	43·2	38·8	14·7	2·7	17·6	37·8	28·3	10·6
Matale . .	47·2	38·2	11·9	2·5	21·0	39·3	25·0	11·3
Nuwara Eliya .	34·0	40·3	20·4	4·4	11·8	35·6	35·7	15·2
Badulla . .	43·3	34·3	17·6	4·5	15·1	24·8	27·3	15·5
Ratnapura .	22·2	33·7	31·0	12·2	5·0	19·4	36·7	29·7
Kegalla . .	28·7	40·8	23·6	6·4	8·7	31·8	37·4	20·3
Ceylon . .	31·4	32·8	21·1	11·2	6·4	16·4	21·6	25·7

Source: *Census of Ceylon, 1946*, vol. i, pt. 2.

of livelihood; in Chilaw District, for example, it is generally less important than coconut cultivation.[2]

As in the Dry Zone, many factors have to be taken into account in any attempt to assess 'land hunger' in any given district, and existing data fail to compose themselves into a clear picture; but, by and large, it can be seen that shortage of paddy land in the Wet Zone in general, and in the Kandyan districts in particular, is more marked than in any Dry Zone district with the possible exception of Jaffna.

4. *Tenure of high land.* As in the Dry Zone, it is not easy to obtain a comprehensive picture of the distribution of holdings of

[1] *Village Survey: Kurunegala*, p. 11.
[2] *Village Survey: Chilaw*, p. 7.

high land. The 1946 Census of Agriculture does, however, furnish data about the number and extent of 'small holdings' (a holding of less than 20 acres and more than 1 acre) and of 'town and village gardens' (of less than 1 acre).[1] 'Small holdings', as thus defined, are relatively far more numerous in the Wet Zone than in the Dry Zone. This reflects the greater physical possibilities for high land cultivation, the more intense pressure on the land, and the stronger tendency towards cultivation of cash crops: for many peasant small holdings are under such crops as coconut (especially in the Chilaw and Kurunegala Districts) and rubber (in the Kalutara and Ratnapura Districts). There are also some small holdings under tea. There are actually more small holdings than owners of paddy land in a number of Low Country districts, and the disparity is especially marked, as might be expected, in the 'Coconut Belt'.[2] There are, however, fewer small holdings than paddy owners in most Kandyan districts (except, curiously enough, Nuwara Eliya): this is partly due to the occupation by estates of much high land, partly to the Kandyan habit of parting with high land in a financial emergency far more readily than paddy land. In Nuwara Eliya, with physical conditions adverse to paddy, there are more high land small holdings than there are paddy holdings. Altogether small holdings, in the areas where they are numerous, do much to mitigate the poverty of peasants who possess them, and they are often the main source of a family's cash income. But a great proportion of them are too small to provide an adequate income (the mean areas vary from 2·04 acres in Nuwara Eliya District to 3·20 acres in Chilaw District);[3] the problems associated with divided ownership are rife;[4] and in many areas outsiders have, as in the case of paddy land, acquired peasant small holdings.

Even smaller, by definition, are the 'town and village gardens' of less than 1 acre, whose mean size varied in 1946 from 0·43 acres in the largely urban Colombo District to 0·60 acres in the Ratnapura District.[5] Even in these tiny gardens there is often divided ownership. Peasants with gardens in addition to paddy land possess a useful means of supplementing their diet and their incomes; but, although such gardens cannot be large enough for subsistence, they frequently represent the primary source of income, as in the

[1] *Census of Ceylon, 1946*, vol. i, pt. 2, p. 386.
[2] Data on number of paddy owners from *SL*, pp. 29–38.   [3] Ibid., p. 28.
[4] See, for example, *Village Survey: Rayigam Korale*, p. 5.   [5] *SL*, p. 28.

quarter to 1-acre coconut holdings of the Chilaw District.[1] A tiny patch of infertile high land may be all that a family has; sometimes, especially Up-country, this may be a 'private' *chena* on a slope which should never be cultivated. (Much Wet Zone *chena* is 'private'.)

TABLE 13

Estimated Percentage of Wet Zone Agricultural Families who were Landless, 1946

District	Percentage	District	Percentage
Low Country		*Up-country*	
Colombo . . .	14·2	Kandy . . .	19·4
Kalutara . . .	22·0	Matale . . .	38·3
Galle. . . .	20·0	Nuwara Eliya .	41·8
Matara . . .	20·2	Badulla . . .	8·8
Chilaw . . .	34·9	Ratnapura . .	32·2
Kurunegala . .	12·1	Kegalla . . .	20·5
		Ceylon Total . .	26·3

Source: SL.

5. *Landlessness.* There are also, as Table 13 demonstrates, many peasant families with no land at all, who are reduced to the role of *ande* tenants or labourers. No very full discussion of such landlessness is possible since Table 13, like Table 6 for the Dry Zone, is based on samples only. The Kandyan Peasantry Commission did, however, collect data for certain D.R.O.'s Divisions, which confirm the general impression given by the table and also reveal certain black spots. In Kotmale (Nuwara Eliya District), for example, 2,723 out of 7,504 peasant families were completely landless.[2] Comparison with Table 6 shows that there are relatively more landless people in a number of Kandyan districts than anywhere in the Dry Zone outside Jaffna and the abnormal Batticaloa District. But there are surprising anomalies, for example the low figures for Kandy and Badulla Districts; these suggest that the sample survey stands in need of broadening, and also that landlessness alone cannot be taken as an index of pressure of population on land, especially in a society which clings to its tiny plots of land as the last insignia of self-respect and in the absence

[1] *Village Survey: Chilaw*, p. 10.
[2] *KPC*, p. 316. It is proposed (Sept. 1953) to carry out a comprehensive survey of landlessness in the Up-country districts.

of full data on the availability of alternative employment (e.g. on estates). Similarly, while the figures for the Low Country are, as might be expected, generally lower than those for the Up-country, that for Chilaw is surprisingly high and that for Colombo surprisingly low.

6. *Conclusions.* From a general glance back at all the data which have been quoted, it will be clear that the agrarian situation in the Wet Zone of Ceylon is everywhere complex, and in many places serious. By a number of the criteria which have been used, the Kandyan villages are in a worse plight than the Low Country. But with data at present available, and assuming the seriousness of the agrarian situation to be the touchstone, it is impossible to say that whereas District 'A' deserves 100 places in a colonization scheme, District 'B' deserves 200; this question of the selection of colonists will be reopened in Chapter 10.

How has the unsatisfactory agrarian situation come about? This is a controversial matter on which it is hard to come to a firm conclusion, especially in the absence of exact data about the state of affairs before Western impact. But it is possible to suggest that a number of interrelated factors were at work. Of these, the most obvious and possibly the most potent is the great increase of population, free from the restraint imposed on the Dry Zone by endemic malaria, with the coming of internal peace and with improved health and other conditions. The population of the Low Country has increased from 1,189,526 in 1871 to 3,313,442 in 1946, and that of the Up-country from 692,025 to 2,252,910 in the same period. (Part of the increase is, of course, due to immigration from India, especially Up-country.) Some of the increase has been taken up by the growth of town employment and, particularly Up-country, by the possibility of work on estates, but a great burden has fallen on the lands of the peasant.

A second result of the opening up of the country has particularly affected the Kandyan districts. This is the movement among an unsophisticated peasantry of Low Country Sinhalese, Moors, and others who have foreclosed on mortgages, and otherwise exacerbated the agrarian problem.

A more controversial factor is the operation of the Crown Lands Encroachments Ordinance of 1840,[1] under which land considered to be 'waste' was declared Crown property, and much of it

[1] See above, pp. 81–82.

subsequently alienated to estate owners, especially in the Kandyan districts. The protagonists of the estates point out, quite rightly, that many of them, especially in the great area of the mono-culture of tea round Hatton, occupy land which was apparently never used for any purpose by the Kandyans and which is be-cause of its altitude incapable of use by their indigenous agri-cultural techniques; while others are on land bought from the Kandyans.[1] It is also pointed out, again rightly, that it is the estates which largely generate the external purchasing power which has enabled Ceylon to import food for its growing population and to give its people a standard of living higher than that of its neigh-bours; that it is the estates which constitute the chief source of the internal capital without which peasant development schemes, including colonization, would be impossible;[2] and that the estates provide employment for Kandyans and would have provided more but for their objections to working for hire. But, for all that, the author is convinced by field evidence that the Crown Lands Encroachments Ordinance, and the estates which grew up be-cause of it, have borne hard on many Kandyan villages and in doing so have accentuated an agrarian problem which would have been serious in any case. Many a Kandyan village has found itself hemmed in by estates, denied access to its customary pasture, forest, and *chenas* (which, having been mistakenly assumed to be 'waste', had been alienated to planters), and unable to expand its paddy or other land as its population increased. And some at least of the 'private' *chenas* and other lands which have been sold to estates were given up by their peasant owners because they were unable to take the risk of claiming for title to be settled in their favour when presumption was in favour of the Crown. It seems likely, too, that land policy and its effects have contributed to a sense of hopelessness among the Kandyan peasantry.

Income, Poverty, and Debt in the Rural Wet Zone

The demographic and agrarian position which has now been outlined would of itself be quite sufficient to account for a down-ward spiral in which increasing subdivision of holdings depresses incomes, increases indebtedness, and leads to the sale or surrender

[1] See, for example, Sir Hugh Clifford, 'Some Reflections on the Ceylon Land Question', *Trop. Agriculturist*, vol. lxviii (1927), pp. 289–94.
[2] See below, pp. 328–30.

of lands to outsiders and consequently to the spread of tenancy and landlessness. But other forces have also been at work. With the impact of a money economy, the peasant came to sell part of his paddy crop for cash, and in due course exposed himself to the effects of a flood of cheap rice imported from Burma. If, as sometimes happened, he began to grow other crops, such as coconuts or tea, in addition to or even to the neglect of his traditionally cherished paddy, then his prosperity became subject to the fluctuations of a notoriously unstable primary-commodities market.[1] If, with a diminished or vanished holding, he worked for hire on an estate or elsewhere, he was drawn further into the modern economic machine. The Wet Zone peasant is less subject than the Dry Zone peasant to drought and disease, though by no means immune; but he is far more vulnerable to economic depressions like that of the 1930's.

To the effects of disequilibrium between people and land there was thus added the effects of an unstable money economy; the situation has, of course, many parallels in Asia and Africa, notably in Indonesia.[2] It is not surprising that the Economic Surveys of the 1930's paint a depressing picture, coming as they did when the villages, living very near starvation in any case, were pushed nearer to it by the malaria epidemic of 1934–5 and by the economic depression. The general lessons of the Surveys have been summarized by Sir Ivor Jennings.[3]

How poor was the peasantry during the pre-war decade when, it is relevant to remember, the colonization schemes were being created largely in an attempt to ameliorate its condition? According to the Economic Surveys, 60–70 per cent. of the peasants in the Low Country villages which were studied had total gross incomes in cash and in kind, including the cash value of their own produce consumed at home, of under Rs. 20 (about 30s.) per month; in the coconut lands of Kurunegala District, the percentage with less than this low income was said to reach 76·7 per cent., nearly 11 per cent. receiving less than Rs. 5 per month.[4]

[1] See UN, Dept. of Econ. Affairs, *Instability in Export Markets of Under-Developed Countries.*

[2] See, for example, E. H. Jacoby, *Agrarian Unrest in Southeast Asia* (New York, Columbia Univ. Press, 1949), pp. 34–69.

[3] *The Economy of Ceylon,* 2nd ed. (Madras, OUP, 1951), pp. 52–62.

[4] For details of all the Economic Surveys, see pp. xxvi–xxvii. The statistics of income must be received with caution.

Unfortunately, the only Up-country villages surveyed were some in the Matale District; if the results are accurate and typical of the Kandyan districts as a whole, they certainly reveal a very bad state of affairs. Of the families surveyed 87·6 per cent. were said to have net incomes of under Rs. 20 per month. (The fact that this figure refers to *net* incomes makes very little difference to the answer.) This clearly reflects not only the depression in the tea estates, where most of the villagers worked for at least part of their time, but also the lack of resilience in an economy characterized by chronic land hunger. The median income in the Matale District was under Rs. 10 per family per month, compared with about Rs. 15 for the Low Country villages and with the figure of about Rs. 12 per month quoted for Dry Zone villages; but even lower incomes have, of course, been recorded for many other Eastern rural communities.

Certain of the Economic Surveys give estimates of the degree to which villages were dependent on supplies of paddy from outsiders; these are an interesting index of the extent to which the old self-sufficiency had broken down, and of the vulnerability of the peasant economy to external economic forces. The degree of dependence varied from about 35 per cent. in the Matara District, through 42 per cent. in the Matale District (the one Dry Zone village surveyed being, significantly, the only one to produce a surplus), to as much as 70 per cent. in the Chilaw and Kurunegala 'Coconut Belt'.

Not surprisingly, the Wet Zone villages surveyed had, like those in the Dry Zone, a heavy burden of debt. The percentage of families whose annual expenditure exceeded their income varied from 33 per cent. in the Matara District to 52 and 59 per cent. in the Matale and Chilaw Districts respectively. (One suspects, however, a consistent tendency, not confined to the East, for incomes to be under-declared.) The percentage of indebted families varied from about 50 to about 75 per cent., the highest figures again being for the Chilaw and Matale Districts. Clearly, then, the dangers of dependence on export commodities must be set against the advantages of estate employment in assessing the need in any given district for economic relief, whether by places in a colonization scheme or in other ways; for the proportion of both deficit and indebted families was, in the pre-war period at any rate, at a maximum in the most commercialized areas. And the extent of indebtedness makes fully understandable the process by which peasant land has been sold or surrendered for debt.

What can be said in the Wet Zone of the post-war improvement which appears to have affected at least parts of the Dry Zone? There seems to have been a general improvement in real incomes, as might be expected in an agricultural community in an inflationary period, especially when government policy guarantees prices for staple foodstuffs.[1] Unfortunately, no detailed results of the 1950 Economic Survey are available at the time of writing; but it is said that in 1950, in the sample villages, 85 per cent. of the families had a gross income of over Rs. 40, and that the average rural family income had risen from under Rs. 20 to Rs. 93 per month.[2] That these increases more than outweighed the concurrent increase in living costs is suggested by the statement that 68 per cent. of families now had an excess of income over expenditure; and that the percentage of indebted families had apparently fallen to about 33 per cent.[3] Specific measures of rural improvement have here supplemented general economic improvement though the figures may not be particularly reliable. But, clearly, a fall in the prices of the basic commodities could soon once again cause serious trouble to the villager; and there are many danger areas, particularly Up-country. The Kandyan Peasantry Commissioners could still report in 1951:

The general standard of living is low and goes down often to starvation level. The income of the peasants falls short of their bare needs and they are as a rule in a chronic state of indebtedness and poverty. . . . The outstanding feature . . . was the progressive backwardness of the peasantry and of their conditions of life as they receded farther and farther away from urban and municipal areas.[4]

Some Features of the Wet Zone Social System

For the same reasons as were set out at the beginning of the corresponding section of the last chapter, it seems desirable to say a little about the structure of Wet Zone Sinhalese society as it affects the behaviour of colonists emigrating to the Dry Zone. As was the case with the Dry Zone, however, one is hampered by lack of data.

It is important to stress, in the first place, that Wet Zone

---

[1] See UN, ECAFE, *Economic Survey of Asia and the Far East, 1948* (New York, 1949), p. 197.

[2] *Prelim. Rep. Econ. Survey Rural Ceylon*, pp. 11–12.

[3] Ibid., pp. 12–13.   [4] *KPC*, pp. 8–9.

Sinhalese society has many of the basic features of Dry Zone Sinhalese society; and, in fact, this section can proceed by taking Dry Zone society as a standard for comparison. Differences have, of course, arisen mainly because of the contrasting physical environment and because of the differential impact of social and economic forces emanating from the West.

Within the Wet Zone, as defined in this chapter, there are social differences between the Kandyan (Up-country) and Low-Country regions, mainly due to the longer and more intense impact of the West on the latter. Early accounts suggest Low Country customs identical with Kandyan;[1] but the Low Country was strongly influenced by the Portuguese and the Dutch as well as the British, whereas the Kandyan kingdom only finally yielded in 1815. So, in spite of the planting of estates since 1815, the Kandyan villages still preserve far more of the old order than their Low Country counterparts. To say this is not to suggest that life in a Kandyan village is an idyll lived according to ancient custom; if hallowed tradition and harmonious social life are inscribed on one side of the penny, backwardness and low educational and medical standards are on the other. Moreover, although the distinction between Low Country and Kandyan Sinhalese is recognized in law and in Census Reports, it is a distinction which can be, and has been exaggerated, and is everywhere today diminishing.[2]

In many parts of the Wet Zone it is still possible to distinguish the village community as the social unit, as in the Dry Zone; this is particularly true Up-country. But in most areas the village may well have originally been more scattered, because of the absence of any special class of high land to which settlement had to be restricted. Certainly it is very scattered today, with bazaars and linear roadside villages superimposed on the older settlement pattern and with many alien elements in the village population. In the Kandyan country in particular there is a contrast of *gama* (village) and bazaar.[3] Moreover, especially in the Low Country, the economic forces discussed in this chapter have made the peasant less village-bound, more individualistic, and, in fact, some- times rootless; he is thus more ready than formerly to migrate. In

---

[1] Hayley, *Laws and Customs of Sinhalese*, p. 24.

[2] See Denham, *Ceylon at the Census of 1911*, pp. 212–13. Denham's report also contains a vast amount of fascinating, if scattered, lore about the inhabitants of Ceylon.   [3] *KPC*, p. 75.

this connexion it may be interesting to quote the percentages of villagers who, asked whether they believed they could better their economic position by going to a colonization scheme, replied in the affirmative; the figures are: for a Jaffna village, 47 per cent.; for an urban-influenced Low Country village, 65 per cent.; for a Kandyan village, 21 per cent.; and for a Bintenne village, 14 per cent.[1] (Other factors besides the village tie, such as ignorance about colonization schemes, or even knowing too much about them, help to create this situation, however.)

In the Wet Zone village, and especially in the Kandyan *gama*, there is the same basic pride in land and in status as a cultivator that one finds in Nuwarakalawiya. Traditionally, too, there is the same despising of hired labour. But only too often land hunger and debt have driven the peasant to swallow his pride and to work for hire. The original Up-country estates could not induce the peasant to work on them, not because he was lazy, but because, like the Malay, he was too proud. Now one finds villages, like those described in the Matale Economic Survey, which depend mainly on employment on estates.[2]

As in the Dry Zone, family solidarity tends to be very strong, and therefore, *inter alia*, unemployment tends to be concealed as under-employment. But, because of decreased attachment to the village and family under economic stress and social change, unemployment in the Western sense has rather more meaning; and its volume grows with every accession to the ranks of those who are being educated for white-collar jobs which simply do not exist. Table 14 shows the incidence of rural unemployment in 1949; the figures are given for what little they may be worth and because, whatever they do *not* mean, they are certainly an indication of a malaise; but social research alone could reveal their true significance. (Urban unemployment is also tabulated for general interest rather than detailed discussion.) It may safely be said, however, that the larger figures for Low Country than Up-country districts are an index of the break-up of the old social order rather than of greater economic distress.

Buddhism is the majority religion in both Low Country and Up-country (but the Indian Tamil estate labourers are, of course, Hindus and there are many Sinhalese Christians in Chilaw and

[1] Ryan, in *Rur. Soc.*, vol. xvii, p. 21.
[2] *Village Survey: Matale.*

13. CROWD AT LAND KACHCHERI, DEWAHUWA COLONY

14. SQUATTERS' *BOUTIQUES*, POLONNARUWA RAILWAY
STATION
Back view

15. AMPARAI TANK

16. KALA WEWA YODA ELA
The ancient Jaya Ganga just below Kala Wewa

other coastal districts). Buddhist attitudes to such matters as the keeping of poultry are forces to be reckoned with in the colonization schemes, and Buddhism, the cement of many a village, is a potential source of harmony, cohesion, and tolerance in the colonies.

TABLE 14

Unemployment, Wet Zone Districts, October 1946

District	Rural		Urban		Estate	
	Male	*Female*	*Male*	*Female*	*Male*	*Female*
Low Country						
Colombo . .	39,802	6,113	32,925	5,981	866	543
Kalutara . .	6,588	1,114	1,296	315	61	50
Galle . .	3,096	639	2,055	449	11	24
Matara . .	1,988	316	948	505	6	3
Chilaw . .	2,342	239	156	10	2	3
Kurunegala .	2,407	355	375	61	19	20
Up-country						
Kandy . .	1,882	354	1,906	384	216	79
Matale . .	351	102	346	40	25	2
Nuwara Eliya .	455	100	426	341	112	48
Badulla . .	745	133	246	26	32	1
Ratnapura . .	1,582	284	400	42	69	38
Kegalla . .	2,695	526	120	18	210	215

Source: Unemployment Census, pp. 240–51.

Caste may originally have played the same part in defining status in the Wet Zone as it still plays, though to a diminishing extent, in the Dry Zone. But many villages consist of people of more than one caste.[1] This may be an ancient feature, related to the scattered settlement pattern, but has undoubtedly been reinforced by modern movements of 'outsiders' into *purāna* villages. Thus Miss Cook found in the village of Hettipola, in Kurunegala District, that there were 800 *goyiyas* and 250 low-caste people, including *boutique-*keepers; but the dhobies lived in a separate village.[2] The peasantry is everywhere still conscious of caste, especially Up-country, but everywhere the services and functions of caste have broken down; the Kandyan Peasantry Commissioners were able to write that

[1] Hayley, *Laws and Customs of Sinhalese*, p. 1. Since this section was written Ryan's *Caste in Modern Ceylon* has appeared.
[2] From manuscript notes left by Miss E. K. Cook, see p. 42.

caste distinctions 'are not as defined as they appear to have been in ancient times and are fast disappearing, but inasmuch as they still exist, they cannot be ignored in a consideration of relevant problems';[1] and this may be taken as a text to be applied to the colonization schemes.

Conclusion

If the Dry Zone of Ceylon is a problem area because of malaria, physical conditions, the state of technology, and general neglect, the Wet Zone of Ceylon is seen to be a problem area for different reasons. Nature appears to be bountiful, and there is no endemic malaria; but physical difficulties nevertheless exist. The main problems, however, are those associated with population increase under Western impact, and with landlessness, land shortage, the breakdown of the old social order, and poverty and indebtedness. Plantation agriculture has made opportunities for employment and given Ceylon its foreign trade, and a commercial economy has provided a means of earning cash by the sale of crops, but the changes of the last century or so appear, on balance, to have made the prospect for the village worse, not better. There has been some improvement since 1946, but this is very dependent on the somewhat uncertain prosperity of the three main export industries.

Finally, it will be clear that everywhere in the Wet Zone country-side there are pressures capable of being reduced if peasants are transferred to Dry Zone colonies; but it will be equally clear that land tenure and general economic conditions are so complex that it is not easy to say whether any given region of the Wet Zone stands in greater need of relief than another; though the plight of many Kandyan areas does stand out.

[1] *KPC*, p. 11.

PART TWO

THE EVOLUTION OF
A POLICY OF
PEASANT COLONIZATION
IN THE
DRY ZONE OF CEYLON

5

The Old Order, 1815–1914

THE British occupied Trincomalee and Colombo in 1795 and 1796 respectively, and by 1815 had extended their rule over the whole of Ceylon, including the Kandyan Provinces. There then developed, slowly at first, but with gathering momentum, the state of affairs which has been discussed in the previous chapter: an extensive, valuable, but narrowly based system of plantation agriculture in the Wet Zone, especially Up-country; and, associated with a great increase of population, the beginning of the pressure of population on land. But, during the same period, there was a growing appreciation of the present emptiness and past glories of the Dry Zone. Chapter 1 has quoted passages which show this process at work. What efforts did the Government of Ceylon and the British Colonial Office make to set the mounting difficulties of the Wet Zone over against the potentialities of the Dry Zone (which were evident though clearly difficult of realization)? In particular, what steps were taken to sponsor and assist peasant colonization of the Dry Zone?

It is proposed in the next three chapters to attempt an answer to this second question. Each chapter will deal with one of three marked phases in the history of aided colonization. In the first phase, from 1815 until 1914, there was very little government-sponsored colonization, but there were important developments in the provision of certain prerequisites to it. In the second phase, from 1914 to 1931, there was a great change. There were active, if not always successful experiments in actual government-sponsored colonization, and in such of its apparent prerequisites as a system of tenure designed to facilitate the acquisition of Crown land by peasants and to afford, *inter alia*, security of tenure for them once they were in possession. In the final phase, from 1931 to 1951, active colonization of the kind still in train was put in hand and the detailed policy of today was evolved.

The author does not pretend to be a historian, and he is very conscious that the evolution of policy is not fully discussed in the context of contemporary ideas. It is hoped, however, that the three chapters will serve as an introduction to the present pattern of peasant colonization in the Dry Zone of Ceylon.

Some General Characteristics

The period from the establishment of British rule over the whole island until the beginning of the First World War was in general characterized by the relative neglect, on the part of the Ceylon Government, of the people and potentialities of the Dry Zone, and the concentration of most of its activities, which increased in scope as *laissez-faire* was abandoned, on the Wet Zone with its larger population and productive plantations. The planters had, directly and indirectly, a great influence on policy, both in the Ceylon Legislative Council and at the Colonial Office, though perhaps not to the extent suggested by some modern Ceylonese historians.[1] Moreover, the Government was always concerned, and sometimes obsessed, with safeguarding and increasing its revenue, as was the case in most other colonial territories; and the malarial, jungle-clad, derelict, and sparsely peopled Dry Zone appeared at first, relative to the Wet Zone, to offer but little prospect of earning a return. But this chapter will show that there were high officers of government who, like Sir Henry Ward, castigated 'that neglect which has characterised the public service in the Eastern Province' and other Dry Zone areas, and maintained that 'it is only by extending to native interests the same attention, and encouragement, that we pay to those of our countrymen, that we shall ever realise the benefits that ought to be derived from British rule'.[2] Gradually, the Government was persuaded, and began 'to abandon its avowed *laissez-faire* policy, and to take more positive action to develop the resources of the country and to improve the people and their condition.'[3]

As has already been said, the period 1815–1914 saw important developments in the provision of certain prerequisites of colonization. These prerequisites will now be considered under the two

[1] For example, A. B. Perera, 'Plantation Economy and Colonial Policy in Ceylon', *Cey. Hist. J.*, vol. i (1951), pp. 46–58.

[2] 'Second Minute on the Eastern Province', Ward, p. 189, and 'Letter of 5 July 1858 to Sir E. Lytton Bulwer', ibid., p. 501.

[3] Mendis, *Ceylon under the British*, 2nd ed. (Colombo, Colombo Apothecaries, 1948), p. 5. This is a valuable work as a source for this and the two succeeding chapters.

main headings of (1) irrigation and communications; and (2) land policy. The peasant settlement which actually took place, and particularly such little of it as can fitly be called 'colonization', will then be reviewed.

Irrigation and Communications

From all that has been said about physical conditions and traditional techniques in the Dry Zone, to say nothing of the evident material basis for prosperity in ancient times, it will be clear that the restoration of irrigation works was essential for a return of population to the Dry Zone (though, towards the end of the period, the more active minds were turning their attention to the possibilities of the permanent unirrigated cultivation of high land).[1] Again, if the Wet Zone peasant was to reach the Dry Zone and to establish something more than a primitive subsistence economy, communications were vital, as, indeed, they were to the irrigation engineer.

The restoration of the magnificent ancient irrigation works of the Dry Zone did not, however, begin with the British. It was the Dutch who turned a *villu* (swamp) into Amparai Tank, now one of the beauty spots in the Gal Oya valley;[2] they also undertook other works in the Eastern Province, and contemplated projects in the Wanni.[3] But it was during the British period, after a very hesitant start, that the great work of restoration was mainly accomplished.

Early British travellers through the newly acquired Kandyan territories were greatly impressed by the ruins of great irrigation systems which they saw, especially in Nuwarakalawiya and Tamankaduwa.[4] At first they were, for the most part, content to express astonishment at the magnitude of the works and to comment on the beauty of such tanks as were still unbreached.[5] Thus Major Forbes wrote of Minneriya Tank:

On reaching the lake, its placid surface, lighted by the evening sun, reflected the varied foliage and forms of the clumps and trees on its promontories, capes, and islands; narrow creeks pierced far into the over-arching forest; and, beyond the waters, rich grassy plains stretched

[1] See, for example, J. C. Willis, 'Rotation of Crops upon Chena Land', *Circulars and Agric. J. of R. Bot. Gardens, Cey.*, vol. iv (1907), pp. 39–40.

[2] J. W. Birch, 'Report on the Irrigation of the Fields dependent on the Pattapola Aar', in Ward, pp. 193–203.

[3] See above, p. 6. [4] See above, pp. 10–14.

[5] See the examples quoted by Brohier, *Tamankaduwa District*, pp. 8–10.

amongst the wooded hills, over which arose in the distance the grand outlines of the Mátalé mountains.[1]

But soon there were also utilitarian attitudes. Thus Skinner, the 'road-maker', concerned at the evident depopulation of the country-side in 1833, urged the Government 'to take active steps for the pre-servation of [what was left] of these great irrigation works':[2] but nothing was then done. Again, in 1845 a Committee recommended the restoration of ancient tanks; but the Secretary of State, 'obsessed by British ideas of Government at the time, refused to allow grants-in-aid to irrigation works unless they increased the productive powers of the island and were likely to yield a fair return on the capital invested.'[3] Yet a third effort to impress the Government was made by Sir Emerson Tennent, who in 1848 submitted a restoration project to the Legislative Council; his scheme was approved, but what he euphemistically called 'events which after-wards disturbed the tranquillity of the island' prevented the carry-ing out of his plans.[4] For in 1848 occurred Ceylon's '45, the last revolt of the Kandyans against the British, and Tennent, who was Chief Secretary, was dismissed as a result of an inquiry into the circumstances of the rising.[5]

Ten years or so later the times were more propitious. Peace had been restored, a trade depression was over, and the Government of Ceylon, and to some extent the Colonial Office, had become con-vinced that administration could not be limited to such subjects as justice, law, and order, whatever might be considered desirable and necessary at home. The change of policy towards irrigation was very largely due to the energy and masterly minutes of Sir Henry Ward, Governor of Ceylon from 1855 to 1860, though it is only fair to add that his attention was drawn to the state of the irrigation works by both officials and members of the public.[6] Ward and his officers travelled far and wide and wrote down very forcibly their views on what they saw. They were particularly

---

[1] Forbes, *Eleven Years in Ceylon*, i. 204.
[2] *Fifty Years in Ceylon*, p. 167.
[3] Mendis, *Ceylon under the British*, p. 67.
[4] Tennent, ii. 432; see also Tennent, *Report on the Finance and Commerce of Ceylon* (London, Clowes for HMSO, 1848), p. 69.
[5] Bailey, *Ceylon*, pp. 107–13.
[6] Notably by John Bailey, who in 1855 wrote a great report on irrigation in Uva; see E. Elliott, 'Paddy Cultivation in Ceylon during the XIXth Century', *Trop. Agriculturist*, vol. xxxvii (1911), pp. 501–7.

active in the Eastern Province (which then included Taman-kaduwa) where they made great efforts to help the peasantry and to develop paddy production.[1] The result of all this activity was the enactment of an Irrigation Ordinance (No. 9 of 1856) and the restoration of many smaller works and of a number of major works in Batticaloa District (including Amparai) and in Southern Province.

But the habit of restoring irrigation works as a matter of course was not yet established. The next Governor, Sir Charles McCarthy (1860–3), reduced expenditure on public works and did little for irrigation; and nothing was done at this time to restore the great works of Tamankaduwa, though they had been visited by Ward and commented upon by a Commission appointed in 1867 to report on 'the existence of any locality in the island where public money or private capital might be advantageously expended on Irrigation, or other works likely to tend to an increased production of the food of the people.'[2] The Director of Public Works, in refusing to undertake work in Tamankaduwa, said that the area was too remote, which is a commentary on the state of communications.

It was in the 1870's and 1880's that irrigation really got under way. Much of the new impetus was due to Sir William Gregory (Governor 1872–7), who was much concerned for the peasantry (especially that of Nuwarakalawiya) and, unlike many of his predecessors, did not insist that public works must be judged solely by their capacity to earn revenue.[3] Throughout the period, however, rates paid for irrigation water were expected to give a reasonable return on the capital invested. The new emphasis on peasant welfare, which can, of course, be matched in late nineteenth-century colonial policy elsewhere, was maintained by Gregory's successors.[4] Much of the work which was done was concerned with village tanks, but a very large programme of major work was also carried out; if one looks at a list of schemes then undertaken,

---

[1] 'Minute on the Eastern Province, 1856', Ward, pp. 69–70; 'Second Minute on the Eastern Province, 1857', ibid., pp. 182–8; and 'Letter of 5 July 1858 to Sir E. Lytton Bulmer', ibid., p. 500.

[2] Quoted by Brohier, *Tamankaduwa District*, p. 11.

[3] Mendis, *Ceylon under the British*, pp. 82–83.

[4] Cf. J. S. Furnivall, *Colonial Policy and Practice* (Cambridge Univ. Press, 1948), pp. 62–64; but one does not readily accept Furnivall's explanation of the reasons for changed policy.

the astonishing fact emerges that almost exactly half of the hundred
or so major works restored or constructed up to 1914 were in fact
completed between 1870 and 1890 and nearly 90 per cent. of them
between 1870 and 1900.[1] Many of these were fairly small in scope;
but most of the tanks and *anicuts* which supply the Batticaloa
coastal paddy fields, and elsewhere such schemes as the great Kala
Wewa and its Yoda Ela to Anuradhapura and the large tank at
Kantalai, were in working order by 1900. (For the location of these
and other irrigation works, see Map 5; see also Map 9.) All this
activity was controlled by the Provincial Irrigation Boards founded
in 1885 and by a Central Irrigation Board founded in 1888.[2] A
separate Irrigation Department was set up in 1900.

Until 1900, however, very little had still been done in Tamankaduwa, with its great ancient tanks of Minneriya, Giritale, and
Parakrama Samudra, which now supply one of the greatest con-
centrations of colonists in the island. The restoration of Minneriya
Tank was completed in 1903, and that of Giritale in 1905; the
first decade of the twentieth century also saw activity on a number
of other works which later came to feed colonies; and the Nachchaduwa scheme was completed in 1914. All of these works reflect
not only continuing concern with peasant welfare but also increasing revenue, and the opening up of the Dry Zone by new
communications.

Clearly, then, a great deal of useful work was done in the sphere
of irrigation in the period from 1870 to 1914; the restoration or
construction of some hundred major schemes, and of very many
village tanks, represent no mean achievement, bearing in mind the
malarial and remote state of the Dry Zone at the time. But it is
possible, from the study of irrigation history alone, to derive an
exaggerated idea both of the shift from *laissez-faire* to welfare in
policy towards the peasantry and of the general activity of the
Government in the Dry Zone. For while all this work was going
on for the peasants in the Dry Zone, far greater sums were being
spent on such things as road and railway construction of direct
benefit to estates in the Wet Zone.

The provision of communications in the Dry Zone, moreover,
lagged behind their provision in the Wet Zone[3] (see Map 2). For

---

[1] See *Admin. Report: Irrigation*, 1949, App. A, pp. 21–23.
[2] Brohier, *Tamankaduwa District*, p. 12.
[3] This section is mainly based on the excellent account, illustrated with in-

some time British-built Dry Zone roads were merely designed to serve strategic or administrative ends, and even these roads were few and far between. The Dry Zone benefited little from early roads of this order, which merely penetrated its marches at Dambulla and Hambantota. And it gained little more from roads built between 1833 and 1843 to join provincial capitals; for, although these linked Puttalam with Kurunegala, and Jaffna, Anuradhapura, and Trincomalee with Dambulla, all but the road to Puttalam were neglected in the 1850's and 1860's, when the Government was concentrating on the provision of communications in the estate areas; most Dry Zone roads, in fact, became mere narrow tracks through the jungle at this time.

Governor Ward followed his predecessors in providing further roads in estate districts (then under coffee); but he also, with his concern for the peasantry, drew attention to the need for roads in the Dry Zone.[1] He actually achieved little more than the widening of the Dry Zone approach roads to Dambulla and the construction of a road in the Jaffna Peninsula; and it was left to his successors to lay down the main outlines of the present Dry Zone road network. Batticaloa had been connected with Colombo via Badulla, and the old roads Jaffna–Anuradhapura–Dambulla and Trincomalee–Dambulla had been reopened, by 1872, in time to provide access at least to the vicinity of the irrigation works whose restoration dates from about the same period. Further branch roads (e.g. Puttalam–Anuradhapura–Trincomalee and Hambantota–Tissamaharama–Wellawaya) were built by 1890; but this still left roadless the whole of Tamankaduwa and the great coastal sector from Batticaloa to Tissamaharama. The late provision of communications is in fact one reason for the late restoration of irrigation in Tamankaduwa; and the building of a road from the Dambulla–Trincomalee road, past Minneriya to Polonnaruwa in 1891 was followed by work on Minneriya and Giritale tanks.[2] Further elements were added to the road network by 1914, and the roads were made more effective by the coming of motor vehicles; but there were still considerable tracts without roads (thus there was no link from Polonnaruwa to Batticaloa) and access from irrigation

teresting maps, in Mendis, *Ceylon under the British*, pp. 16–20, 48–50, 61–66, 78–81, and 108–14.
[1] e.g. 'Minute on the Eastern Province, 1856', Ward, p. 73.
[2] See above, p. 106.

works and villages to the main network was often very unsatisfactory.

The railway line from the Wet Zone to Anuradhapura and Jaffna was not completed until 1895; among a number of motives for its construction was the 'confident expectation' of the development of land then waste;[1] there was also the hope that it would relieve congestion in the Jaffna Peninsula by drawing settlers south to the Wanni.[2] The only other Dry Zone railway to be built by 1914 was the branch to Mannar, designed mainly to bring Tamil labourers from India.

Some Aspects of Land Policy[3]

This section, and the corresponding sections of Chapters 6 and 7, are not intended to form a comprehensive history of land policy in Ceylon, much as such a history is needed; but a brief review of certain aspects of land policy seems relevant. For it is in this field that government interest in the estates, and the gradual swing towards peasant welfare, are particularly evident; and to study the evolution of interest in peasant welfare is to study the history of an attitude of mind without which the Ceylon Government was unlikely to embark upon peasant colonization. Moreover, particular aspects of land policy vitally affect the possibility of successful settlement and colonization. If rights over waste land are such that the Government cannot colonize it, clearly no colonization is possible; if the Government controls waste land, but only issues it to the peasant on terms which are difficult for him, then legitimate spontaneous settlement will be hampered and sponsored colonization is likely to run into such troubles as indebtedness and default on payments due to Government; even if land is easily available, there is, at least in the view of one prominent school of thought, a need for some form of restrictive or controlled tenure if the peasant's new holding is to be preserved for him and his successors, and not sold, mortgaged, fragmented, or eroded. The reader will therefore find that the evolution of policy concerning ownership of waste land, methods of alienating Crown land, and the possibilities of

---

[1] *Railway Extension Northwards*, S.P. 6 of 1893.

[2] Cf. H. R. Freeman, 'Dry Farming', *Trop. Agriculturist*, vol. xli (1913), p. 524.

[3] The author is greatly indebted to Mr. K. Kanagasundram, formerly Land Commissioner, for discussing with him the evolution of land policy from 1815 to the present day. But any errors of fact or inference are the author's.

restrictive tenure, particularly in their bearing on colonization, will be recurrent themes in this and the two succeeding chapters.

Land policy in Ceylon throughout the period 1815–1914 was based on three main principles; there were no real deviations from them, merely amendments and ameliorations in detail as peasant welfare came to the forefront of public policy. The first of these was the principle so frequently applied in colonial and other 'new' territories, that undeveloped land was Crown property. The application of this principle caused considerable hardship to the peasantry, but at least gave Government control of unused land which could in a later phase be used for colonization. The second principle was that the initiative in the alienation of Crown land must come from the individual wanting the land, and the third principle was that Crown land must be paid for; both of these bore heavily on the peasantry in general and on the potential settler in the Dry Zone in particular.

The first principle was implicit in the system of land grants operated in the earliest days of British rule;[1] and was explicitly declared in the Crown Lands Encroachments Ordinance, No. 12 of 1840, which established *inter alia* that 'all forest, waste, unoccupied or uncultivated lands shall be presumed to be the property of the Crown until the contrary . . . be proved'.[2] The presumption in favour of the Crown has led to bitter controversy, centred particularly on the question whether it truly represents a right claimed by the Sinhalese kings.[3] And the land presumed to be Crown property was, as has already been seen, widely alienated to planters, the process being associated with drastic changes both in the external economy of Ceylon and in the environment of the Kandyan peasantry. In the Dry Zone, with its malaria and harsh climatic régime, there was no such development, and the Ordinance bore on the peasantry mainly by giving the Crown the right to control *chenas* (other than 'private' *chenas* with title established), since these were declared 'waste'. There was also the fact that, although a section of the Ordinance established the prescriptive right of the subject to

[1] See below, p. 111, and see Brohier, *Land, Maps and Surveys*, i. 31–33, and Sir Charles Collins, *Public Administration in Ceylon* (London, RIIA, 1951), pp. 32–33 and 39.
[2] The Ordinance is quoted in full in Brohier, *Land, Maps and Surveys*, i, App. F, pp. 101–3.
[3] See, for example, Ceylon Legislative Council, *Debates*, 1927, i. 419–27, 428–72, 477–513, 516–25.

land if he had held it uninterruptedly for thirty years, the onus of proof lay on him; consequent uncertainty of title has ever since had a confusing and economically depressing effect.

The Crown Lands Encroachments Ordinance has also come under fire because, like similar enactments elsewhere, it misunderstood ancient custom and, in particular, rights to waste for such purposes as shifting cultivation, pasture, and timber cutting.[1] But the Ordinance must not be judged too harshly. As political ideas changed and interest in peasant welfare grew, the Government came to regard Crown lands as held in trust for the people; and, if waste land had not been Crown property, it is difficult to see how the alienation of great tracts to peasants in modern colonization schemes could readily have come about. As Harroy said of somewhat comparable African conditions:

La solution apportée est enfin caractéristique d'une tendance générale, partant d'une méconnaissance réelle, à l'origine, des droits et besoins des autochthones, et faisant place, à mesure que la colonisation se développait, à un plus grand respect des intérêts des populations locales.[2]

The second principle of land policy during the period, that of individual initiative in the alienation of Crown land, was held virtually inviolate throughout the period. It found expression in the 'application system', under which, 'when an individual required land, he applied to purchase or lease it'.[3] His application was considered by the local Revenue Officer, who was required to take into account the possibility of land being required for other purposes (e.g. village pasture). If he decided in favour of the applicant, 'the land was surveyed and advertised and the land or lease of it sold to the highest bidder'.[4] This system had disadvantages for the planter (delay might be considerable, or decisions be reversed by a change of Revenue Officer) and for the Government (surveys were made as applications arose, and not systematically, a very uneconomical procedure). But the disadvantages for the peasant were still greater. Quite apart from the financial implications, the complications of the system were usually beyond his ken and unrelated to traditional notions. A Wet Zone peasant, in particular, would be unlikely to know what land was available under a distant

---

[1] Cf., for example, Lord Hailey, *An African Survey*, ch. 12, pp. 712–829; and J.-P. Harroy, *Afrique, terre qui meurt*, 2nd ed. (Brussels, Hayez, 1949), pp. 336–44. See also Pelzer, *Pioneer Settlement*, p. 207.

[2] Harroy, *Afrique*, p. 337.   [3] *LC*, p. 12.   [4] Ibid.

Dry Zone scheme. There were, however, one or two concessions as time went on. Thus, by the 1890's, shareholders under a tank were allowed pre-emption over new lands rendered irrigable by their own efforts (though this clearly did not benefit immigrant peasants).[1] And, in the 1890's came the Kala Wewa experiment in colonization.[2]

There were further disadvantages in the system of individual initiative. There was no officer of Government who could initiate a policy of land classification, either in conformity with ecological principles or in the interests of the economically weak members of society. The Revenue Officers, it is true, referred questions of policy to the Controller of Revenue in Colombo, but he was generally too busy to give due attention to land questions, and, in any case, could not, in general, offer tracts of land to selected peasants on account of their need.

The third principle, that Crown land must be paid for, did not apply in the earliest days of British rule, when free grants of land were made on conditions actually more favourable to Ceylonese than to Europeans.[3] But, by the time that land under restored Dry Zone irrigation works was becoming available, a system of sale and lease was in operation. This, like the application system, was better suited to the estate owner than to the peasant with his characteristic lack of capital. Such relaxation of regulations as was allowed, was designed to make it easier for the peasant to pay, and not to excuse him altogether. Thus Ward in 1866 devised a system of payment by instalments which became known as 'alienation under "Sir Henry Ward's Minute"', and many Dry Zone villages purchased extra land and enlarged their *yāya*.

By the first decade of the twentieth century there were some minds, particularly those under the influence of new ideas on peasant welfare, which held that all was not well with Ceylon's land policy. Leonard Woolf, for example, was concerned with the problem of preventing peasants newly on the land from running into debt.[4] And in 1912 Sir Hugh Clifford, later to be Governor of Ceylon and a potent influence on a new land policy,[5] tried to 'get the entire Land Policy . . . consigned to the melting-pot', but was

---

[1] See *Admin. Report: North-Central Province*, 1895, p. 6.
[2] See below, p. 113.
[3] Brohier, *Land, Maps and Surveys*, i. 31–32 and 97–99.
[4] From his MS. Diary. [5] See Chapter 6.

unsuccessful in his efforts.[1] So in 1914 land policy was still in general adverse to the peasant and to peasant colonization, in spite of small concessions. The presumption of Crown rights to waste land had provided an essential preliminary to colonization, but the individual initiative and capital required even by the modified application system told against peasant settlement. Other measures later thought desirable were not yet in force. There was thus no legislation like the Government Tenants (Punjab) Act of 1893, which embodied a form of protective tenure designed to control the subsequent fate of land alienated to colonists.[2] Experience in the 1920's was rightly or wrongly to convince the Ceylon authorities that such a tenure was essential to successful colonization in the Dry Zone.

Actual Colonization and Settlement

By 1914 the idea of government-sponsored colonization was well known in other Asian countries. In India, for example, the great Punjab canal colonies had been started in 1886; while the Dutch had begun in 1905 to organize very carefully the movement of peasants from Java to Sumatra.[3] But in Ceylon there was in 1914 no policy of government-inspired colonization. It will be evident from what has been said that land policy was adverse to such a process; or, putting the matter in terms of more fundamental causes, the official attitude to peasant problems was as yet unfavourable to the notion of colonization (for if that attitude *had* been favourable, land policy would clearly have been amended accordingly).

It was not, however, that suggestions were lacking that the Government should take a more active interest in colonization. Thus Ward, with characteristic vision and concern for the peasantry, had seen that some form of government initiative was desirable. He said:

> To talk of tank repairs, or of laying out money in any other way than by bringing a fresh population into contact with the treasures, which Nature has lavished on the soil, would be uncalled for, as well as unprofitable. . . . We must therefore colonize, or do nothing.[4]

[1] See Clifford, in *Trop. Agriculturist*, vol. lxviii (1927), p. 286.
[2] See *The Punjab Colony Manual*, rev. ed. (Lahore, Supt. of Govt. Printing, 1933–4), pp. 48–52.
[3] See Darling, *Punjab Peasant*, pp. 111–31, and Pelzer, *Pioneer Settlement*, pp. 160–231.   [4] 'Minute on the Eastern Province, 1856', Ward, p. 73.

He thought that an experiment in colonization might be attempted since there was, already in 1856, a surplus of labour in Jaffna and the 'Seven Korales' (roughly the modern Kurunegala District).

An experiment was in fact attempted at Kala Wewa in the 1890's and appears to have owed a great deal to news of the inauguration of the first Punjab colony in 1886.[1] (In fact, it appears probable that the term 'colonization', meaning government-sponsored peasant settlement in an area away from the settlers' homes, as distinct from spontaneous settlement, either near to or away from the settler's homes, first entered Ceylon from India at this time.) The Government had restored the great tank of Kala Wewa in 1887, and, being concerned at the slow rate of settlement under it, sanctioned a scheme for aided colonization as a special measure. It was arranged for a Tamil gentleman in Jaffna to select two batches of colonists, who received substantial aid in the shape of free transport, maintenance for six months, ready-built houses, free seeds and tools, and facilities for hiring buffaloes and ploughs. It was hoped to recover some at least of the cost of this aid. The colonists were meant to clear the land themselves, but local labour was in fact called out to help the second and somewhat shiftless batch of Tamils. An attempt was also made to settle on newly irrigated land Sinhalese peasants from a local *purāna* village, but the attempt failed when a large block of land adjacent to the new settlement was alienated to a Low Country Sinhalese and the villagers fled because of some prejudice regarding their new neighbour. Aided colonization of Tamils also soon fell through. There was much sickness, some colonists returned to Jaffna, and the Government tired of the scheme as soon as it seemed likely that the lands under Kala Wewa would be sold without resort to colonization. The whole experiment was, however, interesting; in its methods and difficulties it foreshadows the modern colonies.

There was, however, in spite of the physical difficulties and bad reputation of the Dry Zone, and for all the lack of encouragement and the adverse land policy of the Government, a certain amount of new settlement in the Dry Zone, especially in the Batticaloa coastal alluvium, in parts of Nuwarakalawiya, and in the southeast, where Leonard Woolf was able to report in 1909 that the works at Tissamaharama had attracted 'all sorts and conditions of

[1] *Report on the Kaldwewa Colonisation Scheme*, S.P. 4 of 1893.

people' from nearby areas of the Wet Zone.[1] But in these newly settled areas land often went, under the sale regulations then current, to absentee landowners or even to 'land-grabbers', who then let it out on *ande* to immigrant peasants. Such purchasers were in general relatively petty men, however; there was hardly any large-scale capital investment in Dry Zone paddy land because of low prices and the generally uncertain nature of paddy cultivation. Only occasionally was a voice raised in favour of capitalist investment in paddy cultivation.[2]

In some areas there was, because it was so hard for a peasant to acquire land legally, a great deal of squatting, in other words, encroachment on Crown land. This practice, together with the operation of the Ordinance of 1840, increased the tendency to uncertainty of title which has already been mentioned. The Waste Lands Ordinance, No. 1 of 1897, was an attempt to deal with this problem by ensuring the speedy settlement of title to waste land; and a special Land Settlement Department was formed in 1903 ('Settlement' here means the determination of title as between the Crown and the subject). But there are still today great areas where uncertainty of title is a handicap to economic development.[3]

But the scale of new settlement, legal or illegal, was in certain regions, particularly the more remote, very small indeed. Thus, to begin with, the restoration of Giant's Tank in 1902–6 had disappointing results. The 1911 Census Report was able to record twenty-two new villages with 1,500 inhabitants;[4] but detailed analysis showed that increases in new villages were largely due to emigration from nearby old ones, some of which were deserted, rather than to an influx from the Wet Zone. The Karachchi scheme, south of the Jaffna lagoon, also had poor early results. And, worst of all, twenty years after the restoration of Minneriya Tank in 1903, there were still only some 170 acres of paddy directly under it, whereas its estimated irrigable area was 10,000 acres.[5] Quite

---

[1] MS. Diary.
[2] e.g. Elliott, 'Rice Cultivation under Irrigation in Ceylon', *J.R. As. Soc.* (Cey. Br.), vol. ix (1885), pp. 160–70; and it was in 1880 proposed to reserve 10,000 acres under Kantalai Tank for paddy cultivation by the 'Jaffna and Batticaloa Agricultural Co. Ltd.', see *Grants of Government Land*, S.P. 36 of 1880.
[3] See *KPC*, map 8, and pp. 105–6. See also the *Admin. Reports of the Settlement Officer*.   [4] Denham, *Ceylon at the Census of 1911*, p. 74.
[5] Brohier, *Tamankaduwa District*, pp. 25–26.

apart from other considerations, a great deal of government capital was locked up in a completely unremunerative fashion in works such as this.

And yet, while all this irrigable land lay unused, potential pressure on Wet Zone land was mounting; 'potential' because the essentially unstable nature of the Wet Zone economy, both in its external aspect, with its reliance on a very few staple commodities, and in its internal aspect, with a peasantry whose basic economy was being undermined, was concealed by the general prosperity of the estate industries and, in particular, by the fantastic rubber boom of the first two decades of the twentieth century. The area under rubber grew from 1,750 acres in 1900 to 188,000 acres in 1910 and to 460,643 acres by 1920.[1] Depressions there were, but the Edwardian glory of the old order in Ceylon blinded all but the most perspicacious to its inherent dangers and, in particular, to the possibility of serious food shortage. The essential instability of the whole system was only brought home by the food crisis during and immediately after the war of 1914–18, and it was this realization of danger which was initially responsible for the seventeen years or so of intense discussion, experiment, and change, which ushered in the modern era of aided colonization in the Dry Zone of Ceylon.

[1] *Report of the Commission on the Rubber Industry in Ceylon,* S.P. 18 of 1947, p. 3.

6

Experiment and Change, 1914–31

THE period from the outbreak of war in 1914 to the initiation of the 'Donoughmore Constitution' in 1931 forms a very suitable unit in the study of the history of colonization policy in Ceylon. For the war ushered in an interesting period in which land policy and colonization were the subjects of active discussion, experimentation, and reform; the process culminated in the fundamentally important *Final Report of the Land Commission* (*LC*). By 1931 the need for colonization to relieve pressure in congested areas was accepted, although the Dry Zone still had such an unsavoury reputation that it was generally held to be unsuitable for colonization. It was, in fact, only after 1931 that Dry Zone colonization as practised today became an accepted need and an accomplished fact. And it was not until 1935 that the Land Development Ordinance, the basic legislative enactment for modern colonization, gave effect in modified form to some of the main recommendations of the Land Commission.

During the period 1914–31 there were a number of factors which at various times drew attention to the social and economic problems of Ceylon and of its peasantry, and led to suggestions concerning land policy in general and colonization in particular. The first of these, chronologically, was the war-time need for increased food production; and, although the immediate danger receded after 1918, the decreased overseas purchasing power of the country which resulted from the depression in the estate industries in the 1920's kept the need for food production temporarily to the fore. The call for home-grown food in a country like Ceylon does not necessarily improve prospects for the indigenous peasant or for his colonization of Crown land; there may be a demand for food at any price. Thus, in spite of the overcrowding of the Wet Zone, there were proposals in 1920 for the importation of Indian labour to hasten Dry Zone development;[1] and there was a brief period when it was capitalist, rather than peasant activity which was most

---

[1] *Food Supply Committee*, p. 4.

prominent.[1] The food production campaign did, however, benefit the peasantry in a number of ways. As part of the campaign, the Ceylon Agricultural Society did much to ventilate peasant problems;[2] it produced a very valuable report on land development in the Dry Zone which contains many ideas subsequently taken up by the Government in its colonization schemes;[3] and it was the Society which was largely responsible for the experimental Nachchaduwa colony.[4] It was also at a discussion of the Society that Lieut.-Colonel T. G. Jayawardena formulated the reasons which had previously led to slow settlement in the Dry Zone; they were, he said, (1) lack of settled government policy on Crown lands, (2) lack of roads, (3) lack of medical facilities, and (4) want of encouragement.[5] The third factor can hardly be blamed on the Government, for very little could be done to control malaria until the invention of DDT spraying; but the other points were reiterated, discussed, and to some extent dealt with in the period 1914–31.

Benefit to the peasantry and eventually to peasant colonization also came from a government report on food production which was published in 1920.[6] It reviewed the reasons why paddy was not more widely cultivated in Ceylon and proposed such remedies as guaranteed minimum prices, the opening of new lands (including the Nachchaduwa Colony then being proposed by the Ceylon Agricultural Society, and a government scheme under Minneriya), and more progressive policies concerning irrigation and transport. The need for food production also led to a liberalization of land policy which had, as will be seen, important permanent effects.

Sporadically during the food-production crisis, and increasingly as the crisis passed and the nature of Ceylon's basic economic difficulties became apparent, the problem of a rapidly increasing population came to the forefront; and, as a necessary concomitant, there was less talk of Indian labour as a means to land development for its own sake, and more talk of measures deliberately calculated to absorb the local population and to provide employment for

[1] See below, p. 129.
[2] See its reports in *Trop. Agriculturist*, vols. xliv (1914)–li (1918).
[3] 'Report of the Land Development Committee of the Ceylon Agricultural Society', ibid., suppl. to vol. xlix (1917).
[4] See below, pp. 130–2.
[5] 'Land Development in the Dry Zone' (report of a discussion), ibid., vol. l (1918), p. 6.   [6] *Food Supply Committee.*

Ceylonese. Thus in discussions of the Nachchaduwa Colony[1] there were declarations as early as 1919 that settlement, and not mere food production, was the objective: and a similar opinion was expressed in 1921; the object was 'not to get 500 acres cultivated immediately but to get settlers from outside [i.e. Low Country, Sinhalese] into it.' Confusion between the two objectives, food production at any price, or the absorption and welfare of the surplus peasant population, has, however, cropped up periodically throughout the subsequent history of the colonization schemes.

In the later 1920's it was the latter objective which was being mainly kept in view. Thus the energetic and outspoken Governor Sir Hugh Clifford (1925–7), although maintaining the then generally accepted view that the increase in Ceylon's population was a sign of material prosperity, nevertheless was well aware of the danger of 'overcrowding', and wanted 'to provide in good time against this threatened congestion.'[2] And the population problem was considered by the Land Commission to be a main reason for the organization of colonies; they wrote:

The population, particularly in the coastal strip of the Wet Zone, has more than doubled during the last few decades. This increase is still going on, and land in many places has begun to be insufficient for the population that requires to use it. These conditions are causing the migration of more enterprising or restless individuals further afield in search of the land and employment they cannot hope to obtain in their own villages. This movement, though there is little doubt it is constantly going on and indeed increasing, is yet a slow process and does not in any way keep up with the growth of the population which is becoming every year more congested. It therefore appears to us to be a matter of serious consideration whether special measures should not be taken by Government to assist this movement.[3]

There was also, in the period 1914–31, a developing concern for the peasantry as a social institution, and not merely as a producer of food or as a demographic phenomenon. There was, as there is today, relatively little exact information to demonstrate the plight of the peasants. But an inquiry in 1910 had revealed the prevalence of indebtedness;[4] the devoted work of various Revenue Officers

---

[1] See below, pp. 130–1.
[2] Clifford in *Trop. Agriculturist*, vol. lxviii (1927), pp. 301–3.
[3] *LC*, pp. 19–20.
[4] *Report of a Committee appointed by the Governor to consider the whole question of Agricultural Banks*, S.P. 8 of 1910.

had drawn attention to the small size and apparent fragmentation of holdings; and it was becoming apparent that many peasants had disposed of their land to speculators during the rubber boom.[1] The land problem of the peasantry thus forced itself on the Government and on interested private persons, and, not least, on the Land Commission. The problem was conceived to have three main aspects—the difficulty of acquiring new land, loss of land through indebtedness, and fragmentation.

The peasant system was not, as has been seen, in good odour at the time of the food crisis. 'We have waited long enough for colonization by small settlers', said the Ceylon Agricultural Society in 1916:[2] and similar views on the ineffectiveness of the peasant tended to prevail among planters and others in later years. But he was not lacking in champions who considered that the odds had been loaded against him and that he had lacked encouragement;[3] and his cause gained from the transparent failure of large-scale food production projects in the early 1920's.[4] Powerful support also came from Sir Hugh Clifford, who in Nigeria made a frequently quoted statement in support of peasant agriculture, claiming that it was superior to plantations because it was rooted in local custom, 'self-supporting as regards labour', cheap, and capable of rapid expansion;[5] Sir Hugh brought his ideas to Ceylon in 1925, and came out strongly in support of the peasantry. When he left in 1927 he wrote in a farewell message to the Finance Committee, 'No peasant of any tropical country will willingly work for a wage, no matter how tempting the figure at which the wage be placed, if the alternative be open to him of cultivating land of his own', and went on to express concern at the drift of the Sinhalese peasantry towards employment on the estates.[6] He had, in other words, added a social reason for preserving peasant agriculture to the economic one which he advocated in Nigeria; but seems to have been thinking in terms of an egalitarian yet individualistic system of peasant proprietorship very different from the system

---

[1] Clifford in *Trop. Agriculturist*, vol. lxviii, pp. 298–9.

[2] 'Land Development in the Dry Zone', *Trop. Agriculturist*, vol. l, p. 4, quoting the *Ann. Report of the Ceylon Agricultural Society* for 1916.

[3] e.g. the remarks of Mr. K. Balasingham, later a member of the Land Commission, ibid., p. 4.   [4] See below, p. 129.

[5] In an address to the Legislative Council of Nigeria, quoted by Hailey, *African Survey*, p. 982.

[6] *LC*, p. 12.

of interlocking mutual obligations in the traditional village.[1] From 1927 onwards, it became the view of the Ceylon Government and of many eminent Ceylonese that the peasantry had been weakened by the impact of new forces and ought to be preserved; and that individual, independent peasant proprietorship was desirable.

This view found notable expression in the declaration by the Land Commission that the preservation of the peasantry should be considered the main object of future land policy. Crown land was to be 'mapped out', that is, allocated between various classes of use, peasant needs were to have priority, and land was, amongst other things, to be allocated for colonization.[2] (Other proposed uses for Crown land included village expansion, reserved forests, and alienation to 'persons other than villagers', e.g. the middle class.) There was no question, it should be noted, of a thoroughgoing classification of land according to its physical nature, such as is often now advocated; but the Land Commission did consider that 'an agricultural survey of the land mapped out as available for economic development would serve a useful purpose', the survey to include a study of soil, rainfall, and other factors.[3] (It is unfortunate that modern views on land classification did not prevail at this formative period in the history of Ceylon's land policy.)

The preservation of the peasantry, accepted a little uncritically, was the mainspring of the social purpose of land reform in the Ceylon of the 1920's; but there were also subsidiary social motives. Thus some play was made of the fact that 'middle-class' persons found it difficult to obtain land, and that the attraction of such persons to the land was socially desirable in the interests of a balanced rural society.[4] Efforts were also made to help particularly needy communities, such as the 'Malays' of Hambantota, descendants of Javanese and Bandarese who were brought to Ceylon by the Dutch as mercenaries, and who by 1927 were said to be in a desperate state.[5]

The economic and social motives which have been described were brought to bear on the situation in Ceylon largely because of a favourable political climate. There was an unofficial majority in

---

[1] See above, p. 71.

[2] For 'mapping out' procedure see G. B. King, 'Mapping Out of Crown Lands in Ceylon', *Emp. Survey Rev.*, vol. xi (1951–2), pp. 194–204 and 242–7.

[3] *LC*, p. 13.   [4] Ibid., p. 14.

[5] See below, pp. 134–5. The author is indebted to Tuan K. Burah, of Hambantota, for information about his community.

the Legislative Council after 1920;[1] and the unofficial members included a group of very able Ceylonese, including Sir James Pieris, F. R. Senanayake and his younger brother, D. S. Senanayake, Sir Baron Jayatilaka, and K. Balasingham. These men debated land questions in the Council, in the National Congress,[2] and elsewhere, and contributed greatly to the formulation of problems, to suggestions for solutions, and to the assurance of continuity from colonial rule to the virtual self-government of 1931. A number of them served on the Land Commission but had as yet no executive functions. There were also a number of Governors, especially Sir Hugh Clifford, who made notable contributions to discussions of land policy.

The short-term need for food, concern over a rapidly growing population, social motives, and political circumstances thus combined to stimulate interest in land policy and in colonization. The story of work thus encouraged may be told under three headings:

1. The provision of irrigation and communications.
2. Experiment and change in land policy.
3. Experiment and accomplishment in colonization.

The Provision of Irrigation and Communications

Although during this period it was still generally recognized that settlement in the Dry Zone, at least along traditional lines, was dependent on irrigation, not a great deal was in fact done to restore ancient works or to provide new ones. Public works of necessity took a back place during the war, and after it the emphasis was rather on the utilization of land under existing works than on the provision of further irrigation schemes. The new tank at Unnichchai was, however, completed in 1919, and the Verugal *anicut* (feeding Allai Tank) in 1928; work was also done in the period on the Walawe Ganga Left Bank scheme. (All of these now feed colonies.) But the acreage sown under major irrigation works increased only from 142,947 acres in 1922 to 162,797 acres in 1930.[3] The period of maximum rate of expansion was to come after 1931.

There were, however, signs of the times in other directions. A

---

[1] *Report of the Special Commission on the Constitution* (Donoughmore Commission), Cmd. 3131 (1928), p. 14.
[2] A national political organization.
[3] 'Progress in Irrigation', *Ceylon Daily News*, 17 Sept. 1951.

Committee in 1920 not only suggested that 'the programme of new irrigation works, which has been suspended for about ten years, should now be resumed' but made a suggestion which would have shocked an older generation, that 'the Irrigation Department should not in future be regarded so much as a revenue-earning department, but a spending department, like the Public Works.'[1] The notion was not adopted, but later suggestions for the temporary waiving of irrigation rates in new settlements (made, for example, by Sir Hugh Clifford) ultimately became standard practice in colonization schemes.[2]

During the period 1914–31 it became widely recognized that communications as well as irrigation were essential to Dry Zone colonization; and there was a renewed willingness, reminiscent of the enthusiasms of Ward, for the Government to take the initiative in the provision of roads and railways. Lack of roads was, it will be remembered, one of the reasons which Lieut.-Colonel T. G. Jayawardena held responsible for the slow progress of Dry Zone settlement; and the 1920 Committee on food production suggested 'that in future means of communication should precede rather than follow the development of a district', and that, in harmony with this principle, a light railway should be built to Polonnaruwa in order to open up Tamankaduwa.[3] More than this was in fact accomplished, for the railway was extended to Batticaloa, and a branch was built past Kantalai to Trincomalee; one motive in this major piece of construction was undoubtedly the encouragement of paddy cultivation.[4] The new notion of the function of the government railway was expressed by its General Traffic Manager, who is quoted as saying 'that the primary object of the railway should be the development of the country, and not profit'.[5]

But not all was done that might have been done. A projected extension of the railway from Batticaloa to Nintavur, which would have been of great assistance to the present Gal Oya Scheme, was never constructed.[6] There were in various Dry Zone districts

[1] *Food Supply Committee*, p. 5.
[2] 'Message from His Excellency the Governor (Sir Hugh Clifford)', in Brohier, *Land, Maps and Surveys*, i. 119.
[3] *Food Supply Committee*, p. 5.
[4] G. S. S. Gordon, 'Extension of the Ceylon Government Railway', *Geog. J.*, vol. lxvi (1925), pp. 471–2.
[5] *Report of the Karachchi Scheme Committee*, S.P. 5 of 1926, p. 11.
[6] *Railway from Batticaloa to Nintavur*, S.P. 5 of 1924.

many complaints of inadequate local roads, especially when the coming of the motor bus in the 1920's created new peasant demands;[1] thus in 1924 there were complaints about the lack of feeder roads in the Nachchaduwa Colony.[2] And the problem of communications has persisted to the present day.[3]

Experiment and Change in Land Policy

Amongst the most important results of the new economic, social, and political forces of the period were those in land policy, especially in the development of the themes outlined in the previous chapter. There was almost continuous discussion about ways and means not only of enabling the peasant to acquire Crown land, but of preventing both the loss of the holding if he became indebted and its fragmentation when he died. All this was very important for the eventual pattern of colonization.

The food-production motive led to some mitigation for the peasant of the rigours of the application system, and also to discussion of reformed tenures. In 1916 outright sale of Crown land was temporarily suspended.[4] In 1917 a Committee considered an alternative system of leases, and suggested that leases should specify crops to be grown and should forbid inheritance of land in undivided shares (they did not, however, specifically object to subdivision).[5] In 1920 there came a Food Production Minute which allowed Revenue Officers to allot small plots of Crown land to selected applicants on easy leasehold terms; a Crown grant could be obtained after three years on payment of the unimproved value of the land, provided that most of it had been brought under cultivation.[6]

The food-production motive was also a dominant one in the tenurial experiments at the Nachchaduwa Colony.[7] It was the original intention that colonists should receive, after ten satisfactory years' cultivation and after repayment of advances made to them, free grants of up to 5 acres of paddy and 5 acres of high

---

[1] e.g. *Admin. Report: North-Central Province*, 1921, p. 7.

[2] Ibid., 1924, p. 3.

[3] See below, pp. 269–70.   [4] *CUCL*, p. 8.

[5] *Report of the Committee appointed to consider the Terms and Conditions on which Crown Land should in future be leased for Agricultural Purposes*, S.P. 2 of 1917.

[6] For an example of the working of the system see *Report of the Karachchi Scheme Committee*, p. 3 and App. B.

[7] See below, p. 131; the colony is sometimes called Ratmale.

land. But by 1929 the original principle of independent peasant proprietorship had been lost sight of, and much land had passed into the hands of the colonists' creditors.

Outright sale of Crown land had, as the pressing, short-term need for food diminished, been resumed. High postwar prices for paddy put in the hands of the cultivator money which he tended to invest in land, and in 1922 the Government Agent at Anuradhapura was able to report heavy land sales.[1] This temporary phenomenon concealed for a time the fundamental difficulty of the land-sale system; but by 1925 sales in the North-Central Province were less, because the peasants were less prosperous.[2]

Meanwhile, important work on land tenure was being done by C. V. Brayne, Government Agent at Batticaloa.[3] This work began under the Food Production Minute, but another important motive was undoubtedly concern for the peasantry conceived as a class of independent proprietors. C. V. Brayne was a brother of F. L. Brayne, who did such good work in Indian villages and, in particular, in Gurgaon;[4] the two brothers must have learnt much from each other, and from the Punjab Canal Colonies. It must be remembered, too, that this was the time of widespread interest in the agrarian reforms in the new republics of Europe, with their support of the independent peasant proprietor. In the years 1920–5 C. V. Brayne evolved a system of tenure, which finally became the 'Peasant-Proprietor System', designed not only to stimulate food production by making land available, but also, so far as the law then permitted, to keep land in the hands of the peasantry. In the scheme as finally formulated are to be seen the seeds of the Land Development Ordinance and of current practice in the colonization schemes.[5] Land was allotted only to carefully selected applicants, who gained immediate possession without the expenses of preliminary survey. They were given a lease which conferred on them most of the advantages of ownership, but gave the Crown the power to remove unsatisfactory cultivators. The land could not be alienated without permission, or sold for debt. The system

---

[1] See *Admin. Report: North-Central Province*, 1922, pp. 3–4.
[2] Ibid., 1925, p. 3.
[3] See *Admin. Reports: Eastern Province*, 1920–5.
[4] See, for example, F. L. Brayne, *The Remaking of Village India*, 2nd ed. (London, OUP, 1929); *Report on Rural Reconstruction in Ceylon*, by G. de Soyza, S.P. 23 of 1944, pp. 58–62.
[5] See *Admin. Report: Eastern Province*, 1925, p. 8.

went far towards overcoming such obstacles to land development, and hence to colonization, as lack of capital; but the provision later included in the Land Development Ordinance, that land should pass to one heir only, could not be tackled without a change in the law and, it should be noted, a flouting of traditional custom.[1] Brayne was perhaps inclined to be too idealistic and too optimistic, as indeed was his brother in the Punjab;[2] and, for all his undoubtedly good motives, his scheme was an imposed one, based on individual proprietorship and other Western notions alien to traditional tenurial systems.

Brayne's system was extended to other areas, e.g. to the Malay Colony;[3] and by 1926, although land sales continued, they were mainly otherwise than by public auction. 'The Revenue Officers were instructed to sell land outright, at fixed prices, to people who deserved to possess land.'[4] But there were abuses, 'land grabbers' putting up a peasant as the ostensible purchaser and, the land having been bought preferentially, taking it over from him.[5] There was also dissatisfaction with the length of time allowed for payment under Sir Henry Ward's Minute.[6] There was, in fact, plenty of scope for further inquiry and experiment. Thus in 1925 a Committee was set up to advise, *inter alia*, 'what measures could suitably be taken to settle upon Crown land those who were without sufficient land for the support of themselves and their families'.[7] (The Committee did not report until 1931, and was overshadowed by the Land Commission which had already reported in 1929.)

By 1927 all this discussion and experiment had enabled those principles of land tenure which were later to be the basis of peasant colonization to be clearly formulated. Thus Sir Hugh Clifford, in the farewell message already quoted, described the aims of what was to become the Pasdun Korale East Scheme[8] in these terms:

(i) To make easily available to bona fide would-be peasant proprietors land of good quality in sufficient quantity to suffice for the permanent

---

[1] See *LC*, p. 18.
[2] See Darling, *Rusticus Loquitur* (London, OUP, 1930), pp. 120–8.
[3] See below, pp. 134–5.
[4] Mr. J. L. (later Sir John) Kotelawala's speech in the debate on the Land Development Ordinance, *DSC*, 1933, p. 2350.   [5] Ibid.
[6] *Report of the Karachchi Scheme Committee*, p. 11.
[7] *Report of the Landless Villagers Committee*, S.P. 6 of 1931, p. 3.
[8] See below, pp. 135–7.

maintenance of the cultivator himself and of those immediately dependent upon him.

(ii) To render the taking up of such small-holdings not only feasible, but easy, for bona fide tillers of the soil, who desire to become landowners, and who are prepared to contribute toward the development of these small-holdings the labour of themselves and of their immediate dependants.

(iii) To enable these small-holdings to be taken up and brought under cultivation by bona fide cultivators, who are not possessed of any capital, without any undue burden of debt being by them incurred.

(iv) To render it impossible for small-holdings alienated to bona fide cultivators under this Scheme, to be sold or transferred by them to third parties.

(v) To prevent these small-holdings from passing, on the death of the original owners, to a number of heirs in undivided shares.[1]

Sir Hugh also emphasized that it must be made illegal for owners of 'small-holdings' (in his sense) to raise money on their holdings without stringent control.[2]

To Sir Hugh Clifford's list of aims for a new peasant tenure the Land Commission added the need to prevent peasants from leasing their land, and 'to deal with land abandoned or allowed to fall out of cultivation'.[3] The Land Commission was actually appointed just after Sir Hugh left the island, but he had much to do with setting in motion the machinery which should undertake a thorough overhaul of land policy and ensure that what had been 'done sporadically should be done systematically and crystallized into a definite policy'.[4]

The Land Commission reviewed exhaustively every aspect of land policy, together with many administrative matters referred to them by the Government. Some of their conclusions have already been noted; others (e.g. those concerning land settlement and the Kandyan *chenas*) are of considerable interest but not immediately relevant to the theme of peasant colonization;[5] and all that will be attempted here is a summary of the Commission's recommendations concerning tenure in Crown land alienated to peasants.[6]

It will be remembered that it was the Land Commission's view that the preservation of the peasantry ought to be the primary aim

---

[1] Quoted in Brohier, *Land, Maps and Surveys*, i, App. J, p. 121.
[2] Ibid., p. 126.   [3] *LC*, p. 17.   [4] Ibid., p. 13.
[5] See, for example, ibid., pp. 24–32.
[6] Recommendations on colonization itself are considered below, pp. 137–8.

of land policy, and that they recommended a system of 'mapping out' of settled Crown land,[1] that is, allocating it between peasants and other potential users. They further considered that, in contrast to the state of affairs under the old application system and in harmony with the trend evident in the period of experiment, the initiative in the alienation of Crown land should lie with the Government through a specially appointed officer, a 'Commissioner of Lands'.[2]

They recommended three kinds of peasant tenure of Crown land:[3] outright grant, to be allowed where the peasant did not specially require protection; lease under the Peasant-Proprietor System, in the Eastern Province and other suitable places; and a new system of tenure specially designed to 'protect' the peasant in areas where, as the Commission put it, 'he displays the utmost improvidence in parting with land'. This new 'peasant tenure' would be created by Ordinance, since a change in the law was necessary if fragmentation was to be restricted, and was really a development of a normal annual lease, but so arranged as to give security of tenure subject to certain conditions; these were to be that the land was put to good use, that it was not alienated, mortgaged, or disposed of without permission, that it could not be sold on any decree of the Court, and that it passed, on the peasant's death to a nominated successor or to an heir indicated by law. It was also suggested that rent need not be demanded once the holder had paid a certain sum.

In the event, six years elapsed before the Commission's ideas on a new form of tenure finally became law in modified form as the Land Development Ordinance of 1935. The delay was largely due to the preoccupation of Government and of legislators with the constitutional problems which surrounded the inauguration of the Donoughmore Constitution;[4] and there was dissatisfaction with the Government's apparent failure to act on most of the Land Commission's recommendations.[5] The Government did, however, act promptly in certain matters, for example the recognition of the preservation of the peasantry as a paramount aim of their policy and the acceptance in principle of 'mapping out' and of a

---

[1] 'Settled' in the legal sense of Crown title having been established.
[2] See *LC*, pp. 10–11.
[3] Ibid., pp. 17–19.   [4] See Cmd. 3131.
[5] See, for example, Senanayake, *Agriculture and Patriotism*, p. 13.

restricted form of tenure.[1] But, as the Commission itself recognized, the proposed peasant tenure could, in detail, only evolve from working experience.[2] Something approximating to it was, in fact, tried out in the new Tabbowa Colony in 1929, and in the Pasdun Korale East scheme in 1930; but the precise form of tenure which was to dominate the colonies which the author visited in 1951 was only finally determined with the promulgation of the Land Development Ordinance in 1935.[3]

By 1931, then, Ceylon was moving towards a system of tenure which would, it was hoped, at once encourage colonists and protect them and their holdings. Various systems were in force in various areas.[4] But all of the new systems of holding Crown land were based ultimately on the idea that an independent, individualist peasant proprietor, owning a compact block of land, was the ideal —an ideal far removed from the economic co-operation and web of reciprocal obligations involved in traditional tenure, and typified by the *bethma* system; and in consequence all of the new systems, imposed by the law of the colonial power, were apt, especially in the tradition-bound regions of the Dry Zone, to be in conflict with custom. It will later be seen that the conflict of law and custom was to be a potent source of difficulty to the authorities in managing the tenure of Crown land in colonization schemes.[5]

Experiment and Accomplishment in Colonization

In the final section of this chapter it is proposed to see how far the tentative and transitional land policies, aided by other measures which were from time to time devised by the Government, led to peasant colonization in the Dry Zone. It must be stressed at the outset that the changes in land policy which have just been discussed were not necessarily designed as an inducement to Dry Zone settlement. Indeed, Sir Hugh Clifford, who played such a large part in bringing those changes about, thought that 'Any attempt to colonize the dry-zone with immigrants from the wet-zone is . . . foredoomed to failure, at any rate until such time as acute economic pressure . . . has assumed the potency of an

---

[1] See *Decisions of Government on the Recommendations made in the Final Report of the Land Commission*, S.P. 35 of 1929. [2] *LC*, p. 18.

[3] Information on Tabbowa collected in the field; on Pasdun Korale East, see *First Report of Pasdun Korale East Colonization Scheme*, pp. 4–5.

[4] See *ARLC*, July–Dec. 1931, p. 4.

[5] See below, pp. 289–94.

irresistible force.'[1] Sir Hugh went on to show how firm was the grip of malaria on the Dry Zone, and he might have stressed too the poverty of communications in a great part of the region. The Dry Zone was still a region of great difficulty, and pessimism about it was certainly engendered by the fate of efforts to colonize it during the period.

A number of these unsuccessful efforts were made on a large scale in the early 1920's by companies and individual capitalists under the stimulus of the food-production drive and of high rice prices. Thus at Kala Wewa the Ceylon Mills Company took up 5,000 acres of land in 1920, but by 1922 had failed and was forced to surrender its lease.[2] On the Kirindi Oya, the Low-Country Products Association took up land in 1921, but failed to develop large-scale working and by 1922 was leasing on *ande* such of its lands as had been cleared.[3] At Minneriya a most ambitious scheme was launched in 1919 by the Minneriya Development Company, which planned to clear 9,000 acres, using the land mainly in mechanically cultivated 250-acre paddy blocks but also providing high-land allotments for the colonists whom it was planned to employ on a crop-sharing basis.[4] The Government encouraged the project by giving the Company a ten-year rent-free concession, and by undertaking to construct channels and build roads. The Company had no difficulty in raising capital, mainly from European planting interests, but ran into disaster in its first wet season. Malaria struck down many labourers and frightened others away, the rains made the newly constructed roads impassable, and work was almost at a standstill when, rice prices having fallen, the Company went into liquidation. The recommendation of the Food Production Committee that the Government itself should open up at least 1,000 acres at Minneriya with Indian or prison labour having also come to nothing, the lands remained unoccupied for some years.[5] F. R. Senanayake, brother of the future Prime Minister, then proposed to open up land, using discharged prisoners; his scheme came to nought at his death, but had important indirect repercussions which will be noted in due course.[6]

The indirect effects of all the large-scale ventures were, in fact,

---

[1] Clifford, in *Trop. Agriculturist*, vol. lxviii, p. 304.
[2] *Admin. Report: Agriculture*, 1922, p. 5.   [3] Ibid.
[4] Brohier, *Tamankaduwa District*, pp. 26–29.   [5] Ibid.
[6] From an interview with the late D. S. Senanayake.

more important than the direct ones. All of the efforts failed in
their immediate aim of opening up large tracts for paddy; but they
did increase knowledge of the country and of the problem, and
they did, above all, reinforce the social motive for encouraging
peasant colonization with an economic one, fostering the opinion
that 'if paddy cultivation on new areas is to be increased in Ceylon,
it must be through the small cultivator', either through direct sale
or lease to him, or by using him as a tenant (as at Kirindi Oya)
under a capitalist or a development syndicate.[1]

The social motive in colonization produced, in this same war-
time and postwar period, a few notable efforts at colonization by
voluntary bodies. The Salvation Army started a colony for Indians
at Unnichchai, and tried to settle them under Brayne's Peasant-
Proprietor System.[2] Cultivation was carried on for a while, but
there were many deaths from disease and wild animals, and the
colony closed down. And a Sinhalese organization, the *Lanka
Mahajana Sabha*, evolved a scheme for a colony at Minneriya in
1922, but nothing came of it.[3] These voluntary efforts achieved
little at the time, but they do prompt the thought that, with the
main obstacles to Dry Zone development now removed, such
efforts might well succeed today and relieve the Government of
expense and effort.

It was also voluntary effort, in this case on the part of the Ceylon
Agricultural Society, which was mainly responsible for persuading
the Government to start the colony at Nachchaduwa which can
claim to be the first of the line of modern, state-aided peasant-
colonization schemes.[4] The idea of a colony at Nachchaduwa was
first mooted in 1917, in the report, inspired by the food crisis, of
the Land Development Committee of the Ceylon Agricultural
Society, whose chairman was F. A. Stockdale.[5] In 1918 the
Government accepted the Committee's recommendations, funds
were voted, and a special Committee formed. From the outset, there
was some confusion of aims, for there were those who declared
that the object was the settlement of immigrants from other districts, and not merely food production.[6] But by 1919, before

[1] *Admin. Report: Agriculture*, 1922, p. 5.   [2] See *DSC*, 1939, p. 667.
[3] Brohier, *Tamankaduwa District*, p. 28.
[4] Information mainly from personal inquiries.
[5] See 'Report of the Land Development Committee of the Ceylon Agricultural
Society', suppl. to *Trop. Agriculturist*, vol. xlix (1917), and Discussion, ibid.,
vol. l (1918), pp. 3–10.   [6] See above, pp. 117–18.

anything had been accomplished, the whole scheme was in abeyance because of epidemics of influenza and malaria, and it was suggested by the then Government Agent that, with food production now less urgent, the project should be dropped; he also quoted the opinion of R. W. Ievers, who had been Government Agent at the time of the Kala Wewa experiment of 1893,[1] that 'colonization by independent cultivators is infinitely preferable to state-aided colonization'.

In 1920 the food situation was once again serious, and the Nachchaduwa scheme was resuscitated on the recommendation of the Food Production Committee.[2] The Committee also suggested that the terms offered at Nachchaduwa should also be granted wherever not less than twenty-five families were prepared to settle, but little seems to have come of this proposal; there were, however, three small, short-lived colonies in Batticaloa District.[3] The terms offered at Nachchaduwa were essentially those originally suggested by the Agricultural Society.[4] Each peasant colonist received 5 acres of paddy (as in more recent colonies) and 'some' high land. Outright assistance included a temporary house, and meals until the colonist was self-supporting; the Government also supplied roads, free irrigation for five years, a medical service, and a school. The colonist was, in addition, advanced a sum of money together with seed paddy and buffaloes. Later, free coconut and Jak plants, and free tools were added to the list.[5] The colonist, however, had to clear the jungle and prepare his land himself. The Government paid a Colonization Officer (J. W. Robertson) who was responsible for deciding the rate of development and for general supervision. Such Officers were, of course, familiar figures in the Punjab Canal Colonies and elsewhere, but this was the first appearance of one in Ceylon.[6] Robertson was joined in 1922 by a voluntary assistant, that remarkable man H. R. Freeman, a former Government Agent, Anuradhapura, who was always keenly interested in the peasant and his problems, and who was eventually the elected representative on the Legislative Council of the peasantry whose Revenue Officer he had been.

For all this programme of aid, the colony soon ran into serious difficulties. It was not easy to attract colonists to the Dry Zone

[1] See above, p. 113. [2] See *Food Supply Committee*, p. 4.
[3] *DSC*, 1932, p. 334. [4] For tenure, see above, pp. 123–4.
[5] Cf. the scale of aid today, pp. 167–8.
[6] *Punjab Colony Manual*, i. 26–27.

with the evil reputation it then had, and not all of those who were attracted were desirable characters. The Government Agent anticipated modern practice[1] by asking his colleagues in the Colombo, Kandy, and Galle Kachcheries to select 10 colonists each from overcrowded villages, with a preference for landless peasants who were industrious, skilled, and of good character; and he wisely requested batches of 5–10 from the same village.[2] But the results were disappointing; of the first 19 colonists, only 10 came from outside, and some of these soon left. The Colonization Officer reported that the Colombo colonists were poor specimens physically, with little knowledge of cultivation, and that they were refusing to work communally.

Health was a persistent problem. Out of the first batch of 19 families (comprising 91 souls), 2 adults and 15 children had died by the end of the year in which they came; in the first *Maha*, all 5 children of one couple died. It is not surprising that colonists left, and that it was difficult to find replacements.

The finances of the colonists soon fell into a parlous state. With the spread of indebtedness, some holdings passed into the hands of money-lenders and, a sore point with a revenue-conscious government, many of the loans which had been made to the colonists became irrecoverable. The economy of the colony was not helped by the lack of feeder roads.[3]

In 1924 Nachchaduwa was closed down as a colonization scheme and fell under normal administrative machinery like any other village until the modern colony was started in the 1930's. But some of the problems remained. In 1925 the first colonist cleared his debt and won his grant of land; but attempts to recover the debts of others went on down the years, as did the transfer of land to outsiders and also the illegal letting of holdings on *ande*. Attempts to clear up the muddle were still going on in 1931, by which time it was estimated that only half of the holdings were being cultivated by allottees or by their legal successors.

The story of Nachchaduwa has been described in some detail because it brings home very clearly the great difficulties, physical and human, of Dry Zone colonization during the period under review. The troubles of Nachchaduwa in fact cast a cloud over the idea of state-sponsored colonization for some time. Thus in

---

[1] See below, pp. 206–7.   [2] Cf. pp. 298–9 below.
[3] *Admin. Report: North-Central Province*, 1924, p. 3.

discussions of the measures which should be taken to stimulate development of land in the Karachchi scheme (under Iranamadu Tank) H. R. Freeman wrote:

> As a result of two and a half years of residence and work on the Nach-chaduwa Colonization Scheme I am opposed to another State-aided scheme on similar lines. . . . Experience at Nachchaduwa is that coloniza-tion cannot be started artificially. . . . The proposers of this particular scheme [to start a colony in the Karachchi Scheme] look to a grant from Government, but this cannot be expected unless Government has con-trol, and no successful agriculture can be carried on by subsidized colonists subject to Government audit and what is known as red tape.[1]

Freeman's views were typical of those held by many responsible and knowledgeable people. Moreover, the new systems of tenure, especially the Peasant-Proprietor System, were somewhat improv-ing the rate of settlement on Dry Zone Crown land, in spite of the hazards of disease, drought, and wild animals. Thus the Karachchi Scheme Committee concluded that 'in view of the number of applications for land recently received by the Government Agent, there is at present no necessity for a Government-aided scheme of colonization'.[2] The short-term food crisis was over, and, in spite of the mounting pressure in the Wet Zone and of the need to give the island a better balanced economy, there was little tendency in the middle 1920's to accelerate the rate of Dry Zone settlement. It was enough if land under existing irrigation schemes was taken up. Moreover, it was generally considered that a better type of peasant would migrate if colonization was left to the individual; and that a reformed system of tenure would be enough to ensure a healthy economy in a newly settled area.

So it was that the Nachchaduwa experiment was not repeated for a number of years. And although two Dry Zone colonies *were* started before 1931, both had somewhat special motives behind them. However, both survive as colonization schemes today, and bridge the gap between the periods before and after 1931.

The first of these schemes to attract settlers was that at Tabbowa, near Puttalam.[3] Here the special circumstance was that Tabbowa Wewa had been restored in 1926 with the dual aim of supplying

[1] *Report of the Karachchi Scheme Committee*, p. 10.   [2] Ibid., p. 6.
[3] Information on Tabbowa mainly from personal inquiries; see also *Village Survey: Puttalam*, pp. 32–49, which, however, brings the story on to a more recent date.

Puttalam town with water, and of irrigating 5,000 acres of coconuts (Puttalam is at the extreme northern end of the extension into the Dry Zone of the 'Coconut Belt'): paddy cultivation was originally to be expressly excluded. It was recognized that the lease of a small block for coconut cultivation with the inevitable five or six years before the trees came into bearing, would do little, however favourable the tenure, to attract landless men with no capital unless support was given until an income was assured. But the Government, with Nachchaduwa fresh in its mind, was loth to start another aided colony. After much discussion, attempts were made to attract local Sinhalese villagers, but with little success, partly because the villagers disliked the idea of succession by one heir only in the tenure which was proposed in anticipation of the Land Development Ordinance. And persons with capital were slow to apply for land, for coconut prices were by this time ceasing to be attractive. Ultimately, a start was made in colonization in 1926, the Government having been virtually forced, by their determination to stick to coconut, into granting aid. This aid, at the start, took the form mainly of loans, which it was hoped to recover, though seeds and planting materials were free; the Government also provided roads, a school, and medical facilities. Colonists cleared the jungle themselves, and built their own houses. Inevitably (as one sees it with hindsight wisdom) the colonists ran into debt, especially when astute Muslim traders from Puttalam cornered the trade in plantains and other *chena* produce by which the colonists sought to live until their coconuts began to yield; matters were helped when the colonists were encouraged to run their own market stall in Puttalam, but there were the familiar difficulties over the recovery of advances. There was, however, less disease than at Nachchaduwa. By 1930 there were forty-eight allottees, of whom twenty-nine were still aided, and the scheme survived to come under the Land Development Ordinance and the modern colonization procedure;[1] but, the 1930's depression in the import industries having hit Ceylon, the colonists were agitating to be allowed to grow paddy. They were permitted to do so in 1932.

The Malay Colony at Beragama, in the Walawe Ganga Left Bank Scheme, also began for a special reason.[2] The Malay community at Hambantota had never been agriculturally minded, and

---

[1] See below, pp. 165–6.
[2] Information on the Malay Colony mainly from personal inquiries.

had lived by practising such trades as fishing, salt-making in the lagoons of the area, or carting. By 1927 these trades had declined, and the Malays petitioned the Governor for lands so that they could set up afresh. Because of what they claimed to be their 'extra poverty', they wanted the Government, in addition to granting the advantageous Peasant-Proprietor terms, to clear their lands and pay them a maintenance allowance. In the event, and after much discussion, they were merely given lands at a nominal rent for the first three years, and advances for initial expenditure and maintenance. The first colonists were settled in 1930, each on 1 acre of high land and 3–4 acres of paddy land. There were the familiar troubles over the repayment of advances, though these fell mainly in the period covered by the next chapter.

While these events were taking place in the Dry Zone, 'Sir Hugh Clifford's Scheme' was being put into practice in Pasdun Korale East, in the Wet Zone.[1] The problems of this colony are set in such a different physical and human context that they have little relevance to the study of Dry Zone colonization, except for two aspects. In the first place, the choice of the Wet Zone, albeit a difficult, hilly, and inaccessible part of the Wet Zone, by Sir Hugh was in itself an effect of the revulsion which he felt for the Dry Zone after his experience of the malaria and muddle of Nachchaduwa. In the second place, Sir Hugh proposed a system of colonization which, modified by practical experience, attracted the attention of the Land Commission and, through their *Report* and discussions of it, powerfully affected Dry Zone colonization for good or ill in the suceeeding period. Sir Hugh, having said that he would put the area to be colonized under a Colonization Board, went on to enunciate his ideas on the 'economic holdings' into which the colony should be divided. The guiding principles should be, he said:

(*a*) That the area of each small holding should be sufficient permanently to provide an adequate livelihood for one family of average size; it being anticipated that, as they come to maturity, all the sons of the house, save he alone who is registered as the land-owner's heir, will leave the family holding and will each take up a new holding under the Scheme, on his own account.

[1] See 'Message from His Excellency the Governor', in Brohier, *Land, Maps and Surveys*, vol. i, App. J; and *First Report of Pasdun Korale East Colonization Scheme*.

(*b*) That the area should not be larger than a family of average size and energy shall be able, without the assistance of labour from outside, effectively and continuously to cultivate.[1]

Here is not only a potential conflict of law and custom but also, perhaps, the source of the confusion about the nature of an 'economic holding' which has tended to afflict Ceylon's colonization schemes; a holding which can be cultivated by a family may be bigger or smaller than one which can provide an 'adequate livelihood' (whatever that may be). The point will, however, be taken up at more length later in this book. One may also note Sir Hugh's optimism, not echoed by those familiar with demographic trends in modern Ceylon, that the younger sons will always find a place 'under the Scheme'.[2]

Sir Hugh broke new ground by recommending a liberal scale of government aid to the Colonization Board. 'The task entrusted to it,' he said, 'is not the mere execution of some important public work . . . but instead is the building up, upon a solid basis, of the economical prosperity of Ceylon and that of some of the most deserving classes among its population.'[3] And he stressed that the Board should view its finances quite differently from the Revenue Officer anxious to see 'that not one cent of money . . . due to Government . . . should escape collection'.[4] This vision of emancipation from the somewhat narrow traditional financial concepts of the colonial government, interested in revenue rather than in long-term capital investment, only became reality and only affected the Dry Zone in the next period. Sir Hugh, however, anxious to avoid a charge of 'pauperism', still thought in terms of loans to colonists and not outright grants; liberal expenditure was to be mainly a matter of the (very wise) provision of roads, bridges, and other capital equipment.

Finally, Sir Hugh advocated the appointment of a carefully selected Colonization Officer, preferably one experienced in the running of peasant co-operative credit societies, who should have an adequate staff of assistants.

Later chapters will show how many of these ideas, including the

---

[1] 'Message from His Excellency the Governor', in Brohier, *Land, Maps and Surveys*, i. 123.

[2] For Sir Hugh's ideas on tenure, see also pp. 125–6.

[3] 'Message from His Excellency the Governor', ibid.

[4] Ibid., p. 125.

apparently confused ones, were eventually taken up in the Dry Zone colonies. Meanwhile, it must be noted that something very like Sir Hugh's scheme was put into effect in Pasdun Korale East in 1930.[1] A Board was formed in 1929 under the chairmanship of C. V. Brayne, and soon echoed Sir Hugh's general ideas about tenure, the urgency of communications, and the appointment of a good Colonization Officer. They considered, however, that no direct financial aid, even by means of loans, was necessary as the Korale was so near a crowded area whose people were only too ready to take land under the scheme. And they added two additional points, not mentioned by Sir Hugh, which have deserved more attention in some of the Dry Zone colonies; first, that in any conflict of interest in land between local villagers and immigrants, the former should have preference; second, that, for social reasons, care should be taken to build up village nuclei in the colonies and to choose colonists who, by reason of family or village ties, are likely to live happily together.[2]

The Land Commission paid great attention to the views of Sir Hugh Clifford, and also had before them not only data about existing colonies (e.g. Nachchaduwa) but also a whole mass of evidence about the rural economy of the whole island. That they envisaged colonization, in the sense of the government-assisted migration of people from congested to less congested areas, will be evident already from the fact that it was one of the uses for which Crown land should, in their view, be 'mapped out'.[3] And their recommendations on colonization form an excellent summary of ideas current at the time when their *Final Report* appeared in 1929 or, for that matter, current in 1931. These recommendations are best quoted in the Commission's own words:[4]

(1) The congestion of the population in certain localities calls for special measures on the part of Government to assist migration to localities in which peasants, and others of moderate means, can be settled and given the opportunity of forming prosperous colonies upon new lands.

(2) Such special measures are of two kinds—

(*a*) Measures to anticipate and provide for the natural flow of migration by mapping-out and reserving suitable lands for smallholders and persons of moderate means in localities which are developing in proximity to congested areas.

[1] *LC*, pp. 21–22.   [2] Cf. below, pp. 298–9.
[3] See above, p. 210.   [4] *LC*, pp. 21–22.

(*b*) Measures to stimulate the formation and development of colonies in definite selected places.

(3) The smaller colonists should be recruited more from the small land-owning class than from those who work entirely for hire.

(4) Certain qualities are necessary in a colonist and a careful selection must be made from the applicants who come forward.

(5) Grouping is an essential factor to success and must be carefully studied.

(6) Self-help must be encouraged but Government assistance will be required in the construction of various works necessary to open up the country and provide medical, agricultural and other facilities for the colonists.

(7) Some financial assistance will be needed, especially by the smaller colonists, and to provide this we recommend the constitution of a special agency with a special fund of its own so that the progress of colonies may not depend in this matter upon annual votes from the revenue which may prove precarious.

(8) His Excellency Sir Hugh Clifford's scheme referred to us for report is outlined.[1] We recommend it be modified in the following particulars:

(*a*) Men of moderate means should be included as well as small-holders.

(*b*) Colonizing effort should not be concentrated entirely on one spot, but land should be allocated for colonization in suitable places in three Provinces.[2]

(9) The colonies in each district should be under the direction of a board.

(10) The mapping-out of the area selected by Sir Hugh Clifford should be subject to the final approval of these Boards.

(11) Special provision should be made for the agricultural education of the colonists. A preliminary agricultural survey should also be made.

(12) Such safeguards should be adopted as will prevent land taken up by colonists passing to a money-lender or large capitalist.

The Government was prompt to accept that the promotion of colonization, defined as the 'relief of congestion in certain localities by the settlement of peasants on vacant lands outside their own villages', was one of the primary aims of land policy; and went on to lay it down that land should be mapped out for colonization near congested areas, or in regions where immigration was likely in the

---

[1] i.e. in the chapter of the Commission's Final Report of which this is a summary; ibid., p. 21.

[2] i.e. Western, Central, and Southern Provinces, ibid.

not too distant future (the context makes it clear that these were held to be Wet Zone regions).[1] But, they went on, the needs of resident villagers must have first call on such land. They approached the problem of financial assistance with great caution, with Nachchaduwa fresh in their minds, considering that the 'natural process of migration' could be promoted by providing facilities for enterprising settlers to obtain Crown land, and by providing communications. They did not, however, rule out the possibility of financial aid in all circumstances.

Conclusion

Clearly, then, the period 1914–31 was, for the progress of Dry Zone settlement, one of experiment and discussion rather than of actual accomplishment. The Dry Zone in 1931 was still under a cloud; malaria and remoteness combined to give it an evil reputation and to discourage voluntary immigration. And, except for the special cases of Tabbowa and the Malay Colony, and for the suspended animation of Nachchaduwa, there were no colonies in being in the Dry Zone at the end of the period. The *idea* of government-sponsored colonization had been accepted, but for settlement in the Wet Zone only. There was but little dissatisfaction with the slow rate of voluntary settlement in the Dry Zone, at least until the very end of the period; work on the restoration of irrigation works, the essential preliminary to colonization, was in any case very slow.

The scale of aid to colonists was carefully discussed, but in terms which were not very generous compared with those which ultimately became the rule; in particular, there was no effort to clear holdings in advance of settlement. And there was a fear of excessive aid, because of its supposed pauperizing effect and also because of experience with the local bureaucracy. There was also a general reliance on imposed reform of land tenure as an adequate safeguard against the ever-present and heavily criticized tendency of colonists to become indebted and to alienate or mortgage their holdings. Little was said about the simple credit facilities, the Co-operative marketing, and the rural education which were later to characterize peasant colonization in Ceylon; the Landless Villagers Committee did, however, comment on what they took to be

---

[1] See *Decisions of Government on the Final Report of the Land Commission*, p. 4.

the need for Co-operative credit and for reformed rural schools;[1] and towards the end of the period a start was made with the Co-operative movement generally, though Co-operation was not applied to colonization until later.

The main positive achievements of the period 1914–31 were the enunciation of the principle that peasant needs for land should have priority (based on the idea of peasant proprietorship), and the reform of the tenure of Crown land. Even though the latter only became fully effective in 1935, the principle that the Government should take the initiative in the alienation of Crown land had become established. These things were vital prerequisites to the policy of peasant colonization later enunciated. But a broader attack on the problem of Dry Zone colonization, and a more flexible administration, was to come only after 1931 as a result of the impact of realigned forces and new events.

[1] *Report of the Landless Villagers Committee,* pp. 3–4.

7

Achievement in Colonization, 1931–53

ALMOST immediately after the inauguration of the 'Donough-more' Constitution in July 1931 there came a series of rapid developments which culminated in a fixed policy of acceler-ating aided peasant colonization in the hitherto generally despised Dry Zone of Ceylon. A broader attack on the whole problem was mounted, a much more generous scale of aid was approved, a new administrative machine was created, and a whole series of new colonization schemes came into being. It is proposed in the present chapter to discuss briefly the motives which led to those develop-ments, then to outline the developments themselves, and finally to review the steps which were taken to provide what the reader will by now recognize as the prerequisites of colonization as it is today: for example, irrigation, communications, and reformed tenure. To discuss actual colonization before discussing its bases is a deliberate reversal of the order followed in preceding chapters; for the first time the actual colonization of the Dry Zone became a prime consideration, and not merely an expedient for disposing of unsaleable land, or for tiding over a short-term food shortage, or for dealing with some purely local social or agronomic problem.[1]

It was not, however, that the factors at work in the previous period had lost their force; most of them continued vigorously to influence policy. Thus the short-term need for food supplies often lurked in the background of discussion, and came very much to the fore in the war of 1939–45;[2] a number of 'State Farms' then cleared from the jungle and worked by the Government eventually became peasant colonies. Sometimes the Government was accused of the old confusion of aims between food production and colo-nization.[3] But, by and large, there was a general tendency to take

---

[1] Cf. the reasons for the establishment of the Dry Zone colonies mentioned in the previous chapter.

[2] See, for example, 'Food Production', *Trop. Agriculturist*, vol. xcix (1943), pp. 231–56 and vol. c (1944), pp. 20–33; and Min. of Agric. & Lands, *How Lanka fed herself during the War, 1939–1945* (Colombo, 1947).

[3] e.g. remarks of Dr. N. M. Perera, *DSC*, 1939, p. 680.

a wider view of the economic and social problems of Ceylon, and to recognize that there was a close relationship between such problems as the narrowly based external economy, the growth of population, the need for increased home-grown food supplies, landlessness, poverty, indebtedness and under-employment among the peasantry, and urban unemployment. Sometimes one, sometimes another facet of this group of closely related problems caught the light, but from 1931 onwards there was growing appreciation in responsible circles of the need for an attack on a broad front. The development of alternative export crops, increases in yields per acre of food crops, and industrialization were clearly possible lines of attack; and another, very important one was Dry Zone development in general and peasant colonization in particular.[1]

The need to relieve agrarian pressure by all available means was brought home with great force by the depression in the export industries in the early 1930's which, affecting as it did almost all the homes in the island except those based on the most primitive subsistence economy, resulted in general distress in the peasant sector of Ceylon's economy. The situation was well summed up by the Committee of Agriculture and Lands when, in 1932, they stated that the slump, on top of rapid population increase, had thrown the people back on their own resources at a time when they had become too numerous for the land at their disposal.[2]

The depression receded, but the lesson of the inherent instability of the island's economy had been learnt, and there was no relaxation of effort as there had been after the crisis of the 1920's. The war of 1939–45, and the fluctuating prices for export commodities in the unstable postwar world, helped to ensure that the essential problem was kept in view. (The boom, especially in rubber, in the immediate postwar years did, however, lead to over-optimism about the possibilities for government spending, an over-optimism which has latterly received a shock.) A series of inquiries also helped to keep peasant needs in particular in clear focus. Thus the Ceylon Banking Commission reported in 1934, and produced much fresh evidence not only about the national economy as a

[1] See, for example, *DSC*, 1931, pp. 656–8; 1932, p. 334; 1939, p. 595; see also Senanayake, *Agriculture and Patriotism*, espec. pp. 5–9 and 19–20; and Ceylon, *Post-War Development Proposals* (Colombo, Govt. Record Office, 1946).
[2] *DSC*, 1932, p. 334.

whole but also about rural indebtedness.[1] (They also discussed the special need for credit facilities in the colonization schemes by then in process of establishment.)[2] And by 1937 the important series of Rural Economic Surveys was coming in.

That these economic and social forces were brought to bear so effectively on colonization policy was largely a result of constitutional changes.[3] The Donoughmore Constitution for the first time introduced universal adult suffrage, so that members of the new State Council became very sensitive (sometimes over-sensitive) to peasant demands for land and, as colonization schemes became more popular, for land in the Dry Zone. Perhaps more important was the fact that there were now Ceylonese Ministers, each the elected Chairman of one of the Executive Committees into which the State Council divided itself, and each responsible for the government departments which fell within the purview of his Committee and which now became responsible for carrying out, not initiating policy. This was, it is true, a curious and cumbrous system which sometimes caused delay; and, moreover, finance was not the subject of a Committee or of a Minister responsible to the elected Council, but of a colonial civil servant, the Financial Secretary. The Donoughmore Constitution not surprisingly did not satisfy the demands of nationalist feeling and, following the *Report* of the Soulbury Commission, was succeeded in 1947 by a system of Legislatures and Cabinet akin to the British model.[4] Nevertheless, a very important result of the Donoughmore Constitution was that distinguished Ceylonese who had gained invaluable experience as members of the Land Commission and of other inquiring authorities now became Ministers and could apply their knowledge in an executive capacity. And, being Ceylonese, they were thoroughly steeped in the land-consciousness of their compatriots, so that land questions were not likely to be forgotten.

Don Stephen Senanayake, who had served on the Land

---

[1] See the Ceylon Banking Commission, *Report* and *Memoranda and Evidence*, S.P.s 22 and 23 of 1934.

[2] Ceylon Banking Commission, *Report*, pp. 130–2.

[3] This is not the place for a full discussion of recent constitutional change in Ceylon. See, however, *Report of the Special Commission on the Constitution*, Cmd. 3131 (1928); *Report of the Commission on Constitutional Reform*, Cmd. 6677 (1945); S. Namasivayan, *The Legislatures of Ceylon* (London, Faber for Nuffield Coll., 1951); and Sir Ivor Jennings, *Constitution of Ceylon*, 2nd ed. (Bombay, OUP, 1951).

[4] Cmd. 6677; see also Jennings, *Constitution of Ceylon*.

Commission, became the first Minister of Agriculture and Lands, controlling the Departments of Agriculture, Irrigation, Survey, Forestry, Land Settlement,[1] and also the newly created Land Commissioner's Department. The existence at last of a Land Commissioner was in itself enough to ensure a great measure of co-ordination in land policy, but the effect was enhanced by the grouping of all the 'land' departments under one Minister.[2] Thus Senanayake was able, as early as November 1931, to initiate regular meetings of all his departmental heads with the express purpose of speeding up the completion of irrigation works.[3] With the same object, and against departmental opposition, he moved the Irrigation Department headquarters from Trincomalee to Colombo.[4] It was also simpler under the new order to undertake the measures of administrative reorganization which became imperative as the scope of aided colonization broadened.[5]

But it was not only, in Senanayake's Ministry, a matter of these fairly obvious administrative reforms. Behind them, and lending power to them, lay the ability and the personality of the man himself, a man exceptionally gifted by nature and nurture to carry out the work of formulating and applying a policy of colonization. As a landowner at Mirigama, between Colombo and Kurunegala, he was well aware of the peasant conditions for which relief was necessary and thoroughly conversant with agricultural practice. He had had Dry Zone experience in connexion with his brother's abortive scheme at Minneriya. As a practical farmer he was greatly interested in colonization as a means to land development, to the opening up of ground which it irked him to see lying idle; he was, perhaps, more subject to this motive, and to the appeal of re-creating the glories of Rāja Raṭa, than to the more academic consideration of national social and economic conditions. Once he was convinced of the possibilities of colonization, he became a most vigorous campaigner. His transparent integrity and simplicity of character, and his dogged persistence, won the regard of men in key positions, notably of the Financial Secretary; and this was an important matter in Donoughmore days.

[1] See above, p. 114.
[2] A further unifying agent was provided by the Soulbury Constitution in the shape of a Permanent Secretary in each Ministry. See Collins, *Public Administration*, p. 140.   [3] Brohier, *Tamankaduwa District*, p. 13.
[4] From an interview with the late D. S. Senanayake.
[5] See below, pp. 155–6.

But, for all Senanayake's greatness, it must not be forgotten that much was contributed by his officials, notably by C. V. Brayne, his first Land Commissioner, and by an outstanding civil servant, C. L. Wickremesinghe, who later served in the same capacity. Nor must it be forgotten that Dudley S. Senanayake caught his father's enthusiasm and, becoming Minister of Agriculture and Lands in 1947, presided over his father's old Ministry until he in turn became Prime Minister in 1952. During these years Dudley Senanayake worked with great conscientiousness and energetically drove forward the policy of colonization, often in a more scientific spirit than had been shown by that intuitive thinker and practical man, his father.[1]

But it was not only developments inside the island which affected colonization policy after 1931. The idea of aided colonization received a fillip in 1939 from a visit which C. L. Wickremesinghe paid to the Jewish settlements in Palestine; the details of the aid to be afforded owed something to what he saw there, and also to reports on Italian colonization in Libya.[2]

And a fundamentally important influence from outside came in 1945, with the introduction of DDT spraying as a measure of malaria control. The terrible malaria epidemic of 1934–5 in the Wet Zone, it is true, greatly stimulated local investigation (and also increased distress among the peasantry, reinforcing the social motive for colonization);[3] but real progress only came with the introduction in 1945 of DDT spraying, an imported idea.[4] It had long been realized, of course, that malaria was the foremost enemy of Dry Zone development, and some of the colonization schemes in the early 1930's were criticized as attacks on an impossible problem. The results of the new invention will be discussed later.[5] But it must be stressed here (1) that the scale of aid developed in

---

[1] It may be noted here that the Minister of Lands in the new government which was formed after the election of April 1956 is C. P. de Silva, a former civil servant with experience of land development.

[2] From an interview with the late D. S. Senanayake; see also *DSC*, 1939, p. 596. For the Italian schemes, undertaken for social and political reasons with no regard to cost, see Sir E. J. Russell, 'Agricultural Colonization in the Pontine Marshes and Libya', *Geog. J.*, vol. xciv (1939), pp. 275–92. (See also W. V. D. Pieris, 'Experiments in Land Settlement', *Trop. Agriculturist*, vol. c (1944), pp. 4–8.) For the Jewish schemes, see B. A. Keen, *The Agricultural Development of the Middle East* (London, HMSO, 1946), pp. 24–27.

[3] See the references quoted above, p. 19 footnote.

[4] See above, pp. 21–22. See also *The Health of the Nation* (Colombo, Dept. of Information, 1950), pp. 59–63.   [5] See below, pp. 221–3.

the 1930's was considered necessary to attract settlement to a region in which malaria was as yet unconquered, and (2) that the situation was completely transformed, as has already been said in an earlier chapter, by the application of DDT.

The Progress of Dry Zone Colonization, 1931–9

It will be remembered that at the time of the inauguration of the Donoughmore Constitution in July 1931 there was considerable discussion of the need for government-sponsored colonization schemes, but that there was reluctance to establish colonies in the malarial Dry Zone, and that aid was envisaged in terms of loans on a moderate scale rather than outright grants on a generous scale. There were, it is true, the Dry Zone colonies of Tabbowa and Beragama (the Malay Colony), but these were special cases.[1] But twenty-two years later, in 1953, colonists had been established in the thirty-one Dry Zone colonies, some of them very large, listed in Table 15; and the scale of aid was generous in the extreme. Moreover, by 1953 there had arisen a large organization specifically concerned with the work of colonization. It is the purpose of the paragraphs which follow to outline the stages whereby a policy of generously aided Dry Zone colonization, backed by an efficient organization, came about in the years 1931–53. It will be convenient to consider the events of the period in two phases; from 1931 to 1939, a phase of discussion and initial, somewhat hesitant achievement in which, as Table 15 shows, only four new colonies were established; and from 1939 to 1953, when, following the enunciation of the 'New Policy', the rate of development accelerated out of all recognition.

Very soon after the inauguration of the Donoughmore Constitution, discussion on colonization began. On 27 October 1931 S. W. Dassenaike tabled a motion in the State Council: 'That the Minister for Agriculture do take immediate steps to set up aided land colonization to afford work for the surplus population and increase food production.'[2] Mr. Dassenaike, speaking to his motion, drew attention to the plight of the peasantry, and stated that 'we are faced with a situation under which unemployment arises not from any depression or any crisis but simply owing to the natural increase of the population on the land.'[3] He went on to stress the

[1] See Chapter 6, espec. pp. 133–5.
[2] *DSC*, 1931, pp. 656–8.
[3] Ibid., p. 657.

difficulty of establishing colonies with a peasantry devoid of capital, and implied that he was thinking in terms of Dry Zone colonization.

TABLE 15

Date of Establishment of Dry Zone Colonies

Date	Colonies established	Other events
1928 . .	Tabbowa.	..
1930 . .	Beragama (Malay).	..
1931 July	..	Donoughmore Constitution. Creation of Minister and Executive Committee of Agriculture and Lands; and of Land Commissioner's Department.
1933 . .	Kagama (Old), Minneriya, Nachchaduwa.	..
1935 . .	..	Land Development Ordinance.
1936 . .	Iranamadu (Kilinochchi).	..
1939 . .	..	The 'New Policy'.
1940 . .	Beragama, Minipe.	..
1941 . .	Kopakulama (middle class).	..
1942 . .	Parakrama Samudra.	..
1943 . .	Ridibendi Ela.	..
1944 . .	Kagama (New).	..
1945 . .	Elahera, Sangilikanadarawa.	DDT spraying began.
1946 . .	Unnichchai.	..
1947 Sept.	..	Soulbury Constitution. The 'Six Year Plan'.
1948 Feb.	..	Independence of Ceylon.
1948 . .	..	Creation of Land Development Department.
1948 . .	Kottu Kachchiya, Maha Kumbukkadawala, Maha Uswewa, Uriyawa.	..
1949 . .	Bathmedilla, Dewahuwa, Giritale, Pandiyankadawela.	..
1950 . .	Iranamadu (Paranthan), Okkampitiya.	..
1951 . .	Gal Oya.	..
1952 . .	Allai, Huruluwewa.	..
1953 . .	Attaragalla, Kantalai, Soraborawewa.	End of First 'Six Year Plan'.

Note: For each colony date shown is that of first alienation of land to colonists.
Sources: ARLC, 1931–51; *ARDLD,* 1951; various S.P.s quoted in text; inquiries in the field.

The need for developing the Dry Zone was specifically mentioned by C. V. Brayne in his first report as Land Commissioner, and by the Executive Committee of Agriculture and Lands when they reported on Mr. Dassenaike's motion in January 1932.[1] But, while recognizing the need for colonization in view of prevailing conditions, and while expressing the view that the issue was the most important one then before the State Council, they did not favour a general policy of subsidization on the grounds that experience at Nachchaduwa and elsewhere had shown that it attracted the wrong man or, when it attracted the right man, led to demoralization. They did not, however, rule out money subsidies altogether.[2] They also thought that work on village tanks should be undertaken in preference to colonization schemes.[3]

Later in 1932 there was published an important report which recommended a radical change of policy. This was the report of a Committee appointed to consider the development of the unused land under Minneriya Tank, which was set up on the initiative of D. S. Senanayake, and which included C. V. Brayne and C. L. Wickremesinghe.[4] The Minneriya Committee considered that the time was ripe for Dry Zone development because the depression was making the Wet Zone peasantry more willing to emigrate, and also because road and rail communications had been improved since the abortive experiments of the early 1920's. But malaria was still a great handicap, and it was largely this, rather than consideration for the peasant's lack of capital, which led the Committee to recommend what was in fact a revolutionary step, that the Government should clear the jungle for the colonists. It was considered that anti-malarial measures would have a better chance of success if a wide area were cleared in one continuous block. It was further recommended that the cost of clearing should be considered a gift to the colonists, again not so much in consideration for them but because of the muddle that had developed over the collection of advances in the original Nachchaduwa Colony and also at Tabbowa and in the Malay Colony. The colonist was, however, expected to make an increased annual payment in return for ready-cleared land; and a cash deposit was expected of him.

---

[1] *ARLC*, 1931, and *DSC*, 1932, pp. 334–9. [2] Cf. above, p. 139.
[3] J. S. Kennedy, 'Evolution of Scientific Development of Village Irrigation Works', *Trans. Eng. Assoc. Cey.* (1933), pp. 229–92.
[4] *Minneriya Irrigation Scheme Committee.*

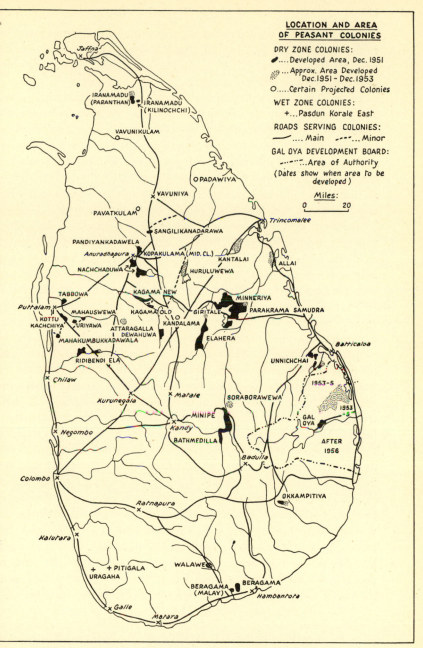

Jaffna
IRANAMADU
(PARANTHAN)   IRANAMADU
                     (KILINOCHCHI)
VAVUNIKULAM
OPADAWIYA
VAVUNIYA
PAVATKULAM
Trincomalee
SANGILIKANADARAWA
PANDIYANKADAWELA
Anuradhapura   KOPAKULAMA (MID. CL.)
                              KANTALAI
NACHCHADUWA   HURULUWEWA   ALLAI
KAGAMA NEW
TABBOWA   MINNERIYA
Puttalam   PARAKRAMA SAMUDRA
                KAGAMA OLD   GIRITALE
MAHAUSWEWA
KOTTU
KACHCHIVA   URIYAWA   KANDALAMA
       ATTARAGALLA
       DEWAHUWA   Batticaloa
MAHAKUMBUKKADAWALA   ELAHERA
                                             UNNICHCHAI
RIDIBENDI ELA
                                                1953-5
Chilaw
                                                       1953
                     Matale   -5
Kurunegala   SORABORAWEWA
                                        GAL
Negombo   MINIPE   OYA
             Kandy   AFTER
       BATHMEDILLA   1956
                            Badulla
Colombo
                                        OKKAMPITIYA
             Ratnapura
Kalutara
                              WALAWE
       + PITIGALA
URAGAHA   BERAGAMA   BERAGAMA
                     (MALAY)   Hambantota
       Galle
             Matara

MAP 6. Ceylon: location and area of peasant colonies (1953).
The map also shows the relation of the colonies to rivers and roads.

The Government was to provide roads and channels, measures for malaria control, and a hospital, but that was to be the limit of aid; colonists were, *inter alia*, to build their own houses. There were also to be middle-class colonists.

In the event, the first colonists moved into Minneriya on 30 April 1933, and the scheme functioned much as recommended by the Committee. The same general pattern was followed at two further colonies opened the same year, Kagama (Old), below Kala Wewa, and Nachchaduwa (taking up unused land around and between the lands of the earlier Nachchaduwa colonists); also at Iranamadu (Kilinochchi), opened in 1936. In most of these cases, colonists themselves worked as paid labourers in the task of jungle clearing. These four colonies were not altogether unsuccessful, but there was serious trouble of a familiar order. Malaria caused much sickness, some deaths, and many desertions. It was, in spite of the Minneriya Committee's optimism, not too easy to obtain colonists, still less to obtain good ones. As D. S. Senanayake himself put it in 1935, diffidence about colonization was aroused by the 'notorious aversion to any form of pioneering enterprise which has been expressed as a characteristic of the Ceylonese peasant'.[1]

But Senanayake himself was by this time convinced of the need for continuing aided colonization; he saw it as an 'economic necessity' because of the growing population and the shortage of land in the Wet Zone.[2] There were others, like Sir Henry de Mel, who thought that further incentives to colonization, and not abandonment of the whole idea, were required.[3] And in 1936 it was decided that all past and future payments to colonists should be considered as outright grants, and that an additional grant should be paid for house construction. Further, in 1937, the Land Commissioner (C. L. Wickremesinghe) issued an important circular on assistance to peasant colonists, based on the principle that the main object was to establish the peasant on the land and to assist him so that he could maintain a 'reasonable standard of living'. The first need, he said, was to ensure that allotments were big enough, then to decide what assistance should be given and what the peasant should be required to do himself, by considering each individual's

[1] Senanayake, *Agriculture and Patriotism*, p. 19.
[2] Ibid., p. 20.
[3] Information supplied to the author in 1951 by the then Land Commissioner, Mr. K. Kanagasundram, who also helped greatly with the contents of this chapter as a whole.

resources and probable income. He also proposed that, if a colonist showed a profit, he should be required to deposit his savings in a bank. Some of these proposals, especially that for a 'means test' and that for compulsory saving, were not and are not particularly practicable, but Wickremesinghe's ideas are nevertheless interesting.

All these moves only affected new allottees in existing colonies; no new schemes were started between 1936 and 1940. There were critics of this apparently slow progress, but the phase is best seen as one of consolidation and of moves towards the 'New Policy' of 1939.

The 'New Policy' of 1939 and After

The final phase of the evolution of a policy of aided Dry Zone colonization, a phase still current today, began with the presentation to the State Council on 23 February 1939, by D. S. Senanayake, of the very important report of his Executive Committee on 'Aided Land Colonization'.[1] This report reviewed progress to date, codified the policy which had been developing, and proposed substantial increases in the scale of aid. It recognized that, for all the aid hitherto given, colonists faced a grim struggle, especially during their first six months; and went on to stress that the problem of unemployment, under-employment, and food production was becoming ever more pressing, while the demand for land was becoming keener. 'Colonization must be accelerated and its complete success assured.' It was suggested that experience in Ceylon and elsewhere had shown that what was required was that the Government should hand over to the colonist a ready-made farm, complete with house. Wickremesinghe's report on procedure in Palestine and Libya was quoted in support of this proposal (indeed, the hand of Wickremesinghe is discernible throughout the Committee's report).

The report then made a statement of proposed policy. It commended the practice which had grown up of making, in advance of the planning of a colony, a soil survey and then an engineering survey, on the basis of which the 'blocking out of allotments could be undertaken while channels and roads were under construction';[2]

[1] *DSC*, 1939, pp. 595–9.
[2] See, for example, Brohier, *Tamankaduwa District*, pp. 21–25, for an account of the soil survey undertaken at Minneriya in 1935.

colonists could then be brought in as soon as construction was completed. Turning to the very important matter of the scale of aid, its main proposals were that clearing should be at government expense, that each colonist should receive a subsistence allowance till he reaped his first harvest, that houses should be constructed at government expense for colonists who had made good (initially they were to be housed in temporary *wadiyas*, large communal huts), and that 'any work required to be done after the first harvest for ridging and stumping the paddy land of a colonist should be paid for' by the Government. Each colonist was also to receive free planting material, a loan for the purchase of implements (to be retained free if he proved satisfactory), and a loan for the purchase of buffaloes, repayment to be wholly or partially waived if satisfactory progress was made. The Government was to be responsible for domestic water-supply, major irrigation channels, roads, the reservation of sites for schools, hospitals, and communal buildings; for the provision of special colonization officers; and, through its Marketing Department and the Registrar of Co-operative Societies, for the organization of marketing.

The report proposed that a 'land kachcheri notice', announcing that land was available in a given district, should be sent to 'every Revenue Officer from whose district persons are likely to apply for land'; each of these officers was then to draw up a list of the potential colonists arranged in the order in which they should be given allotments.

The Financial Secretary, H. J. Huxham, in discussing the financial implications of these proposals, expressed the view that the cost per colonist, excluding irrigation, roads, and kindred items, would be Rs. 700 (about £54), compared with Rs. 250 under the pre-1939 system. He considered that the high cost would be justified by the gain to the country of the increased wealth to be produced by the colonists, and by the fact that without colonization there would be very slow settlement of land beneath restored irrigation works, so that, as he put it, 'the loss of interest on the cost of the irrigation and other works already completed or undertaken . . . would amount to a large part of the proposed additional expenditure without benefiting anyone.'[1] This concept of finance is a far cry from the tight holding of the public purse-strings which had been the rule not very long before.

[1] *DSC*, 1939, pp. 598-9.

The debate on the 'New Policy' was long, interesting, and generally on a high level. There were serious criticisms of the cost of the proposed aid; in particular there was the view that even with the lavish aid proposed success was not assured.[1] The problem of confused motives in colonization[2] was raised; 'the policy that has been pursued', said Dr. N. M. Perera, '. . . is neither a food-produc-tion scheme, nor an unemployment-relief scheme, nor a scheme to put the surplus population on the land', and he quoted a similar view about Tabbowa Colony recorded in the official Economic Survey.[3] Other contributors to the debate were concerned about the difficulty of obtaining reasonable yields of paddy in the Dry Zone;[4] and about the temptation to promote spectacular new schemes rather than humdrum but possibly more effective measures.[5] There was, on the other hand, the view that the pro-posals were not bold enough.[6] All of these criticisms and views are still to be heard today, and most of them will be referred to in subsequent chapters.

The report was eventually carried by a large majority and the 'New Policy' came into force. It soon received a great fillip when, with the outbreak of war in September 1939, food production took on a new urgency. The 'New Policy' is essentially that under which all the many colonies founded since 1939, including those under the 'Six Year Plan', 1947–53, have grown up, and it con-tinues, with but little modification, today.[7] It will be the main purpose of the remaining chapters of this book to assess the achievement and discuss the problems of these schemes. All that need be attempted here is a review of the ways in which policy concerning aid, selection of colonists, and the administrative machine have changed since the 'New Policy' began.

There has been a general tendency until very recently indeed for there to be a further increase in the scale of aid. Thus in 1941 a

---

[1] Ibid., p. 605, speech of G. E. de Silva.
[2] Cf. p. 118 above.
[3] Ibid., p. 680; see also *Village Survey: Puttalam*, p. 48.
[4] *DSC*, 1939, p. 681, speech of Dr. N. M. Perera.
[5] Ibid., pp. 654–5, speech of G. A. H. Wille.
[6] Ibid., p. 665, speech of D. P. R. Gunawardana.
[7] For plans for some of these schemes see the *Reports on the Walawe Left Bank Irrigation Scheme*, S.P. 4 of 1940, and *on the Minipe Yoda-ela Scheme*, S.P. 6 of 1940; *of the Committee on the Parakrama Samudra Scheme*, S.P. 24 of 1941; and *of the Committee of the Ridi-Bendi-Ela Scheme*, S.P. 5 of 1943. For the 'Six Year Plan' see *Economic and Social Development*, pp. 20–33.

Committee reporting on what should be done in the projected Parakrama Samudra scheme recommended that houses should be constructed *before* colonists were brought in, the earlier system of *wadiyas* not, they thought, being conducive to systematic development.[1] They also recommended that paddy fields be 'ridged' (i.e. that the field *bunds* be put in) before colonists arrived, to conserve soil and to prevent waste of water. And they proposed that aid should also include free seed and tools. All subsequent colonies received these measures of aid in addition to those proposed in the 'New Policy'. Again, a subsidy of Rs. 200 became available in 1950 to encourage proper cultivation of high land allotments; this followed a visit by the Prime Minister to Tabbowa, where he found the high land lots 'disgraceful'.[2] In the same year the Minister of Agriculture (Dudley Senanayake) visited Giritale, and, arising from what he saw there, it was decided that it would give the colonists a better start if the Government removed the stumps from 2 acres of the paddy land, the colonist receiving a subsidy for stumping the remainder. The Gal Oya Development Board has gone a stage farther, and provides colonists with completely ridged and stumped paddy allotments and with completely stumped high land allotments. In 1952, however, decreased scales of aid were announced.[3]

The suggestion that land kachcheri notices should be sent out to all districts likely to contain applicants came to nothing. It became the general rule for the Land Commissioner to select certain districts only in which land in a given colony should be advertised. This is a reflection of the spectacular increase in the popularity of colonies (a generally posted notice would today result in an overwhelming spate of applications); but it also raises the point that if colonization is meant to relieve agrarian pressure there is a call for some objective criterion by which the Land Commissioner may judge the need of each D.R.O.'s Division for places in the schemes; it will be apparent, however, that such a criterion is hard to come by.[4]

Finally, the 'New Policy' has meant far-reaching changes in the organization of jungle clearing and construction work. Work in the first colonies to come under it was done by contract and by the

---

[1] See *Report of the Committee on the Parakrama Samudra Scheme*, pp. 6–9.
[2] Cf. pp. 249–55 below.   [3] See below, p. 168.
[4] See above, p. 90, and below, pp. 215–16.

direct employment of labour under the immediate control of colonization officers and under the general direction of the local Kachcheri. Events at Minipe in 1940 were typical of what tended to happen under this system. All started well:

work commenced on the 10th morning. At 7.28 a.m. an auspicious hour the oldest resident of Kandegama, Katandigedera Kirihamy, felled the first tree in the presence of the Ratamahatmaya and the headman and villagers of the place, and after sprinkling of milk and a few words of advice from the R.M. to the villagers regarding the advantages of [this] scheme to the people and country work was adjourned for the day.[1]

Unfortunately the adjournment was interpreted as an indefinite one, the Ratamahatmaya's injunctions having fallen on deaf ears. The Colonization Officer perpetually found great difficulty in recruiting labour; in October 1940 there were 1,602 labourers on the roll but the average daily attendance was below 20 and the men who did turn up were unused to axes. It is an interesting sidelight on D. S. Senanayake that when he visited the scheme a little later he personally 'taught the people how to handle an axe and the proper way to fell the forest'. Work by contract fared little better. After fifty-six letters had accumulated in the Contract File at Kandy Kachcheri only three contractors had been engaged and only 7 acres felled; and soon there were innumerable tangled disputes, two men claiming to have felled the same piece of jungle and some claiming who had felled none.

Allowance must be made for malaria and for the remoteness of Minipe from Kandy. But the simple truth is that an already busy and over-taxed Kachcheri could not control land development on the scale and with the efficiency and imagination required by the accelerated programme of colonization under the 'New Policy'. Consequently a new administrative machine was developed specifically to undertake what became known as 'Land Development', i.e. jungle clearing, ridging and stumping, house building, and the whole business of preparing a ready-made farm for the incoming colonist.

The first revolutionary change came in July 1942. The Irrigation Department was made responsible for the whole task of land development, the work in each scheme being supervised by a

---

[1] From a report by the Colonization Officer, Minipe, dated 7 Aug. 1940. He was rewarded for his pains by being told 'as a measure of retrenchment the C.O. may be asked to write on both sides of the paper'.

Committee drawn from it and other interested departments.[1] Mechanization was introduced when possible, though in war-time it was very hard to obtain equipment, and labour difficulties continued (Italian war prisoners were at one time extensively used). But the advantages of effective, uniform control by a Department used to engineering works in the field were enormous. Rapid progress was made at Minipe, Elahera, Kagama, Beragama, Parakrama Samudra, and elsewhere, in spite of great difficulties over malaria.

But by 1946 the land-development work of the Irrigation Department had assumed such proportions that it was 'interfering with the legitimate work of the Department', and in March 1947 the work was handed over to a special branch of the Land Commissioner's Department.[2] This proved only a temporary arrangement, and in 1948 a separate Land Development Department was created in the Ministry of Agriculture and Lands.[3] It is this Department which now controls all land-development work in the Dry Zone (except that of the Gal Oya Development Board), including the siting and construction of such buildings as dispensaries, hospitals, and schools. It uses its own labour, not that of the Agricultural Corps (another government department), and also that of two special groups whose work will be referred to later.[4] (The Gal Oya Development Board is itself a special machine for promoting colonization, formed in 1949 on the general lines of the Tennessee Valley Authority.)[5]

The Ancillaries of Colonization

It is the purpose of the concluding section of this chapter to review developments in fields which, although important in themselves, are from the point of view of this book prerequisites to colonization; in particular, the fields of irrigation, communications, and land tenure.

In the period after 1931 there was but little discussion of the principles which should govern the Government's interest in irrigation; D. S. Senanayake's dictum that irrigation was 'the nation's

---

[1] See *Admin. Report: Irrigation*, 1943, pp. 3, 12–13, and 22.
[2] See ibid., 1946, pp. 9–10.
[3] See *ARDLD*, 1951, p. 3.
[4] See below, pp. 195–6.
[5] See Gal Oya Development Board Act, No. 51 of 1949, and GODB, *Ann. Reports*.

business' was generally accepted.[1] The history of irrigation in the period is therefore one of planning, of organization, and of achievement.[2] Although in the early 1930's colonization was mainly a matter of the utilization of unoccupied land under existing irrigation works (Huxham's financial argument for colonization will be remembered), work was soon in hand on the restoration of ancient schemes and on the construction of new ones. Some of the schemes, such as the restoration of the great tank of Parakrama Samudra, were particularly ambitious. Not very much had been achieved by 1938, however; the sown area irrigated by major works, which had been 142,947 acres in 1922 and 162,797 acres in 1930, had risen only to 170,426 acres in 1938 (but by 1951 the figure was 217,766 acres). The Six-Year Plan (1947–53) was intended to bring an additional 81,912 acres under major irrigation works. Among the more important technical developments are a tendency to plan works by catchments according to a co-ordinated plan, the construction of great new works like the Gal Oya Reservoir ('Senanayake Samudra') which are reservoirs rather than tanks, and an increased use of mechanical appliances.

Relatively little was done in the period to provide railways or new trunk roads, nor, indeed, was it necessary, at least until the assault in the last few years on such remaining jungle fastnesses as those of the Gal Oya valley. (The Gal Oya Development Board has ambitious plans for new major road construction and is also developing water transport on the Batticaloa lagoon.)[3] But the construction of feeder roads and 'agricultural roads' was throughout the period considered by the Government to be one of its obligations to new colonies, and much work was done, especially by the Irrigation Department; whether the communications net is generally adequate will be considered later.[4] And, to an increasing extent as the period went on, the use of motor transport did much to break down the isolation of the Dry Zone, to develop its economic potential, and to augment its social amenities. Already in 1932 this point had been noticed by the Minneriya Committee;[5] and the lorry and the bus must be counted major factors in the acceleration of colonization in the last decade.

---

[1] Senanayake, *Agriculture and Patriotism*, pp. 36–37.
[2] See *Admin. Reports: Irrigation.*
[3] See GODB, *Ann. Report*, 1951–2, pp. 20–21.
[4] See below, pp. 269–70.   [5] *Minneriya Irrigation Scheme Committee*, p. 4.

During the period 1931–53 work was done in the provision of many other ancillaries of colonization. Thus agricultural education (in the widest sense) became increasingly important, especially when, after the formation of specialized Research Institutes for each of the three main export crops, the Department of Agriculture was able to concentrate mainly on the peasant sector of the island's economy.[1] There was much discussion of the matter of credit facilities for the peasant, and the Banking Commission paid special attention to the problem of credit for the colonist.[2] The same problem and the related ones of marketing and retail distribution became the concern of a revived Co-operative movement which received a great fillip during the war of 1939–45, when the Government's rationing scheme was administered through it.[3] A rural development movement grew up, with active government encouragement.[4] And from time to time there were proposals for colonization by middle-class Ceylonese, partly with the social motive of providing leadership for the peasant colonization schemes.[5] Middle-class colonists were in fact settled at Minneriya, Nachchaduwa, and elsewhere, and there is an entirely middle-class colony at Kopakulama, near Anuradhapura. Many of these matters will be discussed functionally, as they affect the present state of affairs in the colonies, in the chapters that follow; and it will be seen then that they did not all fulfil the hopes of their protagonists.

A little must be said, however, about legislative enactments concerning land tenure, and in particular concerning the alienation to peasants of Crown land; these represent the end-product of the long process of evolution which was discussed in Chapters 5 and 6, and the codification of the policy recommended by the Land Commission. They included the Land Settlement Ordinance of 1931 and the Crown Lands Ordinance of 1947 (the former marked an important step in the evolution of policy, for it partially undid the ill effects of the Crown Lands Encroachments Ordinance by recognizing the need for communal reserves, and by providing a means

[1] For the general subject of this paragraph, see *Economic and Social Development of Ceylon*; also Farmer, 'Programmes and Plans for Rural Development in Ceylon', in INCIDI, *Rural Development*, pp. 208–14.

[2] See Ceylon Banking Commission, *Report*, i. 130–2.

[3] See *Admin. Reports: Co-operative Societies*.

[4] See *Admin. Reports: Rural Development*.

[5] See, for example, *DSC*, 1932, pp. 688–700; see also *Report of the Committee appointed . . . to draw up a Scheme for the Settlement of Educated Young Men on the Land*, S.P. 5 of 1941.

of satisfying what were by 1931 accepted as the rights of the peasants; the latter codified the laws relating to the vast Crown estate and replaced the old land sale and lease regulations).[1] But far more important from the viewpoint of this book, because it provided the legal and tenurial framework for colonization, was the Land Development Ordinance of 1935.[2] Although the Ordinance represents, in only slightly modified form, the views of the Land Commission which reported in 1929, the Land Development Bill was not, for various reasons, given its first reading until 14 March 1933;[3] and the Land Development Ordinance was not enacted until 1935.[4] During this period of delay, tenure in colonization schemes was on a provisional basis, on conditions foreshadowing those eventually laid down in the Ordinance.

The Land Development Ordinance closely followed the Land Commission in defining the duties of the Land Commissioner, and, adopting the Commission's principle of the dominance of peasant interest, in laying down the procedure for the 'mapping out' of Crown land between various users in a strict order of priority.[5] Crown land may be alienated under the Ordinance on a 'permit' or on a 'grant'. As a rule, an applicant (including a potential colonist) receives a permit in the first instance, and a grant after a period of time if he succeeds in fulfiling certain conditions, e.g. that specified improvements and forms of cultivation are carried out, that he resides on the land, that he erects a house on it (or, in the case of a colonist, that he maintains the house provided for him in good repair), that he provides fences and conservation measures, and that he makes a specified annual payment. The ultimate grant may be on a protected or unprotected tenure, but the former is more usual, and includes conditions to ensure that the land is used and used for a specified purpose, to prevent leasing, mortgaging, or sale, and to ensure that the holding passes to one successor only;[6]

[1] See the Land Settlement Ordinance, No. 20 of 1931 (later amended by Nos. 22 of 1932 and 31 of 1933); and the Crown Lands Ordinance, No. 8 of 1947 (later amended by Nos. 9 of 1947 and 13 of 1949).

[2] See the Land Development Ordinance, No. 19 of 1935 (later amended by No. 49 of 1953); see also *Land for the People*.

[3] See *DSC*, 1933, pp. 535–45; for the second reading see ibid., pp. 2345–60.

[4] See *ARLC*, 1933, p. 3.   [5] Cf. above, p. 120.

[6] This is the rule normal in colonization schemes; where larger holdings are alienated under the Ordinance, a minimum size is specified, and succession may be to more than one person providing that none of the subdivided holdings fall below this figure.

and conditions, similar to those governing permits, concerning fences, conservation, residence, and payment. How these and other conditions affect colonization schemes will be discussed in Chapter 14. Grants under the Ordinance may be cancelled if any of the conditions are not fulfilled, so that the Government retains the ultimate ownership of land, but a well-behaved grantee and his successors may be said to enjoy in perpetuity almost all of the advantages of outright ownership, this being the most important feature of the forms of tenure created by this important Ordinance.

The Land Development Ordinance was, by one of its clauses, deemed to apply to leases and permits which, like those at Tabbowa and other 'old' colonies, were made in anticipation of it. By far the greatest part of the Crown land disposed of since 1935 has been alienated on a protected tenure under the Ordinance; this applies to village-expansion schemes and to alienation to middle-class Ceylonese as well as to alienation to peasants in the colonies. The other two types of tenure envisaged by the Land Commission (outright grant and peasant proprietor's lease) have been lost sight of.

PART THREE

THE
COLONIZATION SCHEMES
TODAY

8

The Colonization Schemes Today

Part III of this book will be concerned with the current achievements and problems of the peasant colonization schemes in the Dry Zone of Ceylon. In the present chapter it is proposed to introduce this subject by setting out a number of basic facts about the colonies and their administration; some of these facts will serve the further purpose of establishing a scale in the mind of the reader, both absolutely, in terms of the number of colonists and the size of the area they cultivate, and relatively, by comparing the achievement of colonization with that of the other methods of settling peasants on the land in Ceylon. A sense of proportion will also be gained from the survey of other Asian colonization schemes which concludes this chapter.

At this stage there is a need for a more precise definition of 'colony' and 'colonization scheme'. It will be remembered that the Land Commission drew a distinction between 'village expansion', the settlement of peasants on land near their *purāna* village, and colonization, their settlement away from their native villages.[1] In the event, the distinction has become blurred. Some schemes containing no colonists other than those from nearby villages (e.g. Sangilikanadarawa) are nevertheless officially classed as colonies because they have qualified for the full scale of aid proper to colonization schemes and not the less generous scale appropriate to village expansion. The reason for this is usually that the colonist, although local, is too far from his *purāna* village to rely on his kith and kin for subsistence during the difficult initial phase, and in any case is made to give up all interests in the *purāna* village as a condition of his new tenure. Hence he needs more aid than the man in a village expansion scheme who suffers none of these disabilities. The schemes listed in Tables 15 and 16, and discussed in the chapters which follow, are colonization schemes judged by this criterion of the scale of the aid which was granted them. Some of the smaller schemes are not, however, always included in official lists.[2]

[1] See above, pp. 120 and 137–8.
[2] e.g. *ARLC*, 1939–47, 1948, 1949, 1950, and 1951.

Table 16 shows the state of the Dry Zone peasant colonization schemes on 31 December 1953; the size and distribution of the schemes is shown in Map 6. It will be seen that there were in all thirty peasant colonies which ranged in size from minor schemes with only fifty colonists to giants like Minneriya, Parakrama Samudra, and Gal Oya. The colonies clustered thickest in the classic country of Nuwarakalawiya. But a great transformation of the landscape had also taken place in Tamankaduwa, where Minneriya, Giritale, and Parakrama Samudra together formed a continuous belt of cultivated land 17 miles from north to south and 11 miles from east to west in what had been twenty years earlier little but jungle and *damana* (cf. Maps 7 and 8). It will be seen that relatively little colonization had taken place in the Wanni, where there were only the two adjacent Iranamadu colonies of Jaffna Tamils. But Bintenne and the East Coast were in process of transformation through the medium of the Gal Oya scheme; it is hoped ultimately to develop most of the land north of the Gal Oya, east of a line joining the symbols for Gal Oya and Unnichchai Tanks on Map 6 and west of the Batticaloa lagoon; there will also be development south of the Oya, and independent schemes farther south.[1] In the south-eastern Dry Zone there were only the twin Beragama colonies, but, again, there are possibilities of future development if the Walawe Reservoir scheme is proceeded with.[2]

Altogether there were on 31 December 1953 some 16,532 colonists cultivating about 118,000 acres of paddy and high land.

Colonists *and* their families may be estimated to have totalled about 90,000 at the end of 1953. This represents about 1·1 per cent. of the population of Ceylon; the proportion of colonists in the population tends to rise as time goes on. The total population of the schemes is probably swollen to about 95,000 by permanent lawful residents other than colonists, for instance, by irrigation workers, artisans, and *boutique*-keepers.[3] In the areas around the colonies are further permanent residents, some of them squatters,[4] engaged in agricultural labour and largely dependent on the colony for their existence; and, especially in the larger colonies, there is a

---

[1] See the draft development plan, GODB, *Ann. Report, 1951-2*, facing p. 32.
[2] See, however, below, pp. 193 and 318–19.
[3] Figures from estimates collected by the author in the field in 1951 and corrected in proportion to increase in number of colonists since that date.
[4] See below, pp. 202–4.

large floating population who come, in particular, to work in the paddy harvest; this floating population was in 1951 estimated to

TABLE 16

State of Dry Zone Peasant Colonies, 31 December 1953

Colony	Number of allottees	Estimated area alienated for cultivation (acres)
1. Allai	568	2,391
2. Attaragalla . . .	310	1,395
3. Bathmedilla . . .	288	1,728
4. Beragama (Malay) . .	65	284
5. Beragama . . .	272	2,176
6. Dewahuwa . . .	453	3,577
7. Elahera. . . .	903	7,224
8. Gal Oya . . .	3,565	25,034
9. Giritale. . . .	101	878
10. Huruluwewa . . .	1,051	5,530
11. Iranamadu (Kilinochchi)	61	427
12. Iranamadu (Paranthan)* .	595	3,635
13. Kagama (Old) . .	216	1,779
14. Kagama (New) . .	516	4,228
15. Kantalai . . .	742	3,690
16. Kottu Kachchiya . .	125	1,000
17. Maha Kumbukkadawala .	50	400
18. Maha Uswewa . .	50	400
19. Minipe	492	3,938
20. Minneriya . . .	1,141	10,678
21. Nachchaduwa . .	820	5,385
22. Okkampitiya† . .	154	1,034
23. Pandiyankadawela . .	76	494
24. Parakrama Samudra .	2,780	22,820
25. Ridibendi Ela . .	358	2,913
26. Sangilikanadarawa . .	49	356
27. Soraborawewa . .	117	545
28. Tabbowa . . .	240	1,624
29. Unnichchai . . .	324	2,475
30. Uriyawa	50	400
Totals	16,532	118,438

* Including Iranamadu Extension Scheme.
† Including Kumbukkan Oya Extension Scheme.
Sources: ARLC, 1952, p. 17, and 1953, p. 19; author's field investigations.

number 2,000, 2,500, and 1,500 at Elahera, Minneriya, and Nachchaduwa respectively. There is also always a large labour force working in the Dry Zone in the preparation of new colonies.

Moreover the colonies, quite apart from providing direct and indirect employment, have done much to demonstrate the practicability of living in the Dry Zone, and hence to encourage the voluntary migration which has been such a feature of the last few years. Under the influence of this migration, superimposed on the natural increase, the population of the North-Central Province, which was only 97,365 in 1931, rose to 139,534 in 1946, to 170,164 in 1951, and to 228,759 in 1953.[1] It may then be justly claimed that the colonization schemes are making their mark on the population pattern of the Dry Zone.

There is also the point that the colonists settled so far are but the pioneers of a great host, for the colonization of the Dry Zone is only just getting into its stride. As Table 17 shows, more than 80 per cent. of the colonists placed on the land by 31 December 1953 were in fact settled after the beginning of 1948, and it was only in 1949 that the annual rate of colonization exceeded 2,000 allottees for the first time. Under the Six Year Plan, it was proposed to settle some 5,900 colonists in 1952 and about 6,400 in 1953;[2] although, as the table shows, actual achievement fell seriously short of these figures, mainly because of slower development at Gal Oya than had been anticipated and because the Walawe scheme had not been started, it is nevertheless clear that the rate of colonization is being stepped up.

To turn to other general aspects of the Dry Zone colonization schemes of today, the point must first be made that no colony has emerged from under the wing of the Land Commissioner and his Colonization Officers or of the Gal Oya Development Board and become a social unit subject to normal provincial administration like any *purāna* village; the earliest schemes, like Tabbowa and the Malay Colony, continue to function as colonization schemes just as do the most recent additions to the list. In consequence, the older colonies constitute a palimpsest in which is to be seen the results of the evolving policies which were described in the previous chapter. There is, however, an air of uniformity about colonies which were the result of the 'New Policy' of 1939; in

[1] For 1931 and 1946 figures see *Census of Ceylon, 1946*, vol. i, pt. 1, p. 72; figures for 1951 are Registrar-General's estimates for 31 Dec., kindly supplied by Mr. A. Arulpiragasam; figures for 1953 from preliminary census data. (See *Ceylon News Letter*, 28 Mar. 1953.)

[2] *Economic and Social Development*, Table 28, pp. lxix and lxx, with conversion of statistics as for Table 17 above.

many ways, in fact, standardization has, in the interests of administrative convenience, gone too far. Except in a few colonies, notably at Gal Oya, the peasant allottee up to the end of 1952 received standard allotments of 5 acres of paddy land and 3 acres

TABLE 17

Recent Progress of Dry Zone Peasant Colonization

Period	'Six-year plan' schemes		Other schemes: Colonists settled	Total Colonists settled
	Colonists planned (approx.)	Colonists settled		
Pre-1939	..	..	1,138	1,138
1939–47	..	..	1,971	1,971
1948	1,340	251	462	713
1949	1,630	2,246	58	2,304
1950	1,230	1,543	567	2,110
1951	1,760	1,165	53	1,218
1952	5,900	2,299	384	2,683
1953	6,400	3,791	743	4,534
Total Colonists settled to 31 December 1953 .				16,671
Less recorded cancellations (all pre-1951) .				139
Balance remaining in Colonies . .				16,532

Sources: 'Colonists Planned' from *Economic and Social Development*, Table 28, pp. lxviii–lxx, where (*a*) figures are in terms of areas to be developed, which have been converted into estimated number of colonists above; and (*b*) figures are in terms of financial years (1947–8 has been entered under 1948 above, 1948–9 under 1949, and so on).
'Colonists Settled' from *ARLC*, from data kindly supplied by the Land Commissioner, and from field notes.

of high land. The scale of aid had, as the previous chapter made clear, gradually evolved, but at any one time it, too, tended to apply to the majority of schemes. Thus in all colonies being developed in December 1951 the Government undertook all jungle clearing; the ridging of all paddy land and the stumping of 2 acres of it; the construction of irrigation channels and roads; the provision of houses, latrines, and communal wells; the issue of free seed paddy for the first season, of free planting material for the high land, of tolls, and of railway warrants from home village to colony; and the building of such communal facilities as hospitals, schools, and meeting halls.[1] Financial aid consisted of a subsidy of up to Rs. 200 per acre for stumping paddy land not stumped by the Government, a monthly subsistence allowance of Rs. 15 until the first crop was harvested, and a subsidy of Rs. 200 for the development of the high land allotment; and an initial waiver of water and land charges. Apart from the Gal Oya scheme (where *all* the paddy was stumped in advance in the belief that the presence of stumps is too grave a handicap to the Colonist) only the mode of division of the high land subsidy between such purposes as fencing, soil conservation, and permanent planting was subject to local variation. As an economy measure, however, the standard size of holding has now been cut to 3 acres of paddy and between 1 and 2 acres of high land, the development subsidies have been lowered, and the size and standard of construction of houses reduced.[2] All colonies have, since 1935, been subject to the restricted tenure set out in the Land Development Ordinance;[3] and all colonies today are supervised by Colonization Officers and officially encouraged to run Co-operative societies. The Gal Oya Development Board at present improves on the standard method of supervision by employing village officers, each responsible for one 'village' of 150 families, under a Colonization Officer, who supervises ten 'villages'.[4]

The Administration and Planning of Dry Zone Colonies

It seems desirable at this stage, and at the risk of repeating some of the points made in preceding chapters, to describe the machinery for administering and planning colonization, in order that a number of the problems discussed in succeeding chapters may be more readily intelligible.

The central figure in both the administration and planning of colonies is the Land Commissioner, who, as the custodian of all Crown lands, has, however, many duties not connected with colonization. It may be decided that a certain piece of Crown land shall be used for colonization as a result of the systematic process

[1] See *ARLC*, 1951, pp. 3–4, and 1952, pp. 3–4; it is realized that to set out the modern scale of aid here involves some repetition of what has been said in Chapter 7, but the reader will find it convenient to have the standard scale set out in one single paragraph.
[2] See *Ceylon News Letter*, 20 June 1953, pp. 3–4; and *ARLC*, 1953, pp. 6–7.
[3] See above, pp. 159–60.
[4] See GODB, *Ann. Report*, 1951–2, p. 56.

of 'mapping out' envisaged by the Land Development Ordinance;[1] but more frequently today, when the demand for land has out-stripped the 'mapping out' process, colonization is decided on in advance of formal 'mapping out'. Once the decision is made, the land is handed over by the Land Commissioner to the Director of Land Development so that he may undertake his preparatory work, and so that the Director of Irrigation may construct his *bunds*, channels, and roads. The land is then handed back to the Land Commissioner for alienation through Land Kachcheries. The Land Commissioner, however, retains his general supervision; quite apart from the fact that he is vitally concerned with the part played by the Crown in tenure under the Land Development Ordinance, the Colonization Officers are members of his staff, though they are locally responsible to Government Agents, or to Assistant Government Agents of Districts, who, in fact carry on a great deal of the day-to-day work of supervising colonization schemes. There have also been, since 1948, specially recruited District Land Officers to strengthen those Kachcheries which have a great deal of land work.[2]

The Director of Land Development and the Director of Irriga-tion do not, however, work through Revenue Officers, but have their own chain of command. The former supervises much work direct from Colombo, but has Assistant Directors in areas where there is heavy development work.[3] One major, or two or more minor schemes in the field are entrusted to a Land Development Officer, who controls a number of Farm Managers, each respon-sible for a given area of development or 'farm' (a curious survival from the war-time days of 'State Farms'). Some areas are, how-ever, cleared on contract by special labour organizations.[4] There are special Construction Units which build houses.

The work of the Irrigation Department is of fundamental im-portance to colonization. Many schemes originate in it, especially in its Designs and Research Branch (though some are suggested by other departments and by private persons). Its role in colony planning will become clear in the next paragraph, and the basic nature of its constructional work will be evident. But its organiza-tion need not be discussed in detail, since a knowledge of it is not so essential to an understanding of the problems of contemporary

[1] See above, pp. 120 and 159.
[2] See *ARLC*, 1949, p. 3.
[3] See *ARDLD*, 1951, pp. 8–10.
[4] See below, pp. 195–6.

colonization.[1] And the same applies to the other departments which are concerned at various stages, e.g. the Survey, Forestry, and Co-operative Departments and the Department of Agriculture.

Most of the departments mentioned so far are involved in the all-important planning stage, when the scheme for the future colony is drawn up as a 'Blocking-Out Plan', or 'B.O.P.' The B.O.P. shows the use to be made of all the land in the scheme; channels, roads, paddy, and high land allotments, reservations for purposes of conservation and for temples and other public buildings are all shown. In the past there have been various procedures for the preparation of the B.O.P. The procedure in use in the latter half of 1951, clearly designed for the case in which there had been no previous mapping out, was as follows.[2] The Director of Irrigation sent a tracing of the area of the proposed scheme to the Surveyor-General with a specification of the surveys required. Copies were also sent to the Land Commissioner, who forwarded one to the Revenue Officer concerned so that there might be no further alienation of Crown land (i.e. for village expansion) in the area of the scheme. Having received the surveys, the Director of Irrigation prepared the B.O.P.; this was meant to be completed two clear years before alienation was planned. Since the line taken by irrigation channels fundamentally affects the land-use pattern of the colony by determining whether land is irrigable or not, it appears an obvious solution for the Irrigation Department to prepare the draft B.O.P.; on the other hand, the layout of the colony then tends to be dominated by irrigation considerations, land use, social and other needs being something of an afterthought. There was, however, machinery for reviewing the draft B.O.P. A copy was sent to the Revenue Officer concerned so that he could make any desirable corrections, and decide whether it would be necessary to acquire any private lands or lands occupied under the Land Development Ordinance, whether the reservations for conservation and for communal purposes were adequate, and whether any lots should be reserved for village expansion. Earlier experience had shown the importance of field inquiry, B.O.P. in hand; for

[1] For details, see the *Admin. Reports: Irrigation*, and *WBR*, pp. 434–5 (ii. 204–5). Irrigation, seen as planned use of water resources, will be further considered in Chapter 9.

[2] From a *Land Commissioner's Circular* of 27 July 1951, consulted in the Office of the Land Commissioner.

example, in the absence of such inquiry, a number of houses at Elahera were located on waterlogged ground. In the Punjab, it may be noted, it was originally the rule that the irrigation engineers chose the site for the *abadi* (village) and that the plan was sent to the Colonization Officer (there much higher in the hierarchy than his Ceylon namesake) for acceptance or amendment; but later the C.O. himself made the selection on contoured plans carried into the field, a noteworthy escape from the thraldom of the irrigation engineer.[1]

This procedure was the result of much trial, and of some errors which created problems to be discussed later. Co-ordination in planning, very important to ensure that all relevant considerations were given due weight, was also facilitated after 1948 by the formation of a Standing Committee on Land Development, to replace the *ad hoc* committees, one for each scheme, originally the rule. The Standing Committee consists of the Land Commissioner, Conservator of Forests, and Surveyor-General and the Directors of Agriculture, Irrigation, and Land Development, and has proved an effective instrument of planning.

It may have been noticed that so far no mention has been made of the part played by soil surveys in the planning process. Such surveys have in fact been made from the early 1930's in most schemes (in fact earlier still they were recommended, it may be remembered, by the Land Commission)[2] and the results reported to the appropriate *ad hoc* committee or, later, to the Standing Committee. But it appears to be a fair criticism that the results of these surveys have not been sufficiently applied in the vital stage of drawing up the B.O.P.s. This point will be taken up in Chapter 12.

Very little that has so far been said applies to the administration and planning undertaken by the Gal Oya Development Board established by an Act of 1949 and designed, largely on the model of the Tennessee Valley Authority, to achieve unified, multi-purpose development on a catchment-basin basis;[3] and in particular, to take on the work of land development and colonization which threatened to be too much, in view of the relatively large

---

[1] See the *Punjab Colony Manual*, i. 234.
[2] See above, p. 120.
[3] See the *Gal Oya Development Board Act*, No. 51 of 1949; also Brohier, *The Gal Oya Valley Project* (Colombo, Dept. of Information, 1951). For the Tennessee Valley Authority, see David E. Lilienthal, *TVA* (Penguin Books, 1944).

area to be developed, for the normal departmental machinery.[1] The Board's area of authority is divided into 'Developed' and 'Underdeveloped' areas (see Map 6). It is the latter which, naturally, is to be the scene of colonization, and in developing it the Board has wide powers concerning irrigation, water-supply, drainage, the control of soil erosion, the generation and supply of electricity, fisheries, afforestation, public health, agricultural and industrial development, and 'economic and cultural progress'. It also has power to undertake constructional work of various kinds and to maintain research establishments. It assumes the functions of government in a number of ways and, in particular, replaces the Land Commissioner as the authority responsible for Crown lands within its underdeveloped area.

The Board has set up a number of departments in order to fulfil its functions. Some of them (e.g. the Electricity Branch) are not particularly relevant here; but several are concerned with land development and colonization.[2] There is, for example, a separate Planning Branch which produces the equivalent of B.O.P.s; the Branch has been handicapped by uncertainty about the course to be taken by irrigation channels and by lack of soil data, but its independence of the irrigation engineers has helped it to show a praiseworthy regard for social considerations and for the checking of plans on the ground.[3] The Board has its own Irrigation Branch, though the reservoir itself ('Senanayake Samudra') and certain channels were constructed by an American firm; there is now a separate Roads Branch. Jungle clearing and other land-development work is undertaken by the Board, largely with mechanical equipment, and there are Branches dealing with house construction, sawmills, carpentry workshops, and the manufacture of bricks and tiles. The work of colonization is undertaken by a Peasant Settlement Branch which controls colonization and Village Officers; selection of colonists, apart from middle-class colonists and those local peasants requiring resettlement because of the

[1] The Gal Oya Board also owes something to Sir Hugh Clifford's idea of a 'Development Board' (see above, p. 135); and 'Message from his Excellency the Governor', reprinted in Brohier, *Land, Maps and Surveys*, i. 122.

[2] This paragraph is based mainly on the author's field inquiries; he wishes to record his gratitude for help given by Members and Officers of the Board, particularly Mr. R. L. Brohier (Member), Mr. S. W. Atukorala (Chief Peasant Settlement Officer), and Mr. D. F. Abeyawardena (Chief Planning Officer). For the activities of the Board see also GODB, *Ann. Reports*.

[3] See below, pp. 297–8.

activities of the Board, is, however, undertaken in the normal manner by Land Kachcheries held by Revenue Officers in the colonist's home areas.

The view is sometimes expressed that a separate organization like the Gal Oya Development Board was unnecessary and that the job could have been done more efficiently by the normal departmental organization. On this view, the strain on the administrative machine would have been great, but could have been met by adequate decentralization; and departmental staffs would initially have been hopelessly inadequate, but could have been enlarged by the methods which the Board itself has had to follow, viz. the recruitment of experts from outside Ceylon, or the secondment of officers from departments not normally concerned with colonization. It is further argued that some of the difficulties which have been encountered at Gal Oya, and which will find mention in succeeding chapters, might have been eased if some of these foreign recruits and seconded officers had been more closely in touch with the experience of Ceylon government departments; this closer liaison, it is said, would inevitably have resulted from departmental control. Finally, it is argued that Gal Oya, with its original plan for some 120,000 irrigated acres, is not really such a large scheme after all, even if it does dwarf Parakrama Samudra; and that it does not warrant a separate authority, with the temptation to grandiose thinking and spending which then tends to be involved.

But the author, though at first he inclined to some at least of these views, is now firmly on the side of a separate authority, having been convinced not so much by field work in 1951 (a time when many mistakes were being made) but by reports which have reached him since he left Ceylon of good things now being done. As a geographer, he is taken by the notion of the unified development of a river catchment, bound together as its resources are 'in that unity with which nature herself regards her resources—the waters, the land and the forests together, a "seamless web"'.[1] There is a great deal to be said, too, for what Franklin D. Roosevelt called 'a corporation clothed with the power of government but possessed of the flexibility and initiative of a private enterprise';[2]

---

[1] See Lilienthal, *TVA*, p. 541; see also 'The Integrated Development of River Basins', *Proc. UN Conference on the Conservation and Utilization of Resources* (New York, 1950), pp. 387–403.   [2] Quoted by Lilienthal, *TVA*, p. 53.

both flexibility and initiative have been well to the fore in the Gal
Oya valley, and there have been, as subsequent pages will show,
a number of reforms and experiments which the government
departments, with their more circumscribed nature and functions,
have not found it possible to undertake. Moreover the Gal Oya
Board has succeeded in creating among its staff a remarkable *esprit
de corps*, a feeling of participation in a great enterprise. One hopes
that further tasks will be found for it and for bodies like it.

Colonization compared with Other Methods of Peasant Settlement

It is important, in order to arrive at a sense of scale, to institute
a comparison between the achievement of colonization on the one
hand, and of other methods of settling Ceylon peasants on the
other. The comparison will be by no means exhaustive, for the
author had little time for field study of these alternatives to
colonization.

There are four main methods, in addition to peasant colonization, of effecting settlement on Crown land in Ceylon today; two
of these concern the peasant directly, two indirectly. The first
method is the alienation direct to the peasantry of small lots of
Crown land under the Land Development Ordinance. Such lots
are generally known as 'L.D.O. allotments', and may consist of
paddy or high land, or both. If high land, and in the Dry Zone,
there is an undesirable tendency for lots to be treated as though
they were *chena*, but cultivated year in and year out. The mean
size of allotments is small; those alienated in 1951 averaged just
under 2 acres.[1] Allotments may be alienated in ones and twos on
the edge of a *purāna* village, or in large batches which, in all but
size of holding and scale of aid, resemble colonization schemes.
Thus the scheme at Kattiyawa (near Kagama Colony), originally
intended as a colonization scheme with 101 allotments, was converted in 1951 into a village expansion ('V.E.') scheme with 202
allotments, each consisting of $2\frac{1}{2}$ acres of paddy and $1\frac{1}{2}$ acres of
high land (see Map 12).[2] In this scheme, the Land Development
Department cleared, ridged, stumped, and built houses as in a
normal colonization scheme, but more usually aid to holders of
V.E. allotments is confined to the construction of roads and of
such buildings as meeting halls, with, in all schemes, subsidies to

[1] See *ARLC*, 1951, p. 12.
[2] From notes in the field, and *ARDLD*, 1951, pp. 17–18.

the allottee who constructs his own house, latrine, and well, and who undertakes soil-conservation measures. This scale is a considerable increase on that of a few years earlier.

The second method is the alienation to peasants of allotments made available by government acquisition of private land. Small lots of paddy and other crops so acquired are usually alienated almost straight away to one or more peasants under normal V.E. procedures, but large acquired estates present a different problem and have caused a great deal of discussion. The Government has for some time been strongly pressed by M.P.s and others to acquire estates for alienation to landless villagers;[1] but it is well known that yields per acre tend, at least under current conditions, to drop if this is done, and there is also the point that fear of acquisition has a depressing effect on capital investment in what is, for all its drawbacks, the mainstay of Ceylon's external economy. It was announced in 1953 that in future only small parts of estates would be acquired and then only for such purposes as schools.[2] What to do with estates actually owned by Government has also caused discussion; in particular, whether to work them as government estates, or as peasants' co-operatives, or as a multitude of individual peasant holdings. The general policy today is to work them as government estates while houses are being built for the future allottees, then to alienate holdings in the normal way under the Land Development Ordinance but with a condition requiring the allottee to join a co-operative society which prepares and markets estate produce.[3]

Thirdly, there have been alienations to middle-class Ceylonese, as envisaged by the Land Commission. Some of these were in colonization schemes; the only entirely middle-class colony is at Kopakulama near Anuradhapura, where there are thirty-six colonists, each farming 10 acres of paddy and 15 acres of high land, but there are also middle-class colonists in Minneriya and other peasant colonies.[4] But most middle-class allottees are outside the colonies. Middle-class alienation indirectly aids the peasantry by providing employment, and the same may be said of the fourth

[1] See, for example, *KPC*, pp. 18–19.
[2] In a statement on agricultural policy to the Planters' Association by the Minister of Food and Agriculture, Sir Oliver Goonetilleke, as reported in *Ceylon News Letter*, 6 Apr. 1953, p. 2.
[3] See *ARLC*, 1950, pp. 4–5 and 1951, p. 8.
[4] See above, pp. 148, 150, and below, pp. 306–7.

method of alienation, viz. alienation *outside* the Land Development
Ordinance, by sale and leases; this has only amounted to some
2,000 acres in the last twenty years or so.[1]

Table 18 shows the areas alienated by the various important
methods up to 31 December 1953.[2] The area shown under village
expansion includes land acquired from private owners and sub-

TABLE 18

*Total Areas Alienated under the Land Development Ordinance
to 31 December 1953*

Category	Amount alienated (000 acres)	Percentage of total
Village expansion (Peasant) . .	309	62
Colonization (Peasant) . . .	118	24
Middle-class Ceylonese . . .	68	14
Total	495	100

Sources: CUCL to 31 December 1950; *ARLC*, 1951, 1952, and 1953; author's
investigations.

sequently alienated. It will be seen that 62 per cent. of the land
alienated under the Land Development Ordinance has been under
village expansion schemes, and only some 24 and 14 per cent. to
colonists and middle-class allottees respectively. The balance
is likely to be tipped in favour of colonization as the heavy
programmes of subsequent years become effective; and the proportion alienated to the middle class may increase if the recommendations of a recent inquiry are translated into action.[3] But at present
it is important to realize that while pioneer colonization is more
romantic, more experimental, more novel, and altogether more
interesting, the steady settlement of villagers on land near their
own villages is quietly and unobtrusively going on and that it had
up to the end of 1953 swallowed up over two-and-a-half times as
much land as colonization. Moreover, because of the much smaller
lots in V.E. schemes, it has affected a far larger number of peasant
allottees.

[1] See *CUCL*, p. 11.
[2] It was estimated in 1956 that about a million people were resident on land
alienated under the Land Development Ordinance.
[3] See *CUCL*, pp. 61–63.

Other South Asian Colonization Schemes

To lend perspective to the Dry Zone colonies of Ceylon a brief survey of certain government-sponsored schemes in other parts of South Asia follows. Particular points of comparison and of contrast between many of these schemes and those in the Dry Zone are made in later chapters, when features of a few non-Asian projects will also be discussed. In making these comparisons and contrasts, there is no suggestion that Ceylon should be able necessarily to achieve what has been achieved elsewhere, or that other regions should be able to achieve what has been achieved in Ceylon. The geographer at least is fully seized of the essential uniqueness of a region like the Dry Zone of Ceylon, in both its physical and its human aspects, and hence of the uniqueness of the problems facing colonization in it.[1]

Pioneer settlement, whether due to governmental or to private enterprise, tends to be seen by the Western reader at least as a matter of colonization by white people or, if Asians are considered at all, as a virtual monopoly of the Chinese. Thus, in the three classic studies of pioneer settlement which are associated with the name of the great American geographer Isaiah Bowman, 31 of the 42 regional studies concern white colonists, and of the 8 Asian examples 7 are almost entirely concerned with the Chinese.[2] The remaining Asian example refers to the Japanese, whose official experiments in colonization were singularly infelicitous;[3] for example, their work in Korea was characterized by the attempt to settle Japanese there in spite of the overcrowded state of that country.[4] More recently, however, some attention has been paid to work in South Asia, notably by Karl J. Pelzer, who has written on government-sponsored colonization in the Netherlands East Indies and the Philippines.[5]

There are, in fact, a number of government-sponsored colonization schemes in South Asia. The survey which follows is neces-

[1] See R. Hartshorne, *The Nature of Geography* (Lancaster, Penn., Assoc. of Amer. Geographers, 1939), pp. 393–7.

[2] See Isaiah Bowman, *The Pioneer Fringe* (New York, Amer. Geog. Soc., 1931); W. L. G. Joerg, ed., *Pioneer Settlement* (New York, Amer. Geog. Soc., 1932), and Internat. Studies Conferences (10th), *Limits of Land Settlement* (New York, Council on Foreign Relations, 1937).

[3] See, for example, Pelzer, 'Japanese Migration and Colonization', in *Limits of Land Settlement*, pp. 155–94.   [4] See Lee, *Land Utilization*, pp. 281–9.

[5] See Pelzer, *Pioneer Settlement*.

sarily incomplete but will give the reader some idea of the scale of activity involved. Working from west to east, and saying nothing further at this stage of Jewish work in Israel (which is hardly Asian), the first example may be taken from Iraq.[1] Here in the Dujaila scheme is 'a pilot land settlement project, "the first project of its kind in the Arab Middle East and the forerunner of a large social experiment".'[2] The scheme is managed by a Board, and it is planned to irrigate some 400,000 meshara (about 250,000 acres) and to issue holdings of 100 meshara (about 60 acres) to landless persons on a restrictive tenure similar to that under the Land Development Ordinance.

In Pakistan the Thal Project, among other schemes, is conceived on the grand scale of the Punjab Canal Colonies of pre-partition India.[3] When the project is completed, $1\frac{1}{2}$ million acres will be under cultivation, irrigated from the Jinnah barrage on the Indus. A Thal Development Authority has been created on T.V.A. lines; it is responsible, *inter alia*, for land development, house construction, and the installation of colonists who, however, pay by instalments for what has been done for them.

The Punjab Canal Colonies will be familiar from earlier references. The object of colonization was the relief of population pressure and the creation of model villages.[4] Land was given to a number of classes, the chief of which was that of peasant proprietors. There were various forms of tenure. The work of colonization spans the years from 1886 to the 1920's, and in all about $5\frac{1}{2}$ million acres, equivalent to about one-third of the entire land area of Ceylon, were settled. There were also other schemes in pre-independence India; thus the Madras Government had 'labour colonies', to which members of the 'depressed classes' were moved, in areas newly opened to cultivation.[5] More recently, there have been a number of schemes in very different country from the alluvial lowlands of the canal colonies. Some of these are river valley schemes like that on the Damodar.[6] Others aim at the

[1] See Brad Fisk, 'Dujaila: Iraq's Pilot Project for Land Settlement', *Econ. Geog.*, vol. xxviii (1952), pp. 343–54. [2] Ibid., p. 343.
[3] Information kindly supplied by the Office of the High Commissioner for Pakistan in the United Kingdom.
[4] See Kazi Ahmed, 'Settlements in the Irrigated Area of Recent Colonization in the Indo-Gangetic Plain', *Ind. Geog. J.*, vol. xvii (1942), pp. 183–99; also *Punjab Colony Manual*, and Darling, *Punjab Peasant*, pp. 111–31.
[5] See Cmd. 3132, p. 509.
[6] See W. Kirk, 'The Damodar Valley', *Geog. Rev.*, vol. xl (1950), pp. 415–43;

subjugation with modern techniques of regions of difficulty like the sub-Himalayan Terai;[1] the colonization scheme there has received refugee settlers from West Punjab and East Bengal.[2] More recently has come the announcement of a plan to settle 4,000 families on 20,000 acres of government-developed paddy and an equivalent amount of high land in the Andaman Islands, with aid in the form of loans.[3] Other colonization schemes are in quite a different category and concern the rehabilitation of refugees or of famine victims.[4] But, in the absence of wide tracts of useful but unused land, colonization is likely to play a relatively unimportant part in the future economy of India.

Turning to South East Asia, there is much less activity on the mainland peninsulas than in the islands of Malaysia. In Burma, it is true, the late nineteenth-century conquest by Burmese and some Indian cultivators of the previously almost unoccupied alluvial lands of Lower Burma ranks with the great pioneering feats of the period, unrecognized though it generally is and attended as it was by most unfortunate social results.[5] But it was for the most part a spontaneous movement of individuals, the Government's part being confined to the issue of land on various systems of tenure, especially the *patta* system (free grants of 15–50 acres to selected applicants).[6] It was only after some time, when indebtedness among the new settlers was being tackled by Co-operation, that the Government Co-operative Department itself took up colonization in order to strike at the evil at its source.[7] Crown land was alienated to selected individuals, or to societies to be farmed co-operatively, the Co-operative Department advancing capital loans.

---

for a brief general review of river valley projects see 'Progress on River Valley Projects', *Ind. Trade and Industry*, vol. i (1950), p. 61.

[1] See above, p. 37.

[2] See *Tarai and Bhabar Report*; the author is greatly indebted to Major H. S. Sandhu, Deputy Director of Colonization, U.P., also to Mr. Ritchie Calder, for information on recent developments in the Terai.

[3] See 'Five-Year Development Scheme for the Andamans', *Ind. Trade and Industry*, vol. iv (1953), p. 497; also P. K. Sen, 'Some Aspects of the Recent Colonisation in the Andamans', *Geog. Rev. of Ind.*, vol. xvi (1954), pp. 33–41.

[4] See, for example, 'Rehabilitation Colony at Nilokheri', *Ind. Trade and Industry*, vol. ii (1950), pp. 58–60.

[5] See, for example, Furnivall, *An Introduction to the Political Economy of Burma* (Rangoon, Burma Book Club, 1931), pp. 50–55 and J. R. Andrus, *Burmese Economic Life* (Stanford Univ. Press, 1947), pp. 14–16.

[6] Furnivall, *Political Economy of Burma*, pp. 51–52.

[7] See *Co-operative Societies in Burma, 1915–16 to 1940*.

There were some colonies in Upper Burma (e.g. in Myitkyina District), but most of the large ones, some over 30,000 acres, were in the lower Sittang valley. The colonies survived until the war came to Burma in 1941; but it is not easy to obtain information about the current state of affairs. There was a certain amount of government-sponsored colonization in Siam before the war of 1939–45, and the work has been resumed since; but there appears so far to be no published account.[1] In Indo-China there has been a voluntary movement of Tongkinese into Cochin China comparable to the movement of Burmese into Lower Burma;[2] and, more recently, the Viet Nam Government has encouraged the southward movement from the Red River delta by affording social services and other aid.[3] In Malaya, in addition to the efforts to resettle Chinese squatters, there are government-encouraged settlements in land newly opened up by the Irrigation Department; these irrigated colonies have qualified for aid since 1939, and cultivated 72,950 acres in 1949.[4]

Dutch efforts to encourage the settlement of Javanese in the Outer Islands date back to 1905.[5] The work has been on a considerable scale and, as it is of great interest and relevance, it will frequently be mentioned in later chapters; little need therefore be said here. It may be noted, however, that the depression of the 1930's, which hit the Indies so hard, gave a great impetus to colonization, as it did in Ceylon; at the same time, a new and less costly system was evolved. The rate of settlement in Sumatra at this period increased from 10,000 in 1931–2 to more than 50,000 in 1940.[6] Since the war the independent Indonesian administration

[1] The author is indebted to the Royal Siamese Embassy in London and to Professor R. L. Pendleton for what little information is available.

[2] See Gourou, *L'Utilisation du sol*, pp. 148–51.

[3] See F.A.O., Regional Meeting on Land Utilization in Tropical Areas of Asia and the Far East, Nuwara Eliya, Ceylon, 16–29 Sept. 1951, *Minutes and Sessions* (Rome, 1952), p. 33.

[4] Ibid., pp. 51 and 55–57 and Drainage and Irrigation Dept., *Ann. Report* (Kuala Lumpur, Govt. Press, 1950), pp. 25–29; see also Fed. of Malaya, Dept. of Inform., *The Story of Tanjong Karang* (Kuala Lumpur, 1951) and D. S. Ferguson, 'The Sungei Manik Irrigation Scheme', *Mal. J. Trop. Geog.*, vol. ii (1954), pp. 9–16.

[5] See Pelzer, *Pioneer Settlement*, pp. 160–231 and J. H. Boeke, *The Evolution of the Netherlands Indies Economy* (New York, IPR and Neth. Indies Council, 1946), pp. 144–50.

[6] See Wibo Peekema, 'Colonization of Javanese in the Outer Provinces of the Netherlands East-Indies', *Geog. J.*, vol. ci (1943), pp. 145–53.

has attempted to continue the work under a special department; it has found settlers more ready to migrate but faces new problems due, for example, to unsettled conditions and to shortages of shipping and materials.[1] Much attention is now being directed to Borneo.

Very little government-sponsored colonization has been attempted in British territories in the East Indies. The Government of North Borneo has expressed its willingness to receive a number of Indian families.[2]

Finally, mention must be made of schemes in the Philippines, though, once again, little need be said since a number of points about Philippine efforts will be brought out later.[3] Government-sponsored colonization was started in 1913 with the dual motive of relieving pressure in the overcrowded northern islands by establishing settlements in Mindanao, and of 'Filipinizing' the Muslim and pagan inhabitants of that sparsely peopled island. Colonists cultivated both paddy and high land. The Mindanao colonies went through various vicissitudes, but by 1935 some 30,000 or 35,000 people had migrated to them. Then came a period of stocktaking and in 1939 the Philippines, like Ceylon, initiated a 'New Policy'. Nearly 9,000 people were attracted in 1940 by the newly formed 'National Land Settlement Association'. After the liberation, the Association started up again, on very much the same basis as before the war.[4] No outright grants are made to colonists, except for small gifts in kind, but there is a system of loans. Colonists pay their own passages to Mindanao; an exception is made, however, in the case of surrendered 'Huks' (Communist guerrillas), with the result that many peaceful citizens claim to be ex-Huks.

From one point of view, then, the colonization schemes of the Dry Zone of Ceylon may be seen as an example of a phenomenon which appears in one form or another, and on a variety of scales, in most of the countries of Southern Asia; though, with the

---

[1] The author is greatly indebted to the Indonesian Ambassador in London and to his staff for information on post-independence developments and for obtaining additional data from Jakarta.

[2] Information kindly supplied by the Colonial Office.

[3] See Pelzer, *Pioneer Settlement*, pp. 81–159; and J. E. Spencer, *Land and People in the Philippines* (Berkeley and Los Angeles, Univ. of California Press, 1952), pp. 139–50.

[4] Information kindly supplied by the Legation of the Philippines in London.

transference of the unused lands of the Indus to Pakistan, India is beginning to fall out of the list. But from other points of view the Ceylon schemes are unique, not only because their regional setting is unique but because they affect, actually or potentially, so large a proportion of the area of their country and because of the far larger part played in them by government organization and assistance. But it would, for all that, be foolish to view the Ceylon schemes in isolation, and the chapters which follow will frequently compare experiences, problems, and achievements in Ceylon with those of other colonization schemes.

9

Some General Problems of Planning and Preparation in Irrigation and Land Development

THIS chapter will deal with certain problems which must be faced during the process of planning a Dry Zone colony and preparing it for its colonists. A number of aspects of this process can safely be left until their results emerge, as situations facing the colonist, in the ensuing chapters. But there is room for a discussion at the point of two particular groups of problems. The first of these may be defined as the geographical problem of irrigation; that is, irrigation seen as a technique of harnessing the water resources of an area. Some aspects of irrigation, particularly engineering construction, are outside the scope of this book and well beyond the competence of its author; others will come to light later; but this geographical aspect is best seen as a whole and as an issue to be faced before a colony is even planned. Time was in the Dry Zone when population was sparse and immigration negligible, and waste of water therefore tolerable; but, as Chapter 17 will show, it will not now be long before untapped water-supplies begin to run short, so that the problem today is not merely utilization, but utilization to the best possible advantage in terms of irrigated acres per catchment. It is this aspect which will be specially stressed here.

The second group of problems concerns the functions of the Land Development Department, which were outlined in the previous chapter. The numerous preparatory operations carried out by this Department are so characteristic of colonization in Ceylon that it seems worth while to discuss some of the major problems besetting them, notably those of labour, jungle clearing, and finance. (Comparable problems of the Irrigation Department are, however, only given passing reference, for they are by no means so peculiar to Ceylon.)

The Geographical Aspect of Irrigation

The simplest problems in irrigation planning arise when no more is involved than the construction or restoration of a single work, but these are nevertheless fundamental and include such matters as the calculation of the spill required to take the overflow in flood, and computation of the irrigable area. These things are obviously important; an undersized spill can readily lead to breaching of the *bund* in a region like the Dry Zone which is subject to periodical very heavy rains and floods, and knowledge of the irrigable area is a very obvious first requirement in the planning of a colony. A calculation of irrigable area demands knowledge not only of the capacity of the tank or the discharge of the *ela*, but also of the 'duty' which the water is required to undertake; this is usually expressed as the amount of water required per acre to bring a crop to harvest, and is given in acre-feet.[1] The standard duty required of water in the paddy lands of the Dry Zone is 5 acre-feet in *Maha* and $7\frac{1}{2}$ acre-feet in the arid conditions of *Yala*, but in some places the duty, due to wasteful use of water, may rise as high as 14 acre-feet.[2] Work at Maha Illuppallama has shown that 4 acre-feet will, other things being equal, give as good a paddy crop as 10 acre-feet; the Gal Oya Development Board proposed in 1954 to make 4 acre-feet their standard duty for *Maha* paddy, and one of the most urgent tasks if Ceylon's water resources are to be used to the best advantage is to arrive at more economical use of irrigation water.[3] Not, however, that Ceylon stands alone in this respect; complaints of wastage have also come from India and elsewhere.[4]

It is possible that in one respect at least the ancient Sinhalese achieved a fuller use of water resources than has in the recent past been achieved by piecemeal restoration of their works. For whereas today it is usual to plan a tank to ensure annual replenishment, letting excess water in years of heavy rainfall run to waste, some authorities consider that the small spill of ancient tanks is an indication that these works were designed to hold something

---

[1] 1 acre-foot of water is the amount required to cover an acre of land to a depth of 1 foot.

[2] See *WBR*, p. 428 (ii. 200).

[3] Information from Professor Evan Hardy, leader of the F.A.O. team which was in Ceylon in 1951. The author is grateful to Professor Hardy for a number of useful discussions.

[4] Cmd. 3132, pp. 335–7.

approaching the *maximum* discharge.[1] It is possible to read the same idea into the often-quoted words of Parakrama Bahu (1153–86) (though these may well be really an expression of general intention which does not imply the ability to carry that intention out):

It is my chief duty to gather up an abundance of grain by all that lieth in my power. . . . In the kingdom that belongeth to me there are many paddy lands that are watered chiefly by the water from rain clouds; but the fields that depend upon a perpetual supply of water from the rivers and tanks are verily few in number. . . . In a country like unto this not even the least quantity of water that is obtained by rain should be allowed to flow into the ocean without profiting man.[2]

If there was indeed an arrangement for holding up flood waters, there would clearly be the possibility of sowing a greater area in wet years than in average or dry years. It is interesting to speculate whether the greater social cohesion and strong political control in at least parts of ancient times enabled the population to survive dry years not only by practising *bethma*[3] but also by storing grain from good years (there were certainly stern laws making this obligatory); and whether it was *rājakāriya* labour, made surplus by such dry years, which the king fed from the royal granaries and utilized for constructing great works.[4] Certainly a system of maximum utilization of water in wet years, with some provision for dry years (crop insurance is a theoretical modern possibility) is eminently desirable in a country of variable rainfall and river discharge.[5] It is by no means certain, however, that the ancients had the right answer; for there is good evidence that much disastrous breaching of tanks was due to lack of suitable spills, which may have been designed with just this end of maximum storage in view.[6] And, in view of what will be said later on the subject of economic co-operation in colonization schemes it is doubtful whether

[1] See A. P. Weir, 'The Relation between Storage Capacity of Tanks and Catchments', *Trans. Eng. Assoc. Cey.* (1929), pp. 546–8, and J. P. Balfour, Pres. Address to the Engineering Association of Ceylon, ibid. (1914). Recent planning at Gal Oya has been based on the inflow in the three driest consecutive years on record; see GODB, *Ann. Report*, 1952–3, pp. 70–83.

[2] See the *Mahávansa*, pt. 2, trans. L. C. Wijesinha (Colombo, Govt. Printer, 1889), p. 147.

[3] See above, p. 45.

[4] For this concept of *rājakāriya* see Balfour in *Trans. Eng. Assoc. Cey.* (1914).

[5] Since these words were written the Ceylon Government has announced a scheme of crop insurance (see *Ceylon News Letter*, 22 Nov. 1954).

[6] See A. P. Weir, 'Notes on the Investigation and Improvement of Village Tanks', *Trans. Eng. Assoc. Cey.* (1933), pp. 293–328.

society as organized beneath major irrigation schemes today could work the disciplined system which is required. But so important is it to obtain the maximum use from Ceylon's water resources that the matter is worthy of careful thought, and deserves social as well as civil engineering. It is worthy of note that the possibility of conserving flood waters has attracted a great deal of attention in India and Pakistan. The Bhakra-Nangal works inaugurated on 8 July 1954 are, for example, designed to impound and use the monsoon flood of the Sutlej.[1]

So far, the problems and possible improvements which have been considered arise when the guiding principle is piecemeal restoration of individual works. But the early adoption of this principle is likely to lead to three kinds of difficulty when, in the interests of maximum utilization of water, later planning takes in a broader view. The first is a result of the fact that in many places the major ancient works are constructed in the lower parts of river valleys, often to command alluvial lowlands. When new works are constructed higher up the rivers, in the interests of maximum use of the waters, the ancient work, if it has already been restored earlier, may become obsolete, and the capital sunk in it would then be lost. Parakrama Samudra would become obsolete, and its tank bed cultivable, if ever the Sudu Kande reservoir is constructed a little higher up the Amban Ganga. Even if the ancient work does not become obsolete, it may run into difficulties; thus, although the Gal Oya scheme is intended in part to improve irrigation conditions in the fertile coastal lowland area watered by the older Pattipola Aar scheme, it will also cut off the Pattipola Aar fields from the silt which made them fertile. As will be seen, this kind of problem recurs in one form or another in various parts of Ceylon. The point is that it is much more economical to plan the use of a river from source to mouth than from mouth to source. Work can then begin with conservation of soil and water on the watersheds, to reduce siltation and flooding and to provide a more even flow, and it can proceed downstream, from dam to dam until the water is fully utilized. Clearly such planned basin development is likely to be the most economical of capital, since no work is made obsolete by new construction or reconstruction above it, but unforeseen

[1] See, for example, Ritchie Calder, *Men Against the Jungle* (London, Allen & Unwin, 1954), pp. 164–5; and 'The Bhakra-Nangal Project', *Ind. Trade and Industry*, vol. vi (1954), pp. 63–68.

difficulties due to technological changes[1] must always be reckoned with, and planned basin development is a counsel of perfection, demanding a detailed knowledge of a catchment's resources and a complete absence of functioning irrigation works before planning starts.

The second problem concerns the use of channels or *elas*. These, apart from distributaries, were traditionally built to take water from an *anicut* direct to the fields (as at Minipe), or from an *anicut* to a tank (as at Parakrama Samudra), or from one catchment to another (as in the case of the Kala Wewa Yoda Ela). The first method is of abiding value when small patches of irrigable land are scattered along a large river (as on the middle Mahaweli Ganga), or where low relief makes tank construction difficult or wasteful (as on the lower Mahaweli Ganga). It also has the advantage of relative cheapness and of avoiding the worst evils of siltation, since much of the flood load of silt passes over the top of the *anicut*. But so does most of the water, which therefore runs to waste. The second method ensures that some water at least can be stored for the dry season, or even from year to year; but, as with the first method, much water runs over the *anicut*. Both methods are likely to be adversely affected by the construction of great reservoirs, beyond the capabilities of the ancient engineers, higher up the river, except where water from such a reservoir is deliberately led back into a river channel to be tapped lower down by an *anicut*. The third method of *ela* construction seems to have been adopted by the ancient Sinhalese as an *ad hoc* measure when it was desired to augment the water in an existing system; for example, the cleverly engineered Kala Wewa Yoda Ela, the ancient Jaya Ganga, runs from Kala Wewa across the watershed into the next major catchment to the north in order to feed the 'city tanks' (Tissa Wewa and Bassawakkulama) at Anuradhapura, watering fields on the way (see Map 9). Were one planning *de novo*, such a long channel might be justified where there was water but no land in one catchment and land but no water in another; or where Wet Zone water could be diverted into the Dry Zone, as through the excellent Nalanda scheme now under construction. But, because of the capital cost per irrigated acre and the loss of water by evaporation and seepage, any such scheme should be looked at

---

[1] e.g. the ability to construct reservoirs on a site previously beyond the scope of engineers.

twice. It might have been more economical, for instance, if Kala Wewa water had all been used immediately beneath that tank, and not sent to Anuradhapura. It is true that, as things stand, only surplus flood water is sent to the 'city tanks', but Kala Wewa is normally expected to feed fields beneath its Yoda Ela, some of which are as much as 56 miles from the tank.

The third problem encountered when irrigation schemes are based on the piecemeal restoration of ancient works is a result of the fact that one cannot necessarily assume that all the derelict works in a catchment ever functioned simultaneously.[1] There may well not be enough water for all of them if all are restored. The difficulties which have beset the Kala Wewa catchment and system provide a case in point, and one of great relevance here because a number of colonies are involved (see Map 9). Kala Wewa supplies not only lands immediately beneath it (including the two Kagama colonies) but feeds many paddy fields from its Yoda Ela. But, in spite of the fact that the Kagama tracts are today possibly more extensive than in ancient times, it would appear that on balance Kala Wewa is called upon to irrigate a smaller area than in the past; for a number of channels formerly served from it remain disused. Yet Kala Wewa today has difficulty in meeting its commitments although its spill was raised in the 1930's. There may be several factors in this state of affairs, such as loss of capacity due to silting (which is strongly in evidence) and lack of a social and political discipline to enable reduced acreages to be sown in dry years. In spite of the difficulties which have in recent years attended cultivation under Kala Wewa, Dewahuwa Wewa, on the Hawanella Oya which feeds Kala Wewa, has been restored, apparently under local political pressure, and on the assumption that it functioned with Kala Wewa in ancient times and therefore should so function today. As might be expected, Dewahuwa has added to the difficulties of Kala Wewa; it has also been short of water itself. Now it is very doubtful whether the two tanks ever did function together, even under different conditions of siltation and of society. There is an interesting local legend that Dewahuwa was in fact built by the Sinhalese king Duttha Gāmani (Dutu Gemenu, *c.* 161 B.C.) in order to deny water to his Tamil enemies who were then in occupation of the Kala Wewa land, and presumably also to supply his own forces with rice. Still more

[1] See, for example, *WBR*, pp. 414–15 (ii. 191).

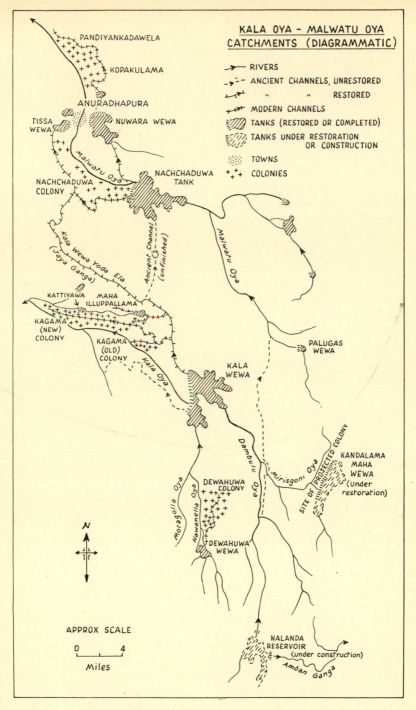

MAP 9. Interlinked Irrigation Works in the Kala Oya and Malwatu Oya
Catchments (diagrammatic) (1951).

water will be abstracted from the Kala Wewa catchment by the restoration of Kandalama Maha Wewa, now nearly complete.[1] It is hoped, however, that this scheme will not be completed until after the construction of the Nalanda reservoir, on the Amban Ganga, which will feed Kala Wewa via a col leading to the Dambulu Oya catchment (this may be an ancient connexion).[2] But it may well be that even with this augmentation Kala Wewa will only be able to water its own fields and those under its Yoda Ela, and would be unable to contribute, through a channel to Nachchaduwa Tank, to a solution of the problems of the Malwatu Oya catchment,[3] at least in the absence of flood-water storage and a strict discipline.

This example, then, brings out not only the particular and complex way in which the water-supplies of a number of colonies are related, but also the important general point that one cannot necessarily restore all ancient works, in any order and under current conditions, on the simple assumption that they all formerly functioned together. Ideally, and given a fresh start, it would be advisable to create the Nalanda reservoir first, then to work downstream in the Amban Ganga and Kala Wewa catchments. In the latter, Kandalama and Dewahuwa should come next, the latter probably on a reduced scale because of the rocky nature of the site; then Kala Wewa should be restored, and full use made of the land under it. Then, and then only, should the possibility of sending water out of the catchment be considered. But all this is an impossible counsel of perfection. Kala Wewa and its lands have been there since 1887; soon afterwards the Yoda Ela was restored, and now Anuradhapura depends on it for much of its water-supply. And Dewahuwa, although it should never have been attempted until Nalanda was completed, is in being. All that can be advised now is that the use of Kandalama should be most carefully considered and that the Kala Wewa catchment must have first call on Nalanda.

In the future planning of irrigation works in Ceylon as a whole all that can in fact be expected, in view of the amount of development that has already taken place, is that the principles of catchment planning and of maximum utilization of water resources

---

[1] Mar. 1953.
[2] See Brohier, *Ancient Irrigation Works*, pt. 2, pp. 5–6.
[3] See below, pp. 232–3.

should be borne in mind, and that the best possible compromise under existing conditions should be arrived at. What is desirable must be reduced to what is practicable.

What has been said about the planning of irrigation in Ceylon is not to be construed as general criticism of at least recent policy. The concept of catchment planning has been a guiding principle for at least a decade;[1] and reviews of the water resources of the whole country have not been lacking.[2] But the Irrigation Department has been sadly hampered by a number of factors, especially lack of fundamental data about river discharges and their variability and about loss by evaporation. There is now an efficient gauging organization, but it is impossible to retrieve quickly the omissions of the past, since river gauging must cover thirty to forty years to be effective. Only about a quarter of the river discharges tabulated by the World Bank mission were based on actual gaugings, and of these only a few went back twenty or thirty years.[3] Evaporation measurements only began in 1951. It will be obvious that until more is known of Ceylon's hydrology no basis exists for the efficient planning of irrigation. The Irrigation Department's forward planning has been further hampered by the heavy strain put upon it by the vastly accelerated scale of its actual construction and maintenance work in recent years, a strain made all the worse by persistent shortages of equipment and of trained men.[4] There is, as the Director of Irrigation and the World Bank mission have pointed out, everything to be said for the establishment of a special Planning Section, undistracted by day-to-day problems; indeed, the same may be said of most government departments concerned with colonization.

Finally, one special problem of irrigation already mentioned a number of times deserves separate consideration. This is the problem of siltation, which has caused a great deal of discussion in Ceylon, particularly in its bearing on the life of the Gal Oya reservoir.[5] Early optimism, based on the mistaken idea that the

[1] See, for example, *Admin. Reports: Irrigation* 1943, p. 4; and *Post-War Development Proposals*, p. 65.
[2] See, for example, M. C. Abraham, 'Water Resources of Ceylon', *Trans. Eng. Assoc. Cey.* (1946), pp. 1–24.
[3] See *WBR*, pp. 403–11 (ii. 183–90).
[4] See *Admin. Reports: Irrigation*; and *Report on the Training of Irrigation Engineers*, S.P. 9 of 1939.
[5] See, for example, Ceylon House of Representatives, *Debates*, vol. x (1951), cols. 973–4 and 1221–2.

Gal Oya catchment was protected by dense jungle, gave way to dismay when the Government's Soil Conservation Officer estimated the useful life of the reservoir as possibly less than twenty years because so much of the catchment was under destructive forms of land use that heavy loads of silt were carried down, especially in heavy storms.[1] A detailed land-use survey was made in May 1950 and showed that only about a fifth of the catchment area was under *damana* or forest, most of the remainder, much of it on steep slopes, being under either *patana* (hill grassland) or under *chena* in various stages of regeneration. It was further considered that periodic burning of the grassland made it singularly liable to erosion, and estimates were made of the erodibility of the various classes of land. But no actual measurements appear to have been made either of the rate of loss from this land or of the load carried by streams. A little later samples were taken by the Irrigation Department in the Gal Oya itself, but not in such a way, or over a long enough period, to be in the least conclusive. In 1951 the Gal Oya Board's own staff reviewed the available observational evidence, and also studied data from other countries, and reached the conclusion that it would require some 1,350 years of siltation to reduce the reservoir's capacity by 50 per cent. This was, in the author's opinion, almost certainly an over-estimate of the time required since it rested, *inter alia*, on a statement in an F.A.O. publication that 'normally with comparable slopes, soils in the tropics are less erosive [*sic*] than those in temperate regions'.[2] This is certainly not true of many tropical soils, including the loose sands resulting from the weathering of the Bintenne gneiss of Gal Oya.

Not surprisingly, opinion became somewhat confused when experts differed in their estimates of the useful life of the reservoir from under twenty to over 1,350 years. The Board wisely decided to have further tests made, and at the same time to go ahead with plans for afforesting parts of the catchment and for ensuring the adoption of less destructive forms of land use in other parts. It may be noted that *patana* burning does not appear to be as destructive

[1] For a general review of the controversy see Brohier, 'Spotlight on Gal Oya', *Ceylon Daily News*, 19 Dec. 1952; see also GODB, *Ann. Report*, 1951–2, pp. 74–83; and R. W. Szechowycz, 'Forests in the Catchment of the Gal Oya Reservoir', *Ceylon Forester* (New Series), vol. i (1953), pp. 58–66. For the original view of the nature of the catchment see *A Report on the Gal Oya Reservoir Scheme*, S.P. 9 of 1948, p. 16.   [2] F.A.O. *Soil Conservation* (Washington, 1948), p. 117.

as was once thought because young shoots soon spring up and slow down run-off. Tests already carried out give a useful life for the reservoir of 450 years, but these are admittedly inconclusive; still more tests are desirable, and there is no room for easy optimism. Now that the reservoir is in existence it will be interesting and useful to watch the rate of delta formation where rivers enter it.

But in spite of the interest in siltation aroused by the Gal Oya controversy, it would appear that insufficient attention is still being paid to this important long-term consideration. Thus the scheme for a reservoir on the Walawe Ganga was going ahead rapidly until the World Bank mission advised caution, on grounds which included the danger of siltation.[1] The author can confirm from personal observation (necessarily, however, qualitative rather than quantitative) that the Walawe's load can be very heavy, and that its headstreams, rising as many of them do in tea estates, are most noticeably discoloured after normal rains. Observations also showed that the area round the Nalanda reservoir site contained many *chenas*, apparently illicit, encouraged by high tobacco prices. Tobacco cultivation is again causing visibly serious erosion in the catchment of Dewahuwa. And the story can be repeated for many other tanks feeding, or about to feed colonization schemes; even on gentle slopes, like those of the Wanni above Iranamadu, gullying is to be seen. The problem appears to be threefold. In the first place, it has been the business of no one in particular to consider the state of soil erosion in the catchment of a proposed new tank. Here is one of the tasks of a Planning Branch of the Irrigation Department or, better, since the problem is part of the broader one of studying existing and potential land use, for a new Department of Land Use Survey like that now so successfully operated in the Gold Coast.[2] A survey of siltation in existing tanks would also be very informative. In the second place there is the question of forest policy.[3] Some forest reserves are so sited that they protect watersheds, and the mapping-out of forests for purposes of conservation was envisaged by the Land Commission

---

[1] See *WBR*, pp. 431–2 (ii. 202–3).

[2] See also below, p. 347 and see C. F. Charter, *Methods of Soil Survey in Use in the Gold Coast* (Boma, Belgian Congo, 1948). Cf. *Soil Conservation and Land Use in Sierra Leone* (Freetown, Govt. Printer, 1951).

[3] See *Admin. Reports: Forests*, also W. M. McNeil, 'Land Planning in Ceylon with Special Reference to the Selection and Reservation of Forest Areas', *Emp. Forestry J.*, vol. xviii (1939), pp. 65–73.

and by the Land Development Ordinance. But most forest reserves in Ceylon have been in fact located by a combination of accident and of the economic attraction of good stands of timber. Forest Officers today are noticeably aware of the need for further conservational reserves, and modern schemes envisage the resiting of forest reserves as part of a general process of catchment planning; but it is not easy to rearrange the landscape when either commercial estates or *chena*-practising peasants are in occupation. Locally, as in the hill range of Sudu Kande which overlooks Parakrama Samudra and Giritale and threatens to send silt into them, they are able to recommend the reservation of a considerable area for conservational reasons. But even where there are practical difficulties it is very necessary to watch most carefully the preservation of forests on hills in tank catchments, and the afforestation of bare places. In the third place, the effects of siltation can be minimized by carefully planned irrigation works. A string of tanks on a river may, for example, be preferable to one huge reservoir, though possibly more costly.

These, then, are some of the main difficulties which attend any effort to achieve maximum use of the water resources of even a single catchment for irrigation purposes, difficulties which are already affecting the colonist directly in such colonies as Dewahuwa and Kagama and which will affect his descendants even more. Ceylon is at once an old country and a new country. Because it is an old country, there are all the difficulties due to the existence of ancient and restored works, which are not necessarily compatible with modern catchment planning nor efficient compared with works which can now be constructed; and there are also difficulties, such as excessive siltation, due to established settlement and land-use patterns, modified it is true by recent demographic trends. Because it is also a new country, it so far lacks the detailed and accurate knowledge both of its resources and of their present use which is essential to wise planning. Few needs in Ceylon are greater than the need for research, and this is especially true of research concerned with the utilization of land and water resources.

Problems of Land Development

When the Irrigation Department has done its planning and prepared the final B.O.P.,[1] there steps on to the scene the Department

[1] See above, pp. 170-1.

of Land Development; concerned as it is with preparation rather than planning, its problems are immediate and practical rather than long term and theoretical; and its task is the essentially straight-forward one of working on a plan already prepared.[1] That is not to say that the work of the Land Development Department is unimportant; it is fundamental to the scale of aid considered necessary for the Ceylon colonist; its methods can have important repercussions on soil conservation; and the rate at which it can work is an important limiting factor to the speed at which coloniza-tion can be accomplished.[2] And very much the same is true of the corresponding branches of the Gal Oya Development Board. The broad organization of the Department and of the relevant branches of the Board having already been discussed,[3] the rest of this chap-ter will be devoted to problems of labour, method and cost in the actual work of land development, house building, and so on.

It will be clear from the accounts which have been given of early efforts at organized jungle clearing such as those at Minipe[4] that the recruitment and maintenance of a labour force was then a most difficult matter. The situation in 1951 was certainly easier in some ways, particularly because of improved malaria control and because of the greater mobility of labour due to the war and to improvements in transport; but the accelerated voluntary emigration of squatters and others to the vicinity of the colonies was not paralleled by a commensurate movement of labour willing to work in jungle clearing. For the jungle is still a much more unpleasant place than a cleared area, and in its conquest it is the land-development labourer who is today the true pioneer. In many schemes the shortage of unskilled labour was serious; there was an even more serious shortage of skilled workers, particularly masons and carpenters, and of supervisors.

Apart from the employment of contractors for a very small pro-portion of the house construction (less than $\frac{1}{2}$ per cent. in 1951), ordinary contractors are no longer used by the Land Development Department. Certain special agencies, essentially Co-operative labour societies whose members work for a wage and also earn any dividends that are declared, are, however, used on contract in

---

[1] The author is most grateful to Mr. M. Srikhanta, formerly Director of Land Development, for the benefit of a number of valuable discussions.

[2] *WBR*, p. 425 (ii. 198–9).　　　　[3] See above, pp. 169–74.

[4] See above, pp. 154–5.

land-development work. These are the Essential Services Labour Corps Co-operative Labour Society Limited, and the Ex-Royal Pioneer Corps Society.[1] They consist respectively of former members of the Essential Services Labour Corps, a war-time body which did valuable work in maintaining essential services and supplying the labour demands of the Royal Navy at Trincomalee; and of the Royal Pioneer Corps. Both function largely under their former military officers, and have done useful work not only in supplying labour in a critical field for the country, but in providing employment for their members and hence easing the transition from war to peace which has proved difficult for so many newly mobile Oriental and African peoples.[2] The view has been expressed, however, that the work done by these bodies cannot be so efficiently supervised and controlled as that done by the Land Development Department, though their efficiency is said to be increasing.

The land-development work and other activities of the Gal Oya Board have also been hampered by shortage of labour, both skilled and unskilled. As in the case of the Land Development Department, the shortage of skilled artisans has been particularly acute. Thus the requirements of the Board in September 1951 were stated to be 2,000 masons and 1,650 carpenters, but only 837 masons and 1,912 carpenters had registered themselves for employment with the Labour Department in the whole island, and by no means a large proportion of these were willing to travel to Gal Oya.[3] The Board had a training scheme for various categories of technical personnel, but the difficulty of recruiting artisans was a grave one. It was partly a matter of increased opportunity for employment in the Wet Zone in both government works and in the then booming estate industries, partly a matter of the rate of Dry Zone development generally; but it must also be remembered that the artisan is not honoured in traditional Sinhalese society, and few from higher castes would be willing to join his ranks.

Turning to methods of jungle clearing, the outstanding feature of the work of the Land Development Department is that it is still essentially based on the techniques of the Dry Zone cultivator. As

[1] The author is grateful to Mr. G. L. Kotelawala for information on the Essential Services Labour Corps.

[2] The same may be said of the Ex-Service Men's Colony at Parakrama Samudra.

[3] See *Ceylon Daily News*, 27 Sept. 1951.

in a *chena*, clearing goes on in the dry weather, and the burning of the felled timber and brushwood takes place just before the rains. (As much useful timber as possible is extracted, but there is inevitably some waste, particularly of firewood.) The wet season is occupied mainly with stumping and ridging. There is mechanical transport, and a relatively small number of tractors and other machines, but in both the Department and the special agencies the emphasis is on manual labour. The Gal Oya Development Board, on the other hand, is much more in favour of mechanical methods. Jungle is cleared largely by the technique evolved in the East African groundnuts scheme.[1] A heavy ship's cable is attached at each end to a pair of caterpillar tractors in tandem; the two pairs of tractors move through previously cleared parallel lanes in the jungle, and most of the jungle trees are easily pulled over as the cable moves in a loop behind them. Some of those which resist are pushed over by two roving tree-dozers, known appropriately as 'scrum-halves', but some large trees are left to provide shade. The machines are worked entirely and with great skill by Ceylonese operators, and it is exciting and impressive to see a great swath being mown through high jungle. Afterwards the debris is piled in wind rows along the contour as a conservation measure, and later burnt (in the case of potential paddy fields) or left as a continuing check on erosion, as a source of humus, and as firewood (in the case of potential high land). Between 50 and 125 acres can be cleared in a day by a team attending two pairs of tractors and a cable. Mechanical equipment such as bulldozers is also used for ridging and levelling potential paddy fields.

At first sight it might be thought that the Gal Oya mechanical technique was impressively superior to the mainly manual technique practised elsewhere, but the matter is not as simple as that and, in view of the interest in mechanical methods of land development in Ceylon and elsewhere (e.g. in Pakistan's Thal scheme), it may be worth reviewing some of the arguments for and against them. In the first place, there can be no doubt that mechanical methods are much quicker and that they are more efficient in terms of output per man-hour. It was just because of the need for speed and of an expected labour shortage that they were adopted at Gal Oya. It may be that they will have to be adopted elsewhere

[1] Great Britain, Overseas Food Corporation, *Ann. Report and Statement of Accounts for Period ending March 31, 1939* (London, HMSO, 1949), p. 17.

in Ceylon and in Southern Asia where speed of development is slowed down by a lack of available labour which can, of course, easily coexist in a peasant society with chronic under-employment.

On the other hand, mechanical clearing is not necessarily cheaper. The approximate average cost per acre of the three main operations undertaken manually by the Land Development Department and its agencies was stated in 1951 to be Rs. 135, Rs. 105, and Rs. 200 for felling and burning, ridging, and stumping respectively (the sterling equivalents of these three figures are, roughly, £10, £8, and £15);[1] the actual cost, of course, varied from scheme to scheme, according to the nature of the jungle and of the local topography. These figures may not be reliable, but, if they are, the total approximate cost per acre of the three essential processes was Rs. 440 (or about £34). No figures have been published by the Gal Oya Development Board of the cost of clearing by their method, but in 1951 it was claimed that felling and burning could be done for Rs. 86–106 per acre (cf. Rs. 135 by hand), and rooting, roughly equivalent to stumping, for Rs. 34 per acre (cf. Rs. 105 by hand). These would appear on the face of it to establish the supremacy of the machine. On the other hand, inquiry suggests that the figures for mechanical means made no adequate allowance for maintenance and depreciation, which are excessively heavy under tropical conditions, as the Overseas Food Corporation found to their cost.[2] Cables, tracks, and other parts in contact with the heavily quartzitic soil abrade very quickly, repairs are often needed, and maintenance may be slipshod. Adequate cost accounting might well suggest that, with wage rates as they were in 1951, and, with the relatively poor maintenance facilities, the machine is dearer than the man. That this is so is suggested by the fact that the figure quoted by an American contractor as the bare cost of mechanical clearing (exclusive of profit) was said to be Rs. 660 per acre, 50 per cent. more than the average cost of the same processes as quoted by the Land Development Department.[3] Moreover, the total cost of clearing, ridging, and stumping by hand in

[1] See *ARDLD*, 1951, Schedule A, p. 20.
[2] See Great Britain, Overseas Food Corporation, *Ann. Report for Period ending March 31, 1949*, p. 9.
[3] For the maintenance problem at Gal Oya see C. S. L. Frances, 'Some Notes on Machine Management on Large-scale Land-Development Projects', *Trans. Eng. Assoc. Cey.* (1953).

Ceylon was almost exactly that which has been given for clearing alone by mechanical means in the Terai.[1]

Some doubt must also be expressed about the wisdom of thorough-going mechanization from the point of view of soil conservation. The contour wind-rows of the mechanized method are of course good conservation devices, but they are not necessarily functions of the machine; they could easily be produced by manual methods. In any case, there are certain disadvantages in the wind-row; decaying wood tends to harbour insect and reptile pests.[2] But the main evil likely to be effected by indiscriminate mechanization arises not so much from jungle clearing as from land preparation by bulldozers and similar devices. Anyone in the least familiar with the fact that tropical soils hold what little humus they have in the top few inches, and aware of the ease with which their structure may be destroyed, is bound to have the gravest misgivings when he sees them being pushed around by great machines as though their composition were constant throughout and as though their structure were proof against rough treatment. This is particularly true in the sandy soil of Gal Oya, and it will be small consolation to the authorities if they achieve the fastest rate of development in the island, only to find that the soil is ruined, or at least gravely affected. Much more care and much more research are needed, and the example of the Terai scheme, where an ecologist worked with the bulldozers, might be followed.

Nevertheless, it cannot be denied that speed is an important criterion in a country with a rapidly increasing population and an unstable external economy. As has already been said, it is the rate at which land-development work can be undertaken which may well be a factor limiting the rate of colonization. It is therefore vitally necessary to use speedy methods, provided that they can be afforded, provided that sufficient allowance is made for depreciation and maintenance, and provided that research devises a method which does not harm the soil.

[1] See Calder, *Men Against the Jungle*, pp. 147–8.
[2] Cf. Ferguson, in *Mal. J. Trop. Geog.*, vol. ii (1954), p. 13.

10

The Selection of Peasant Colonists

WHEN the work of the irrigation engineers and of the Land Development Officers is nearing completion, there arises, under the present system in the Dry Zone of Ceylon, the important problem of selecting the peasant colonists who shall occupy the completed allotments. In describing methods of selection which are used today under conditions of increasing peasant mobility, the question of their efficiency in realizing the two aims underlying present policies is considered. However, of these two aims that of alleviating agrarian distress is given fuller attention than that of increasing the production of food, and an attempt is made to discover if present methods of selection do, in fact, alleviate distress where it is most keenly felt. It is possible to show the ways in which present methods of selection are or are not likely to select efficient producers, but whether such producers are in fact selected is a question which cannot be decided in advance of the discussion which will be given in the chapters which follow. The mutual compatibility of the two aims, about which various critics have expressed doubts, cannot properly be considered until the final chapter of this book.

Selection in the Older Colonies

It will be apparent from what has been said in Chapter 7 that the problem of selection hardly arose in the colonization schemes of the early 1930's, such as Minneriya, Nachchaduwa, and Kagama Old; the problem was one of persuasion rather than selection. Settlers in a colony tended to come mainly from regions not very far from it, though there were individuals and small groups from most parts of the island, and a characteristic of such colonies as Tabbowa is the astonishing mixture of communities and creeds.[1] It cannot be doubted that the early colonists included many unsuitable types, including criminals, fugitives, and ne'er-do-wells

---

[1] See *Village Survey: Puttalam*, p. 44; the statement is also based on the author's field observations.

and a number of men with no great knowledge of agriculture. Theoretically the Land Kachcheries considered capacity to develop the land, agricultural experience, character, and physical fitness;[1] but in practice the number of applicants was often so small that these principles could not be applied if allotments were to be tenanted at all. However, some good cultivators were selected, and some of the criminals became reformed; the author met at Tabbowa an engaging character, apparently a good colonist, who had spent twenty-one years in the Andamans for murder.

There is the further point that many of the unsatisfactory colonists deserted early on, so that their inefficiency is not there to be observed in the colonies today. But desertion was a very serious problem at the time, meaning as it did the expense and effort of selecting a new colonist and installing him in his allotment. No fewer than 53 of the 124 colonists selected at Minneriya in 1938 had abandoned their allotments by the following year; and many of the present colonists at Kagama Old Colony are the third or fourth to occupy their allotments. It must not be thought, however, that desertion is a fault peculiar to the Ceylonese colonist of the 1930's. A similar problem existed in the early colonies in Sumatra and Mindanao;[2] and there was considerable desertion and absenteeism in the Punjab, for example in the Lower Chenab Colony.[3]

At the time of the inauguration of the 'New Policy' in 1939 there were signs of a greater willingness to migrate, in spite of the fact that malaria remained unconquered. In 1938 the Land Commissioner was able to report that the demand for land at Minneriya exceeded the supply, and that Nachchaduwa had become popular. And in 1940 over 2,000 applications were received from landless peasants in the nearby Kandyan Divisions of Uda and Pata Dumbara for lands at Minipe.[4] The increasing popularity of the colonization schemes meant the beginning of more systematic selection, and in particular of the practice of drawing colonists from defined source areas. Thus the Committee on the Minipe scheme recommended that colonists there should come only from Uda and Pata Dumbara:[5] and it was originally intended to choose colonists for

[1] Ibid., pp. 33–34.
[2] See Pelzer, *Pioneer Settlement*, pp. 132 and 198.
[3] See *Punjab Colony Manual*, i. 12 and 72.
[4] See *Report on the Minipe Yoda-ela Scheme*, p. 5.   [5] Ibid.

the first tracts of Parakrama Samudra from Anuradhapura and Batticaloa Districts only.

The Modern Attitude to Migration

Gradually there developed the new peasant mobility which has already been commented on. Increasing pressure on the land, forcing labour for hire and movement away from home on a peasantry which had hated and despised these things; war-time opportunities for military service or employment in remote places; the increasing popularity of the motor bus; the attention given to the Dry Zone and to the colonies in the vernacular press; and above all the victory of DDT over endemic malaria, made the Sinhalese peasant, even the Kandyan peasant, more ready to migrate; the Jaffna Tamil peasant is, however, still chary, as are peasants in Kalutara District and other areas from which few colonists have hitherto been selected and where there is no tradition of migration. And, after 1939, there was the attractive and increasing scale of aid offered to the colonist. (It is interesting that a similar new mobility is reported from other Asian countries, notably Indonesia and the Philippines.[1]) But the spontaneity of the new mobility must not be exaggerated; it has been enforced by circumstances. Kandyan colonists bound for Parakrama Samudra wept as they left their villages in 1951,[2] and there is evidence that movement to a colony is a counsel of despair if status is lost by leaving ancestral homes for a mixed-caste community.

One by-product of the new mobility and of the new attractiveness of the Dry Zone has been a considerable increase in the amount of illicit encroachment on Crown land. 'Squatting' is, of course, a common phenomenon in most countries with unoccupied land and a reasonably mobile population and is no new occurrence in Ceylon. But organized colonization, by providing communications, employment, and trade and by reducing fear of the unknown, often stimulates squatting. This has been the experience in a number of Asian regions (notably in Iraq, the Punjab, and the Philippines).[3]

Squatters in and around the Dry Zone colonies are of two

[1] The author is indebted to the Indonesian Embassy and to the Philippine Legation in London for information on postwar conditions in their respective countries.   [2] *Ceylon Daily News*, 4 Oct. 1951.

[3] See Fisk, in *Econ. Geog.*, vol. xxviii, p. 346; *Punjab Colony Manual*, i. 50; and Pelzer, *Pioneer Settlement*, p. 134.

categories. The first category is made up of *boutique*-keepers and other petty traders, mainly Low Country Sinhalese, who set up rickety *cadjan* stalls along the main roads of most colonies, usually in Crown jungle reserved for conservation or as a roadside margin, and sometimes, one suspects, with the tacit approval or even the connivance of colonization officers and village headmen; in the large schemes there are whole streets of these *boutiques* (see Plate 14). These squatters provide a considerable administrative problem; they break the law, they destroy amenities and conservational requirements, and they encourage habits of usury and debt. Yet they provide a very necessary medium of retail trade and, like the European café and pub, supply crude social centres. It is no answer merely to bulldoze them away. They exist largely because the Government has not so far provided sufficient shops and other buildings for service occupations, nor controlled private enterprise wishing to enter this field. This omission is one example of the general neglect of social considerations to which further attention will be directed in Chapters 14 and 15.

The second category of squatters in colonies is made up of Sinhalese who hope to work as labourers for colonists or in land development, or to procure an *ande* tenancy (though this is forbidden under the Land Development Ordinance), or, somehow, to obtain an allotment themselves. These people build huts for themselves in patches of uncleared land in the larger colonies, and usually clear a patch of jungle to cultivate *chena* crops or, if possible, a little paddy fed by rain-water or by water derived by seepage from an irrigation channel. In not a few cases the diligence and skill of these illicit migrants shows up the work of the official colonists. Cultivating and labouring squatters are particularly prominent in the Tamankaduwa colonies. There were said to be no less than 5,000 families (probably 30,000 individuals) squatting at Minneriya in 1951; and there were, it seems, some 600 families at Parakrama Samudra. Once again, the problem is a grave one for the authorities, especially as havoc is wrought on carefully designed systems of wind-belts and protective jungle. Occasionally the situation becomes ugly. In September 1951, for example, squatters in Parakrama Samudra Colony, becoming desperate because they had not been considered for allotments at a Land Kachcheri and because land-development work, on which they had largely depended, was closing down, threatened to occupy new colonists' houses by force. The whole phenomenon of squatting in the modern Dry Zone is, however, far more than a mere nuisance to the administrator. It is a symptom of current change, of the new mobility, of the mounting pressure in the overcrowded areas; and it is, in many ways, an effect of the success of the policy of Dry Zone colonization, which has done so much to dispel the Dry Zone bogey.

Another result of the same group of forces is the rapid decline in the practice, so frequent twenty years ago, of abandoning allotments. There are still desertions due to special reasons, but the wholesale flight characteristic of the original Minneriya is a thing of the past. Even at luckless Pandiyankadawela, which received no irrigation water in the first two years of its existence (1949–51),[1] the colonists stood firm.

In fact, the new forces at work have created an entirely novel situation to which policy has not yet properly adjusted itself. The problem is no longer to attract settlers to the Dry Zone, but to control the flood of peasants who wish to move there. One very important aspect of this control must under existing policy be the selection of colonists, for there are now always many more applicants at any time than there are holdings. For instance, there were 7,000 applicants for twenty-five allotments reserved for parts of the Western Province in 1950, and it took twelve days to hold a Land Kachcheri; this example can be matched with others drawn from many parts of the island. In these circumstances the machinery of selection becomes a matter of fundamental importance.

The Modern Machinery of Selection

When allotments become available, the Land Commissioner prepares a scheme for their allocation. The first item in his calculations is the reservation of allotments to meet the needs of some at least of the peasants who have been dispossessed of their lands because they were required for irrigation or other works, or in order to avoid the inclusion in the colony of small parcels of private land whose irrigation and administration might cause difficulty. Peasants whose lands have been so acquired by the Government receive compensation in cash, but it is obviously right and proper to allow those who are left landless to qualify for allotments

[1] See below, pp. 232–3.

in the new scheme. Colonists who have received allotments in this way are included under the heading 'Compensation' in Table 19.

The next category to be provided for is made up of other members of the local peasantry who are landless or nearly so (the numbers included under the heading 'Local' in Table 19 are those from the D.R.O.'s Division or Divisions in which the colony concerned is situated). It is an established principle in the Ceylon colonies that an effort should be made to meet local needs before calling in outsiders.[1] (The same principle has been widely used elsewhere, e.g. in Sind.[2])

An allocation may also be made, particularly in the bigger schemes, to labourers who have worked for at least 500 days in preparing the scheme; many of these are outsiders, some of them are squatters who have moved to the colony in the hope of qualifying for an allotment. (Colonists in this category are included under 'Labourers' in Table 19.)

Finally, the remaining lots are allocated to those often considered to be primarily entitled to allotments, namely landless peasants from overcrowded areas away from the colony. (Colonists in this category, who came from D.R.O.'s Divisions other than that in which their colony was situated, are shown under 'Immigrant' in Table 19.) The modern practice is for the source districts of these immigrant colonists to be selected by the Land Commissioner from overcrowded regions in which there is insufficient local Crown land for adequate village expansion schemes. The allocation to D.R.O.'s Divisions within these districts is made by the Local Revenue Officer. The number of lots available for immigrants from overcrowded areas in general has tended to be relatively small in recent years, partly owing to generous allocations to the categories previously mentioned, partly owing to the need to reserve some 475 lots for refugees from Kotmale, which had been badly hit by landslides, and partly because nearly 600 lots in Parakrama Samudra were reserved for ex-servicemen. Many of the latter in fact came from overcrowded rural areas but some were townsmen (not normally eligible) and in any case none were chosen according to a definite plan to relieve pressure in specific regions where relief was needed.

When the Land Commissioner's scheme for the allocation of available lots between categories of colonist and, where necessary,

[1] *KPC*, p. 99.   [2] Cmd. 3132, pp. 356–8.

between source areas has been submitted to and approved by the Minister, it becomes the duty of the Revenue Officers in the source area of each category to invite applications from suitable candidates. These applications are made in a standard form, the applicant being asked questions about his family, lands already held, and so on, and applications are generally required to be submitted during the August before the *Maha* in which alienations are to be made. Each application form is then sent out by the Kachcheri to the D.R.O.'s of the applicant's home area, so that Village Headmen may check the details given and report especially on the applicant's character and ability as a cultivator. When the forms are returned to the Kachcheri it is generally possible to weed out a fair proportion of applicants as prima facie ineligible; the remainder are then summoned to a Land Kachcheri.

The qualifying condition which an applicant must satisfy if he is to be successful at a Land Kachcheri is that he should be landless or at any rate have very little land. Those who qualify by this test are then rated according to their apparent ability to develop the land and to produce food from it; age, physical condition, number of grown-up or adolescent children who can help, and reputation as a cultivator are clearly relevant considerations. There may, however, be special cases; the author witnessed a Land Kachcheri for local villagers at Dewahuwa (see Plate 13) where special attention was given to applications from a village which had a small and most unsatisfactory tank, and where there was a sorry record of deaths from malnutrition and from enteric and other fevers. And in the case of special categories there are additional considerations; it must be ascertained, for example, that labourers really have worked their 500 days, and that compensation cases are genuine.

Land Kachcheries are governed by three main principles: that the conditions on which land will be granted shall be clearly explained at the outset; that all applicants shall be present in person, able to witness the whole proceedings, and able to complain about any application or decision which they claim to be falsely based (M.P.s, Chairmen of local government bodies, and Presidents of Rural Development Societies are also invited to attend to see fair play); and that all decisions shall wherever practicable be made by the Revenue Officer on the spot, his reasons being announced to the assembled company.

Each applicant is interviewed in order to check his statements and those of his Headman in the hearing of his fellows, and those disqualified through being proved ineligible are first ruled out (as are absentees). Successive eliminations are then made, until the successful candidates remain. Detailed procedure varies slightly, but within an established framework, with the locality and Revenue Officer. Thus Jaffna District peasants thought to be 'doubtfully competent' as potential colonists at Iranamadu (Paranthan) were considered by a special board consisting of the Assistant Government Agent and the Divisional Agricultural Officer, and the D.R.O.s were required to check applications personally and not to rely on Headmen. Colonists for Gal Oya are selected in the usual way by the Revenue Officers of source areas, but at one time it was proposed that an officer of the Development Board should sit with the Revenue Officer; and the conditions for selection have been codified thus: 'The applicants must be peasant villagers who are genuine cultivators, physically fit and of good character, and have at least two children over 8 years of age.'[1]

Sources for and Reliability of Tables 19, 20, and 21

The final section of this chapter will take the form of a critical examination of the methods of selection currently used in Ceylon. It is first necessary, however, to outline the sources on which Tables 19, 20, and 21 are based, and to discuss their reliability. Certain figures in the tables are based on published sources: the numbers of V.E. allotments shown in Table 20 are based on the Administration Reports of the Land Commissioner, 1949–51, supplemented by figures for 1952–3 kindly supplied by the Land Commissioner; and the populations and cultivated areas in Table 21 are based on the Census returns noted at the foot of the tables. But the only comprehensive published figures of numbers of colonists merely give the total for each colony.[2] The author pieced the remaining statistics together partly from occasional mentions in published sources, but mainly by inquiry in the field and in Kachcheries and, in the last resort, by inquiry at the Land Commissioner's office ('in the last resort' because one hesitated to put an over-worked department to the trouble of a tedious search).

The statistics as they appear in the table are not completely reliable because, in a number of cases, they represent a compromise between two or more versions, which differed for a

---

[1] See GODB. *Ann. Report*, 1951–2, p. 53.   [2] See *ARLC.*

number of reasons: e.g. the tendency of some Colonization Officers and other officials to 'please' the inquirer by giving the first figure that came into their head rather than confess ignorance, and the

TABLE 19

Origin of Peasant Colonists by Categories (to 31 December 1953)

Colony	Selected by source area		Otherwise selected			Total
	Immi-grant	Local	Com-pensation	Labourers	Others	
1. Allai . . .	276	177	..	115	..	568
2. Attaragalla . .	91	219	..	..	..	310
3. Bathmedilla . .	106	179	..	3	..	288
4. Beragama (Malay) .	..	65	..	..	..	65
5. Beragama . . .	51	221	..	..	..	272
6. Dewahuwa . .	142	91	150	70	..	453
7. Elahera . . .	660	113	11	119	..	903
8. Gal Oya . . .	1,758	1,507	300	..	..	3,565
9. Giritale . .	25	65	..	11	..	101
10. Huruluwewa .	653	181	217	..	..	1,051
11. Iranamadu (Kil.) .	61	..	..	..	..	61
12. Iranamadu (Par.) .	503	77	..	15	..	595
13. Kagama (Old) . .	..	..	..	..	216	216
14. Kagama (New) .	136	229	75	76	..	516
15. Kantalai . . .	348	302	..	92	..	742
16. Kottu Kachchiya .	85	40	..	..	..	125
17. M. Kumbukkadawala.	28	22	..	..	..	50
18. Maha Uswewa . .	..	50	..	..	..	50
19. Minipe . . .	45	447	..	..	..	492
20. Minneriya . .	360	54·	..	112	615	1,141
21. Nachchaduwa .	..	..	..	..	820	820
22. Okkampitiya .	83	71	..	..	..	154
23. Pandiyankadawela .	..	36	40	..	..	76
24. Parakrama Samudra .	1,198	483	178	350	571	2,780
25. Ridibendi Ela . .	165	183	..	10	..	358
26. Sangilikanadarawa .	..	49	..	..	..	49
27. Soraborawewa . .	..	117	..	..	..	117
28. Tabbowa . . .	..	..	..	..	240	240
29. Unnichchai . .	67	237	..	20	..	324
30. Uriyawa . . .	..	50	..	..	..	50
Totals . . .	6,841	5,265	971	993	2,462	16,532
Percentage of totals .	41	32	6	6	15	100

Sources and note on reliability: see pp. 207–8; explanation of categories: see p. 205; full name of colonies: see Table 16, p. 165.

confusion created by desertions, cancellations, and reallotments. Compromise and adjustment were inevitable; but the result is not thought to be seriously in error; the largest numbers (those for the most recent years) are the most reliable.

TABLE 20

Distribution by Districts of Colonists Selected by Source Area to 31 December 1953

| Colony | Wet Zone Districts | | | | | | | | | | | | Dry Zone Districts | | | | | | | | Total |
| | Low Country | | | | | | Up-country | | | | | | | | | | | | | | |
	Colombo	Kalu-tara	Galle	Matara	Chilaw	Kuru-negala	Kandy	Matale	N. Eliya	Badulla	Ratna-pura	Ke-galla	A'pura	Vavu-niya	Jaffna	B'caloa	Trinco	Man-nar	Putt'm	H'tota	Total
1	..	..	..	..	..	105*	25	..	25	..	..	..	80	..	..	..	218*	..	..	..	453
2	..	..	..	..	..	310	..	..	..	..	..	..	..	..	..	..	..	..	..	..	310
3	..	..	..	..	..	..	..	..	..	285*	..	..	..	..	..	..	..	..	..	..	285
4	..	..	..	..	..	..	..	..	..	..	..	..	..	..	..	..	..	..	..	65*	65
5	..	..	..	..	..	..	..	..	..	..	..	..	..	..	..	..	..	..	..	272*	272
6	22	..	..	..	57	..	43	20*	..	..	..	..	91*	..	..	..	..	..	..	..	233
7	68	..	..	..	..	..	79	626*	..	..	..	..	..	..	..	..	..	..	..	..	773
8	113	..	..	..	20	..	413	..	117	250*	..	575	..	..	..	1,602*	..	..	..	175	3,265
9	..	..	..	..	..	..	..	..	..	..	..	25	65*	..	..	..	..	..	..	..	90
10	..	..	..	..	..	45	189	150	50	..	..	..	400*	..	..	..	..	..	..	..	834
11	..	..	..	..	..	..	..	..	..	..	..	..	..	..	61*	..	..	..	..	..	61
12	..	..	..	..	..	..	..	..	..	..	..	..	..	..	580*	..	..	..	..	..	580
13	..	..	..	..	..	..	..	..	..	..	..	..	..	..	..	..	..	..	..	..	0
14	48	..	..	..	..	..	2	1	..	..	..	..	313*	..	..	1	..	..	..	..	365
15	100	..	..	..	..	..	..	..	200	..	..	..	..	..	..	..	350*	..	..	..	650
16	..	..	..	..	25	..	..	..	..	..	..	..	..	..	..	..	..	..	100*	..	125
17	..	..	..	..	28	..	..	..	..	..	..	..	..	..	..	..	..	..	22*	..	50
18	..	..	..	..	..	..	..	..	..	..	..	..	..	..	..	..	..	..	50*	..	50
19	..	..	..	..	..	..	492*	..	..	..	..	..	..	..	..	..	..	..	..	..	492
20	..	..	..	..	..	..	..	..	255	..	..	105	54*	..	..	..	..	..	..	..	414
21	..	..	..	..	..	..	..	..	..	..	..	..	..*	..	..	..	..	..	..	..	0
22	..	..	..	..	..	..	..	..	..	154*	..	..	..	..	..	..	..	..	..	..	154
23	..	..	..	..	..	..	..	..	..	..	..	..	36*	..	..	..	..	..	..	..	36
24	206	..	20	..	..	54	286	..	369	..	..	263	483	..	..	..	..	..	..	..	1,681
25	..	..	..	..	..	348*	..	..	..	..	..	..	..	..	..	..	..	..	..	..	348
26	..	..	..	..	..	..	..	..	..	..	..	..	49*	..	..	..	..	..	..	..	49
27	..	..	..	..	..	..	..	..	..	117*	..	..	..	..	..	..	..	..	..	..	117
28	..	..	..	..	..	..	..	..	..	..	..	..	..	..	..	..	..	..	..*	..	0
29	..	..	..	..	..	..	..	..	..	..	..	..	..	..	..	304*	..	..	..	..	304
30	..	..	..	..	..	..	..	..	..	..	..	..	..	..	..	..	..	..	50*	..	50
Totals	557	..	20	..	130	862	1,529	797	1,016	806	..	968	1,571	..	641	1,907	568	..	222	512	12,106
Percentage	5	..	0	..	1	7	13	7	8	7	..	8	13	..	5	16	5	..	2	4	100

Comparative table: Peasant V.E. Allotments alienated 1949–53

	Colombo	Kalu-tara	Galle	Matara	Chilaw	Kuru-negala	Kandy	Matale	N. Eliya	Badulla	Ratna-pura	Ke-galla	A'pura	Vavu-niya	Jaffna	B'caloa	Trinco	Man-nar	Putt'm	H'tota	Total
No.	2,937	8,727	8,254	1,993	3,494†	6,506	2,535	3,621	1,199	3,750	4,094	916	15,423	5,885	1,588	5,114	3,216	1,714	‡	8,307	89,273
Percentage	3	10	9	2	4	7	3	4	1	4	5	1	17	7	2	6	3	2	‡	9	100

* Local District or Districts of Colony.
† Figures includes those for Puttalam District.
‡ Figures included in those for Chilaw District.

Sources and note on reliability: see pp. 207–8; full names of districts: see Tables 2 and 9, pp. 57, 83. (Anuradhapura District is here taken to include Tamankaduwa, now Polonnaruwa District); names of colonies here represented by numbers: see Table 19, p. 208.

The terms used in Table 19 have for the most part been explained. It should, however, be noted that the column headed 'Other' includes the ex-service colonists at Parakrama Samudra, and colonists in early (1928–33) colonies; neither category was deliberately chosen to represent certain source areas. (Some aban-

TABLE 21

Indices of Agrarian Pressure Compared with Allocation of Allotments in Colonies and V.E. Schemes

District	Indices of agrarian pressures				Allocation of allotments		
	(a) Rural popn. (000) 1946	(b) Rural popn. per cultd. acre 1946	(c) % Landless	(d) % Holdings < 1 acre	Colonies to 1953 (inc.)	V.E. 1949–53	Total
Colombo .	830	2·5	14·2	68·0	557	2,937	3,494
Kalutara .	366	2·6	22·0	44·9	..	8,727	8,727
Galle .	384	2·6	20·0	48·9	20	8,254	8,274
Matara .	303	2·0	20·2	37·4	..	1,993	1,993
Chilaw .	127	1·7	34·9	53·8	130	3,494*	3,624*
Kurunegala .	452	1·1	12·1	59·6	862	6,506	7,368
Kandy .	393	2·8	19·4	82·0	1,529	2,535	4,064
Matale .	104	2·2	38·3	85·4	797	3,621	4,418
N. Eliya .	91	2·9	41·8	74·3	1,016	1,199	2,215
Badulla .	215	3·5	8·8	77·6	806	3,750	4,556
Ratnapura .	243	2·0	32·2	55·9	..	4,094	4,094
Kegalla .	332	1·9	20·5	69·5	968	916	1,884
Anuradhapura† .	119	1·7	21·9	74·2	1,571	15,423	16,994
Vavuniya .	23	1·3	25·6	17·1	..	5,885	5,885
Jaffna .	362	4·3	31·7	75·5	641	1,588	2,229
B'caloa .	190	2·6	57·8	2·2	1,902	5,114	7,016
Trincomalee .	43	3·7	20·0	17·1	568	3,216	3,784
Mannar .	32	1·3	11·1	26·5	..	1,714	1,714
Puttalam .	35	0·7	27·2	68·8	222	‡	222‡
Hambantota .	139	1·6	34·0	25·6	512	8,307	8,819

* Including V.E. allotments in Puttalam District.
† Including Tamankaduwa, now Polonnaruwa District.
‡ V.E. allotments included in figures for Chilaw District.

Sources: Census of Ceylon, 1946, and *Census of Agriculture,* 1946; and Tables 5, 6, 12, 13, and 20; explanation of terms and note on reliability: see pp. 207–10.

doned allotments in the early colonies have in recent years been filled by modern systematic selection, but the numbers are small.) It should also be noted that 'Local' and 'Compensation' are not mutually exclusive categories; some of the former should, if data were available, be included in the latter, and, on the other hand, all 'compensation' cases are 'local' if one is interested in the benefit to *purāna* villages in the vicinity of the colony.

Table 20 shows the approximate distribution by source districts of colonists deliberately selected to represent specific areas, i.e. the 'Immigrant' and 'Local' categories of Table 19. The districts in the table have been grouped by geographical regions, but it must be realized that a number of districts lie in more than one geographical region. A breakdown into D.R.O.'s Divisions would overcome this difficulty (it will be remembered that 'Local' in Table 19 is defined in terms of such Divisions) but would clearly produce an unwieldy table.

The term 'Rural' in Table 21 must be defined. The rural population here shown is meant to represent that from which peasant colonists are drawn, and is the total population *less* the estate population (since the latter may be assumed to be fully employed at present and hence not to need relief: it, in any case, does not receive it) and *less* the urban population as defined by the 1946 Census.[1]

Critique of Methods of Selection

Turning to an appraisal of the methods of selection now used in Ceylon, there can be little objection to the important position of the Land Commissioner. He, of all the officers of Government, is in the best position to take a wise, overall view of the situation. It can, in fact, be argued that, if fair allocation according to need is to be a criterion, his position should be further strengthened by leaving him free of political control in the administration of the selecting machinery. It is sometimes alleged that his choice of source areas is influenced by the Minister for political reasons, to the disadvantage, for example, of opposition constituencies (allegations of similar political influence have also been made elsewhere, e.g. in the Philippines).[2] So long as choice of source area is subject to ultimate ministerial control, there must remain the suspicion that political considerations weigh heavily, even if they rarely do, or at least that the choice is arbitrary. If the Land Commissioner were free to allocate source areas according to a recognized and publicized formula, and if his administration were free from political control, there could be no grounds for such suspicion; the justice which is not only done, but seen to be done in many Land Kachcheries would be done, and be seen to be done in the Ministry.

[1] See *Census of Ceylon, 1946*, vol. i, pt. 1, p. 74.
[2] See Pelzer, *Pioneer Settlement*, p. 154. The new Prime Minister, Mr. S. W. R. D. Bandaranaike, has promised not to discriminate against opposition constituencies.

What of the categories actually selected by the existing machinery ? There can be no serious criticism of the numbers which have been selected in the 'Compensation' category, which amount only to about 6 per cent. of the whole. It should be noted, however, that recent policy has tended to increase the proportion per scheme of these cases, because of its insistence that private lands which will be surrounded by the colony should be acquired. It cannot be doubted that this is in general a wise practice;[1] but it, together with the submergence of villages by the reservoir, led to the absorption of *all* allotments available in the first year of Gal Oya by 'compensation' cases.

There can also be no criticism of the proportion of allotments awarded to labourers, which again amounts only to some 6 per cent. of the total and in any case relieves pressure in unknown but certainly overcrowded areas. But one would be hard put to it to arrive at an objective method of computing the correct proportion of labourers in any one scheme.

It may, however, be thought that the proportion of places allotted to local peasants is excessive; it will be noted from Table 19, bearing in mind the definitions of terms already given, that nearly a third of the total number of colonists installed before 31 December 1953 were deliberately chosen to represent 'local' Divisions; the proportion of 'local' colonists becomes about 38 per cent. if one adds the 'compensation' cases, and probably something approaching 50 per cent. if one remembers that an unknown but considerable proportion of the 'other' colonists were also 'local' in origin. The figures for 'local' colonists give a slightly exaggerated impression, it is true, because certain D.R.O.'s Divisions (e.g. Buttala and Matale North) are large enough to include parts of the Up-country as well as of the Lowland Dry Zone, so that some colonists recorded as 'local' for colonies in such Divisions have in fact come from a very different physical and human environment, and should properly be regarded as immigrant. But the numbers concerned are small, and do not invalidate the broad conclusion that between one-third and one-half of the colonists hail from the vicinity of the colonies in which they now live. This fact may appear surprising, in view of all that was said in the formative period of colonization policy about the need to relieve pressure in the Wet Zone (including the Hills), and also in view of the

[1] Cf. below, p. 309.

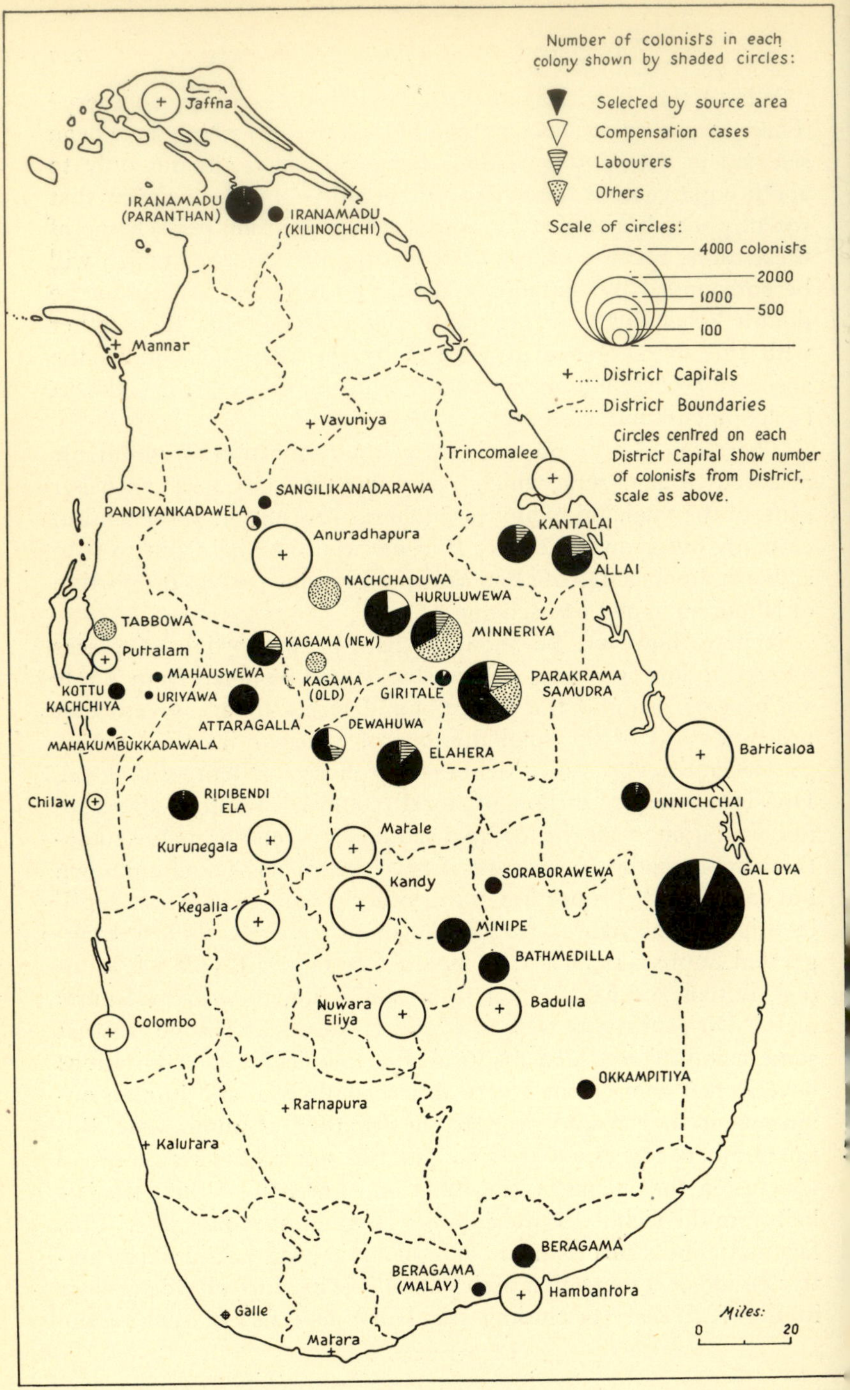
Number of colonists in each colony shown by shaded circles:
Selected by source area
Compensation cases
Labourers
Others
Scale of circles:
4000 colonists
2000
1000
500
100
+..... District Capitals
..... District Boundaries
Circles centred on each District Capital show number of colonists from District, scale as above.
Jaffna
IRANAMADU (PARANTHAN)
IRANAMADU (KILINOCHCHI)
Mannar
Vavuniya
Trincomalee
SANGILIKANADARAWA
PANDIYANKADAWELA
Anuradhapura
KANTALAI
ALLAI
NACHCHADUWA
HURULUWEWA
TABBOWA
MINNERIYA
Puttalam
KAGAMA (NEW)
MAHAUSWEWA
KAGAMA (OLD)
PARAKRAMA SAMUDRA
KOTTU KACHCHIYA
URIYAWA
GIRITALE
ATTARAGALLA
DEWAHUWA
MAHAKUMBUKKADAWALA
ELAHERA
Batticaloa
Chilaw
RIDIBENDI ELA
UNNICHCHAI
Matale
Kurunegala
Kandy
SORABORAWEWA
GAL OYA
Kegalla
MINIPE
BATHMEDILLA
Nuwara Eliya
Badulla
Colombo
OKKAMPITIYA
Ratnapura
Kalutara
BERAGAMA
BERAGAMA (MALAY)
Hambantota
Galle
Matara
Miles:
0
20

MAP 10. Ceylon: Numbers and Sources of Peasant Colonists (to end of 1953).

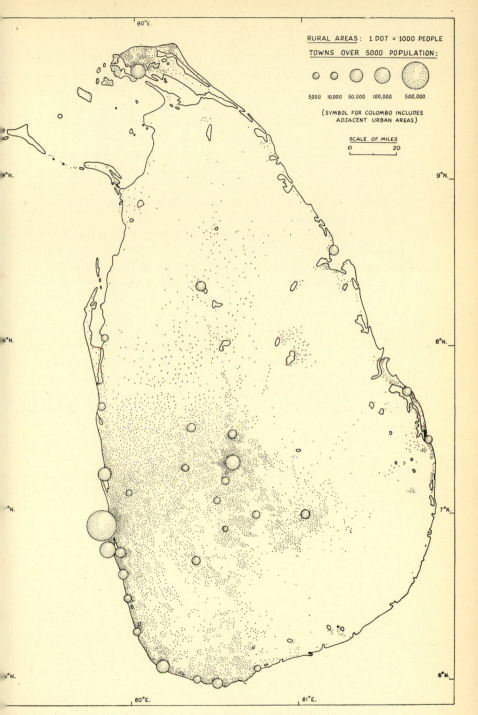

RURAL AREAS: 1 DOT = 1000 PEOPLE

TOWNS OVER 5000 POPULATION:

5000 10,000 50,000 100,000 500,000

(SYMBOL FOR COLOMBO INCLUDES
ADJACENT URBAN AREAS)

SCALE OF MILES
0   20

MAP 11. Ceylon: Population (1953).

figures for other Asian colonies (in two of the larger Punjab schemes, the Lower Bari Doab and Nili Bar Colonies, the proportion of local peasants was only 10 and 16 per cent. respectively;[1] and the colonies in the former Netherlands Indies existed primarily for the immigrant). It may fairly be said, in fact, that a distinguishing characteristic of the Ceylon Dry Zone colonies is a marked solicitude for the local peasant.[2] It must be recognized, however, that in the larger schemes in previously very sparsely peopled areas (e.g. Parakrama Samudra and Gal Oya) there are, or will be, a larger proportion of immigrants than in the average colony of today (see Table 19).

In spite of the solicitude which has been shown for the local peasant, there are regions of opinion in Ceylon which would reserve still larger segments for him. One thing is certain—that it is generally impossible to meet *absolute* local demand, however it be measured. To do so would not only leave little or no room for immigrants, it would also make nonsense of any effort to select only proficient colonists, and would also discourage the movement of labour from agriculture to other occupations which is a necessary concomitant of efforts to increase *per capita* production.

In addition to the fact that so many colonists hail from the D.R.O.'s Division in which their colony is situated, there is also the fact, brought out in Table 20, that even the 'immigrant' colonists have tended to move a relatively short distance to the colonies. This is, of course, sensibly economical in transport costs, both for the Government in the initial move and for the colonist and his family in the old village when they wish to exchange visits; such visits, moreover, play a useful part socially. But it will be noted that the larger colonies tend to receive far-travelled colonists, and thus to produce a number of social problems.

Table 20 and Map 10 may at first sight give the impression that colonists are very unevenly distributed between source areas. Thus Dry Zone districts have supplied nearly one-half of the colonists, partly, but not entirely a result of the preferential treatment of 'local' villagers; Up-country districts have supplied a slightly lower proportion, and Low Country districts only about one-eighth. There is, further, an apparently uneven distribution

---

[1] See *Punjab Colony Manual*, i. 86–88.
[2] In this connexion see the Government's decisions on the recommendations of the Land Commission (p. 139 above).

within the three main geographical divisions. Thus Anuradhapura District (for this purpose including Polonnaruwa District, conterminous with Tamankaduwa) and Batticaloa District have between them supplied some two-thirds of the colonists hailing from Dry Zone districts, Kurunegala more than one-half of those from the Low Country, and Kandy, Matale, and Nuwara Eliya Districts between them nearly three-quarters of those from Up-country.

How can one judge whether this apparent unevenness has some justification, or whether, as is sometimes alleged in Ceylon, political allegiance, and confusion between loudly voiced demand and objective need, are behind it? It is reasonable to suppose that, if colonization is designed in part at least as a means of reducing agrarian pressures, then the distribution of colonists by source areas should bear some relation to the incidence of these pressures; provided always that the alleviating effort in any particular area should be judged not by colonization alone, but by colonization and village expansion combined. There is, however, one cause of uneven allocation which must be mentioned at the outset; it has been amply demonstrated in earlier chapters that Dry Zone colonization is a very recent process, so that the recruitment of colonists from a district may merely be awaiting the completion of a suitable scheme. For instance, there were only 123 colonists from Batticaloa District by the end of 1951, and this fact might well have aroused adverse comment in an appreciation written at that time; but two years later the 123 had become 1,907, mainly as a result of recruitment into Gal Oya, and it would be possible to argue that the 'locals' had by then been unduly favoured were it not for two special conditions: one, that normal alienation of land under the Land Development Ordinance has been suspended within the area of authority of the Gal Oya Development Board, so that some of the apparent colonization is really village expansion; and, two, that the element of compensation is involved, since a portion of the land taken up for development each year was previously used by villagers for rain-fed paddy cultivation.[1]

By what criteria are we to judge whether the allocation of places in colonization and village expansion schemes bears any relation to the distribution of agrarian pressures? It will be clear from the

---

[1] The author is indebted to the Chairman of the Gal Oya Development Board for this information.

discussion in Chapters 3 and 4 that to measure these pressures is easier said than done. A comparative survey of landlessness would tell us much about rural conditions which at present we can only judge from samples; but it is quite insufficient merely to count the number of landless peasants, for those with holdings which are uneconomic (in the sense that a family cannot be supported on them at current living standards and with current technology) also need relief. And any local index of landlessness would in any case have to be weighted, for reasons that will be clear from Chapters 3 and 4, according to the local system of tenure, the possibilities for alternative employment, and the need not merely to accept local technology but to improve on it (thus the *chena* villages of Bintenne would need more liberal treatment than the *yāya-gangoda-chena* villages of Nuwarakalawiya).

As has already been suggested[1] an index of under-employment is perhaps the best single index of need for relief, since it is a measure of the surplus population, to which it is reasonable that allocations in resettlement schemes should be proportional. But under-employment is not easy to measure, especially where seasonal idleness is a social necessity, at least seasonally.

All that can be done here is to attempt an assessment of the situation against the yardsticks which are at present available, even though some of them are not particularly reliable. Some of these are shown in the first four columns of Table 21. (*a*) Clearly, *other things being equal*, allocations in resettlement schemes should be proportional to rural population (this being computed, it will be remembered, to exclude the estate population).[2] (*b*) Rural population per cultivated acre is a measure, but a very crude one, of agrarian pressure; crude because it takes no account of such factors as soil fertility, local technology and tenure, the staple crop, and opportunities for alternative employment, but has some intrinsic interest (the relatively small fluctuation from district to district should be noted) and some slight utility for the present purpose. (*c*) The percentage of the agricultural population which is landless, and (*d*) the incidence of very small holdings, are also relevant indices. But it will be clear that, in the present state of our knowledge of agrarian conditions in Ceylon, no single numerical index which is the product of some or all of these quantities can have practical utility; and discussion can at this stage only usefully

---

[1] See above, pp. 76–77. [2] Map 11 shows *total* population.

proceed by visual comparison of the quantities in Table 21. The reader may feel that even this is a completely academic exercise; but to adopt this attitude is to forget that in many parts of Ceylon today the allocation of places in the colonies is a matter of very live interest (the same may well be true elsewhere in Asia) so that a reasonably objective view of the situation may not be without interest in Ceylon and in other countries where these problems arise. Such, at any rate, is the author's hope.

It does seem that some effort is being made to allocate allotments in colonization schemes to districts where there is acute agrarian pressure but where there is little Crown land for village expansion (see Map 10 and Table 20); this is well marked for the Up-country districts, though their share of the total has dropped slightly between 1951 and 1953; but Ratnapura's absence from the list may not be thought to be justified either by low agrarian pressure or by headroom for village expansion, and Kegalla's share is not, perhaps, high enough. In the Low Country, Colombo and Matara Districts have come off badly in terms of total allotments, while the latter had not earned a single place in a colony in the period covered by the tables.[1] In Colombo District there is, of course, the largest single source of urban employment in the island, though data on rural under-employment would be necessary before one could say whether it sufficiently counterbalances the low figure for allotments. But in Matara District there is no such source, and it is sometimes alleged in Ceylon that this is the result of political discrimination against a region which returns 'Leftist' M.P.s. It may by held that 'Leftism' in Ceylon is a potentially revolutionary force, and that discrimination against its apparent strongholds is justified on the assumption that colonists from them would hold revolutionary ideologies and spread subversion and possibly violence in the colonies. But this is, in general, a false assumption; constituencies away from the Colombo conurbation tend to vote Left because of the personal popularity of a Leftist candidate, or because of ties of caste or community with him. If Matara and similar areas are indeed being discriminated against, and not merely being kept waiting for allotments in the Walawe or some similarly convenient scheme (as is quite possible), then trouble may ensue;

[1] It is learnt that Matara District was subsequently allocated 150 places in colonies. (The numbers involved in the small Wet Zone colonies mentioned on p. 3 are insufficient to affect the argument in this paragraph.)

Communism may not now be ideologically strong, but to ignore agrarian pressures is to render distress, and ensuing revolutionary tendencies, all the more likely in the future.

The figures for some of the Dry Zone districts confirm the view that local villagers may well have been too kindly treated in a situation where scarce means have to be divided between a number of clamourers for attention. The absence of colonists from Vavuniya and Mannar Districts need cause no heart-burning in the light of conditions there, but it is very possible that Jaffna is under-represented; there is, however, considerable alternative employment there, and a certain reluctance to emigrate permanently.

If the tables suggest only a rough and ready adjustment of allocations to source areas, and even some apparent injustices, there are, in addition to the fact that current colonization is an early stage in a continuing process, certain points which may be made in extenuation. One is that in recent years a great proportion of allotments have been necessarily allocated to special classes, such as ex-servicemen and refugees from landslides in Kotmale (though it may be noted that the latter do not unduly swell the total for Nuwara Eliya District). There have thus been insufficient allotments for systematic allocation according to the needs of source areas. On this view, it has been sufficient to consider that certain districts do not require any places at all (e.g. Mannar, Vavuniya) while others are adequately served by local or nearby colonies (e.g. Jaffna by the Iranamadu colonies), so that it is only the congested parts of Western, Central, Southern, Sabaragamuwa, and North-Western Provinces which demand places in the large, 'reception-area' colonies. This, however, is a very crude *modus operandi*; and, once Gal Oya and Walawe in particular move past the stage when they are satisfying a proportion of local need, and so long as the relief of agrarian pressure remains an aim, there is every reason for the introduction of a system under which allocations are based on some objective index of need, however hard this may be to arrive at; the system, moreover, should be made public property and freed from the suspicion, however ill-founded, of political control. The actual formula would have to be based on more data than now exist, and the collection of these data is an urgent task for Ceylon today; and a complication might be caused by the application of the principle of grouping.[1]

[1] See below, pp. 298–9.

The selection of the individual colonist at the Land Kachcheri may now be briefly discussed. There can be no doubt of the essential fairness and justice of the process, so long as one regards landlessness and possession of a suitably large family as the criteria. And there is no doubt that the local Revenue Officer, with his knowledge of local conditions, is the obvious person to conduct the Land Kachcheri. The Revenue Officers were, it should be noted, used for a similar purpose in the Punjab, with considerable success.[1] There are, however, in the author's view three main weaknesses in the present Land Kachcheri system. The first is that since ability to cultivate the standard allotment is largely measured in terms of the size of the family labour force, a premium is placed on the large, working family. This not only excludes the enterprising man whose family are of the wrong size or age, but may at some future date hinder efforts to encourage family limitation, especially as there is a tendency to select a man with a large family because they increase his *need* rather than because of their effect on his *ability*.

The second weakness is that, by and large, insufficient attention is paid to those qualities, other than the possession of a suitable family, which make for a good cultivator. Ability and initiative tend to be cursorily assessed on the basis of Village Headmen's reports. It is not easy, however, to see how the method could be improved without enormous trouble and delay, because of the numbers of candidates involved; it would be difficult to apply the method used in the Jaffna District[2] to areas where there is a much keener demand for allotments. In the Zuider Zee scheme, officers actually visit the farms of applicants to see them at work;[3] such a method would hardly be applicable to the selection of landless peasants, but it might be possible, if Land Kachcheries were held in two stages, to select in the present manner, but provisionally, and then to visit the provisional allottees in their own or in their *ande* holdings. Certainly any extra trouble which can be taken over this aspect of selection would be well worth while.

The third weakness concerns Village Headmen's reports in general; it is clear that they are not always prepared conscientiously. Undesirables are recommended in order that the village

---

[1] See *Punjab Colony Manual*, i. 97.   [2] See above, p. 207.
[3] Information obtained by the author during a visit to the Netherlands in Sept. 1953.

may be rid of them, and persons actually owning land or other property are certified to be landless. Here there is no real remedy except the hope that with better education headmen will prove more responsible and villagers more willing to object to injustices at the Land Kachcheri. Similar problems have, of course, been reported elsewhere.[1]

Conclusions

Those responsible for selecting peasant colonists in Ceylon today are thus faced with a very different problem from that which faced their predecessors twenty or so years ago. Then, the problem of selection barely arose, for it was difficult to persuade the peasant to migrate to the new colonies.* Now, a number of forces have produced an increased willingness to migrate, and, with policy as it is, the problem of selection is acute. This chapter has shown that, in this situation, a real attempt is being made to select colonists from areas where agrarian pressures are highest though it is possible that the peasantry in the vicinity of colonies are being over-favoured, and those of certain Wet Zone districts such as Matara, under-favoured; it is also apparent that selection of source areas by some more systematic and objective method is desirable, so long as relief of agrarian problems is a primary aim of the colonization policy.

On the other hand, this chapter has also shown that it is to be doubted whether existing methods of selection are calculated to select the most efficient cultivators among the landless applicants; and this is clearly important if food production is to be an essential aim of colonization. But the reader will not be able to decide how efficient the cultivator really is until he has read the survey of conditions in the colonies today with which subsequent chapters will be concerned; and the question whether the social aim of choosing colonists from among landless peasants conflicts with the economic aim of food production is also best left until after this survey.

[1] See, for example, Pelzer, *Pioneer Settlement*, p. 196.

11

Some Current Natural Difficulties: Diseases and Water-Supply

IN the present chapter it is proposed to examine the extent to which the techniques now available have enabled present-day colonists to overcome at least the more obvious natural hindrances, such as disease, drought, and the jungle. (Problems associated with the use of Dry Zone soils will be left to the next chapter; they fall into a different category, and, being altogether more subtle, are also more insidious.)

Diseases

The point has already been made that residual spraying with DDT has, as elsewhere in the tropics, proved a generally effective measure of malaria control in the Dry Zone, so that what was formerly a main obstacle to colonization is now of much less consequence. It is not possible to quote comprehensive figures; but the author made careful inquiries in each colony in 1951 and was nearly always told that there was little or no malaria among the colonists, even in the *Maha* fever season. It was claimed, for instance, that no more than 3 per cent. of the colonists in Stage III (the newest part) of Minneriya Colony were annually treated for malaria. Though there may be some over-optimism in these claims, it is nevertheless clear in the field that there is a complete contrast with the state of affairs which prevailed no more than twenty or even ten years ago. There are no longer harrowing tales of high rates of infant mortality or of families forced back to the Wet Zone by some fever-induced disaster, nor is the peasant labour force crippled at a critical season in the agricultural calendar. It is very evident that the measures which are taken by the Department of Medical and Sanitary Services are generally adequate; and that the advice of the World Bank mission, that 'DDT spray measures should be . . . extended to newly developing areas of colonization' is superfluous, for the job is already being efficiently done.[1]

[1] *WBR*, p. 740 (ii. 406).

But there is nevertheless no room for complacency. There are a number of actual and potential colonies where malaria still causes some trouble. Thus at Dewahuwa in late August 1951 ten or twelve people were reporting daily with malaria; most of these were only slightly affected, but there was one very bad case. The trouble was thought locally to be due to the breeding of mosquitoes in the pools of water which tend to lie alongside new irrigation channels still subject to loss by seepage; contributory factors were thought to be the existence of poor latrines and insanitary labour lines. Predisposing malnutrition and lack of resistance among the immigrant Kandyan peasantry may also have been involved; lack of resistance amongst new-comers was said to lie behind such malaria as existed at Nachchaduwa.

But some of the most serious malaria in the colonies today is to be found among Irrigation and Land Development Department labourers; particularly is this true where the men are working in swampy jungle during *Maha*. Thus at Allai, unhealthily situated in the Mahaweli Ganga delta, it was said in 1951 that more than 10 per cent. of the labourers were going down with malaria in the rains. Failure to spray temporary lines may also cause a sudden rise in the malaria rate, as at both Minneriya and Parakrama Samudra in April–May 1951. It is clear that malaria control amongst labourers in the jungle constitutes a special problem.

These survivals and recrudescences of malaria serve as reminders that, good as the control measures are, the disease is by no means eradicated from the Dry Zone; because of the existence in the dry season of pools in river courses far from human habitation, and because *Anopheles culicifacies* does not depend solely on human blood, absolute eradication is bound to be far more difficult than in such countries as Cyprus.[1] Eradication may come in time, for there are signs of a decrease in the mosquito population;[2] but danger is likely to continue for many years ahead, and control measures must not be relaxed. Confidence may lead to simplified procedures and to economy (the period between successive sprayings was increased, by stages, from three weeks to three months until, finally, routine spraying was given up in favour of

---

[1] See Calder, *Men Against the Jungle*, p. 142.

[2] *WBR*, pp. 739–40 (ii. 406): see also Rajendram and Jayewickreme, in *Ind. J. Malariology*, vol. v, pp. 1–124, and their 'Malaria in the Maha Oya Basin', *Cey. J. Med. Sci.*, vol. viii (1951), pp. 85–124; and *Admin. Report: Medical*, 1951, pp. 156–84.

spraying in areas of sporadic recrudescence of malaria). It is also essential, in Ceylon as elsewhere, to secure adequate supplies of DDT. Help from outside has supplemented normal government purchasing power; thus, in 1951, Unicef (United Nations International Children's Emergency Fund) made an allocation of $152,000 to Ceylon for the purchase of DDT. But, in the same year, there was a world shortage of DDT, and reserve stocks had to be supplemented with substitutes such as BHC (Gammexane P. 520). Clearly the serious consequences of a breakdown in imported supplies of DDT make it desirable that this vital insecticide should be manufactured in Ceylon, even if such factors as the absence of a supporting major chemical industry make the plant not strictly economic. It is, in fact, proposed, with the help of Unicef, to build a DDT factory at Elephant Pass, just south of the Jaffna Lagoon. (Similar factories are also to be built in India and Pakistan.[1])

It must perhaps be stressed that such problems as the survival of malaria among special groups of colonists affect relatively few individuals, and do not invalidate the general conclusion that the Dry Zone environment has suffered a true revolution which has put an entirely new complexion on colonization in it. There are, of course, many Asian regions which have been similarly transformed, and most Asian colonization schemes which were stricken with malaria in their early years are now much less afflicted. To take two examples of former malarial conditions, the co-operative colonies in the Mon Canals Tract, in Burma, suffered a disastrous epidemic in 1915, one village almost completely succumbing;[2] while in the Javanese colonies in Sumatra in 1914 it was largely owing to malaria that deaths exceeded births (medical services were, however, sadly lacking).[3] It is not known what measures of malaria control are now being undertaken in the Burmese areas of colonization, but in the Indonesian colonies in Sumatra the use of DDT has begun;[4] and spectacular results have been claimed in the notorious Terai, at the foot of the Himalayas, by a combination of jungle clearing, prophylactic paludrine, and DDT spraying.[5]

[1] Calder, *Men Against the Jungle*, p. 218.

[2] *Co-operative Societies in Burma* (1917), p. 5.

[3] Pelzer, *Pioneer Settlement*, p. 194.

[4] Information kindly obtained from Jakarta by the Indonesian Embassy in London.

[5] The author is greatly indebted to Major H. S. Sandhu, Deputy Director of Colonization, Uttar Pradesh, for information on the Terai scheme.

It would appear, however, that in few Asian colonies is the contrast between an originally desperate situation and the present amelioration so marked as in the Dry Zone of Ceylon; and that this is so reflects the application of a new technique under conditions of political stability and administrative efficiency which are, unfortunately, rare in Asia.

It is also clear that the general unhealthiness, quite apart from malaria, which formerly hung over the Dry Zone has largely been dispelled. Malnutrition and intestinal diseases such as amoebic dysentery do, it is true, continue to cause trouble and must shortly be discussed; but general unhealthiness seems to be a localized phenomenon. Sometimes it is associated with swampy conditions, as at Allai and in that part of the Gal Oya scheme which lies on the alluvium bordering the Batticaloa lagoon. (The impossibility of finding suitable healthy sites for houses on this alluvium is, in fact, a major factor behind a decision of the Gal Oya Board not to restrict development to the customary pattern of peasant holdings containing 'high land' allotments as well as paddy; and absence of high land in other regions, such as the Mahaweli delta, is likely to enforce new development patterns there too.) Sometimes unhealthiness is the result of particularly insanitary habits, such as those which are unfortunately characteristic of some members of the Moslem colonist communities (i.e. the Malays of Beragama and the Tamankaduwa Moors in Block 'D' at Parakrama Samudra).

It is clear, too, that the removal of general unhealthiness from the Dry Zone is the result of the gradual extension by the Government of its network of dispensaries and hospitals, and of a much greater willingness to use these facilities which has spread through the population in the last decade or so. There is strong evidence of this willingness in the colonies; and it applies not only to the use of dispensaries and hospitals but also to the use of maternity homes, where, as at Gal Oya, Kagama, and Minipe, these are available. The popularity of maternity homes may surprise those used to Indian conditions, and it must be stressed that it is to be found mainly among Sinhalese women; the Malay women of Beragama will not use the homes.

The provision of a full complement of medical facilities, including branch dispensaries, rural hospitals, and maternity homes, is clearly bound to be difficult in a country like Ceylon, with a shortage both of trained personnel and of funds. (It is, however, a further interesting commentary on the attitudes prevalent among at least a section of Ceylonese women that there is no shortage of would-be nurses.[1]) And, although it has always been an aim of policy that the modern colonization schemes should be adequately provided with medical facilities, it is not surprising, in view of the size of the problem in the country as a whole, that provision lags behind need, especially in the smaller colonies. Thus in 1951 there seemed to be adequate provision of both dispensaries and hospitals in such colonies as Kagama and Minneriya, but no dispensary had as yet been provided in Giritale, hospital patients from Elahera had to go to Matale or Dambulla (about 34 and 30 miles away respectively), and ex-servicemen colonists in Parakrama Samudra had 8 miles to go to hospital in Polonnaruwa, no means of transport being available.[2] Again, in the small colony of Maha Kumbuk-kadawala, there was a new hospital, but no staff had as yet arrived. This tendency for medical provision to lag behind land development is, in fact, a problem of some magnitude, and the need for better facilities is still, in spite of all that has been achieved, keenly felt by the colonists.

The revolution in health in the Dry Zone has been achieved with means which would be considered inadequate in a Western country; in this connexion it must be remembered that the dispensaries in the colonies and in other rural areas are largely manned, in the absence of fully qualified doctors, by 'apothecaries' who have combined 'a full course in pharmacy with an elementary training in medicine and surgery'.[3] Much, therefore, remains to be done; if it is done the revolution in health will be accelerated.

The question may well be asked with reference to Ceylon and its colonies whether it is ethically justifiable to improve medical care when the result of the measures which have already been taken has been a sudden upward surge in the population curve, a surge of such magnitude that it is very doubtful if we can feed the extra mouths whose owners have already been kept alive.[4] This question is relevant to South Asia as a whole. The author's attitude may well be gauged from what has already been said; it is, in a word, that the relief of sickness and suffering is a worth-while

---

[1] *WBR*, p. 719 (ii. 393).

[2] For a map of hospitals, &c., see *Admin. Report: Medical*, 1951, facing p. iii.

[3] *WBR*, pp. 719–20 (ii. 393–4).

[4] The implications of recent demographic changes in Ceylon will be discussed in more detail in Chapter 17.

end in itself, and that it is an unthinkable solution to deny to regions of actual or potential population pressure the best medical techniques available, still less to allow the scanty facilities available to lapse. But the demographic implications of these techniques must be understood, and steps taken to ensure that the increasing populations can be fed; and, if food supplies and living standards are in jeopardy because of the new rates of increase, then attempts must be made to bring down the birth-rate, not to limit medical care and to condemn those who are born to a life of miserable sickness.

It is in this spirit, and in awareness of at least some of the broader implications, that it is suggested that improved medical facilities are needed, and attention is drawn in particular to what appear to be two of the chief health problems remaining in the Dry Zone colonies today, malnutrition and intestinal disorders.

Malnutrition is, as might be expected, all too common among immigrant colonists, especially among those from the poorer and more overcrowded Kandyan districts. It was noted in 1951 at Bathmedilla, Dewahuwa, Giritale, Kagama, Nachchaduwa, and in parts of Parakrama Samudra; but it was even more marked among the very poor colonists at Gal Oya who had been evacuated from the tank-bed and who were mainly *chena* cultivators with little or no paddy. Malnutrition is not, however, only a matter of the past history of the immigrant colonists. In several places, notably in Parakrama Samudra and at Tabbowa, it was present among established colonists and was put down to over-reliance on manioc, which gives a food consisting almost entirely of starch. Here, clearly, work remains to be done. An attempt is being made in some colonies to fight malnutrition among children by setting up milk feeding centres; there are, for example, three such centres among the generally underfed Kandyan colonists at Bathmedilla.

It is, however, the prevalence of such diseases as amoebic dysentery, diarrhoea, and 'stomach troubles' generally which really strikes the inquirer into present-day conditions in the colonies. One or other of these troubles was reported to the author in nearly all the colonies, though not all of them were suffering all the time (thus Kilinochchi had had an epidemic of dysentery in 1949). Intestinal diseases are, of course, all too common in the tropics, notably in the Dry Zone's climatic analogue, Tamil Nad.[1] They

---

[1] See Gourou, *Tropical World*, pp. 8–9; for Tamil Nad see, *inter alia*, Cmd. 2905, p. 474.

have frequently been encountered in other South Asian colonization schemes, for example those of the former Netherlands East
Indies and of the Philippines.[1] The general prevalence of these
diseases may be put down on the one hand to the effect of tropical
warmth on bacterial and amoebic activity, and, on the other, to
poor sanitation, to the use of a single water-supply for watering
cattle, for washing, and for drinking, and to the neglect of such
simple precautions as the boiling of drinking water. All of these
causes may be seen at work in the Dry Zone colonies, but they are
reinforced by the special problems of domestic water-supply which
are engendered by the hydro-geological peculiarities of the region;
in particular, by the tendency of many wells to dry up completely,
or to yield inadequate supplies, during the dry season, so that the
colonist has to fall back on such readily tainted sources as tank and
channel water. It is no accident that at Giritale and elsewhere the
incidence of intestinal diseases is highest in the dry season.

Domestic Water-supply

The problem of domestic water-supply in the Dry Zone colonies
could fairly easily be overcome if techniques available in the West
could be generally applied; modern methods of treatment, filtration, and piping would, for example, enable water from irrigation
tanks and channels to be made available in a safe and convenient
form in every colonist's cottage. But these techniques are costly,
and high costs are not easily met in a country like Ceylon. Thus a
piped water-supply to a colony has several times been suggested
in the last two decades, but has never materialized, because of the
cost, except in atypical instances such as the new town of Amparai,
in the Gal Oya scheme, which is to be fed from Amparai Tank.
The colonies therefore have to fall back upon other and cheaper
methods. Surface water being all too readily polluted, the well is
the only practicable solution; and, provided that there is ground-
water, it does at least provide a safe supply if simple precautions
are taken.

A communal well is, in fact, provided at a rate of one to every
four to fifteen colonists. And each individual colonist is encouraged
to dig his own well, with the help of a subsidy of some Rs. 40 or of
a loan from his Co-operative Agricultural Production and Sales
Society. (He may not always respond; but it was interesting to

[1] See Pelzer, *Pioneer Settlement*, pp. 141, 194, and 219–20.

see Tamil technology at work in Kilinochchi Colony, where almost every house had its well.) Only occasionally, as at Dewahuwa and Maha Kumbukkadawala in 1951, are there no wells at all; and then there are usually constructional or labour difficulties to be pleaded.

But the colonist's well all too often fails to yield an adequate supply all the year round. He is, in fact, up against a double problem: the small quantity of water which can be stored in the relatively thin layer of decayed rock, subsoil, and soil above the barren, impermeable crystalline material,[1] and the liability of even that small quantity to disappear during the dry season. The author's observations on wells in the colonies amply confirm the general rule that only where the water-table is preserved by per-colation into it from a perennial river, or from a tank or channel, will a Dry Zone well yield all the year round. Exceptions to this rule are rare in the extreme, and appear to be related to peculiar local geomorphological conditions; thus water persisting in wells at Elahera in the dry season may be related to percolation into the rock mantle from a forest-covered ridge above. Wells away from surface water, especially those in true 'high land', thus generally fail in the dry season, and those near channels fail when, for instance, the channels are closed for cleaning. In such circum-stances the colonists fall back on surface sources, carting water, often for considerable distances, from the nearest tank or channel with water in it. This cannot but be bad for health; and in the portion of Parakrama Samudra known as Pudur it led, in 1951, to a noticeable absence of the personal cleanliness normally so charac-teristic of the Sinhalese villager. In the struggle to obtain domestic water, moreover, ugly disputes are apt to arise. And in some cases, notably at Gal Oya in 1952, the actual settlement of new colonists may be delayed by the absence of domestic water. The difficulties of domestic water-supply, moreover, particularly hinder the estab-lishment of those colonists who hail from the Wet Zone with its generally favourable ground-water conditions.

It seems that only some such expensive measure as the construc-tion of a piped-water grid can completely solve the problem of domestic water-supply. But a great deal could be done if the principles which have just been outlined were more universally taken to heart. It is true that there have been many occasions in

[1] See above, p. 30.

the colonies when cognizance has been taken of the reliance of the dry season water-table on percolation from surface water, and when domestic water-supply has been planned in terms of 'seepage wells' and 'filtration wells' near a tank or channel; but the author found other cases in which a great deal of time and money, private and public, had been wasted on the sinking of wells on or near watersheds, well above the reach of the essential percolation from surface-water sources. The only thing to be said for a number of wells at Uriyawa, for example, was that they were near the houses; but this is small consolation to the householders when the wells are dry. It would be far more satisfactory if wells were first sited according to sound hydrological principles (as is now being done at Gal Oya) and the houses then built around them. Failure to appreciate the principles of Dry Zone well siting probably springs from a number of causes; for example, the transference to the Dry Zone of ideas culled from experience in the Wet Zone, where wells on high land are much more reliable, and the small part played by science and geography in the education of many administrative officers.[1]

Water-table preservation, and consequently the reliability of wells, would be greatly improved if there were a wider distribution in the Dry Zone of stored surface water in high land; if, in fact, there were more tanks, so that a greater proportion of the high land could approach *gangoda* conditions. Moreover water-table preservation would not only help to provide domestic water; the next chapter will show that it would also help towards a solution of the vexing question of perpetual high land cultivation. Now, jungle-clearing operations frequently reveal a great number of small, derelict *bunds* which must formerly have held up small tanks or ponds, possibly for paddy cultivation as in Tamil Nad,[2] possibly for water-table preservation. It would be a relatively simple matter to restore these *bunds*, or where no *bund* exists, to construct a new one. The Ministry of Agriculture and Lands in fact directed in 1950 that tanks *in the irrigable command* of major works should be preserved in the interests of domestic water-supply. But, although such minor tanks can aid the general conservation of water by supplementing the main source, by collecting drainage and seepage, and by enabling irrigation water to be used twice

[1] The Government Mineralogist now (1956) advises on the siting of wells.
[2] See above, p. 53.

over, they can only really exert a useful influence on the water-table when the paddy fields are all dry; for, at other times, even in *Yala* when only part of the paddy tract is likely to be cultivated, a minor tank in the irrigable command can do but little more for the general water-table than is already done by the flooded fields.

If any effectual aid is to be brought to the general water-table under the high lands, and hence to the inadequate domestic water-supply, it is the *high land bunds* which must be restored. Something is being done in this direction in the new 'dry-farming' colonies[1] and by the Gal Oya Development Board, which is in this connexion, as in others, well ahead of government departments (though even in Gal Oya cisterns fed by the channels form the basic provision for domestic water-supply). But in the colonies generally little has so far been done to attend to high land *bunds*, and then usually with some other motive than the preservation of the water-table. (Thus there is a small high land tank at Dewahuwa provided mainly for cattle.) Generally old *bunds* stand unused amid the allotments.[2] Something might also be done with ancient channels not now required for the irrigation of paddy. The ancient Raja Ela at Minneriya has, in fact, been restored to supply limited irrigation to high land allotments, and in doing so is bound to have a useful effect on the water-table; but elsewhere ancient channels remain derelict; sometimes, however, local practical difficulties would prevent restoration, as in the case of the enigmatic Kalinga Ela in the Parakrama Samudra scheme.[3]

A policy of restoring all ancient small tanks and at least some of the old but unwanted channels would, however, raise a number of difficulties. A great deal of the high land, perhaps up to a third of its total area, would need to be under water for at least part of the year.[4] High land allotments near to tanks would be liable to waterlogging in *Maha*; for grave as are the effects of the dry season, it must not be forgotten that there is also a wet season. Another difficulty would be the liability of small tanks to dry up completely just when their preservative effect on the water-table is most needed; this difficulty could be partly, if not completely

---

[1] See below, pp. 343–4, and Plate 24.

[2] A directive has now (1956) been issued that high land *bunds* should be restored; it is not everywhere being followed.

[3] See Brohier, *Ancient Irrigation Works*, pt. 1, p. 12.

[4] Cf. the remarks of A. T. Grove in the discussion on Farmer, in *Geog. J.*, vol. xii (1954), pp. 31–32, as corrected ibid., p. 256.

overcome if evaporation could be reduced by deepening the tanks and thus reducing the surface area per unit volume; though it is always claimed that the process would be too expensive. Finally, abstraction of run-off in a multitude of small tanks necessarily affects the water economy of each catchment; this makes for difficulty in a catchment with irrigation works in action, but merely serves to emphasize the importance of catchment planning.[1] But, for all these difficulties, it cannot reasonably be doubted that conservation of water in the high lands is an essential prerequisite to the provision of perennial supplies of well water in these lands (and, as will be seen in the next chapter, to their fuller utilization by cultivated crops). Even if some proportion of the high land has to be sacrificed, through submergence or waterlogging, and even if planning of the catchments is complicated, the sacrifice and complication are worth while; and, even if a tank dries out eventually, it will leave a higher water-table than there would otherwise be.

Some colonization schemes have particular difficulties of domestic water-supply over and above those connected with an impersistent water-table. In a number of them (e.g. Giritale, Kottu Kachchiya, Parakrama Samudra, Nachchaduwa, Okkampitiya, Tabbowa, and Uriyawa), the water which is tapped when wells are sunk or deepened is sometimes found to be alkaline or brackish. In some low-lying wells this may be due to the same cause as alkalinity or salinity in paddy fields,[2] but elsewhere there seems no rhyme or reason in the incidence of these troubles. Thus at Tabbowa Paddy Station (near the colony) there are three wells in a line within a few score of yards of each other; one of them yields pure water, the other two are brackish. This apparently capricious phenomenon may be due to differences in rock composition, but more research on the problem is very necessary if effort is not to be wasted on useless wells.

In fact, as has already been said, more research is needed into the whole problem of underground water in the Dry Zone. An admirable research project is already in hand in the Dry Zone Research Station at Maha Illuppallama;[3] the Vavuniya well survey, with its very limited and somewhat misleading results, has

---

[1] See above, pp. 186–7.
[2] See below, pp. 234–5.
[3] See *Admin. Report: Agriculture*, 1952, pp. 37–38.

already been mentioned;[1] and some useful work has been done by the Department of Mineralogy.[2] But what is needed is a systematic study of water-table conditions in all of the sub-regions of the Zone; and a prerequisite to the interpretation of such a study is a comprehensive and detailed geological map. In this connexion the work done under generally analogous conditions in South India is worthy of study.[3]

Irrigation Problems of the Colonist

It will by now be realized that reliable irrigation is not only the *sine qua non* of paddy cultivation in the Dry Zone colonies but is also, in present circumstances, both directly and indirectly linked to the problems of domestic water-supply. Fully reliable irrigation cannot, of course, be expected in *Yala*, when most tanks, except in years of exceptional inter-monsoonal rains, contain only the water which is left over from *Maha*; and the *bethma* system[4] is essentially a sensible reaction to the need to cultivate only a part of the paddy tract in *Yala*. Reliability of irrigation must therefore be primarily discussed with relation to the situation in *Maha*. The reader will already have encountered[5] some of the problems that arise in the planning of irrigation systems in a region of variable rainfall and run-off, where modern, *de novo* catchment planning is hindered by pre-existing works and land-use patterns, where maximum utilization of water resources is further hindered by a lack of social cohesion and social discipline, and where, further, the situation is complicated, in some cases, by lack of data, by faulty judgement, and, possibly, by politics.

By and large, the colonist is able to grow his *Maha* crop without serious fear of water shortage, so that modern irrigation is, generally speaking, an efficient safeguard for him against the perils of drought. The colonies which, like Minneriya and Parakrama Samudra, depend on large tanks, suffer the most rarely from irrigation failure,

---

[1] See above, p. 30, based on File No GNP. 104, Surveyor-General's Office, Colombo.

[2] See, for example, C. H. L. Sirimanne, 'Some Problems in the Hydrogeology of Ceylon' (Abstract), *Proc. 4th Ann. Sess., Cey. Assoc. Sci.*, pt. 2 (1948), p. 13. The author is indebted to Mr. Sirimanne for the benefit of some valuable discussions on hydro-geological problems.

[3] See, for example, Geological Survey of India, *Records*, vol. lxxxii (1949), pp. 177–8 and vol. lxxxiii (1950), pp. 287–99 for accounts of hydrological surveys in Coimbatore District and in the Ceded Districts respectively.

[4] See above, p. 45.   [5] See above, pp. 184–94.

though it is not unknown at the end of their long distributaries; and there may be, in the early days of a colony, troubles due to seepage losses from new channels as yet unsealed by the natural deposition of silt in them. In the remaining colonies, those which depend on tanks with small catchments, as at Maha Kumbukkadawala and Sangilikanadarawa, suffer all the troubles of Nuwarakalawiya villages in years of low rainfall. The first-named colony had no *Maha* in 1951–2 and only 25 acres in 1950–1; the second-named had no *Maha* in 1950–1, and a *Mäda* (*Meda*) in 1951 was only completed by pumping the last few gallons of water from the shrunken tank. One of the worst failures, however, has been that at Pandiyankadawela, which is fed by an extension of the Right Bank Channel from Nuwara Wewa, which is fed in turn by any surplus waters of Nachchaduwa Tank on the Malwatu Oya. Nachchaduwa spills only at irregular intervals and so can rarely help Nuwara Wewa's own inadequate catchment. Pandiyankada-wela had no paddy crop at all during the first three years of its existence, the colonists being forced to subsist by growing manioc and by hiring out their labour. They would be helped if it were found possible to reinforce the resources of the Malwatu Oya catchment by the completion of the unfinished ancient channel from the Jaya Ganga;[1] but in view of the troubles of the Kala Wewa catchment, it is clearly impracticable to draw on it in this way, and one is forced to the conclusion that Pandiyankadawela was based on an over-optimistic view of the water resources available.

Fortunately, however, failures like these are relatively rare; nor are such failures as do occur peculiar to Ceylon, for there have been, quite apart from recent troubles in Pakistan due to Indian control of irrigation headworks, a number of cases of water shortage in other Asian colonization schemes.[2] In any case, complete reliability is impossible in a region of variable rainfall, at least in the absence of arrangements for storing flood waters and issuing them in ensuing years. The colonist, moreover, is not altogether blameless; for, as has been seen,[3] he is prone to waste water and, lacking social cohesion and discipline, and the will to co-operate, is not

[1] See above, pp. 188–90.
[2] e.g. in the Co-operative Colonies in the Môn Canals Tract of Burma in 1915–16 (see *Co-operative Societies in Burma*, p. 5).
[3] See above, p. 184.

readily adaptable to lean years. Nevertheless, failure of irrigation, when it does occur, has serious effects on the morale of colonists, especially those from the Wet Zone, and engenders innumerable disputes over the division of scarce water. The colonist's life, in fact, for all the high scale of aid today, still has its hardships and still smacks something of the pioneer fringe.

Moreover, the colonist may, especially in certain colonies, run into difficulties due to flooding or waterlogging, and due to salinity and alkalinity. Flooding particularly affects such low-lying flat regions as those flanking the Mahaweli Ganga in Minneriya and Parakrama Samudra Colonies, but it also occurs elsewhere, for example at Tabbowa. Where the flooding is due to remote causes, such as heavy rainfall in a steep catchment largely under cultivation (as in the case of the Mahaweli), very little can be done in the colony except to abandon the flooded allotments, to alienate new ones to the displaced colonists, and to hope for better planning in future. In other cases, flood control may be an essential part of a multi-purpose scheme, as at Gal Oya (and as in the Damodar valley in India),[1] or waterlogging may be due to a local rise of the water-table or to increased surface watering, in each case as a result of irrigation, and such local remedial measures as improved drainage channels may suffice.[2]

This last condition of waterlogging is, however, most serious because of the alkalinity and salinity which may be associated with it. The problem of the accumulation in or on the soil of salts and alkalis is a well-known and critical one in most areas won from the waste by irrigation, notably in Pakistan, of which Spate has recently written 'the problem of keeping irrigated land from ruin by waterlogging and salt impregnation is perhaps as urgent as that of winning new ground'.[3] Waterlogging is apt to bring near to the surface salts and alkalis normally present at depth; then, in the dry season, or when the soil is not being irrigated, capillarity and high evaporation concentrate these salts and alkalis at the surface until, eventually, a visible 'pan' may be formed. The process may be accelerated if the irrigation water itself contains salts. Increasing concentration of salts is not only in itself harmful to crops,

---

[1] See Kirk, in *Geog. Rev.*, vol. xl, pp. 415–43.

[2] See R. Kahawita, 'Water-logging of Irrigated Lands and Remedial Measures', *Trop. Agriculturist*, vol. xcv (1940), pp. 278–87.

[3] Spate, pp. 251–2.

including all but salt-resistant varieties of rice, but may, through base-exchange, produce sodium clays and hence cause reduced permeability and other difficulties, and also increase the concentration of sodium carbonate, an alkali.[1] In Ceylon, fortunately, the problem affects small areas only, and does not take the extreme form of 'black alkali' (sodium carbonate) concentration. 'White alkali' (the chlorides and sulphates of sodium and magnesium) has, however, caused loss of crops in patches of ground in such colonies as Minneriya, Parakrama Samudra, Kilinochchi, Elahera, and Unnichchai. The problem was particularly acute at Minneriya in 1939 and caused a suspension of development work while research was undertaken by Joachim.[2] It was found at Minneriya and has likewise been found in other colonies, that salinity is nearly always due to poor drainage and seasonal evaporation. Sometimes the poor drainage is partly a result of bad levelling of fields by colonists, and this is a good reason for the levelling of fields being done as part of land-development operations; it may also be a result of the application of insufficient water to flush the rising salts from the fields into the drainage channels; and this is a warning against over-zealous economy of water. The remedy in nearly all cases is more effective drainage, to carry the salts away, with better levelling and a higher issue of water if necessary.

The Jungle

If modern methods have gone a long way towards the conquest of disease and drought in the Dry Zone colonies, they have, in presenting the colonist with a ready-cleared allotment, completely conquered the jungle as a direct enemy of settlement. But the colonist has not altogether escaped conflict with its resurgence; the secondary growth and weeds which eventually defeat the *chena* cultivator may infest his allotment when he takes it over, if there has been an interval between clearing and alienation, or creep into both his high land and his paddy as he cultivates them. The problem of weeds is always a serious one in tropical agriculture; but it is particularly serious when there is an invasion of the grass *Imperata cylindrica*, the *illuk* of the Sinhalese;[3] fortunately, this

---

[1] See Sir E. John Russell, *Soil Conditions and Plant Growth*, 8th ed., rev. by E. W. Russell (London, Longmans, 1950), pp. 559–64.

[2] See Joachim, 'The Alkali Soil Problem and Reclamation Methods in India and Ceylon', *Trop. Agriculturist*, vol. xcvii (1941), pp. 202–14.

[3] See above, p. 32.

scourge does not frequent paddy lands, being killed by flooding. *Imperata cylindrica* is an almost universal problem in the tropics; it is widely distributed, especially in abandoned cultivated land, in a number of varieties throughout the tropical and inter-tropical lands of the Old World.[1] It is the variety *major*, sometimes known as *I. arundinacea*, which plagues the Asiatic tropics and extends also into South-East Africa and Australia. The Dry Zone of Ceylon is, however, fortunate, for at present at any rate *illuk* is only a serious problem in the colonies east of the Mahaweli Ganga, notably in Bathmedilla and Okkampitiya. It is a much less serious problem in colonies just west of the river and hardly a problem at all in other regions. The reasons for this restricted distribution are not fully known; it is tempting to point out the correlation with the outcrop of the Bintenne gneiss and to infer a causal relationship with the poor, sandy soils which develop from this rock, especially where there has been cultivation and burning;[2] it may be that *illuk* is absent from the bulk of the Dry Zone colonies merely because its seed has not reached them, the south-west monsoon wind fortunately tending to blow the seed let loose in Bintenne away from them. It is also said that the seed of *illuk*, though easily carried by wind in open country, is halted by a belt of jungle and, not being very viable, soon dies.[3]

Where *illuk* has invaded the high lands of a colony, it is a great nuisance to the cultivator. Spreading as it does by tough, extensively creeping rhizomes, it is invulnerable to attack by hoeing and to fire. It can be controlled, it is said, by pulling up the new green shoots in the wet season; but the colonist at this time is too busy with his *Maha* paddy. In government farms it has been found possible to eradicate *I. cylindrica* by applying sodium arsenite, or by ploughing and disk-harrowing in the dry season (with, however, a possible adverse effect on the soil); but these methods are expensive and beyond the reach of the peasant. More success may ultimately attend control by means of cover-crops such as the creeper *Passiflora foetida*, which has been used in Africa, or by growing closely spaced manioc, or by planting some rapid-growing tree or shrub useful for green manure, like

[1] See, for example, Imp. Agric. Bureaux, *Imperata cylindrica*; Harroy, *Afrique*, p. 78; and Gourou, *Tropical World*, pp. 41–42.

[2] See Farmer, in *Geog. J.*, vol. cxx, p. 28.

[3] The author is indebted for this and other points to Dr. M. F. Chandraratna.

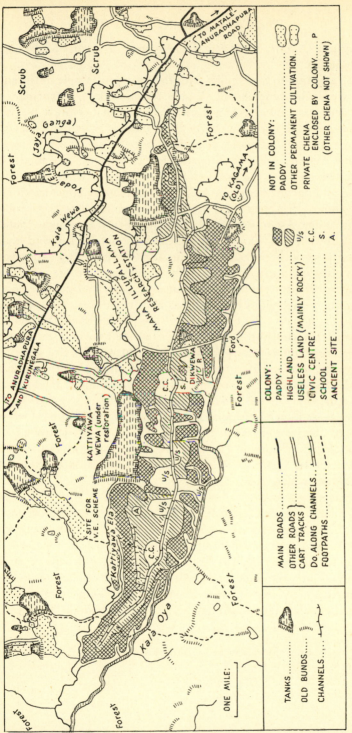

MAP 12. Kagama (New) Colony: Layout and Setting (1951).

Leucaena glauca; for *Imperata cylindrica* is destroyed by shady conditions.

In addition to the conflict with the resurgent jungle in the shape of weeds in general and, locally, with *illuk* in particular, the modern Dry Zone colonist still in many places finds his fields subject to the depredations of wild animals which the surviving jungle shelters. This is, of course, only to be expected since so many colonies are, like Nuwarakalawiya villages, girt about with thick jungle; and the problem is all the greater where a colony is long and narrow, its shape being determined by considerations of irrigation (cf. Map 12). The Ceylon colonies share this problem with other Asian settlements which are set in jungle, notably with the Terai scheme.[1] In the Ceylon colonies, the wild boar is almost everywhere the biggest nuisance, grubbing up and devouring great quantities of crops. The elephant is a more spectacular doer of damage, but does not so often affect so many colonies; reports of incursions by elephants have to be treated, in any case, with caution, for the colonist (and the Colonization Officer) have learnt that the European is always pleased to hear tales of the creature which fascinates him so much. Damage is also sometimes done by wild buffalo, deer, and leopard amongst larger animals, and by monkeys, parrots, and various small birds; these smaller creatures may, in fact, do more damage and be less easy to exclude than their larger brethren, as was found by the British Overseas Food Corporation recently when weaver birds destroyed over 3,000 acres of sorghum at Kongwa (Tanganyika).[2] And damage may not be confined to the attacks of wild animals; the herds of cattle which roam the jungle can also do a great deal of damage.

All this means a considerable, sometimes a disastrous, loss of crops, and a considerable waste of effort both in cultivating without reward, and in watching crops by night in the hope of being able to use some ancient fire-arm to project old nails or similar objects into the hide of a retreating elephant or boar. Night watching may also be, as a report on the Terai pointed out, a considerable strain on the vitality.[3] The erection of fences can do

[1] See *Tarai and Bhabar Report*, p. 33. See also Calder, *Men Against the Jungle*, p. 148.

[2] Great Britain, Overseas Food Corporation, *Ann. Report for period ending March 31, 1953*, p. 8.

[3] See *Tarai and Bhabar Report*, p. 14.

something, and does do something, to exclude some types of animals at least; even elephants were said to be excluded by barbed wire at Giritale. In the Terai it was proposed in the 'northern vulnerable area' to fence the perimeter and then to clear a belt half a mile wide outside the fence in order further to discourage attack.[1] This method would be wasteful of land in a small scheme but might be emulated in the larger Ceylon schemes. The Gal Oya Development Board, working on different lines, propose to permit shooting all the year round in a 3-mile wide belt parallel to the *bund* of Senanayake Samudra in order to protect the developed areas from the nature sanctuary of the tank and upper catchment. Small pests are, however, another problem altogether, and the only answer in many colonies is to employ small boys as bird-scarers in the traditional manner, to the detriment of their schooling. On the whole, however, it is to be expected that the problem of wild animals will diminish as the cleared area in the Dry Zone grows and as communications open up farther regions. In fact, the situation today is, in many areas, already a great improvement on the state of affairs which formerly prevailed. Thus the second batch of colonists to be settled in the abortive Kala Wewa Colony in 1893 had their entire crop destroyed by birds and beasts;[2] today, Kagama (Old) Colony in the same region reports that attacks from wild life are very infrequent. And Elahera, Minne-riya, and Nachchaduwa also reported an improvement. In fact, the danger today is that the opening up of the Dry Zone by colonization and other means will lead to a diminution in its wild life, and even to the extinction of such creatures as the elephant. An active policy of conservation is therefore necessary and is being pursued.

All things considered, it is, then, evident that the modern Dry Zone colonist escapes many of the physical hardships and dangers which beset his predecessors. Malaria is conquered, and ought, given good luck and good judgement, to remain subdued; government irrigation works have done much, though not everything, to secure yields at least from the *Maha* paddy lands; and most colonists have no longer to wrestle with wild beasts. But, although all this is true, the average colonist does not live a life of ease. The

[1] Ibid., p. 33.
[2] See above, p. 113 and the *Report on the Kaláwewa Colonization Scheme*, p. 7.

domestic water problem almost everywhere, and locally the problem of *illuk* and of the depredations of wild beasts, serve to remind us that a number of aspects of the Dry Zone environment still cause difficulty. More subtle, and in many ways more serious difficulties are, however, caused by problems of soil and land use, which will be discussed in the next chapter.

17. GAL OYA DAM
With gap still to be filled (1951)

18. KAGAMA: THE COLONIST, HIS FAMILY, AND HIS HOME

19. BERAGAMA COLONY: 'MUDDING' PADDY FIELDS

20. BERAGAMA COLONY: PLOUGHING PADDY FIELDS
With new 'light iron plough'

12

Problems of Land Use

THE question of how far land-use techniques in the colonies are adequate to ensure perpetual cultivation in the face of the difficulties and peculiar problems of the Dry Zone environment will now be considered and the efficiency of agricultural production will be discussed.

Some General Problems

In two important respects the Government has a direct responsibility for conservation; for it ought (1) to ensure that the land handed over to the colonist has not been degraded by its negligence, and (2) to plan such a system of tree-belts that the colonist's land is protected against wind and other agents of erosion.

Some of the conservational aspects of land development, particularly the apparently unappreciated dangers of using soil-handling machines, have already been mentioned; and it has also been seen that one theoretically desirable method of ensuring conservation during jungle clearing, that of leaving uprooted or felled vegetation along the contour, has the practical disadvantage that the debris harbours pests.[1] Not very much damage does in fact probably result from conventional methods of jungle clearing by hand provided that alienation and planting take place very soon after clearing is completed. Damage is, however, likely to be done if there is a delay between clearing and alienation, unless a thick weed cover fortunately develops; and the damage is likely to be especially serious if, as in some of the war-time 'state farms', the cleared land is worked before colonization as a *chena*. There have been frequent warnings against this latter practice, and colonists dislike it because of the adverse effect on the fertility of their allotments; but there are high lands in Ridibendi Ela, Sangilikanadarawa, Unnichchai, and elsewhere whose infertility to this day is at least in part the result of a period spent as a 'state *chena*'.

Turning to the second sphere of government responsibility, the

[1] See above, p. 199.

present practice is to leave a belt of uncleared jungle along all streams and on steep and rocky ground; to leave shade trees along roads and, at the rate of one large tree per acre, in cultivated land; and to leave wind-belts wherever more than 500 acres are cleared. These measures, as planned, are now usually adequate; but they only became the rule in 1950, and earlier colonies contain very inadequate protection against the sun and wind. And in more recent colonies tree-belts planned are not always tree-belts in practice, largely because of clearing by colonists for firewood and by squatters for cultivation. This is particularly serious when it is a wind-belt which is attacked; for the effects of wind erosion, revealed by such signs as little winnowed clusters of quartz grains, are only to be found on careful inspection, so that the danger is often overlooked.

Paddy Land

There can be no doubt at all that the allocation of a major part of each colony to paddy cultivation represents a basically sound system of land use (see Plates 19–20). It may be argued that paddy is grown because of a social and dietetic preference for it, and bearing in mind the expense and difficulty of irrigation, it may be suggested that paddy should be replaced by dry crops; but it is extremely difficult to maintain soil fertility when these crops are grown under Dry Zone conditions, as will be shown in Chapter 17. Paddy cultivation is, in fact, in spite of its expensive and exacting irrigation requirements, an ideal way of using Dry Zone soils, perhaps the only certain way at present of producing a field crop from them in perpetuity with but little trouble beyond that which is traditionally taken.[1] While it is true that better field *bunds* and the application of smaller quantities of water at critical seasons would improve conservation in many paddy fields in the colonies, these facts must stand, whatever criticisms of colonists' methods one may have on other grounds.

Unfortunately, however, the prevention of erosion by means of *bunds* and terraces does not necessarily mean the maintenance of the pristine fertility of the fields. Although it is difficult to collect figures for yields in the colonies, and even more difficult to believe figures when they have been collected, there is evidence that yields

---

[1] The reasons for this state of affairs have already been discussed; see p. 46 above.

in the older colonies, like Minneriya, are falling off. This is, of course, a serious state of affairs, if only in view of the national need for maximum food production, and is primarily a matter of inadequate technology; but it does in fact constitute a further reason for devoting as much land as possible to paddy cultivation, for while efforts are being made to improve techniques some yield at least will always continue to come from the fields, and no irreparable damage is likely to be done to the soil.

A list of the technical deficiencies of paddy cultivation in the colonies is distressingly like the corresponding list for the *purāna* village[1] in spite of the fact that, because of the presence of Colonization Officers and other officials on a lavish scale, the colonies ought on the face of it to be models of improved paddy cultivation. But, as the Gal Oya Development Board have found, 'the progress, as reflected by the present level of agricultural efficiency, and in yield, is disappointing'.[2] What are the technical deficiencies of current practice, and what chances are there of improvement?

In the first place, very few colonists are in the habit of manuring their fields, except by ploughing in straw and weeds and by allowing cattle to graze while land is lying fallow. It was only at Kilinochchi, it appears, that cow dung, compost, artificial manure, and bone-meal were all applied to paddy fields in 1951; here is a clear example of Jaffna Tamil technology transferred from village to colony. Elsewhere, in the Sinhalese colonies, some colonists in Kagama (Old and New) and older fields at Minipe, and some colonists (especially the refugees from the Kotmale landslides) in Parakrama Samudra were reported to manure their fields; elsewhere little or nothing was done. This conclusion is confirmed by a random sample survey at Minneriya, which suggested that over 92 per cent. of the fields received no manure at all in 1951.[3] The general reluctance to use manure may in part be the result of a belief that no good will come from all the hard work involved, and for this view there is some justification; for as D. H. Grist has pointed out, 'the manuring of paddy is such a complicated problem and the evidence as to its efficacy so conflicting that it is unwise to be too dogmatic on the subject.'[4] There have been cases where manuring has actually lowered the yield; in fact, in trials in Ceylon

[1] See above, pp. 45–46. [2] See GODB, *Ann. Report*, 1952–3, p. 7.
[3] See *Ceylon Daily News*, 1 Dec. 1951.
[4] See D. H. Grist, *Rice* (London, Longmans, 1953), p. 182.

in *Maha* 1951–2, transplanting plus fertilizers, or transplanting plus organic manure, in a number of areas gave a *smaller* percentage increase over the yield of control plots than did transplanting alone![1] It might therefore be argued that the caution of the cultivator springs, as in the case of *chena* cultivation, from a wisdom which is unscientific but nevertheless soundly based. On the other hand, enough work has been done in Ceylon to suggest that certain manures do improve yields in certain soils. A further factor in some cases may be the poverty of the cultivator, which may prevent him from buying artificial manure even at subsidized prices, and prevent him from owning cattle, the obvious source of organic manure.

The rotation of other crops with paddy is an accepted method of maintaining soil fertility in many countries.[2] The tendency in the Ceylon colonization schemes is, however, to grow two paddy crops per annum if there is sufficient water, or, if there is not, to let some or all of the fields lie fallow in the dry season. The fallow period between two cultivations is therefore the only equivalent of a rotation crop, and, because of the poverty of the vegetation which springs up, a poor equivalent at that. Many suggestions have from time to time been made for using colonies for large-scale experiments in rotation cropping in *Yala* partly to improve fertility and partly to conserve water by growing some crop less demanding than paddy. Thus when the future working of what was to be Parakrama Samudra Colony was under discussion in 1943 it was proposed that in *Yala* the 5-acre paddy allotment should be under peas, gram, and other legumes (3 acres) and under chillies, tobacco, and onions (2 acres). But official realization of the value of rotation crops and a great deal of intensive propaganda have produced but little result in the colonies. In all the colonies he visited in the *Yala* of 1951 the author saw only one field of rotation crops in paddy allotments, a field of green gram at Nachchaduwa. An even more intensive propaganda effort is now being made; and the Gal Oya Development Board intends to enforce *Yala* cultivation of crops other than paddy under its Left Bank Channel. It remains to be seen what will be achieved in the face of resistances which

---

[1] See *Admin. Report: Agriculture*, 1952, pp. 10–11.
[2] See Grist, *Rice*, pp. 137–9. For the use of rotation cash crops in the Malayan colonization schemes, see Fed. of Malaya, Dept. of Information, *The Story of Tanjong Karang* (Kuala Lumpur, 1951), p. 18.

spring *inter alia* from tradition, from the social esteem in which paddy is held, from suspicion about the value of rotation, and from the desire to benefit to the full from the guaranteed price of paddy.

As Grist has stated, 'the weight of evidence throughout the paddy areas of the world is that transplanting is beneficial to the plant and results directly in increased yields';[1] there is the further point that transplanting enables the ground to be cleaned of weeds at the last moment to the further benefit of the rice plant. Neither transplanting nor weeding is, however, extensively practised in the colonization schemes. The author was only told of extensive transplanting in the Malay Colony at Beragama, at Elahera, and in certain parts of Parakrama Samudra, and the random sampling at Minneriya in 1951 showed that only 16 per cent. of the *kumburas* had been transplanted.[2] Many Kandyan colonists fail to practise in the colony the transplanting technique usual in their home *deniyas* and Tamils who weed in Jaffna fail to do so at Kilinochchi.[3] An important exception is to be found, however, in the Kotmale landslide refugees who, in the Pudur and Kalinga Ela parts of Parakrama Samudra, have established a reputation for good and careful cultivation, including transplanting; since they come from an area of chronic landlessness, they serve to give the lie to the suggestion of the World Bank mission that landlessness and efficiency may be incompatible.[4] It is now to be a condition of the allotment of paddy land in a colony that at least one acre shall be transplanted each season; but it remains to be seen whether the rule can be enforced, for there are considerable resistances; for example, not only is there no tradition of transplanting, but labour is often scarce; and the colonist is hard put to it merely to cultivate his five acres and to sow broadcast, and neither he, nor his womenfolk (on whom transplanting normally devolves) have time to transplant; and he may often be concerned lest transplanting will increase the time from sowing to maturity, a critical factor in a region of scarce water.

On the whole, standards of actual cultivation in the colonies appear to be better than those in most villages; the light iron plough, based on the traditional implement and drawn by buffaloes or bulls, is used by colonists in a number of colonies, though not

[1] See *Rice*, p. 121. [2] See *Ceylon Daily News*, 1 Dec. 1951.
[3] The author is indebted to Mr. M. Y. Banks for this and other information on the Iranamadu colonies. [4] See *WBR*, p. 391 (ii. 175).

by as large a proportion as some Colonization Officers would have one believe (see Plate 20). The Burmese harrow, which improves yields by thinning the standing crop, has proved less popular. In the improvement of cultivation techniques, one severe limiting factor is shortage of cattle, which will be discussed below.

Finally, another technical improvement which has made considerable strides is the use of pure-line seeds; thus just over half of the acreage studied in the Minneriya sample survey was sown with a pure-line variety, which gave a yield 11 per cent. higher than that from the unselected varieties.[1] But only 23 per cent. of the cultivators had sown one variety only, as is desirable, for the colonist finds difficulty in preparing the whole of his lot in time for, say, a $3\frac{1}{2}$–4 month variety of paddy so that he is forced to sow part with a shorter-maturing kind when at last his ground is ready. Adulteration of government pure-line seed also discourages its use.

From this review of technical problems in the Dry Zone colonization schemes, three important points emerge. In the first place, the colonist takes most kindly to improvements which can be most readily grafted on to his traditional methods, e.g. pure-line seed and the light iron plough. In the second place, the relatively large, 5-acre paddy lot, combined with lack of labour at crucial times, causes difficulty and puts a premium on extensive rather than intensive methods, so that even some of the Kandyans, like other highland peoples who have descended to the plains, have given up their traditional intensive methods.[2] In the third place, the more intensive propaganda which can be brought to bear on the colonist has to function in very much the same intellectual climate as effort in the villages.

It is impossible to quote yield statistics to reflect the differential distribution of technical skills in the colonies. Quite apart from the unreliability of the basic data, there is the important point that there are enormous differences in soil; for the paddy lands of the colonies vary from the fertile, flat fields of Beragama, with a clay content in places as high as 63·8 per cent., through the less clayey but still good paddy soils of parts of Parakrama Samudra to the relatively poor, sandy soils of Kilinochchi, Okkampitiya, Unichchai, and Gal Oya. Figures collected by the author may, however,

---

[1] See *Ceylon Daily News*, 1 Dec. 1951.
[2] Gourou, *Tropical World*, p. 91.

be of interest; average yields varied from 20 bushels per acre at Kilinochchi to 40 bushels per acre at Elahera, Minneriya, parts of Parakrama Samudra, and elsewhere; while a figure as high as 70 was claimed for one ex-service colonist at Parakrama Samudra. Other sources support the general picture given by these figures. Thus the yield per cultivated acre at Gal Oya in *Yala* 1953 was found to be 25·9 bushels, a figure which rose to 40 bushels per acre in one more-favoured village and to 57 bushels per acre in some good parts of it;[1] while the Minneriya sample survey indicated an average yield of 43·5 bushels per acre, and a yield as high as 113·5 from some fields; these figures compare with the results of an extended sample survey of the whole island which produced 30·8 as a national mean and 43·6 for Anuradhapura District.[2] The average Minneriya figures are, therefore, higher than the national mean but no higher than the mean for the district in which the colony is set. In fact, the general inference may perhaps be drawn for the colonies as a whole that their paddy yields do not differ markedly from those obtained in nearby villages, and that where there are differences they may so far be explained in terms of the exploitation on virgin soil. There is clearly still much room for the application of improved techniques.

It may be asked why so far no mention has been made of mechanization, so often considered the panacea for agronomic ills, as a possible means of technical improvement in the Dry Zone colonies. This subject has been left till the last because mechanization has so far been little used, and because grave doubts must be expressed about its applicability. Tractor ploughing might appear the obvious answer to the lack of labour in relation to size of allotment and to the need for early ploughing and for better cultivation of the soil; and it might also be thought that there were possibilities for mechanized harrowing and harvesting. Some efforts have in fact been made to encourage the use of tractors, mainly through the establishment of government tractor pools which make machines available to Co-operative societies, and by encouraging the societies themselves to purchase machines. In a number of colonies, considerable use has already been made of the facilities

[1] From a memorandum of the Gal Oya Development Board, quoted by kind permission of the Board.

[2] See *Ceylon Daily News*, 1 Dec. 1951, and *Admin. Report: Agriculture*, 1952, pp. 7–8. One colonist at Minneriya obtained 127 bushels per acre in *Maha* 1955–6; and one's general impression in 1956 is of some improvement.

thus made available. Thus tractors ploughed at Ridibendi Ela in *Maha* 1950–1, with resultant economy of water;[1] tractor ploughing and disking have been practised at Iranamadu (Paranthan);[2] at Kottu Kachchiya tractor ploughing was organized through the Rural Development Society; and at Minneriya, Stage I, there has been considerable demand for tractors for early ploughing. It might appear, then, that mechanization, at least of ploughing, is growing more popular, perhaps because of the saving in personal effort. On the other hand, it is very much to be doubted whether mechanization is really economic either in the general sense, that it is of doubtful present utility in an economy in which labour is a superabundant factor of production; or in the particular sense, that it does not pay, because of the fact that tractors are so far used almost exclusively for ploughing and lie idle when there is no ploughing to be done, and because of inefficient maintenance. And as Grist has recently shown, many agronomic difficulties have attended comparable efforts to mechanize peasant rice cultivation in Malaya.[3] It is true that the Dry Zone of Ceylon is not afflicted by the constantly wet conditions of the Malay paddy fields, but other problems, such as the need for highly efficient water control and for specially designed implements suited to small peasant plots and to local soil conditions, are common to both regions. Mechanization may also have an adverse effect on the soil. Moreover where, because of relatively steep relief, terraces are small, as at Bathmedilla or Dewahuwa, mechanization may be impossible; elsewhere it may demand a rearrangement of field *bunds* or collective or Co-operative cultivation to provide a large enough unit of land. In fact, under present circumstances it appears that mechanization may only function where land is farmed in large units; in other words, under conditions other than those implicit in peasant colonization. This raises the broader issue of possible alternatives to peasant colonization as a means of opening up the Dry Zone, which will be discussed in Chapter 18. Mechanization within the existing framework of peasant colonization is another matter, a matter of untried agronomic experiment. Work should proceed with caution; the Government and the peasant must beware of the pushful

---

[1] See *ARLC*, 1951, p. 6.
[2] Ibid., p. 7; *Admin. Report: Agriculture*, 1952, p. 62; and author's field notes.
[3] See *Rice*, pp. 62–63, and 155–71.

commercial pedlars of the apparent panacea of mechanization, and even look in the mouths of the gift-horses which arrive under the Colombo Plan.[1]

High Land Cultivation

Paddy cultivation in the Dry Zone colonies is, then, essentially sound from an ecological point of view, although capable of improvement in detail. The same cannot, unfortunately, be said of high land cultivation; for in the majority of allotments a method of land use has not yet been developed which will with certainty conserve the soil and maintain its fertility, and at the same time enable crops to be grown on a sustained yield basis. The intention behind the provision of high land allotments was the excellent one of using the class of unirrigable land which, on any view of Dry Zone resources, is more plentiful than irrigable land, in order to provide the colonist with a homestead lot in which he could grow fruits, vegetables, and dry grains; he could thus, it was thought, provide a very necessary supplement to his rice diet, produce a surplus for sale, and obtain some feed for his cattle. In other words, the high land allotment was meant to fulfil the functions of the high land garden of the Wet Zone village, and of *gangoda* and *chena* in the Dry Zone village. There are some excellent allotments, it should be said, fully planted, and producing a useful and sustained yield (see Plate 21). But there are others, the majority in many colonies, in which there are signs of actual or potential erosion, in which crops die before they produce a yield, and in which bare earth, weeds and useless secondary growth fill up the three acres around the colonist's house (see Plate 23). The unsatisfactory state of high land allotments has frequently attracted attention; thus the late D. S. Senanayake, as has already been stated, visited Tabbowa in 1950 and found the high lands 'disgraceful' (it was out of this visit that there arose the policy of paying a subsidy of Rs. 200 per colonist to encourage high land development); and the sorry state of high lands was also commented upon by the Kandyan Peasantry Commission.[2] But the problem is not merely one of the colonist's original sin, or even of his inadequate technology; it has deep roots in physical geography. For the essence of the trouble in high lands is that they

---

[1] A hundred tractors were, for example, given to Ceylon by Australia; see *Ceylon News Letter*, 18 Oct. 1952. [2] See *KPC*, pp. 133 and 270.

are being asked to function as *gangodas*, whereas most of them are without the ground water which alone can make a *gangoda* fruitful; and that nearly all of them are asked to function as *chenas* in perpetuity, without a periodical phase of regeneration. (This applies also to the high land allotments in V.E. schemes in the Dry Zone.) The high land problem can thus be conveniently considered under two main headings; first, the problem of creating a garden of tree crops and vegetables like that of the *gangoda*; and, second, the problem of growing field crops like those in a *chena*, but on a permanent basis. The second problem is mainly one of erosion and loss of fertility, to be countered by conservation, cover crops, rotations, and so on; the first, though erosion may occur readily before trees are established and to a lesser extent afterwards, is primarily that of establishing the trees.

Various tree crops are nearly always included in cropping schemes for high land allotments. Thus, when Parakrama Samudra Colony was being planned in 1943, it was thought that the 3-acre high land allotment should include ½ acre under coconuts, ½ acre under miscellaneous fruits, and ⅝ acre under plantains. And the model layout for the Iranamadu colonies, conformity with which is one of the conditions of the L.D.O. permit, includes 1 acre containing 54 coconuts and 125 palmyras and surrounded by 25 kapok trees and, in a further acre immediately round the house, 10 *murungā*, 15 king coconuts, 100 plantains, and a few mango, jak, breadfruit, orange, lime, and pomegranate trees. Almost all planting schemes in other colonies include some or all of the trees in the Iranamadu list, with the exception of the palmyra, although proportions vary greatly from place to place. Most of the planting material required is issued free from Department of Agriculture nurseries. The list of seeds and seedlings advanced by the National Land Settlement Administration in the Mindanao colonies bears a strong resemblance to the Ceylon list; this is not surprising, for the cultivation of tree-gardens is, of course, a general feature of Southern Asia.[1]

Now the trees which have been mentioned fall into two well-marked groups, one which includes trees which are not tolerant of drought, the other those which are. The first group includes coconut, the various citrus fruits, plantains, jak, and breadfruit; the second group includes most of the remainder, notably mango and

---

[1] See Pelzer, *Pioneer Settlement*, pp. 146–7.

murungā and, hardiest of all, the palmyra (see p. 252). It will be noted that the plants which have the greatest economic importance unfortunately fall into the first group; especially is this true of coconut, plantains, and citrus fruits. For the coconut is very dependent on adequate soil moisture; citrus crops cannot draw moisture from a greater depth than four to five feet, and depend on irrigation in countries such as Palestine which suffer seasonal drought;[1] and plantains suffer the disadvantage under Dry Zone conditions that they not only suffer from moisture deficiency in the dry season but are liable to rot during the wet season.

It is not surprising, therefore, that these drought-susceptible trees only flourish, in colonization schemes and elsewhere, where the water-table is fairly near the surface in the dry season; that is, in *gangoda*-like situations. It is, in fact, striking to observe how rarely this rule is broken. And *gangoda*-like situations, it will be clear from the previous chapter, depend on exactly the same conditions as perennial wells, that is, on proximity to surface water in the shape of river, tank, or channel. Thus excellent and delightful tree plots are in fact to be found in the older parts of Parakrama Samudra under the *bund* of the great tank itself; or in the Beragama colonies, either near the perennial Walawe Ganga or under the main distributary channel; or under the main *ela* at Elahera or Minipe; or under the Raja Ela at Minneriya.[2] Some of these plots are as luxuriantly green as any in the Wet Zone or in Indonesia. There are a few good groups of tree plots in sites not obviously *gangoda*-like, as at Giritale or, outside colonization schemes, in some orange groves of Bibile; here one can only guess that there are exceptional hydrological circumstances or, as at Bibile, a higher and differently distributed rainfall. But on the vast majority of high lands away from surface water it is extremely difficult to keep trees, especially young trees, alive in drought. Watering may help in some cases, if the peasant is willing and able to take the trouble; there is a good high land allotment at Maha Uswewa kept green by this means. But, quite apart from the lack of any Sinhalese tradition corresponding to that which centres on the wells of Tamil Nad,[3] watering becomes difficult if not impossible if the colonist's own

[1] See, for example, Joachim, 'Some Notes on the Citrus Industry of Palestine', *Trop. Agriculturist*, vol. lxxxvi (1936), pp. 323–31; and D. W. R. Kahawita, 'Citrus Culture in the Dry Zone', ibid., vol. xci (1938), pp. 266–79.

[2] See *ARDLD*, 1951, p. 13.   [3] See above, pp. 53–54.

well is dry; and it will be clear that a dry well is a very likely phenomenon in an allotment which is not *gangoda*-like in situation. Many warnings have, in fact, been given of the difficulty of high land cultivation of tree crops in the Dry Zone.[1]

There seem to be a number of lines towards a solution. In the first place, the conservation of surface water in small tanks which is so necessary to domestic water-supply[2] is bound to help the establishment of tree crops; this is a further argument in favour of the policy discussed in the previous chapter. In the second place, in colonies whose water resources exceed those necessary for the watering of the paddy tract it may be possible to install pumps or lifts and to irrigate some high lands, at least lightly, as in an experimental scheme to be instituted at Gal Oya. In the third place, replanning of colonies in some places would enable more high land allotments to be placed in *gangoda*-like situations with respect to *existing* surface water. In the fourth place, it may be necessary increasingly to fall back on drought-resistant trees in some allotments; thus the palmyra, the mainstay of arid Jaffna, may have in such cases to replace the more paying coconut. The palmyra is a remarkable palm, and the Jaffna Tamil is fond of recounting its many uses: its nutritious fruit, its useful fruit juice, the flour made by grinding shoots from the newly planted nut, and so on.[3] But it is not now popular in the Sinhalese districts (indeed, the Tamil colonists at Kilinochchi usually prefer coconut) and takes 20–30 years to produce fruit compared with the 7 years or so required by the coconut. (The palmyra may, however, have been more important than the coconut in the Dry Zone in classical Sinhalese times; for, according to Ferguson, there are more references to it than to the coconut in the *Mahāvaṃsa*.[4]) Another drought-resistant tree that might be grown on high lands is the cashew nut (*Anacardium occidentale*), in whose products there is an expanding trade; Indian exports of cashew-nut kernels have increased from 50 tons in 1925 to 27,417 tons in the year 1952–3.[5] The injunction of a

[1] See, for example, Ievers, p. 176; Leonard Woolf's MS. Diary; and the *Fruit Development Committee Report*, S.P. 20 of 1941, p. 14.

[2] See above, pp. 229–31.

[3] The author is indebted to Mr. V. Krishnapillai, Colonization Officer at Iranamadu in 1951, for information on the palmyra and on other matters.

[4] See J. Ferguson, 'The Coconut Palm in Ceylon', *J.R. As. Soc.* (Cey. Br.), vol. xix (1906), pp. 39–68.

[5] See 'Cashewnut Industry in India', *Ind. Trade and Industry*, vol. vi (1954), pp. 24–26.

British colonial servant in the early days at Tabbowa that 'if they can't grow coconut they should grow cashew' is thus not now quite so Marie Antoinettish as it must have sounded at the time.

In any case, what seems to be needed in the high land allotments is a greater degree of adaptation to local conditions. There are, it is true, considerable variations between schemes for different colonies; but what is needed is a variation, according to soil and hydro-geological conditions, *within* the colony.

The problems connected with the growing of field and garden crops with bare earth exposed between the plants must now be considered. These crops include the usual range of dry grains grown on *chenas* such as *kurakkan* and other millets, maize, sorghum, and gingelly; and vegetables such as manioc, yams, gourds, brinjals, chillies, and onions.[1] It is also sometimes suggested that fodder grasses, groundnuts, cotton, and other crops should also be grown.

The first problem raised by attempts to grow field crops is that erosion and soil degradation are all too prone to result from the exposure of bare soil (see Plate 23); this also applies to the cleared but as yet uncultivated allotment, and to the tree plot in which an arboreal cover has not yet been or cannot be established. The need is for some cover to protect the soil, and for contour *bunds* to check run-off and hence to conserve soils (and also water). It will be remembered, from the brief account which was given in Chapter 3, what damage was done in experiments in India under conditions similar to those of the Dry Zone.[2] The danger of erosion on high land allotments has been fully recognized by the authorities in Ceylon. D. S. Senanayake himself used to draw attention to them; quite early in the days of the 'New Policy' towards colonization he made statements on the necessity of protecting the soil from the start. And in most recent colonization schemes a subsidy in the region of Rs. 40 has been payable to the allottee on the completion of adequate conservation works.

Yet poor results have in fact been achieved. The author saw reasonably good conservation works in some allotments in a few colonies, notably in Giritale and Kottu Kachchiya. But elsewhere (and this applies to the majority of allotments) very little has been done to construct conservation works, and still less to provide

[1] For the identification of these crops see above, p. 48.
[2] See above, p. 55.

cover crops. One of the main reasons for this state of affairs is undoubtedly the colonist's preoccupation with his paddy allotment. Coming to the colony for the first time just before *Maha* cultivation is due, the social prestige and monetary value of the paddy crop mean that it tends to receive his undivided attention just when high land conservation and planting should be in progress. The same situation tends to recur each *Maha*, with labour shortage at least locally to be reckoned with. Another reason is that there is amongst the colonists, except for some of the Kandyans, no real tradition of soil conservation on high land, used as they are either to the *chena* of the Dry Zone or to the tree-garden of the Wet Zone. Further, it is often very difficult for climatic reasons to establish a cover crop which will survive the dry season and protect the soil from the first onslaughts of the rains, even if the colonist is willing to try. In view of all this, and since soil is irreplaceable capital, it might well be worth while for land-development work to include at least the construction of contour *bunds* as it does in the new 'dry-farming' colonies;[1] allotments should also be planned to conform to topography, and not to a geometrical pattern.[2] Research on cover crops must go on, and propaganda be used on the colonist from his boyhood onwards; but propaganda must expect to meet all the familiar resistances.

What of the problem of maintaining fertility? This is, of course, not only a matter of the prevention of erosion, but also of rotations and manures; in fact, more so than in the paddy lots. Here, as might be expected, a number of the Jaffna Tamils in the Iranamadu colonies have something to teach the Sinhalese. These colonists not only manure their allotments with compost and cow dung but some of them also practise a four-course rotation on the one acre which, under the model plan, they allot to field crops. The rotation is: (1) cereals; (2) legumes (green gram, cowpeas, &c.); (3) manioc and yams; (4) cash crops such as tobacco, chillies, onions, gingelly, and vegetables. (Not all, however, can be made to follow the model plan.) But elsewhere one very rarely sees signs of manuring, it again being outside Sinhalese tradition. Many are the plans for green manuring, cattle-keeping, and rotations, but few are the results so far. In any case, it is by no means certain, as has already been pointed out,[3] that a technique has yet been devised which can assure fertility in high lands for all time.

---

[1] See below, pp. 342–4.   [2] Cf. *CUCL*, p. 60.   [3] See above, pp. 49–50.

This, then, is in outline the general problem of the high land allotments of the Dry Zone colonies, a problem which must no doubt be matched in many other regions with markedly seasonal rainfall and little underground water. There are, however, few parallels in other South Asian regions of colonization. The Dry Zone high land problem becomes more serious in certain circumstances which occur locally. Thus very steep slopes are sometimes foolishly mapped out as high lands, as at Bathmedilla, where erosion is painfully visible and the only satisfactory answer is to reafforest the steep slopes (see Plate 22). Elsewhere poor soils may exaggerate the difficulties of holding water, of establishing crops, and of erosion; areas of great poverty were originally mapped out as high lands at Tabbowa, and old *chenas* not yet regenerated cause trouble elsewhere. Or, in the far end of ribbon colonies like Kagama (New), the colonist is so far from a market that he has no economic incentive, beyond his own needs and the subsidy, to attend to his high land (see Map 12).[1] Or the difficulty of working both paddy and high land in *Maha* may be increased where, as at Dewahuwa, the local relief makes it necessary to place the two classes of land some way apart.

It can thus be seen that, so far at any rate, the high land allotment is usually a poor substitute for *gangoda* or for a Jaffna garden, and a very dubious successor to *chena*;[2] and that the setting in of conditions which might turn the Dry Zone into a badly eroded waste, like parts of the Deccan, is a very real danger indeed. In some cases the trouble could be rectified by simple action, in others it is a matter of research and of the discovery of methods of influencing the colonist. By and large, however, the problem is more manageable in the closely controlled conditions of the colonies than in V.E. schemes or in other places in which it occurs and it is possible to see the colonies in this, as in other cases as the pioneers in the conquest of the Dry Zone.

Pasture

The colonist's animals are mainly, as might be expected, buffaloes and draught cattle; many, perhaps a majority of colonists, have, in spite of loans from the Government or from Co-operative

[1] There is now (1956), however, a road of sorts north from the channel road across the *bund* of Kattiyawa Wewa to the main road.
[2] Cf. above, pp. 47–50.

societies, insufficient cattle to enable them to cultivate properly, thus enhancing the difficulties which have been mentioned earlier in the chapter; others, usually a minority made up of Dry Zone villagers who have brought their cattle with them or of colonists who have grown wealthy in the colony, have too many, as in Minneriya Colony, and their cattle then become a great nuisance. But, whether there are too few or too many, there ought to be pasture for plough animals as long as they constitute the primary source of agricultural power. Moreover, though milch cattle are extremely rare except in the Tamil colonies of Iranamadu, there being a strong prejudice against them among Buddhists, it is very desirable, on nutritional grounds, that their number should be increased; and their demands on pasture are more exacting than those of draught cattle. Goats are, not surprisingly, even more rare among Buddhist colonists, since their main use is for meat; they are, however, to be found in the Malay Colony, at Iranamadu, amongst the Moors of Parakrama Samudra and the Tamils of Nachchaduwa, and also amongst the curious mixed society of Tabbowa; where goats are kept they again need pasture, though they are tolerant of much poorer conditions and, for that matter, of uncleared land.

The traditional Dry Zone answer to the problem of pasture is, of course, to use fallow paddy fields and the jungle. The former is available in the colony, but on a restricted scale if there is a full *Yala* cultivation. And the use of jungle is impossible in the larger colonies where it is too far removed from the central allotments, and undesirable in all because of the uncontrolled breeding, loss to wild animals, and slack animal husbandry which are encouraged. One partial solution, the grazing of animals and growing of fodder on high land allotments, has already been mentioned; and other possible answers have been debated from the date of the experimental Nachchaduwa Colony (1920) onwards. But it cannot be said that the problem has as yet been solved. In a fair number of colonies (notably Bathmedilla, the Beragama colonies, Dewahuwa, Giritale, Kottu Kachchiya, Maha Kumbukkadawala, Maha Uswewa, and Sangilikanadarawa) there was no provision at all in 1951. In most others the area set aside was inadequate for actual or potential needs, either in size or in quality or in both. Thus at Minneriya pasture was confined to the area of poor *damana* christened 'Windsor Park' by the members of the R.A.F. who lived

21. ELAHERA COLONY: PRODUCTIVE AND TIDY HIGH
LAND LOT

22. BATHMEDILLA COLONY: HIGH LAND LOT
Far too steep for safe cultivation

23. UNNICHCHAI COLONY: HIGH LAND LOT
Parched by dry season

24. RELAPANAWA: ANCIENT MINOR TANK RESTORED
To preserve the water-table

near it in the war. Now Ceylon is not alone in this respect among
the South Asian countries which organize colonization. No provision at all is made for pasture in the Indonesian and Philippine
colonies;[1] while, although 20 per cent. of the Lower Chanab
Colony was originally reserved for pasture, fuel, and other common purposes, this was of little use because it was confined to the
highest and worst land (later, however, after much discussion, a
definite reservation for each village was made).[2]

Now the inadequate provision of pasture by no means arises
from a failure to appreciate the need for it; but it is very largely a
matter of the difficulties which attend the establishment of pastures in a tropical country, especially one characterized by seasonal
rainfall. These difficulties have recently been adequately discussed for Ceylon by the World Bank mission;[3] and they were
discussed for India by the Royal Commission on Agriculture.[4]
They are of two kinds, physical and human. The physical problem
in the Dry Zone is largely a climatic one, that of finding a nutritious grass which will survive trampling in the dry season. So far,
opinion favours molasses grass (*Melinis minutiflora*), Napier grass
(*Pennisetum purpureum*), and *Brachiaria* spp. with the legume *Stylo-
santhes* spp. But much work remains to be done. The human
problem is that even if suitable grasses and legumes can be found
there is no local tradition of pasture management whatsoever; the
colonist comes from a world which is far removed from one of grass
leys, managed pasture, and silage. The current scheme in the
colonies is for the Government to clear an area for pasture, and
then to turn it over for management to peasant Co-operatives or, at
Gal Oya, to village committees. It is to be doubted whether this is,
at present at any rate, a satisfactory solution; quite apart from the
fact that new techniques are needed, Co-operatives themselves tend
to be an imposition from outside on the social structure of the
colonies.[5] Some time ago the Government cleared and fenced 100
acres for pasture for the Tabbowa colonists; today the field is a
tangle of secondary growth, and it will require a great deal of social

[1] Information kindly supplied by the Indonesian Embassy and Philippine
Legation in London. [2] See *Punjab Colony Manual*, i. 153–7.
[3] See *WBR*, pp. 317–22 (ii. 124–8).
[4] See Cmd. 3132, pp. 201–2. For the general problem of tropical pasture,
see Gourou, *Tropical World*, pp. 53–64, and B. H. Duclos, *Pâturages et fourrages
tropicaux* (Paris, Maison Rustique, 1952).
[5] See below, pp. 295–7.

and technical change if the new policy of Co-operative pastures is not to produce the same result. The Gal Oya Development Board propose to reserve considerable areas of pasture for the first ten years or so, mainly for *purāna* villagers. Ultimately it is hoped to reduce the size of the herds owned by these villagers and to limit each colonist to one pair of draught cattle and a cow (buffaloes being excluded because of the damage they do to channels). It is then ultimately hoped to reserve only a few swampy areas for pasture and otherwise to rely on fallow, on fodder crops grown in paddy fields in *Yala*, and on high lands. It will be interesting to see whether the technical and social difficulties which stand in the way of this policy can be overcome. It may be of interest to note that in the Indian Terai scheme also it is proposed to limit the number of cattle, and to grow fodder crops.[1]

Forest

Ideally, at any rate, each colony needs 'village forest', to use the terminology of the mapping-out proposals of the Land Commission;[2] the function of this forest is to provide timber for fencing, building, firewood, and so on, much as in the medieval European village. The Wet Zone Low Country immigrant is, of course, unlikely to have had this amenity in his old home, neither is the Kandyan if he has come from an estate-girt village; but the Dry Zone peasant is used to a forest on his doorstep. A number of proposals have from time to time been made for the allocation of forest to the Ceylon colonies; and there are a number of colonies (notably the Iranamadu colonies, Kagama Old, and Ridibendi Ela) where there are definite reservations for colonists' use. But elsewhere there is no specific provision, and colonists are wont to help themselves from jungle or from conservational reservations, not a very satisfactory state of affairs. The problem of 'village forest' is, in fact, one which needs attention.

Conclusion

There are thus a number of complex problems connected with land use in the Ceylon Dry Zone colonies; in many cases, the authorities are aware of them but, no obvious solution being in sight, the problems remain. As a means of soil conservation, paddy

---

[1] See *Tarai and Bhabar Report*, p. 32.
[2] See p. 120 above; cf. *WBR*, p. 342 (ii. 142).

cultivation is generally satisfactory and would be more so if customary techniques paid more attention to the maintenance of the
pristine fertility of the fields; high land cultivation is generally
much less satisfactory except where hydrological conditions permit
the establishment of permanent tree crops. That is not to say that
it is foolish to try and establish high land allotments; the alternatives are not to use high land at all, which would be to waste the
greater part of Dry Zone land, or to allow the colonists to practise
chena, which would be a dangerous anachronism. Provided that
proper conservational precautions are taken (and this may prove
to be a job for the land-development authorities) the high lands
may well prove to be a useful laboratory for studying the use of
unirrigable land; but there must be more small-scale adjustment
to local conditions, and a willingness to try new ideas.[1]

If the criterion is the ability of the colonist to contribute fully to
Ceylon's population and food problems, then clearly there is room
for improvement in both paddy and high land allotments. In the
case of paddy, it is mainly a matter of applying techniques already
known; in the case of the high land, techniques will also have to
be discovered. But in both the major problem is to induce the
colonist to change his traditional ways; for however undesirable
his practices may be from the point of view of conservation or of
food production, he will not willingly change them if, as at present,
he usually sees no incentive. The colonist, in other words, may
well be content with the state of affairs which has been discussed in
this chapter. But the attitude of the colonist cannot be understood,
and the present contribution of the colonies cannot properly be
appreciated, without some consideration of the economic and
social conditions in which he finds himself: and to these discussion
must now turn.

[1] Cf. below, pp. 342–8.

13

The Economy of the Colonist

IN general, the observations made in this chapter refer only to colonies which had become fully established by 1951; that is, to those in which irrigation had by that date been properly provided, and in which the colonist, having done the hard initial work of completing the preparation of his allotment, was successfully cultivating it, at least in terms of the relatively unimproved techniques described in the last chapter.

The Colonist's Income

It is not easy to arrive at accurate figures for colonists' incomes. The author did, however, by inquiring from Colonization Officers in June–December 1951, attempt to ascertain for the average colonist at each colony (1) the proportion of the total produce sold for cash, and (2) the total annual net income, in cash and in kind. The results of this reconnaissance survey are shown, for the well-established colonies, in Table 22. There are, of course, considerable variations between one colony and another, and quite apart from faulty estimates these are bound to arise owing to variations in soil, water resources, technique, and other factors. There is, however, a certain consistency about the results; almost all colonies sold, on an average, one-half to four-fifths of their crops, and in many of them the colonist could expect a total annual net income of Rs. 1,500–3,000 (about £115–230). Most of this income arose from the paddy crop, though in some colonies with well-cultivated, *gangoda*-like high lands as much as Rs. 800 per annum (gross) might derive from high land cultivation.

A certain amount of confirmation for these figures comes from official sources. The peasant colonist whose budget was published in the report on *Agricultural Wages and Earnings of Primary Producers in Ceylon* derived from his land an annual net income of Rs. 1,800 per annum.[1] But this was in 1949, when the price of

[1] See *Agricultural Wages and Earnings of Primary Producers in Ceylon*, Table 15, p. 49.

paddy was Rs. 8 per bushel instead of the Rs. 9 which obtained in
1951. No comprehensive figures have yet been compiled by the
Gal Oya Development Board, but a *Yala* cultivation in one village
yielded nearly Rs. 950 (gross) per colonist in 1953; the gross
income for the whole year might be expected to exceed twice that
amount.[1]

TABLE 22

Estimated Income of Colonists, 1951

Colony	Proportion of produce sold	Estimated total income (rupees)*
Beragama	About ½	600–700†
Beragama (Malay) . .	Over ½	600–700†
Elahera	About ½	4,000 downwards
Giritale	¾	2,500–3,000
Iranamadu (Kilinochchi) .	⅘	1,800–2,500‡
Kagama (Old) . . .	⅔	1,500 aver.
Kagama (New) . . .	⅔–¾	1,500–2,500
Minipe	⅘	4,000?
Minneriya, St. I. . .	¾	3,000–4,000
Nachchaduwa . . .	¾	3,500?
Parakrama Samudra:		
Blocks A, B, C . .	⅔	2,000–3,000
Blocks D, E, F . .	⅔	1,350–3,000
Ex-servicemen's . .	½–⅔	3,000 downwards
Ridibendi Ela . . .	?	2,400 aver.
Sangilikanadarawa . .	About ½	800?
Tabbowa	V. variable	V. variable
Unnichchai . . .	?	1,100?

* Rs. 13·33 = £1 sterling.
† Probably an under-estimate.
‡ May be an over-estimate.
Source: author's inquiries of Colonization Officers—see text.

Though it is difficult with such inadequate data to draw firm
conclusions about the prosperity of one colony as compared with
that of another, one thing is clear: in most established colonies
the average colonist is much better off than the average villager.
The average *gross* income of Ceylonese families dependent on
agriculture was given in 1950 as Rs. 95·31 per month, or about
Rs. 1,150 per annum, well below the *net* annual income of the

[1] Quoted by kind permission from a memorandum of the Board.

average colonist in most of the colonies shown in Table 22.[1] And there is, of course, an even greater gap between the income which a man earns as a colonist and that which he formerly earned as a landless or near-landless villager. Whatever opinions others may hold on the success of colonization, for the established colonist it is certainly an economic success, and he has every reason to be grateful to his Government. Often, indeed, he *is* grateful.

The ability to produce a surplus and to earn a relatively high income is a familiar phenomenon in some, but not all, Asian colonization schemes. Sir Malcolm Darling called attention to the prosperity of the Punjab Canal Colonies; and in the modern Thal scheme it is said that the cultivator can earn Rs. 1,000 net from a single harvest.[2] Colonists at Tanjong Karang, in Malaya, are able to sell some 60 per cent. of their rice crop.[3] But, although it was the aim of the Philippine colonization programme 'to create a class of agriculturists who would be more than subsistence farmers working to cover their barest needs', recent information hints that colonists in Mindanao are not necessarily better off than other Filipino peasants, because of lack of initial capital and other concomitants of a low scale of aid.[4] And, although it is reported that Indonesian colonists are in general better off than peasants in Java, they are not necessarily better off than peasants in the Outer Islands; further, the average Indonesian colonist is said to need most of his produce for his own consumption, and to have a cash income, over and above the value of food needed for subsistence, of only some £40 (Rs. 520).[5]

The contrast between the income of peasant and colonist that has been demonstrated for some at least of the Ceylon colonies is thus by no means universal in South Asia, and hence is not a simple result of such generally distributed features of colonies as the existence of a virgin soil. Clearly, too, from what has been said in the previous chapter, it is not a result of a great improvement in technology; except in certain directions (e.g. the adoption of pure-line

---

[1] See *Prelim. Rep. 2nd Econ. Survey Rural Ceylon, 1950*, S.P. 11 of 1951, p. 17.

[2] See Darling, *Punjab Peasant*, pp. 111–37; and Jehangir A. Khan, 'Thal', *Pakistan Q.*, vol. ii, no. 3 (1952), pp. 20–26.

[3] See Fed. of Malaya, *The Story of Tanjong Karang*, p. 16.

[4] See Pelzer, *Pioneer Settlement*, p. 156. Recent information kindly supplied by the Philippine Legation in London.

[5] The author is indebted to the Indonesian Ambassador in London for obtaining data on this point from Jakarta.

seed) the intensive supervision which has been lavished on the colonies has yielded disappointing results. The relative prosperity of the colonist arises from peasant agriculture, in spite of its technical deficiencies and, often, in spite of an unprofitable high land allotment. The reason for this must be sought in other factors now to be discussed; particularly in size of holding, scale of aid, provision of credit and marketing facilities, and system of tenure. In the course of the discussion, it will become apparent that there are ways in which the influence of some of these factors upon incomes could be increased; in other words, the difference between incomes in colony and in village is not as great as it might be.

Factors Tending to the Prosperity of the Colonist

(a) *The size of holdings*. The greatest single factor contributing to the relative prosperity of the colonist is obviously, in most colonies, the size of the holdings. By about 1940 the standard allotment had become fixed at 5 acres of paddy and 3 acres of high land; the prevalence of the 5-acre/3-acre allotment in 1951 will be evident from Table 23. The variants fell into three principal categories: (1) survivals from older arrangements, as in Nachchaduwa and the Malay Colony and in the somewhat confused situation at Tabbowa; (2) modifications of the older colonies, mainly made with the object of giving colonists more than the half-acre or so of 'homestead allotment' which was in some cases all the high land that was originally allotted (thus each colonist at Kagama Old and some of those in the oldest part of Minneriya were given an extra 5 acres of high land); (3) variations from the standard pattern made necessary in some newer colonies by lack of land (e.g. lack of paddy *and* high land in the steep and rocky conditions at Bathmedilla, lack of high land at Pandiyankadawela and Okkampitiya).

But, for all these variants, it will be clear that the 5-acre/3-acre allotment, and in particular the 5-acre paddy allotment, were distributed very widely indeed; rarely, moreover, was the paddy allotment smaller than 4 acres. If one compares this situation with that in *purāna* villages and V.E. schemes,[1] it will be clear that here is a very important cause of the relatively high income of the average well-established colonist; he had only to sow a *Maha* crop and obtain a yield of 20 bushels per acre to earn the

---

[1] See above, pp. 56–66 and 82–90.

equivalent in cash and kind of Rs. 900 at the guaranteed price of Rs. 9 which prevailed in 1951. In some cases at least it is clear that the increase in his income is not commensurate with the increase in the size of the holding.

TABLE 23

Sizes of Holdings, 1951

	Established colonies*			Other colonies		
Colony	Paddy (acres)	High land (acres)		Colony	Paddy (acres)	High land (acres)
Beragama . .	5	3		Bathmedilla . .	4	2
Beragama (Malay) .	3–5	1		Dewahuwa . .	5	3
Elahera . . .	5	3		Gal Oya . .	4	3
Giritale . . .	5	3		Iranamadu (Par.) .	4	3
Iranamadu (Kil.) .	5	2		K. Kachchiya .	5	3
Kagama (Old) .	5	5½–5¾		M. Kumbukkadawala .	5	3
Kagama (New) .	5	3		M. Uswewa .	5	3
Minipe . . .	5	3		Minneriya, St. II .	5	3
Minneriya, St. I .	5	Small plot plus 5 acres for some		Minneriya, St. III .	5	3 appr.
Nachchaduwa . .	3–5	1 appr.		Okkampitiya . .	5	2
Parakrama Samudra:				Pandiyankadawela .	5	1½
Blocks A, B, C .	5	1½–3		Parakrama Samudra:		
Blocks D, E, F .	5	3		Pudur, &c.‡ . .	5	3
Ex-servicemen .	5	3†		Uriyawa . . .	5	3
Ridibendi Ela . .	5	3				
Sangilikanadarawa .	5	1½ or 3				
Tabbowa . .		Variable				
Unnichchai . .	5	3				

* For definition, see text.
† Three acres applies to former 'other ranks'; former officers have 5 acres of high land.
‡ Pudur, Onegama, and Kalinga Ela.

Source: author's investigations.

(b) *The scale of government aid.* The scale of initial aid which the Ceylon Government was granting to colonists in 1951 has already been set out in some detail[1] and need not be repeated here.[2] There can be no doubt that the high scale of government aid was important in attracting colonists to the Dry Zone in the days when it bore an evil reputation. Moreover, it has been a factor of some importance in the colonist's prosperity by removing from him the burden of making anything but the tiniest capital investment in his holding; and this burden is one which, because of his poverty, he is singularly ill-equipped to bear. Just how poor the colonist tends to be initially is revealed in striking fashion by figures collected by

[1] See above, pp. 167–8.
[2] See also *ARLC*, 1951, pp. 3–4, and GODB, *Ann. Report*, 1951–2, pp. 53–54.

the Gal Oya Development Board, which show that the average
family settled by the Board in 1950–2 owned only Rs. 11·84 worth
of household goods, Rs. 22·60 worth of personal goods and assets,
Rs. 5·55 of agricultural goods, and Rs. 21·46 worth of livestock.[1]
And it is the high scale of aid which enables the landless, penniless
immigrant to take over a virtually ready-made farm and to go into
production straight away; it also gives him an income to tide him
over until he has reaped his first harvest.

TABLE 24

Land and Water Charges, 1951

Colony	Water charge per irrigated acre (rupees)	Land charge per acre (rupees)
Beragama (Malay)	2·00	1·00
Beragama	nil	1·00
Elahera	nil	2·00
Iranamadu (Kilinochchi) . . .	1·00	1·00
Kagama (Old)	5·00	0·50
Kagama (New)	0·50 or 5·00*	0·50 or 10·00*
Minipe	5·00	10·00
Minneriya, St. I	5·00	10·00
Nachchaduwa	2·50	0·50 paddy / 0·25 high land
Parakrama Samudra, Blocks A, B, C, E .	nil	10·00
Tabbowa	1·50	5·00 paddy / 2·50 high land
Unnichchai	nil	10·00 paddy / nil high land

* According to Tract.

Source: author's inquiries.

The assistance given to the new colonist is further increased
because he is initially excused payment for irrigation water and
for the tenure of his land. The initial period during which these
concessions hold is liberally interpreted. In fact, in 1951 charges
were only being levied in the colonies and parts of colonies shown
in Table 24. Moreover, when charges *are* eventually levied, they
are apt to be very low; as Table 24 shows, water charges varied
from 50 cents to Rs. 5 per acre (they are not meant to cover more
than mere maintenance costs) and charges for paddy land from

[1] From a memorandum of the Board, quoted by kind permission.

50 cents to Rs. 10 per acre.[1] Clearly, even the highest *total* charges tabulated (Rs. 15 per acre at Minipe and in Stage I at Minneriya) can easily be met from the proceeds of the crop. And the low general level of the land charges serves to enhance the differential between the colonist and the villager who does not own his land, particularly the villager who is an *ande* tenant handing over half his gross crop to the landlord.

(*c*) *Credit and marketing facilities.* The Government of Ceylon has made special efforts to provide its colonization schemes with credit and marketing facilities, notably through Co-operative societies. The results on the income of the colonist and on the difference between his income and that of the villager are not as spectacular as the results of the factors already discussed; but because there are various interesting complexities the discussion of credit and marketing will have to be a little more extended.

In spite of the aid which he receives, the colonist is likely to need credit fairly early on in his career, for example, to buy seed for his second crop, or to hire buffaloes, or to buy consumer goods. In the village, the traditional sources of credit are the *boutique*-keeper and local man of substance, with their high rates of interest. In the colony and reformed village the answer, in theory at any rate, is the Co-operative society.

But credit cannot be separated from marketing. The finding of a market, and the prices ruling in that market, are obvious factors in the prosperity of the colonies, especially in view of the fact that they sell such a high proportion of their crop. But, just as in the village the *boutique*-keeper is both money-lender and buyer (or at least absorber) of crops, so in the colony (and for that matter in the reformed village) recent government policy has made the Co-operative Agricultural Production and Sales Society (C.A.P.S.) a mechanism for both credit and marketing. The two aspects, credit and marketing, must therefore be considered together.

Co-operation, is, of course, the fashionable remedy for the diseases of Asian peasant economies.[2] As has been seen,[3] there was little talk of it in the early days of colonization in the Dry

---

[1] There is no land revenue, as distinct from payments for Crown land, in Ceylon.

[2] For co-operation in general see W. K. H. Campbell, *Practical Co-operation in Asia and Africa* (Cambridge, Heffer, 1951), and Margaret Digby, *Agricultural Co-operation in the Commonwealth* (Oxford, Blackwell, 1951).

[3] See above, pp. 101–15.

Zone, but there was much interest in it during the discussions of the 1930's, it was an integral part of the creed of D. S. Senanayake and of the 'New Policy' of 1939, and it received a great fillip during the war of 1939–45. In Ceylon it has in general been the policy of the Government to encourage the formation of a number of societies, each for a different purpose, within each village or colony;[1] multi-purpose general-service societies have not been encouraged, although the Gal Oya Development Board have established them.[2] The types of society which are relevant here are credit societies and Co-operative Agricultural Production and Sales (C.A.P.S.) societies. Credit societies, with the simple function of making small loans at low rates of interest, largely dominated the scene in the early days of Co-operation in Ceylon, but they are by no means universal in the colonies. In 1951 they only existed at Elahera, Giritale, Kagama (New), Minneriya, Okkampitiya, Parakrama Samudra, Sangilikanadarawa, and Tabbowa (it will be noted, however, that this list includes some of the larger colonies). In some other colonies attempts were being made to form credit societies, in others like Dewahuwa the time was not considered ripe.

C.A.P.S. societies are intended 'to promote the economic interests of their members and to arrange for the better development of agriculture, animal husbandry and the marketing of produce'.[3] They have in recent years multiplied very rapidly in Ceylon as a whole, in fact from only 47 societies in 1947–8 to 337 in 1950–1. This multiplication was largely a result of very active government stimulus of two main kinds. In the first place, the Land Development Department lends money to C.A.P.S. societies at only 2 per cent. interest, on both a short-term and a long-term basis, for such purposes as the purchase of seeds, manure, buffaloes, and implements, the construction of mills and warehouses, and the sinking of wells; in addition, cash loans are available to members in areas where there is a surplus of produce (and this clearly applies to established colonies) in order to enable them to undertake transplanting, reaping, threshing, and preliminary cultivation; and, where societies have proved their capacity, additional cash loans

---

[1] For Co-operation in Ceylon in general, see *WBR*, pp. 198–205 (ii. 46–50); Digby, *Agricultural Co-operation*, pp. 93–103; and the *Admin. Reports: Co-operative Societies*.

[2] See GODB, *Ann. Report*, 1952–3, p. 5.

[3] See *ARDLD*, 1951, p. 43.

of not more than Rs. 500 per member may be made against the security of the standing crop.[1] C.A.P.S. societies are also used for the distribution of subsidized manure, barbed wire and, as already mentioned, for attempts to introduce tractors (though with relatively little effect so far on technology in the colonies, as will already be apparent). It will be evident that these provisions to a large extent remove the need for separate credit societies, except that a man may still need a loan for non-productive purposes, or for productive purposes where the amount required is more than the maximum which he can obtain through his C.A.P.S. society.

The Government uses C.A.P.S. societies as its agents for the purchase of commodities, such as paddy, maize, *kurakkan*, and chillies, for which it offers guaranteed prices.[2] A number of societies also operate their own rice-hulling mills, notably at Nachchaduwa and Minneriya Colonies.

The very favourable financial arrangements made available to C.A.P.S. societies, together with active propaganda in their favour, resulted in their establishment by 1951 in all the colonies except Beragama (Malay) and Dewahuwa, though in some (e.g. Maha Uswewa) the society was shared with a nearby *purāna* village. This does not mean, however, that the colonist has necessarily dispensed with the old-style middleman, for reasons to be discussed a little later on.

In spite, however, of the continuing activity of the private trader, and in spite of various other difficulties, it would nevertheless appear that Co-operatives have contributed sometimes to the high income of many colonists by providing cheap credit and by paying relatively high prices for basic products, and possibly also, though with less frequency so far, by stimulating investment in productive enterprises. Assuming that a colony and a village both have their incomes increased in the same proportion by these causes, then the absolute gap between the two is bound to widen. But it must be stressed that, in the absence of an objective, outside study of the working of Co-operation in the villages, it is not possible to test the validity of the assumption which has just been made. Three things are, however, clear; that Co-operatives tend to increase the absolute income of colonists where they are effective; that Co-operation is at work in a higher proportion of colonies than of villages; and that the special provisions for 'surplus areas'

[1] *ARDLD*, pp. 44–47.   [2] Ibid., pp. 47–49.

affect all colonies, but only a fraction of the villages. But it must be admitted that a large part of the effect of Co-operatives derives from the fact that they are used to operate the guaranteed-price scheme, and not essentially from the fact that they are Co-operatives.

Marketing in the colonies is, however, not merely a matter of guaranteed prices and Co-operatives. Not all commodities are subject to guaranteed prices; this applies especially to vegetables, plantains, and coconuts, all, it will be noted, high land products. Although there is nothing to prevent C.A.P.S. societies from selling these, in practice the private trader usually steps in and the price to the colonist correspondingly falls. True, there is a government Marketing Department which purchases vegetables and pays good prices in some areas, but in 1951 it had extended its activities to very few colonies. Vegetables are usually sold either to itinerant traders or in the local fair or bazaar, and in all these cases the demand and the price depend very much on proximity to a town or large bazaar. The bazaars at Minneriya and Parakrama Samudra are large enough to constitute a market in themselves, and other colonies are conveniently close to Anuradhapura or some other urban centre. But as yet no such centre has grown near the remoter colonies, such as Kagama; and even in Minneriya and Parakrama Samudra it is a cause for complaint that government construction of shops has lagged behind colonization.

Some colonies, too, suffer from lack of good road access to the actual allotments, so that, even if a market is not far away, lorry transport cannot be used; traders may in such circumstances not call at all, or may offer only low prices. Lorry traffic is in fact prohibited by the Irrigation Department in the Iranamadu colonies, in the remoter parts of Kagama (see Map 12), and in parts of Nachchaduwa and Parakrama Samudra; in the ex-servicemen's colony in the last-named scheme, tomatoes which fetch 40 cents per pound in the bazaar may, it was said, bring only 4 cents to the colonist. These difficulties serve to accentuate the remoteness and reduce the prosperity of certain colonies. The problem tends to be complicated by divided responsibility for roads: main roads are attended to by the Public Works Department, but the Irrigation Department maintains what are known as 'agricultural roads', and also constructs and maintains roads in the paddy blocks and along distributary channels, while roads in the high land blocks are constructed by the Land Development Department but maintained by the Land Commissioner. There is, however, a general awareness of the need for good access if a colony is to be prosperous, and, in addition to internal roads within colonies, there have recently been a number of proposals for new main road links in the Dry Zone (see Map 2). The Gal Oya Development Board, moreover, operates boats on the coastal lagoons, and has considered an extension of the railway which at present ends at Batticaloa.

Where marketing and transport difficulties occur, they to some extent offset the factors making for a high income in the colony, and, since they affect mainly high land produce, may discourage high land development. Remoteness, of course, also retards social and educational change.

It may finally be noted that Co-operative credit and marketing facilities are generally provided in other Asian colonization schemes. Co-operation in various forms became a basic tenet of colonization in the Punjab, where, as in Burma, there were even colonies in which the land was held co-operatively.[1] In Indonesia much attention is paid to Co-operatives.[2] In the Dujaila scheme in Iraq there were in 1951 farm Co-operatives through which tractors were lent, and it was hoped to start marketing societies in 1952; opposition was, however, being encountered from merchants and landlords.[3] In the Philippines, on the other hand, only modest beginnings had been made by 1952.[4]

Other marketing methods have not been forgotten in these schemes; in particular, elaborate *mandis*, or markets, were laid out at suitable points in the Punjab colonies.[5] And most colonizing authorities have, in recent days at any rate, recognized the need for communications in a colony which has to dispose of surplus produce. In the Nili Bar Colony in the Punjab, for example, well-planned, metalled roads were laid out in advance, and had a marked effect on the successful development of new market towns.[6] And the Philippines are notable for a great programme of 'National Highways' in the colonization area of Mindanao.[7]

[1] See Darling, *Punjab Peasant*, espec. pp. 154 and 228–45, and *Co-op. Societies in Burma*.
[2] Information kindly obtained from Jakarta by the Indonesian Ambassador in London.　　　　　　　　　　　　[3] See Fisk, in *Econ. Geog.*, vol. xxviii, p. 346.
[4] Information kindly supplied by the Philippine Legation in London.
[5] See Cmd. 3132, p. 384.　　　　　[6] See *Punjab Colony Manual*, i. 25.
[7] Information kindly supplied by the Philippine Legation in London.

But Ceylon would appear to be outstanding for the energetic use which has been made of Co-operatives as a means of carrying out government policy concerning food production and marketing. The establishment of successful Co-operatives for these purposes is not without its difficulties, but at least it may be said that an interesting experiment is being carried out in the villages and colonies of Ceylon.

(*d*) *Tenure.* The system of tenure under the Land Development Ordinance (L.D.O.), the evolution and main provisions of which have already been outlined,[1] was almost universal in the Dry Zone colonization schemes in 1951. Only at Tabbowa, that scene of rich confusion in many fields, were tenures under older systems still being changed into tenures under the L.D.O. It will be remembered that L.D.O. tenure has provisions designed to prevent leasing, mortgaging, or sale, and to prevent fragmentation by instituting inheritance by a sole successor. Very similar systems of tenure have been evolved for similar reasons elsewhere though few of them are as thoroughgoing as the L.D.O. Thus in the Gezira scheme there are provisions against fragmentation, absentee landlordism, and sale to merchants.[2] In the Dujaila scheme land may not be sold or leased during the ten probationary years, though when, after that time, a definite grant is made there are no such restrictions.[3] The Punjab Canal Colonies were the scene of the complicated evolution of a tenure suited to peasant conditions. Early on, however, by the provisions of the Government Tenants (Punjab) Act of 1893, tenants could only sell, give away, or mortgage their land with the sanction of the Financial Commissioner;[4] while in 1912 government tenants, but not peasant proprietors, were required to nominate a successor.[5] And the Colonies Commission recommended in 1908 that though tenants should be subject to restricted tenure, there should be no restrictions, apart from those of the ordinary law, after the granting of proprietary rights.[6] In the Terai scheme 'the settler possesses the hereditary rights for cultivating the land but cannot mortgage or sell it. The land cannot be subdivided or further leased out. The state has

---

[1] See above, espec. pp. 159–60.
[2] See Keen, *Agricultural Development of the Middle East*, p. 18.
[3] See Fisk, in *Econ. Geog.*, vol. xxviii, pp. 343–4.
[4] See *Punjab Colony Manual*, i. 49.
[5] Ibid., pp. 65–69.
[6] Ibid., p. 69.

the proprietary rights'.[1] A similar system of tenants in hereditary lease on public land characterizes Zionist colonization in
Israel.[2]

The system of tenure under the L.D.O. has tended to make a
substantial, though not readily assessable, contribution to the
prosperity of the colonist, not only through the waived or reduced
rentals which have already been mentioned, but also by making
it impossible for him, through misfortune or improvidence, legally
to lose or reduce the basis of his prosperity by selling, leasing, or
mortgaging his land or by inheriting a fragmented holding. However, as will be seen in the next chapter, some of these things are
tending to be done illegally, and the L.D.O. has its disadvantages
(notably the impossibility of raising credit from private sources
on the security of land held under it). And in any case the holder
of an allotment in a village has the same advantages.

These, then, are some of the main reasons for the relatively high
income of the colonist, which locally could be still higher, quite
apart from improvements in agricultural practice, if there were
improvements in such things as communications, the marketing
of high land produce, and the working of Co-operation.

Expenditure

How, it may be asked, does the colonist in the established colonies spend the relatively high net income which comes to him?
And, in particular, does he save it, or invest it in ways which will
increase his or someone else's production?

Taking first the question of thrift, it will be appreciated that
this is important, *inter alia*, because it is one of the ways in which
domestic capital may be made available to a national economy
which is inevitably not too well provided with capital of any sort.[3]
Ceylon has of recent years made efforts to promote savings in the
Post Office Savings Bank and in savings certificates, and to encourage Co-operative thrift societies, which may also make loans
to members.[4] Some success has attended these efforts if one looks

[1] Information kindly supplied by Major H. S. Sandhu, Deputy Director of
Colonization, Uttar Pradesh.

[2] See A. Bonné, 'Problems of Rural Development in Israel', in INCIDI,
Rural Development, pp. 243–4.

[3] See UN, ECAFE, Working Party of Experts on the Mobilization of Domestic Capital, *Mobilization of Domestic Capital* (Bangkok, 1953), and pp. 328–34,
below.

[4] Ibid., pp. 51 and 59–61; and *Admin. Reports: Co-operative Societies*.

at the nation as a whole, but thrift in the colonies is sadly lacking. In 1951 there were thrift societies in only seven of the colonies, and some of these had very few members and were making but slow progress. In five other colonies it was reported to the author that some colonists were saving through the Post Office Savings Bank. On the whole, it was very clear that there was no local tradition of saving, and that a possible source of considerable domestic capital was lying untapped. In most established colonies, however, a certain amount of money was being ploughed back into the colony, either for productive purposes (e.g. through the purchase of carts) or for improvements to amenities (e.g. through the purchase of bicycles, electric torches, furniture, and paint for the house).

But considerable sums were also being invested outside the colony, for instance by the purchase of land or houses in a *purāna* village, or invested in enterprises, such as *boutiques*, of doubtful economic or social value. There was also a great deal of what by Western standards at any rate was extravagance (e.g. the buying of old cars, gramophones, and the undertaking of journeys to distant places), which tends to rouse jealousy in *purāna* villages; and in some colonies drinking and gambling were said to be rife (though it is not easy to say whether conditions were any worse than in many a village). One must be careful not to be too critical of apparently wasteful expenditure; some long journeys, for example, were to distant shrines and served a religious purpose which, quite apart from its inherent value, made for social harmony and stability. And by no means all the established colonists are wasteful. Yet many observers of the Ceylon colonies, including thoughtful Ceylonese, confess to some disappointment with the volume of expenditure on things which neither add to the permanent amenities of life nor to future productivity; such expenditure, being conspicuous, also arouses jealousy in the villager.

The Ceylon colonies are, however, by no means unique in this respect. Sir Malcolm Darling describes the effects of sudden prosperity on some (but not all) of the Punjab colonies and concludes that 'the prosperity . . . was too easily won, and a great part of the wealth that came with it was thrown away upon unproductive, and often unworthy, ends'.[1] In the Indonesian colonies 'settlers do not save money for investment; their natural aptitude

[1] See *Punjab Peasant*, pp. 224–7.

is not suited for that purpose'.[1] It must be remembered, too, that European pioneers are also apt to be wasteful, and that the phrase 'conspicuous waste' was invented to describe an attribute of a Western society.

Indebtedness

It has been seen earlier in this book that indebtedness is characteristic of the Ceylon village, as of other Oriental peasant societies, though its incidence may recently have somewhat diminished. But it may surprise the reader, in view of what has been said about the income level of colonists and about the widespread distribution of Co-operative societies, to learn that indebtedness to private persons was reported to the author in 1951 in nearly all colonies and that, moreover, in not a few it was being found difficult to recover loans made by Co-operative societies. The private creditors were mainly local *boutique*-keepers, or relatives, or people in the colonist's *purāna* village, but occasionally they were other colonists. Sometimes it appeared that a majority of the colonists had private debts (70 per cent. was the proportion quoted at Unnichchai). Though exact data are lacking, the incidence of debt does seem to be high. How has this come about?

In a number of colonies pioneer conditions and other causes of temporary hardship still seemed to be at work: for instance, at Nachchaduwa there had been crop failure and a consequent inability either to pay back Co-operative loans or to raise fresh ones; at Unnichchai colonists had become indebted in trying to purchase seed for a second crop after the first, from free seed, had failed; at Beragama a paddy pest had gravely reduced yields. In other cases indebtedness existed because though a Co-operative had yet been formed old private loans were still unpaid; this was so at Iranamadu (Kilinochchi). In still others, as at Dewahuwa, no Co-operative had yet been formed.

In several colonies, notably at Iranamadu and at Minneriya, debts had been contracted for purposes beyond the scope of Co-operatives, notably for dowries and for weddings, anniversaries, and other social and ceremonial occasions. And quite possibly the same cause was at work elsewhere.

But in a number of cases where none of these causes seemed to

---

[1] From information kindly obtained from Jakarta by the Indonesian Ambassador in London.

be at work, colonists preferred the private money-lender to the Co-operative. There may be a number of reasons for this. Larger sums may be borrowed, without restriction on the purpose of the loan; the colonist may be subjected to some sort of pressure by the *boutique*-keeper, or he may feel safer with the familiar dealer than with the impersonal, unfamiliar Co-operative. In all these eventualities, repayment will usually be in kind, and produce will evade the C.A.P.S. society. Sometimes, also, the dealer may pay a high price and so attract produce from men who are not indebted to him; thus at Iranamadu in 1951 Jaffna dealers were paying Rs. 11 per bushel for rice although the guaranteed price was Rs. 9. The dealer may also attract produce by paying ready cash.

But behind all these reasons for private debt and private trade there is the very important point that Co-operation is an alien introduction, not a natural growth from the felt needs of society; and detailed investigation might well show that some debts at any rate were viewed by colonists as part of normal, reciprocal social relations.

Indebtedness is by no means unknown in other Asian colonization schemes in which Co-operation has been fostered. But Darling showed clearly, with the aid of statistical data which are unfortunately not available in Ceylon, that although there was considerable debt in the Punjab Canal Colonies, it was much less heavy than in other parts of the Province; and he diagnosed that the reduced weight of debt was due to an increase in the size of holdings and a new-found security in agricultural and pastoral activities (though a further cause of debt, the cost of marriages and ceremonial, remained in operation).[1] It is hard to say, in the absence of comprehensive quantitative data, whether the Ceylon colonies have already followed the same pattern, or are in process of doing so. But it is certainly true that debt to private traders and the consequential or independent sale of produce to them is by no means absent from the Ceylon colonies, whatever claims may sometimes be made to the contrary.

Two important problems in the economic organization of the Ceylon colonies as they are at present conceived arise out of the foregoing discussion; they are (1) the problem of an 'economic unit' of land for the colonist; and (2) the problem of aid to the colonist. These problems may be conveniently considered here.

[1] See Darling, *Punjab Peasant*, pp. 124–31.

The Problem of an 'Economic Unit'

The notion that an allotment of 5 acres of paddy and 3 acres of high land should be provided whenever possible in the colonies was rooted in the belief that this constituted an 'economic unit'. But, so far as the author has been able to discover, there has never been a thorough investigation of the matter; and there has been some confusion about the nature of an 'economic holding'. Sometimes it was said to be the amount cultivable by means of the un-aided efforts of a peasant family;[1] sometimes it was said to be the area which would provide an adequate livelihood for such a family,[2] at times both definitions were combined in one statement of aims, as in the guiding principles enunciated by Sir Hugh Clifford, which have already been quoted;[3] at other times it is not clear which definition was being adopted, as in the Land Commission's statement that they would fix the unit 'at the extent of land which is sufficient for one peasant and his family'.[4] Now, the area of an economic holding based on one definition will not necessarily equal that based on the other; for the amount cultivable by a peasant family may be more than is necessary for subsistence or for some other given standard of living; or it may even, in adverse circumstances, be less. Moreover, as is indeed implicit in what has just been said, it is necessary if the second definition is adopted to define the 'adequate livelihood' which the economic unit is to win for the peasant; and this appears never to have been done.

A number of arguments, however, appear to support the view that the standard 5-acre/3-acre allotment is too large, at least if it is to be cultivated by a colonist and his family. Taking the broad viewpoint demanded by the national situation in Ceylon today, a great need, because of the mounting pressure of population re-sources, is to increase production per acre. With this in mind, it appears desirable not only to fix the standard allotment at a size which can be cultivated by the peasant family with present tech-niques, but also one which will tend to stimulate improvement; always provided that the size is not so small that the family is pushed below subsistence level. Now it has been seen that shortage

---

[1] See, for example, *Village Survey: Puttalam*, p. 38.
[2] See, for example, remarks of Dr. N. M. Perara, *DSC*, 1939, p. 682; *Agricultural Wages and Earnings of Primary Producers in Ceylon*, p. 11; and *KPC*, p. 92.
[3] See above, pp. 135–6. [4] See *LC*, p. 19.

of family labour in relation to standard allotment size is one important factor working against such technical improvements as the
transplanting of paddy and, indeed, against high land development
where this is possible. Moreover, the present size puts a premium
on the large family, which is undesirable on demographic grounds.
And, with present colonists' incomes at the high level just quoted,
a considerable reduction in the size of future holdings could be
effected without hardship, provided that rice prices do not fall
greatly. In any case, the application to paddy lots of techniques
already known would enable present income levels to be reached
from a considerably smaller area, prices remaining stable. Now it
does not follow, of course, that smaller holdings will necessarily
lead to technical improvement and to smaller families; they do not
do so in the villages; but smaller standard holdings would appear
to be one of a number of conditions for both desirable results,
always assuming that colonization is to be by peasant paddy cultivators using family manual labour.

Various suggestions for new standard holdings have been made
from time to time with the aim of improving efficiency. The author
heard a good case for 3 acres/2 acres, and another for 3 acres/1 acre,
put forward by experienced Colonization Officers in Minneriya
and Parakrama Samudra respectively. The World Bank mission
suggested 3 acres/2 acres, with more land for good colonists.[1] The
Gal Oya Development Board made their standard holding 4 acres/
3 acres in 1951, and later reduced the paddy allotment to 3 acres
on the ground that this represents the extent which a peasant
family can cultivate unaided without machinery, with the chance
of earning by intensive cultivation the same income as the larger
lots had yielded by extensive cultivation. General change was,
however, eventually precipitated by a financial crisis, and standard
allotments were reduced to 3 acres/1–2 acres in 1953 in order to
reduce the *per capita* cost of colonization. Fortunately this approximates to the size which would appear to be desirable on other
grounds. It certainly does not, given current paddy prices, depress
the colonist below subsistence level, even with existing techniques;
but, whatever size of holding is fixed as standard, there ought to
be great flexibility, because of the variable soils and water conditions in the Dry Zone. There is something to be said for the
World Bank mission's suggestion of enlarging the allotment of a

[1] See *WBR*, p. 389 (ii. 174).

cultivator who proves himself competent. For some colonists at least this might prove an incentive to efficiency and against the temptation to invest in land outside the colony and in non-agricultural enterprises within it.[1] But the suggestion raises other issues which must be discussed later.[2]

To the Western mind, accustomed perhaps to the grants of 160–640 acres made under the American Homestead Acts, a 4- or 5-acre lot will seem very small indeed (an American authority on South Asia has in fact recently stated categorically that 'a 5-acre farm is too small for economic operation'),[3] and to argue that it must be *reduced* in the interests of efficiency may appear absurd. Moreover, a 4- or 5-acre lot is certainly small when compared with holdings in some other Asian colonization schemes, as will be apparent from the following figures for areas of basic units: Punjab Canal Colonies, 12 acres minimum, 20 acres normal; Thal, 15 acres; Terai, 10 acres, increased if the cultivator has tractors; and Dujaila (Iraq), approximately 60 acres.[4] But these are all schemes which do not depend on rice, and which have not the benefit of truly tropical temperature conditions. In South Asian schemes in which physical and technical conditions approximate more closely to those of the Dry Zone, for instance those of Malaya and Indonesia, support will be found for the size of the new allotment. Thus in a number of the Malayan colonies the basic paddy allotment was of 3 acres, with 1 acre for 'domestic cultivation', while in Indonesia the colonist is given about 5 acres altogether of which $2\frac{1}{2}$ acres are, if possible, paddy land.[5] But there is no final solution to the problem—as is, indeed, inevitable in a region where attitudes, technology, and prices are liable to change; and very recently in Malaya it has been found that 'the more industrious of the families in the Sungei Manik area could cultivate more than four acres', so that some 4-acre/2-acre allotments were given out and, later, some 6-acre/2-acre blocks.[6] 'This total of eight acres is now considered

---

[1] Cf. above, p. 273. [2] See below, pp. 284–7.
[3] See Robert I. Crane, *Aspects of Economic Development in South Asia* (New York, IPR, [1954], mimeo), p. 3.
[4] See *Punjab Colony Manual*, i. 159; Khan, in *Pakistan Q.*, vol. ii, no. 3, pp. 20–26; Calder, *Men Against the Jungle*, pp. 148–9; Fisk, in *Econ. Geog.*, vol. xxviii, p. 343.
[5] See Fed. of Malaya, Drainage and Irrigation Department, *Annual Report*, 1949, pp. 26–27, and Fed. of Malaya, Dept. of Information, *Tanjong Karang*, p. 5; information on Indonesia kindly obtained by the Indonesian Ambassador in London. [6] See Ferguson, *Mal. J. of Trop. Geog.*, vol. ii, p. 14.

to be an economic unit for a Malay family to cultivate without mechanical aid, and from which to gain a livelihood.'[1] It is, moreover, dangerous to try and draw exact parallels between one region and another when physical and human conditions are so variable, and still more dangerous, *pace* the American authority, to generalize over such a vast field; and one can only repeat that for the Ceylon Dry Zone colonies, there seem to be many reasons for adopting a standard 3-acre/1–2-acre allotment under present conditions, provided that flexibility is allowed and the possibility of enlargement borne in mind.

Problems Arising from the Scale of Aid

The 1951 scale of aid was very costly; but, quite apart from that, it had grave disadvantages. It was unnecessary because it is no longer essential to offer spectacular inducements to attract people to the Dry Zone: witness the great army of squatters. And a high scale of aid fosters the ever-present attitude that the Government is the giver of all things, and that little needs to be done by the colonist's own exertions. A high scale of aid tends also to reinforce the traditional resistances to individual endeavour which undoubtedly stand in the way of the increased production *per capita* which the modern demographic situation demands; in fact, it may reasonably be held partly responsible for the relative failure of attempts to improve techniques in the colonies.

The scale of aid was, however, cut for financial reasons in 1952. The colonist was given a smaller and more cheaply constructed house, costing Rs. 1,700 instead of Rs. 3,200, and a number of reductions were made in the subsidies paid for development of his allotment. But a thorough-going review of the whole system of aid is required, for more than the mere cost is involved.[2] Such a review would have to consider what were the right spheres of capital investment for the Government and the colonist, striking a balance between the adverse effects of subsidization and its evident merits in bringing land rapidly into production. It may be suggested here that there are certain obvious spheres of government action: for example, the construction of roads, irrigation works, and at least rudimentary houses, some at least of the clearing, and initial

---

[1] Ibid.
[2] Cf. *WBR*, p. 392 (ii. 176–7). The mission was, however, mainly concerned with the cost factor.

conservation works to protect the vital capital contained in the land itself. (In fact, it was suggested in the previous chapter that the Government should do more than it now does in the high lands; perhaps to compensate for this less could be done to ridge the paddy fields, since the colonist is sure to give these first priority.) The colonist, on the other hand, might be expected to do some clearing, to add to the rudimentary house, and to complete the ridging of his fields. And part of the financial assistance to him might be considered as a loan, repayable in instalments over the years. Chapters 5 and 6 have, it is true, shown the difficulties that formerly arose when loans were made to colonists; but, with malaria conquered and with modern income figures before one, it is difficult to believe that these difficulties would necessarily arise today.

In this connexion much is to be learnt from study of other modern South Asian colonization schemes.[1] So far as the author has been able to discover, in each of these cases the Government concerned takes responsibility for roads, irrigation, and other normal public services; in the Thal and Terai schemes, all clearing and land preparation is done for the colonists, but in the Andamans only the paddy allotments are cleared, the 5 acres of high land being left in jungle, while in Indonesia the settler still undertakes his own clearing, though the Government is said to have plans for taking over some of the work. In no case does the state present the colonist with a house; he either builds his own, with or without a loan from the state, or repays in instalments the cost of a house built by the state. There may be a grant for draught animals, or seed, or tools, or initial subsistence, but for other purposes loans replace the outright grants made in Ceylon. Certainly a field study of the working of these systems should form part of the thorough review of Ceylon practice which is now overdue.

Such a review ought also to consider the very low charges for water and land which are customary and which also constitute a subsidy to the colonist.[2]

---

[1] Information on the Thal scheme kindly supplied by the High Commissioner for Pakistan in London, also from Khan, in *Pakistan Q.*, vol. ii, no. 3, pp. 20–26; on the Terai scheme kindly supplied by the Deputy Director of Colonization, Uttar Pradesh, also from the *Tarai and Bhabar Report*; on the Andamans scheme from *Ind. Trade and Industry*, vol. iv (1953), p. 497; on Indonesia kindly obtained from Jakarta by the Indonesian Ambassador in London; and on the Philippines kindly supplied by the Philippine Legation in London.

[2] See above, p. 265 and cf. *WBR*, pp. 393–4 (ii. 177).

Conclusion

The evidence which has been brought forward in this chapter has shown that the techniques of colonization which have been evolved in Ceylon have, in conjunction with largely unimproved land-use systems, made it possible for prosperous communities to dwell in what was for so long a region of difficulty, shunned by human settlement. This is no mean achievement.

But, as in other aspects of Dry Zone colonization and of land policy in Ceylon, it is time to take stock, for all is not well. Indebtedness is apparently present even in long-established colonies, though more data are needed; the income of many an established colonist is possibly greater than is good for his moral welfare, and is certainly too big, with 1951 guaranteed prices and with the 1951 scale of aid and size of holding, to offer any financial incentive to the improvement of husbandry in the directions which the previous chapter suggested were desirable. The financial incentive will be increased for new colonists now that holdings are smaller and scales of aid lower. But will these incentives be enough to bring about a more intensive method of growing rice and a more satisfactory method of cultivating high land allotments (always remembering the physical limitations of the latter and the local difficulties of marketing their produce)? It is difficult enough to arrive at adequate incentives in a Western society; but this is an Oriental peasant society, and it is not enough to consider financial inducements such as might be offered in the West. The nature and values of Sinhalese and Tamil society must be taken into account in an adequate discussion of these and other problems of colonization in Ceylon; and an attempt to take them into account, admittedly in a limited context, will be made in the next chapter.

14

The Social Factor

IT has already been stated that an appreciation of the social system in the villages of Ceylon is essential to an understanding of the problems of peasant colonization. In summing up some of the most important ways in which the social factor seems to be at work, especially in the setting up of resistances to current policies, it is necessary to state that the author does not pretend to be a sociologist, and his field work was undertaken from the point of view of a geographer interested in a general ecological study. The comments which follow thus have no pretensions to finality, or even to a high degree of precision; but the subject is far too important to be omitted. In spite of the mass of existing literature,[1] the effects of the values and attitudes of indigenous peoples are still insufficiently appreciated. This is confirmed by the finding of a recent conference that 'it is evident from a study of existing development projects that insufficient attention has been paid to the social factor'.[2] Only too often the economic problems which Asian and

[1] See, for example: from the point of view of the humane administrator, F. L. Brayne, *The Remaking of Village India* (London, OUP, 1929) and *Better Villages*, 3rd ed. (London, OUP, 1945), and Darling, *Punjab Peasant*; from the point of view of the welfare worker, D. Spencer Hatch, *Towards Freedom from Want* (London, OUP, 1949); from the point of view of the social anthropologist, M. Fortes, 'An Anthropologist's Point of View', in R. Hinden, ed., *Fabian Colonial Essays* (London, Allen & Unwin, 1945), pp. 215–34 and A. C. Mayer, *Land and Society in Malabar* (London, OUP, 1952); from the point of view of those economists and economic historians who have 'a persistent concern with the social textures with which the threads of economic enterprise are interwoven', S. H. Frankel, *The Economic Impact on Under-Developed Societies* (Oxford, Blackwell, 1953), the review article by Sir W. K. Hancock, 'The Under-developed Economies', *Econ. Hist. Rev.*, 2nd ser., vol. vi (1954), pp. 310–15 (the source of the quotation above), and J. H. Boeke, 'Agrarian Reforms in the Far East', *Amer. J. Soc.*, vol. lvii (1952), pp. 315–24. The subject is one of the main preoccupations of the Research Centre on Economic Development and Cultural Change at the University of Chicago: see Bert F. Hoselitz, ed., *The Progress of Underdeveloped Areas* (Chicago, Univ. of C. Press, 1952) and has occupied the attention of international conferences; see, for example, INCIDI, *Rural Development*, espec. pp. 350–6 and 398–402. Since this book was written there has appeared W. Arthur Lewis's remarkable synthesis, *The Theory of Economic Growth* (London, Allen & Unwin, 1955).

[2] INCIDI, *Rural Development*, p. 399.

African societies present are seen merely in terms of their apparent technical incompetence and economic inefficiency, and the remedy is conceived merely in terms of technical improvement and capital investment. If the human resistances to technical change are considered at all they tend all too often to be considered in terms of such alleged attributes of the indigenous people as their 'laziness'. Yet, to take the Dry Zone peasant as an example, the same family which is too 'lazy' to conserve its high land allotment will walk 30 miles or more in the heat of the dry season to a great Buddhist festival at Anuradhapura, carrying its children, its food supplies, and its firewood.[1] The truth is that 'underdeveloped' societies have a different view of the things which are worthy of effort, and these things do not necessarily include technical change for its own sake, or as a sign of modernity, or as a means to more efficient production. The Westerner thinking about economic affairs in an Oriental setting cannot too often remember that, if one considers the whole known range of human attitudes to work and wealth, then the modern Western attitude is seen to be highly abnormal; and that Western technology and capital cannot be applied to Oriental societies without reference to the indigenous culture: nor does it help to adopt a censorious attitude, or an attitude of moral superiority to the human resistances which the 'improver' encounters.

The social factor, moreover, seems to have been largely neglected in the formulation of colonization policy in Ceylon. It is true that, as earlier chapters have demonstrated, present colonization policy has in part sprung from 'social' motives, notably in response to the desire of a peasant society for paddy land; and it is true that many Ministers and officials in Ceylon are aware of at least some of the views of the peasantry, and there are signs that this awareness is increasing. But many aspects of the organization of the colonies have involved the imposition of ideas alien to indigenous peasant society. That is not to say that policy in Ceylon has been particularly inept; there are perfectly good reasons for its social blind spot. In the first place, as has already been pointed out, there is but little organized knowledge of the structure and values of Ceylonese societies; and there have been very few studies of the social factor in Ceylon's economic affairs.[2] In the second

---

[1] Cf. the remarks of Meyer Fortes on the fallacy that non-Europeans are lazier than Europeans, in Hinden, *Fabian Colonial Essays*, p. 218.

[2] See, however, P. T. Ellsworth, 'Factors in the Economic Development of

place, the idea that the nature of an indigenous society must be taken into account in economic and administrative matters is of fairly recent currency, since it is so largely a product of the modern science of anthropology. In the third place, the fact that so much of the structure of the colonies has been imposed on peasant society from outside is itself partly the result of a social phenomenon; for, as Chapters 5–7 have shown, many of the imposed features, notably the system of tenure, have their roots in the colonial period and reflect current ideas in Britain or in other parts of the British Empire, while others, together with the day-to-day administration and instruction of the colonist, are the work of a Ceylonese élite which has to a greater or lesser extent lost the values of peasant society. In other words, many of the present problems are rooted in the characteristic features either of a colonial or of a plural society.

The Social Factor and Resistance to Technical and Economic Change

Even given favourable circumstances—which can seldom exist— many colonists tend to fall far short of the productivity which would be possible given the best-known land-use techniques; and it is clear in the field that this is largely due to a failure to depart from traditional methods and to adopt new ones. In fact, how often resistance to change has been a factor in the various problems of colonization has emerged from topics discussed in previous chapters; for example, in wastage of water, in the application of fertilizers, rotations, and transplanting to paddy cultivation, and in the whole problem of the utilization of high land.

Often, much more often than is generally conceded, resistance to technical change has a rational basis, as when, for example, the proposed new technique is untried, or unsuitable, or even unusable.[1] For the colonist, it must be stressed, is by no means the fool he is sometimes made out to be, and he has some grounds for rational doubt when he is expected to cultivate high lands with field crops in perpetuity, or even when, in certain circumstances at

Ceylon', *Amer. Econ. Rev.*, vol. xliii (1953), pp. 116–25; Ponna Wignaraja, 'The Conflict between Economic Rationality and Cultural Values', *Civilisations*, vol. iii (1953), pp. 51–60; and Murray A. Straus, 'Cultural Factors in the Functioning of Agricultural Extension in Ceylon', *Rur. Soc.*, vol. xviii (1953), pp. 249–56.

[1] Cf. R. Firth, 'Some Social Aspects of the Colombo Plan', *Westminster Bank Rev.*, May 1951, pp. 5–6.

any rate, he is asked to manure and to transplant his paddy;[1] and Murray Straus cites an instance at Parakrama Samudra, where an 'improved' iron plough could not be shifted by the buffalo, so that confidence in this particular 'improvement' was shattered.[2] It cannot, in short, be too strongly emphasized that in Ceylon, as in the tropics generally, the right technical answer to many problems remains unknown, and, even if it is known, the colonist needs to be persuaded that it is financially worth his while to adopt it.

The fact remains, however, that in many instances there seems no valid rational objection to a technical change, and yet the colonist resists it, or merely goes through the motions of conformity to it. In some cases faulty selection of colonists, or their selection because they are landless and not because they are good cultivators, is the reason for such resistance. But it is possible tentatively to suggest that a number of attributes of Sinhalese society help to produce resistance to change and it seems likely that similar factors are at work, with modifications, in Tamil society. It is also possible in some cases to suggest remedial lines of action, given the present aims and general method of colonization.

There may be, in the first place, the superior attitude adopted towards the colonist by Colonization Officers and others whose job it is to teach new methods. The tendency is for these officers to issue the orders of higher authority to the colonist without consulting him about his needs and views; to the colonist, technical change is then an imposition the need for which he does not see. Murray Straus sees the reason for this state of affairs in the stratified organization of Sinhalese society which makes it 'difficult for Ceylonese to order their relationships with persons of lower status on any other basis than that of superior–inferior';[3] there is also the fact that this is a plural, ex-colonial society, with a great gulf in status, educational background, and system of ideas and values between government officer and peasant. Straus, in the author's view, over-weights the importance of the 'top-down' approach, but the fact remains that the problem of giving a lead in technical change is an important one, and, as part of the general problem of leadership, will receive consideration in the next chapter.

A second probable factor in the colonist's resistance to technical change is his attitude to wealth; this may well be more important

[1] See above, pp. 243–5.
[2] In *Rur. Soc.*, vol. xviii, pp. 255–6. [3] Ibid., see espec. p. 252.

than the factor just discussed, and is certainly very frequently brought into discussions of the problems of 'underdeveloped' countries. In the West the desire of a producer to improve his financial position, both in order to increase his current consumption and in order to make capital investment possible, is clearly one of the strongest of the motives which lead him to change his techniques. It must be said straight away that most Dry Zone colonists *are* subject to economic motives, *pace* those who believe that Buddhism leads to an 'other-worldly' attitude to worldly goods.[1] Most colonists, in fact, are mercenary in their outlook and wish to improve their living standards, particularly to be able to purchase cherished articles like bicycles, umbrellas, and electric torches. That is the main reason why they need to be persuaded that new techniques will bring sufficient financial returns. There are, however, two important points to be remembered. The first is that some colonists at any rate do not appear to pursue their desire for wealth to the exclusion of their interests in other things, notably in religion, in observances required by society, and in leisure. If they can reach the standard of consumption which they have in mind without the additional care and effort which are required by technical change, then they continue to use the old methods. Frankel has suggested that this tendency of the cultivator to devote most of his effort to the satisfaction of needs determined by custom is characteristic of 'underdeveloped' societies.[2] In the Ceylon colonies this phenomenon may be one of the reasons why the larger holding, far from encouraging more efficient methods and a larger product per acre, leads in some cases at least to less efficient methods than the colonist practised in his village, and hence to a *lower* yield per acre.[3]

A further facet of the colonist's attitude to wealth is that, as Chapter 13 has shown, the desire to raise the level of production high enough for capital investment to be possible is one that rarely affects the colonist; here again the colonist is not alone, for capitalist economic motivation is, after all, extremely uncommon outside certain sectors of modern Western or Westernized societies.

Another possible cause of resistance to technical change is that

[1] See, for example, Ellsworth, in *Amer. Econ. Rev.*, vol. xliii (1953), p. 117, which, like many Western opinions on Ceylonese village attitudes, does not ring true.
[2] See *The Economic Impact on Under-Developed Societies*, p. 35.
[3] Cf. above, pp. 276–9.

colonization policy gives little extra inducement to the colonist who *is* subject to a more Western type of economic motivation. He cannot invest his profits in a larger allotment, though it has sometimes been suggested that he should be able to do so.[1] And, as Chapter 13 has shown, he tends to put his money into enter- prises, such as *boutique*-keeping, which may then be frowned on by authority because a breach of L.D.O. conditions is involved, and frowned on by others because of alleged trespass against traditional or Gandhian values, or because of jealousy, or because he has got out of step with the rest of his family group (the last reason for disapproval is, however, obviously more likely in a village than in a colony). Here, perhaps, is another aspect of the confusion of purpose which has frequently been commented on in this book. Maximum food production would seem to demand incentives to economic individualism, the preservation of tradi- tional peasant society would seem to demand the subjugation of the individual to the group. Neither is in harmony with the egali- tarianism which is implicit in the L.D.O. as applied to the colonies.

These and other conditions, then, appear to damp down eco- nomic activity in at least some of the colonists; and together they are probably among the strongest of the forces which resist techni- cal change. But is it possible to suggest a number of other factors which may be at work? For instance, work being seen only as one of a number of necessary activities, a mere means of acquiring 'concrete needs determined by custom', there is no overriding pride in workmanship for its own sake, and such devices as prizes for the best allotment do little to stimulate improvement. It is quite possible also that the attitude of the Sinhalese family towards young children tends to induce docility and reverence for authority. A comprehensive study of the influence on the Sinhalese mind of cultural influences in early childhood, like that which Carothers has made for the African mind, has yet to be made;[2] but it would be interesting to know whether such factors as late weaning, early indulgence, and traditional verbal instruction tend to produce a mind which is, by Western standards, unquestioning and un- enterprising.[3]

---

[1] See above, pp. 277–8.
[2] See J. C. Carothers, *The African Mind in Health and Disease* (Geneva, WHO, 1953), espec. pp. 41–47.   [3] Cf. *WBR*, pp. 773–4 (ii. 428–9).

So far, discussion of the role of the social factor has centred on its effect on the willingness of society to adopt new methods, especially new agricultural methods. There are, however, two other groups of forces which derive from indigenous culture and which also play a part in creating current conditions in the Dry Zone colonies; they are (1) the attitude to the Government, and (2) the attitude to imposed solutions to economic and social problems, especially in the field of land tenure.

Some Attitudes to the Government

The Dry Zone colonist, whether he be Sinhalese or Tamil, tends to look on the Government as the giver of all things, no effort on his part being called for. The author recalls a meeting of a Rural Development Society at Kagama which was allegedly called to consider ways in which local needs could be met by self-help, but which in fact drew up a long list of measures which it wanted Government to take. This attitude probably has its roots in the hierarchical organization of society and the autocratic rule by the king and his agents which formerly went with it, and which required little initiative and no participation in central government from the peasant. It was certainly reinforced, as in other colonial territories, by the paternalism of colonial rule. In this connexion Spencer Hatch calls attention to the comparatively large place Government plays in Indian life;[1] and the same might have been said of the colonial government of Ceylon. More recently the tendency to expect everything from Government has been strengthened by the foolish irresponsibility of those members of Parliament who make very free with promises of 'help' to their constituents and who measure their parliamentary success in terms of the amounts they have induced Government to spend. Superimposed on all this there is, in the colonization schemes, the effect of the high scale of aid; if the Government has done everything to prepare for the colonist before he enters the colony, he will expect the standard of attention to be maintained. For instance, the colonist is notoriously bad at replacing tiles blown off his roof, and expects Government to come and replace them. The colonist's attitude to aid from the Government, then, serves to sap his none too great reserves of initiative.

[1] Hatch, *Towards Freedom from Want*, p. 3.

Attitudes to Imposed Solutions, especially in Land Tenure

A number of instances have already been given of the difficulties which are caused because institutions and solutions to problems are imposed on the colonist without reference to his values and attitudes; for instance, difficulties in agricultural extension and in Co-operation. In no field is the fact that the official solution is an imposed solution so clearly brought out as in the field of land tenure. The L.D.O., having few roots in local custom, can be enforced only by constant vigilance; this inevitably breaks down here and there, through the inaction of officials or, more often perhaps, where senior officials are thinly spread on the ground. The most serious resultant problems for the authorities, apart from those concerning the enforcement of rules about conservation and good husbandry, are those which concern (*a*) illegal leasing of holdings, and (*b*) succession on the death of the colonist.

The tendency of colonists to let all or part of their paddy lot on *ande*, notwithstanding the terms of their permit or grant under the L.D.O., is of long standing; as long ago as 1939 at Minneriya defaulting colonists were replaced by men who were openly recognized to be former *ande* tenants.[1] The tendency is based, fundamentally, on traditional practice in Sinhalese villages by which a man with more land than he wishes to cultivate himself does not employ wage-labour (which is held to degrade both employer and employee) but parcels out some of his land on *ande*. Here, in fact, is an obvious example of a clash between custom and imposed legislation.

The author's investigation in 1951 showed that *ande* was probably in vogue in about half of the colonies, and quite possibly also in some of the remainder. *Ande* tenants are sometimes villagers, sometimes squatters, sometimes even other colonists.

Ande tenure and other leasehold systems are very hard to detect; *ande* tenants working on a colonist's fields may be explained away as hired labourers, who are perfectly permissible. The arrangement of the tenancy may be purely verbal, or there may be deeds which are concealed, and often the existence of *ande* only comes to light when there is a dispute between a landlord and a tenant, or when there is an aggrieved third party who acts as an informer. Technically, of course, the colonist who so lets out his

---

[1] See *ARLC*, 1939, p. 5.

land is liable to ejection, as is the tenant if he also is a colonist; but rarely is there sufficient evidence, especially if the Colonization Officer turns a blind eye; and legal ejection is, in any case, a painfully slow process.

Ande tenure in the colonies is an embarrassment to the Government because it brings the law into disrepute, encourages squatting, and defeats the aim of establishing peasant proprietorship, especially where, as in certain instances at Nachchaduwa, the colonist becomes an absentee landlord or even, it is suspected, secretly 'sells' his allotment. *Ande* also tends to discourage technical improvement: a progressive colonist who has grown wealthy will tend to lease out his land to *ande* tenants on whom his progressiveness will be lost. This point must be weighed against the possible positive incentive in considering any proposal to enlarge the allotments of competent colonists.

The second major problem, not yet grown to its full potential dimensions, is that of succession, which arises out of the attempt to prevent fragmentation by arranging for the colonist to nominate a sole successor during his lifetime. In practice the colonist usually nominates a son or a daughter, or his wife; thus out of a batch of 43 colonists at Uriyawa, 19 nominated a son, 13 a daughter, and 7 a wife. Even before the death of a colonist, the problem of succession may cause trouble; there is in some colonies, notably Iranamadu, a strong complaint about the provisions designed to check division. It has, moreover, quite frequently happened in the older colonies that all the children of a family have, as they have grown up, helped their father to prepare his allotment, a harder task, it must be remembered, in the days of low scales of aid than it is today. When it is learnt that, contrary to custom, only one child has succeeded, or can succeed, there may be serious family disputes, as has happened at Iranamadu, Minneriya, and in the older blocks of Parakrama Samudra. The dispute may become very complicated if, as not infrequently happens, a man has had several 'wives' all of whom survive him with their respective children, but none or only one of whom were legally married to him.

In other cases, some or all of the deceased colonist's family may come to an agreement with the legal successor that they will share the produce of the holding on some basis or another; they may even all agree to live together on the holding, though if this involves the construction of additional buildings there is then a breach of the terms of the L.D.O. permit or grant. These cases, which occur, for example, at Tabbowa and Kagama, of course involve a sort of concealed fragmentation or concealed *tattumāru*, arrangements with considerable social advantages; but once again, of course, there is a conflict between custom and the provisions of the L.D.O. Custom leads to fragmentation (not necessarily inefficient with present techniques); the L.D.O., if enforced, would lead to landlessness among sons who could not succeed.

There have also already been a number of minor complications of succession; for example, a daughter may be nominated as the sole successor but marry a non-cultivator; in fact, the land may be settled on her as a dowry purposely to attract a non-cultivator. This is alleged to have happened at Minneriya. Technically, of course, if the woman succeeds but is non-resident the holding should revert to the Crown; in practice, absentee landlordism probably results (though by their very nature these cases are hard to track down).

In fine, useful as the L.D.O. has been in securing the rights of the colonist and hence in improving his economic and social position, the simple fact is that it is, like Co-operation, an imposed solution which has not grown out of indigenous society; and the problems which have already attended its operation may be expected to mount as succession becomes a real issue in each colony.

There is, moreover, a further consideration which links the imposed character of the L.D.O. to peasant productivity and therefore to the subject-matter of the earlier part of this chapter. It is now being said in well-informed quarters in Ceylon that the system of lease in perpetuity which the L.D.O. involves is completely alien to Sinhalese ideas and that many colonists do not understand that the land is theirs and their heirs' for all time provided that the conditions of the grant are obeyed; they feel, it is said, that they are only renting the land from the Government, and hence do not bestow on it the care which they would give to their own land, held freehold or by customary tenure. This feeling gains strength, on this view, from the fact that the annual charge is payable in perpetuity, for the only such charge which they know is the rent which a tenant pays his landlord, and from the way in which certain Colonization Officers are for ever holding over the tenant's head the threat of ejection for some breach of the conditions of his permit or grant. It is possible that the advantages of freehold tenure outweigh the disadvantages of fragmentation, of possible sale for debt, and of a recurrence of phenomena which the L.D.O. was designed to prevent. There is, however, this to be said: that local ideas about land are very important because so much of a man's status and sense of purpose hinge on them; and that if, as has been demonstrated, the official honouring of the L.D.O. is accompanied by unofficial breaches, then it may not only be a waste of time to try and enforce certain clauses of the Ordinance, but it may release latent energies and give a firmer base to society if alienations are outright and unrestricted except, perhaps, for an embargo on sale and a condition about conservation. There can be no doubt that many colonists would prefer outright alienation;[1] but one would need further evidence to convince one that insecurity of tenure is universally a potent economic factor. After all, peasant proprietors owning their land in *purāna* villages show no great desire for technical or other change, which suggests that more fundamental factors are at work on them.

Nevertheless, the proposal to introduce freehold is an interesting example of a welcome desire to base progress on local custom; and this is undoubtedly one of the solutions to present difficulties provided one is forced to work within the framework of colonization policy. It is noticeable that the colonist takes most easily to technical and other changes which fit readily into his cultural pattern; an earlier chapter has, for instance, shown that the use of pure-line seed and of the light iron plough, although liable to encounter resistances, is accepted far more readily than, say, transplanting, which demands far more disturbance of customary procedures. These are, of course, only examples of a phenomenon of social change which is well known to students of society and which has been suggested as a basis for action by a number of recent writers on the problems of underdeveloped areas.[2] In this connexion a study of 'felt needs' is a praiseworthy aspect of the work done by Spencer Hatch under the auspices of Unesco at Minneriya;[3] but much more could be done in the whole field of agricultural instruction. Much might also be done to base other aspects of colonization on the culture of

[1] See, for example, *KPC*, p. 85, and cf. above, pp. 127 and 159–60.
[2] See, for example, K. L. Little, 'Social Change in a Non-literate Community', in P. Ruopp, ed., *Approaches to Community Development* (The Hague, van Hoeve, [1953]), pp. 87–96, espec. pp. 91–92.
[3] See 'Fundamental Education', *Ceylon Today*, vol. ii (1953), pp. 8–13.

the people who are involved in it. Thus research might well reveal means of harnessing the tremendous religious energy which colonists manifest. Here a great deal of imaginative work is needed; not that it is always lacking, for when the first colonists arrived at Parakrama Samudra in October 1942 they were conducted to the colony in *Perahera* (procession), while in the evening ten priests chanted *pirith* in a specially constructed hall, and an 'excellent sermon' was preached. But the reception which the author witnessed in the same spot in 1951 was cold and bureaucratic. When a tract is colonized use might well be made of an adaptation of the ancient Sinhalese ritual for founding a new village which Codrington recorded.[1] In Tamil colonies it might prove possible to conform to Hindu custom, which requires astrological determination of the layout of the compound, for there is evidence from Iranamadu colonies that some colonists are unhappy that the entire site is planned by the Government irrespective of a man's star.[2] A technique of conformity to local custom on migration seems to have produced enthusiasm in Polynesia.[3]

Much might be done on a broad front, in fact, if every policy were preceded by thorough and expert economic and social research to see not only what social resistances must be overcome, but also what energies of peasant society can be harnessed.[4]

But it may be asked, especially by those primarily interested in the economic and demographic situation, is it enough to merely try to harness these energies? Is not a fundamental change in society itself the only way by which sufficiently rapid technical and economic change can come about?

In this connexion it might be expected that conditions in the colonization schemes would help in time to bring about such a fundamental social change. The colonist is, clearly, geographically separated from his traditional family society, and the general effect of the succession clauses of the L.D.O., as they stand at present, can only be to disrupt kinship relations still further: for although

---

[1] See *Ancient Land Tenure*, pp. 63–65.

[2] The author is indebted to Mr. V. Krishnapillai for a valuable discussion on this point. See also R. Chelvadurai-Proctor, 'Some Rules and Precepts among Tamils for Construction of Houses, Villages, Towns, and Cities during the Mediaeval Age', *J.R. As. Soc.* (Cey. Br.), vol. xxx (1927), pp. 337–60.

[3] See H. E. Maude, 'The Colonization of the Phoenix Islands', *J. Polynesian Soc.*, vol. lxi (1952), pp. 62–89, espec. p. 79.

[4] Cf. Boeke, *Amer. J. Soc.*, vol. lvii, p. 324.

there are occasional pleas for allotments for the sons of colonists;[1] and although in large schemes like Gal Oya the part of the family group which cannot inherit may remain in the area as hired labourers for 'capitalists'; and although concealed *tattumāru*[2] may temporarily at any rate keep the family together, in practice sons who leave the father's allotment during his lifetime or after his death tend to drift into casual labour or into squatting, not necessarily in or around the colony. Moreover, colonies are subject to other forces making for social change to a greater extent than many villages; for example, full provision of educational facilities (though here action is apt to lag behind planning). Are there any signs that these and other forces are tending already to produce social changes which in turn are having an effect on productivity and on economic organization? Certainly there are already a number of colonists who have shown some of the attributes valued in more dynamic economies. But the social changes which are undoubtedly occurring are not necessarily all to the good, even from a narrowly economic point of view; for latent energies as well as resistances tend to be worn away, as will appear from evidence to be presented in the next chapter. Certain of these social changes, moreover, tend to cast doubt on the social success of colonization, that is, on its success as a method of establishing healthy, functioning peasant societies. However, the very fact that the conclusions drawn here are, for sheer lack of data, so tentative should serve to draw attention to the need for intensive and localized field studies seeking to discover just what are the motives actuating the living community in village and colony.

[1] Cf., for example, the optimistic views of Sir Hugh Clifford that sons of colonists would themselves become colonists on their own holdings, above, p. 135.   [2] See above, p. 57.

15

Some Social Problems

THE social problem of colonization in Ceylon is not only that the nature of Ceylonese society complicates the execution of existing policy, but also that that policy in its turn reacts on social conditions in the colonization schemes.

Economic Interdependence and Co-operation for Economic Purposes

The traditional Ceylon village seems to have housed a community whose members were economically interdependent, co-operating for a great many processes of cultivation. Today the ancient pattern is most nearly found in the Dry Zone, especially in Nuwarakalawiya, where economic interdependence is seen in the organization of co-operative labour teams, especially in ploughing and harvest, and in the eminently sensible custom of *bethma*.[1] Co-operative agricultural practices may also often be witnessed Up-country.[2] But co-operative custom is weaker in the Low Country of the Wet Zone and, according to M. Y. Banks, in Jaffna;[3] and Margaret Digby has gone so far as to say of Ceylon, apparently with Low Country villages in mind, that 'the temper of village life is individualist, and little remains of the old mutual aid of the clan.'[4]

The physical and economic setting of the Dry Zone colonies lends to co-operation a number of particular economic advantages. For example, irrigation difficulties and labour problems at critical seasons of the agricultural calendar could be eased, though probably not solved, by co-operation. Again, co-operation for economic purposes is essential to the success of Co-operative and Rural Development Societies.[5] The same applies, but with even greater force, to the system of Co-operative cultivation of pooled holdings which has from time to time been proposed as a solution to some

[1] See above, pp. 71–72 and see Ryan, *Caste*, pp. 239–60.
[2] Ibid., pp. 196–238, espec. p. 205.
[3] The author is indebted to Mr. M. Y. Banks for a personal communication about conditions in the Jaffna Peninsula.
[4] See *Agricultural Co-operation*, p. 93.
[5] Cf. *Rural Progress through Cooperatives*, p. 15.

of the technical problems of Dry Zone colonization.[1] The original plans for the ex-servicemen's colony at Parakrama Samudra involved communal cultivation, as does the system in the new 'dry-farming' colonies.[2] It will be recalled that there were Co-operative colonies in Burma,[3] and they have also been tried in India;[4] in fact, Co-operative cultivation is widely recommended as a remedy for the troubles of petty peasant proprietorship, and it is important to realize that in a non-totalitarian state it stands or falls with the reaction to it of the cultivating society.

How far, then, are colonists willing to combine for economic and other purposes? In some colonies, there appeared to the author in 1951 to be a considerable amount of co-operative effort; in the Malay Colony at Beragama, for instance, a society, the Kudabolana Muslim Society, had been spontaneously generated and had built a permanent mosque, while among groups of Kotmale refugees in Block E and in Pudur at Parakrama Samudra there was a fairly high degree of co-operation. In others, there was some co-operation; at Kilinochchi, for example, colonists each gave Rs. 1 towards funeral expenses if one of their number died, and M. Y. Banks reports that colonists there are co-operating in ways which are unknown in Jaffna;[5] but at the same colony, the Colonization Officer complained that communal activity was difficult to stimulate, each man caring mainly for himself and his family, and it certainly appears that co-operation does not reach the high levels which it attains in Nuwarakalawiya or Up-country. In many other colonies social cohesion and community spirit are sorely lacking. In 1936 it was stated of Tabbowa that 'mutual assistance, which is a feature of paddy cultivation in other areas, has not developed here yet', and it was hoped that it would 'come later with the growth of greater community spirit';[6] but the author found that there was still a lack of mutual assistance fifteen years later. In most colonies, in fact, including older ones like Minneriya and Nachchaduwa, and smaller ones like Uriyawa, there was little co-operation for economic purposes, and most colonists were individualists.

The more perspicacious among the public servants in Ceylon

[1] Cf. ibid., p. 28.   [2] See below, pp. 342–5.   [3] See above, pp. 179–80
[4] See W. R. S. Sattianadhan and J. C. Ryan, *Co-operation* (Madras, OUP, 1946), pp. 25–26.
[5] In a personal communication to the author.
[6] See *Village Survey: Puttalam*, p. 38.

realize that Co-operative societies rest on an unsure foundation in these societies of individualists. A wise public servant wrote a sensible memorandum on the subject in 1945, pointing out that colonies are essentially different from villages because people do not know one another, and even more different from the Western societies in which Co-operation was a spontaneous growth. And Mr. C. P. de Silva's ambitious scheme of 1946 for a great ex-servicemen's colony at Parakrama Samudra to be worked largely by Co-operative mechanical cultivation, foundered for reasons which are said to include waning *esprit de corps*.

It will be remembered that the vast majority of colonists hail from Dry Zone and Up-country districts in which co-operation for economic purposes is still, by and large, customary, and only a relatively low percentage from the more individualistic societies of Jaffna and the Low Country.[1] Choice of source area cannot there-fore be blamed for the lack of co-operation which characterizes most of the colonies today. It is often suggested that this is only a temporary phenomenon which will constitute a much less serious problem as the colonists get to know one another and generally 'shake down'. This may happen in a second or later generation, but it is evident, from the fact that 'old' colonies still lack co-operative practices, that if time tells at all it tells very slowly; and because it is important to solve the problem quickly the question of applying a suitable stimulus arises. It is sometimes suggested that the formation of Rural Development Societies can supply such a stimulus;[2] but the author's experience in the colonies leads him to conclude that, whatever these societies may accomplish in the villages, they fail, or supply a façade only, in most of the colonies just because of the prior absence of a willingness to combine. To quote an unusually candid comment on one of these societies from a civil servant, 'It serves no purpose, and people are dragooned into joining it without being the least bit interested.'

Something might be done if the authorities took a leaf out of the Gal Oya Development Board's book and planned the domestic plots in 'village units', a group of houses arranged around a circle or square.[3] For, even given the strongest of motives for co-operation,

---

[1] See above, pp. 211–15.

[2] For Rural Development Societies in general see *Admin. Reports: Rural Development*.

[3] See GODB, *Ann. Report*, 1952–3, p. 5; and cf. *Punjab Colony Manual*, i. 235.

it is hard to see how it can readily develop in a long ribbon-colony like Kagama (New), strung out for miles along a channel, and lacking any focal point whatsoever (see Map 12); here is a strong argument against domination of colony planning by the irrigation engineers.[1] But the fact that co-operation is also lacking in small colonies with convenient focal points, like Uriyawa, shows that although the layout of a colony may be a prerequisite of community spirit, it is in itself not enough.[2]

It is very probable that the high scale of aid which was current until very recently, together with the Government's policy of providing meeting halls and other central buildings, serves in some cases to weaken incipient co-operation by removing motives for colonists to band together for communal purposes; this point is, however, not an easy one to establish.

But the factor of overriding importance in this problem seems quite clearly to be the break-up of village ties of kinship when peasants leave their *purāna* villages for the colonies and dwell among strangers not of their kin. The clearest proof of this is that it is just those colonies or parts of colonies to which whole groups of relatives from the same village have moved that co-operation in economic matters is strongest; for example, the parts of Parakrama Samudra colonized by Kotmale refugees. Further evidence is provided by experience of colonization in other familial societies. Thus it is reported from Indonesia, 'The social cohesion of the settlers [family, clans, village, &c.] is very strong. Settlers as a rule are strongly linked up with each other',[3] and it was the Dutch custom to encourage original settlers in the Outer Islands to send to Java for further members of their families.[4]

The principle of grouping colonists by families and localities has not been altogether lost sight of in Ceylon. Thus the Land Commission concluded, probably after study of practice in the Punjab:[5]

Another important matter is grouping. Suitable grouping may make all the difference to the happiness and success of a colony. People of the same village and community, connected by ties of relationship and association, are more likely to work and live happily together than a

---

[1] Cf. above, pp. 170–1.
[2] Meeting halls are not now (1956) provided.
[3] Information kindly obtained from Jakarta by the Indonesian Embassy in London.   [4] See Pelzer, *Pioneer Settlement*, p. 198.
[5] See *Punjab Colony Manual*, i. 60 and 102.

heterogeneous collection brought together by mere chance from half a dozen different localities.[1]

The same point was made a few years later by the Pasdun Korale East Colonization Board;[2] while the Kandyan Peasantry Commission reported that requests were made to them by peasants that villagers should be settled in colonies 'according to their groups of origin'.[3] Some attempt has been made to group colonists, e.g. at Elahera, but on the whole not enough attention has been paid to this important principle, which is clearly based on indigenous custom. It is true that the application of the principle would complicate the administration of the methods of selection recommended in Chapter 10; if 100 places were allotted to a D.R.O.'s Division on the basis of the objective formula which, it was there suggested, should be devised and applied, it would not be easy to decide from which villages to select groups large enough to be viable in a colony; it might well be necessary to choose the major villages with the highest agrarian pressure, and jealousy might be caused. But unless the principle of group selection is applied, other remedies seem very unlikely to produce social cohesion except by very slow growth.

Social cohesion is, however, liable to be weakened by other factors not yet mentioned and to one group of these, communalism, creed, and caste, discussion will now turn.

Communalism, Creed, and Caste

Communalism causes relatively little trouble in the colonization schemes, in spite of the marked divisions within the national population; for in all recent colonies it has been the practice more or less to segregate the communal groups. But in the older colonies, Minneriya, Nachchaduwa, and Tabbowa, the population is very mixed, and petty disputes still sometimes take communal lines. The late D. S. Senanayake, genuinely anxious that a feeling of Ceylonese nationality should replace communalism, was apparently for some time not convinced that segregation was desirable; in 1943 he was still asking whether the proposed reservation of Block D at Parakrama Samudra for Moslems alone was desirable. In the event, however, most subsequent small colonies and most

[1] See *LC*, p. 20.
[2] Cf. above, p. 137 and see *First Report of the Pasdun Korale East Colonization Scheme*, pp. 3 and 5.   [3] See *KPC*, p. 85.

sections of large ones have been filled mainly with members of one of the major communities. And although segregation of this sort may conflict with the long-term aim of creating a Ceylonese nation, it removes one possible obstacle to the growth of social cohesion.

Three types of communal phenomenon do, however, still arise. The first of these involves clashes within a colony between Kandyan and Low Country Sinhalese or between Sinhalese of local origin and those who are not. The grouping of colonists by source villages prevents such clashes but where there is no such grouping there may be trouble; thus in 1948 the colonists at Sangilikanadarawa banded together to petition against one of their number who was alleged to have stolen cattle, diverted water, and given hospitality to drunken relatives from his native village, but whose real offence was merely that he originally came from the Low Country. There has also been friction between local and immigrant colonists at Beragama, though here, as will be seen, there were undertones of caste.

The second communal phenomenon arises from Tamil reactions to proposals to settle Sinhalese colonists in Tamil areas (the converse problem has not yet arisen). The Tamil Federalists, for example, who desire 'home rule' for the Tamil provinces, wanted in 1951 to reserve the whole Gal Oya scheme for Tamils on the grounds that it lies in Eastern Province, which is predominantly Tamil.[1] And a similar issue arose over Kantalai.

The third phenomenon is the very evident difference in technical level between adjacent tracts in the same colony occupied by different communal groups. But it is not possible to arrange Sinhalese, Tamil, and Moslem in an order of merit; for while, to quote a few examples, the Puttalam town Moslems in Kottu Kachchiya Colony are in general poor cultivators and, it is suspected, still work in the town, the Eastern Province Moslems in Gal Oya are considered to be better and more energetic cultivators than either Sinhalese or East Coast Tamils. The 'Sinhalized Veddas' from the tank-bed who were given lands in the Gal Oya scheme had never previously grown anything but *chena* crops, and are problem children indeed; but the eighteen 'Coast Veddas' at Unnichchai, although originally fishers and apt to make grave mistakes, are far keener to learn than the East Coast Tamils, and

<hr />

[1] Ceylon, House of Representatives, *Debates*, vol. x (1951), pp. 1224–5.

far less prone to the habit of deserting their allotments and return-
ing to the coast. Again, Jaffna Tamils are generally more efficient
cultivators than East Coast Tamils.

There is, of course, a marked correlation between communal
group and creed; the majority of Sinhalese are Buddhists, the
majority of Tamils are Hindus, and all the Moors are Moslems.
The usual policy of communal segregation, therefore, does a great
deal to ensure that religion cannot cause internal dissension in a
colony. Even in communally mixed colonies like Tabbowa, however, religious differences appear to do little to weaken the admittedly none too strong social cohesion, and mixed marriages are
not unknown; while in communally unitary colonies the presence
of Christians among Buddhists or Hindus does not cause serious
friction. And, given suitable circumstances and the right type of
priest, religion can do much to promote social cohesion.

Communalism and creed thus cause only minor problems, on
the whole; caste is a very different matter.[1] There are two main
reasons for this state of affairs. One is that, whereas it has been
recent official policy to segregate communities (and therefore
creeds), the Government has chosen officially to ignore caste when
selecting colonists and allotting them their holdings. This contrasts with practice in the Punjab Canal Colonies where bodies of
colonists were so chosen as to be homogeneous by caste as well as
by community.[2] Because of the official policy in Ceylon, there are
very few colonies, or tracts of large colonies, which are homogeneous by caste; Uriyawa, whose colonists are all *goyigama*, is
one of them. Elsewhere, a tract or colony is likely to contain
members of several castes, and *goyigama* are usually located
cheek-by-jowl with members of other castes. (There may also be
a few artisans selected as such, and, like most artisans, these are
likely to be *navandanna* by caste; the discussion which follows
refers specifically, however, to ordinary cultivator-colonists.)

The second reason for caste friction is that such a large proportion of the colonists are Kandyan Sinhalese from Up-country and
the Dry Zone, in whose villages the traditional functions of the
castes and the traditional values inherent in the caste system are
still to be found, though in emasculated and disappearing form.
The ancient pride of the *goyigama*, the superior caste of cultivators,

[1] For caste in Ceylon see Ryan, *Caste*; see also above, pp. 72–74.
[2] See *Punjab Colony Manual*, i. 162.

in particular remains; and it is not surprising that in the colonies *goyigama* are apt to resent the equality thrust upon members of other castes who have become colonists with the same amount of land, the same status in the eyes of officialdom, and the same earning power as their *goyigama* neighbours, but with none of their traditional duties. The lower castes react in a variety of ways; for example, by changing their names and pretending to be *goyigama*, by marked sensitivity, or, especially if they have lost the traditional respect for *goyigama*, by aggressive behaviour.

The existence of inter-caste friction in the colonies is not always admitted, for one of the results of the assimilation of Western political ideas and of knowledge of the kind of society which a Westerner would wish to find is that educated Ceylonese tend to ignore caste and to deny its force when talking to Europeans whom they do not know well. Careful inquiry does, however, show that caste is by no means an insignificant factor in creating friction and weakening social cohesion.

In some colonies, it is true, inter-caste friction appears to be but slight. This appears to be the case in the fairly sophisticated Low Country society of the ex-servicemen's colony at Parakrama Samudra, where friction takes the form more reminiscent of a Western class society, for the ex-'other ranks' complain of privileges accorded to ex-officers. Again, there is little trouble at Tabbowa, and there have even been inter-caste marriages.

In the other colonies, there is more friction. At Kilinochchi, the issue of untouchability arises in the predominantly Hindu society, and colonists are, in the words of their Colonization Officer, 'equal under the Government but not in social life'. As a result, the organization of Co-operative meetings requires great tact. The issue of untouchability does not arise in the Sinhalese colonies, although the nearest approach to the untouchables in the Sinhalese system, the *rodiyā*, are represented at Ridibendi Ela, and their presence, as may be imagined, caused trouble at first.[1] The normal state of affairs in most Sinhalese colonies is perhaps approached at Dewahuwa, where goldsmiths (*navandanna*), washers (*henayā*), tom-tom beaters (*beravā*), and others of non-*goyigama* caste tend to be socially ostracized.

It is perhaps at Beragama that caste troubles have arisen in their most acute form and in a manner which has the most obvious

---

[1] For the *rodiyā*, see Ryan, *Caste*, espec. pp. 132–4 and 225–38.

effects on co-operation for economic ends. Here, in part of the colony, the very unusual situation occurs that *goyigama* are in a minority, the majority consisting of local villagers and others of fisher (*karāva*), cinnamon-peeler (*salāgama*), washer, and tom-tom beater caste. For a long time the *goyigama* made it very difficult to reach agreement at the statutory meeting called to fix dates for the various operations in cultivation, for they systematically opposed any proposal emanating from another caste or castes. Conditions have improved, partly, it is said because of the help of a Rural Development Society, but the *goyigama* still do not mix socially with the other castes and there is still a needless exaggeration of petty incidents over straying cattle and the like.

Finally, it should be noted that economic co-operation is not all that suffers from caste frictions. It is not unknown for a Colonization Officer to find that his leadership is ineffectual because it has been discovered that he is not of acceptable caste. At Parakrama Samudra, for instance, a Colonization Officer became very unpopular and was the victim of trumped-up charges because it was alleged that he was of *padu* (*batgam*) caste. This caste stands very low in the traditional system, and the fact that its members could not acquire permanent rights in land under the Sinhalese kings helps to explain the resentment of the *goyigama* colonists that an alleged *padu* should be placed over them to administer the land laws.[1]

The simplest way to remove caste as a serious source of friction between colonists would be the policy of grouping kinsfolk together which is so desirable on other grounds; for kinsfolk are automatically of the same caste, and to use kinship as a social cement is to use caste for the same purpose. The problem of the caste of Colonization Officers and other paid officials is a more difficult one. A policy of recognizing caste in selecting these officers would doubtless commend itself to most groups of colonists; but it would be contrary to the commonly expressed opinions of the Western-educated though perhaps not to the less overt beliefs of some of them.

Leaders and Leadership

Those concerned with the problem of trying to encourage change in a peasant society have often stressed the importance of

[1] See Denham, *Ceylon at the Census of 1911*, p. 192; see also Ryan, *Caste*, pp. 127–8.

finding suitable indigenous leaders who, by their personal status and influence, can leaven the mass;[1] and a recent international conference concluded that 'the traditional and other leaders of local society should be the first to inspire the work of rural development' and that 'in reorganizing disintegrated groups, or groups without sufficient leadership, . . . a nucleus will have to be built up by the selection and training of efficient social leaders.'[2]

In traditional Sinhalese society there were, of course, a number of categories of accepted leaders, notably *bandāras* (noble chieftains) and *gamarālas* (village elders) who, by virtue of their status, had a great influence on village society. There are many villages where the writ of such authorities still runs, and where the technique of seeking out the traditional leaders and influencing them in order to influence the peasantry would still be perfectly practicable. In the colonization schemes, however, it is otherwise; there one is, in fact, face to face with one of the 'groups' without sufficient leadership'. In the average Dry Zone colony, with its collection of individuals unrelated by kinship, starting at similar levels of poverty and landlessness, and separated rather than bound together by caste, there can be no one who stands out *ab initio* by the distinction of his family, or by his caste, or by his wealth in lands, or by any of the other means by which prestige and a position of leadership are inherited in traditional society.

In these circumstances, some at least of the functions of the village leaders tend to devolve on the Colonization Officer. But experience shows that although some of these Officers do give coherence to the 'disintegrated groups' in their colony, and do stimulate technical and economic change, others fail to do so. What reasons may there be for this state of affairs?

The difference in outlook between officer and colonist, which is one of the reasons for the 'top-down' attitude, is also one reason for poverty of leadership. For even if the Colonization Officer is receptive to 'felt needs' coming from the colonist, he may not fully understand what is at issue. This partly arises from the fact that many, but not all, officers have had a predominantly literary and academic education, for reasons that are deeply rooted in the values

[1] See, for example, Hatch, *Towards Freedom from Want*, espec. pp. 15–22 and 115–45; Sir E. John Russell, 'India's People and their Food', *Geography*, vol. xxxvii (1952), pp. 125–41, espec. p. 141; Little, in Ruopp, *Approaches to Community Development*, pp. 87–96, espec. pp. 91–93.

[2] See INCIDI, *Rural Development*, p. 400.

of Ceylon's plural society, and which have often been discussed.[1] Their knowledge of both agriculture and the peasant may thus be theoretical and second-hand; yet their academic-style education has not been academic enough to stimulate their intellectual curiosity about the roots of their day-to-day problems. These 'marginal men' thus fall firmly between the two stools of academic and practical interest in the job in hand.[2]

A second possible reason for the deficiencies of many Colonization Officers is the relatively low status accorded to the post by society; this is partly, as Straus has suggested, because the work is practical and not clerical;[3] and partly because in Ceylonese eyes the Colonization Officers have a much lower standing than members of the civil service (which corresponds roughly to the Administrative Class of the British civil service).

Colonization Officers, like most members of the public service in touch with the people in Ceylon, are often, further, accused of bribery and corruption; but, even if the charges took concrete form, they would be difficult or impossible to prove. One Colonization Officer at Kagama was found guilty of bribery and corruption by the Bribery Commission of 1948–9;[4] the author's suspicions were strongly aroused in two cases in the course of his field work, once over apparent complicity between a Colonization Officer and a *boutique*-keeper, the other over the affairs of a Co-operative Society; but beyond that, there is little of value to be said about these accusations.

It must be stressed, however, that even where a Colonization Officer suffers from few or none of the defects which have been mentioned, he is still not the leader which the situation requires. Even at his best a Colonization Officer is an outsider, who is in the colony for a short time only, and who is imposed on the colony by authority. As such he can never fulfil the role of a natural leader who is a member of the colonist community; the ideal officer, probably, is one who has been a colonist and who has showed merit as such. One or two middle-class colonists have in fact become Colonization Officers, and the Gal Oya Development Board

---

[1] See, for example, R. Pieris, 'Bilingualism and Cultural Marginality', *Brit. J. Soc.*, vol. ii (1951), pp. 328–39, and *WBR*, pp. 769–73 (ii. 425–8).

[2] The phrase is Pieris's (p. 332).

[3] In *Rur. Soc.*, vol. iii, pp. 252–3.

[4] See *Report of the Bribery Commission, 1948–9* (Colombo, Govt. Press, 1951), pp. 23 and 161–4.

intends to use peasant colonists as assistants, on a voluntary basis; but the removal of the gap between colonist and officer cannot take place until the educational standard of the colonist improves.

It used to be frequently suggested that a solution to the problem of leadership in the colonization schemes lay in the establishment of middle-class colonists in or alongside peasant colonies. Thus, as has already been seen, the Land Commission recommended that 'men of moderate means should be included as well as small-holders'.[1] D. S. Senanayake, writing in 1935, more specifically envisaged the middle-class colonists as leaders, or 'rural gentry', as he called them, and saw in the role an 'opportunity for truly patriotic endeavour'.[2] The idea of providing leadership by settling the middle class has been a favourite one elsewhere from time to time, notably in the Punjab, where at one time it was the custom to settle 'yeomen', to form useful members of society, and 'capitalists', who, it was hoped, would form the 'natural leaders' of the new society.[3] But it was found that the 'yeomen' were, on the whole, not very satisfactory, tending to develop their land slowly and to become involved in disputes, but not to make any material contribution, to the welfare of the colony. In fact, the idea of 'including colonists of a class above the ordinary peasant as an integral part of a colonization scheme' was later dropped.

Middle-class colonists had in fact been settled in only two peasant colonies in Ceylon by 1951; there were 23 of them in Minneriya and 13 in Tabbowa. In addition, the 36 colonists in the entirely middle-class colony at Kopakulama adjoined the peasant colony at Pandiyankadawela; there were middle-class allottees (not strictly colonists) on land adjoining the Iranamadu colonies, and the ex-officers in the ex-servicemen's colony at Parakrama Samudra had more land than the 'other ranks' and, it was hoped, would provide leadership. It will be noticed that only in the rather special case of the ex-servicemen's colony was middle-class colonization at all recent. For a number of years, in fact, middle-class colonization has been under a cloud. This is partly for general reasons, for example, government concentration on the peasant, and shortage of suitable land in the face of peasant needs.[4]

[1] See *LC*, p. 22.
[2] See Senanayake, *Agriculture and Patriotism*, p. 23.
[3] See *Punjab Colony Manual*, i. 114–15.
[4] See *ARLC*, 1953, pp. 3–4.

But there is also the fact that middle-class colonists have, as a rule, not been particularly satisfactory from the Government's point of view. As early as 1937, land allotted to middle-class colonists at Minneriya had to be reallocated because of the failure of earlier allottees to cultivate their land, and absentee landlordism soon became rife.[1] When the author was working in Kopakulama Colony in 1951, 32 out of the 36 'colonists' were not in residence and the standard of cultivation was generally very low. There are, it is true, a number of mitigating circumstances, especially lack of capital.

Middle-class colonists have not only been unsatisfactory cultivators; they have on the whole done little or nothing to provide any form of leadership for nearby peasant colonists. Punjab experience has thus been repeated, and few authorities in Ceylon would now envisage middle-class colonization as a solution to the problem of leadership. There is now some attempt to revive middle-class alienations, but the motive is the economic one of harnessing private capital.[2] If social motives are mentioned at all, as they are in a recent memorandum of the Gal Oya Development Board, it is merely in terms of 'balanced development'.

It is becoming increasingly clear, in fact, that leadership in the colonies will eventually have to come from the colonists themselves. The same conclusion had already been reached nearly fifty years ago in the Punjab Canal Colonies, for the Colonies Committee reported in 1907–8 that 'the colonies would probably do better to rely for their future leaders amongst the agricultural community on men raised from the peasant class'.[3] So far, unfortunately, there is a tendency for leadership amongst colonists themselves to be in the hands of bullies and demagogues, who dominate Co-operative and Rural Development Societies, sometimes, it is suggested, to their own material benefit. This, of course, only goes to show once again that such institutions are artificially imposed, and to underline the point that valuable leaders are only likely to arise gradually. It may here be suggested that the colony consisting of the groups of kinsfolk, which has been advocated in this chapter, is more likely to throw up 'natural'

---

[1] See, for example, ibid., 1937, p. 8 and *Admin. Report: Irrigation*, 1943, pp. 3–4.

[2] See *CUCL*, pp. 61–63, and *ARLC*, 1953, pp. 4–6.

[3] Quoted in *Punjab Colony Manual*, i. 298; and cf. *CUCL*, p. 60.

leaders than one holding an amorphous mass of unrelated colonists. But the transition from authoritarian to 'natural' leadership will not be an easy one.[1]

Relations with Purāna Villages

A set of problems of a somewhat different nature is created by the fact that almost all colonies are set down adjoining or even encircling *purāna* villages which, though mainly small, are tending to grow rapidly and which, moreover, are peopled by peasants who are most tenacious of their rights in *purāna* lands and of the status that goes with their ownership. At the very least, colonization in these circumstances means disturbance of peasant rights to *chena*; it may mean very much more if paddy lands are affected, or if social relations between colony and village are bad.

Relations with existing settlers have, of course, caused difficulty in many different colonization schemes. The Italians solved the problem ruthlessly in Libya, displacing Arabs from the coast plain to make room for Italian settlers, and paying compensation 'where deemed necessary'.[2] In most Asian schemes, however, the object has been to hurt local interests as little as possible, and to achieve some sort of fusion of local peasants and incoming colonists. Reports from Indonesia suggest that this problem, involving as it does relations between shifting and sedentary cultivators, is causing more difficulty than social cohesion within the colony.[3] In the early Punjab Colony on the Lower Chenab, hostility from the nomadic Janglis was long a thorn in the flesh of authority, and many colonists failed to reach their land at all, having been waylaid by the nomads.[4] Later it became settled policy to give lands to local people, grants being liberal and 'proportional rather to their prolific qualities than their present needs'. Here, perhaps, is the germ of the Ceylon policy, whose effects on the selection of colonists have already been discussed in Chapter 10. Certainly, tenderness for local interests has always characterized colonization in Ceylon, from the early days of the Pasdun Korale East

[1] Cf. R. A. J. van Lier, 'Les Aspects Sociaux du Développement Rurale', in INCIDI, *Rural Development*, pp. 334–5.

[2] See Sir E. J. Russell, 'Agricultural Colonization in the Pontine Marshes and Libya', *Geog. J.*, vol. xciv (1939), pp. 280 and 288.

[3] The author is indebted to the Indonesian Embassy in London for obtaining these reports from Jakarta.

[4] See *Punjab Colony Manual*, i. 12–13.

Colony onward.[1] But problems and difficulties have nevertheless arisen.

Some of these problems have already been mentioned; for instance, the jealousy aroused in the villager by the prosperity and subsidization of the colonist, and his tendency to look down on the colonist, because of his lack of kinship status and because of his mixed caste society. Most other problems in this field arise over land. No very consistent policy has been followed in the treatment of private land, whether *purāna* or *akkarai-wel*, which is found to be included in or to adjoin the area which it is intended to colonize; and all of the various solutions which have been tried bring their own problems in their train. If all such private land is acquired and reorganized to conform with a consistent pattern of development, *purāna* holders are likely to absorb a large proportion of the available holdings. Indeed, if an attempt had been made to give holdings in the colony to all the villagers affected by the Allai scheme there would not have been enough land to go round. Thus, quite apart from the feelings of villagers about their ancestral lands, the tidy solution may be physically impossible. Sometimes, as at Bathmedilla, policy has taken account of feelings about ancestral lands, and villagers have been given the option of retaining them. Then there are colonies like Nachchaduwa and Ridibendi Ela, which are a jigsaw of *purāna* holdings, former Crown land alienated before the modern colony was started, and modern paddy and high land allotments. It is in these colonies that overt trouble between colonist and villager is at a maximum. There are innumerable disputes, some of them petty, many of them ugly, over land, water, straying cattle, fences, theft, and women. These disputes are readily avoided if private holdings are acquired and arranged; but it is a moot point whether they make for greater economic inefficiency than the loss of incentive when a villager loses his *purāna* holding, with all that that means in pride of possession and in status.

Apart from these particularly troublesome colonies, relations between colony and village tend to be complicated in any colony where certain additional factors are at work. Thus, if, as at Dewahuwa and in parts of Gal Oya, it has been thought necessary to push on with colonization before Crown title has been established, legal disputes may multiply; temples are particularly liable to

[1] See the *First Report of the Pasdun Korale East Colonization Scheme*, p. 3.

appear with claims to large acreages (and, sometimes, to be successful, as at Minipe). Where colonists and non-colonists share a
supply of irrigation water as at Kilinochchi, there may be much
trouble at cultivation meetings. Where, in spite of the general
policy on the segregation of communities, a colony of one community is set down near a village of another, relations may become
very strained; thus a great deal of trouble developed over the
presence inside the Malay Colony of Sinhalese sacred sites;[1] and
there has been friction between the Moslem village of Onegama
and Kandyan Sinhalese colonists in Parakrama Samudra.

The ultimate aim of policy in Ceylon is the integration of colonies with the surrounding villages; and this is, indeed, the only aim
which can reasonably be held in view. In some of the older colonies, notably in Stage 1 at Minneriya, it is claimed that integration
is an accomplished fact, but elsewhere it is obvious that colony
and village are very different, and that relations between them are
distant or even strained. In a region like the Dry Zone, an old
region with a long-established settlement pattern and with a
peasantry whose life revolves around the possession of *purāna* land,
it is difficult moreover to envisage any cut-and-dried land policy
which would eliminate disputes and hasten integration.

A Diseased Society?

The reader, especially if he has African experience, may be
tempted to see in many of the Ceylon Dry Zone colonies examples
of a maladjusted society composed of an uprooted peasantry, devoid of social cohesion and natural leadership, and divorced from
the social system of the settlements around them. And he may
wonder whether there are also present what Fortes has called 'the
common symptoms of a maladjusted social system—crime, prostitution, corruption, and unbridled acquisitiveness ... prominent to
an extent never known in the traditional social order'.[2]

Are, then, these 'symptoms of a maladjusted social system'
present in the colonization schemes? Certainly 'unbridled acquisitiveness' is not generally in evidence; in fact, some might go so far as
to say that its absence is an obstacle to maximum production. Corruption is certainly present, but it is hard to say whether it is more
common than in the villages. One heard nothing of prostitution

[1] See *DSC*, 1932, pp. 1053–4.
[2] In Hinden, *Fabian Colonial Essays*, p. 225.

though in some places marital ties seem to have grown lax away from the restraint of the village. Allegations are occasionally made that crime, particularly gambling, tends to increase when a colonization scheme is established in an area.[1] It is not easy to test the accuracy of such allegations by analysis of statistics. There are no data at all for some colonies, and a number of colonies are in unpoliced areas, so that reporting of crimes may be incomplete: indeed, it may be incomplete even in policed areas. And, since colonies contain relatively few people, compared with whole districts, it is a little unfair to compare their crime rates (i.e. number of reported crimes per 100 population); for one more crime in a colony might well inflate the rate markedly. Table 25 has, however, been compiled, and is presented here for what it is worth.[2]

The table does allow some comparison to be made between crime rates in a colony and in the district in which the colony is set. It will be noticed that some colonies have a crime rate no more than, or even less than their district; and that the relatively high rates for some other colonies (notably Giritale and Minneriya) are reduced by taking the author's estimate of population, which includes squatters and other non-colonists, instead of the official estimates. But a number of colonies remain with relatively high crime rates even if the author's figures are used; in nearly all of these, the rate is two to three times that in the relevant district, though in the case of such colonies as Giritale and Kottu Kachchiya, no firm conclusion can be drawn because of the small population and low number of crimes concerned. Of the large colonies for which the figures probably have more meaning, Minipe and Minneriya stand out. Now, both are colonies in which there are large numbers of squatters and/or migrant labourers, so that there is here some confirmation for the view which was expressed to the Kandyan Peasantry Commission, that trouble in certain colonies begins with 'an influx of undesirables' who induce colonists to gamble and to lose their earnings.[3] Figures for crime at Gal Oya also show crime rates of 0·7 per cent. among the 'floating population' of labourers, a higher rate than in most of the colonies in Table 25.[4] All this confirms that impression

[1] See, for example, *KPC*, pp. 217 and 313.
[2] The author is greatly indebted to Sir Richard Aluwihare, Inspector-General of Police in 1951, for data on crime rates and for elucidating a number of points.
[3] See *KPC*, p. 217.
[4] Data supplied by the Inspector-General of Police, Ceylon.

which one forms as one walks about the colonies, that here is no uprooted, crime-ridden society; in fact, it seems that the population of labourers, squatters, and outsiders approaches far more closely to the 'maladjusted social system' of Africa than does the relatively quiet and law-abiding population of colonists.

TABLE 25

Crime Rates in Certain Colonies, 1951

Colony	No. of grave crimes in colony	Crimes per 100 population in district in which colony stands	Crimes per 100 population in colony	
			*	†
Bathmedilla‡ . . .	2	0·2	0·1	0·1
Dewahuwa. . . .	2	0·4	0·1	0·1
Elahera‡	15	0·2	0·2	0·2
Giritale	8	0·4	1·5	0·9
Kagama§	3	0·4	0·1	0·1
Kottu Kachchiya . .	3	0·2	0·4	0·5
Minipe‡	15	0·2	0·6	0·5
Minneriya	80	0·4	1·4	1·0
Okkampitiya‡ . . .	4	0·2	1·6	1·7
Pandiyankadawela‖ . .	3	0·4	0·7	0·6
Parakrama Samudra . .	86	0·4	0·6	0·5
Tabbowa	3	0·2	0·2	0·3
Unnichchai‡ . . .	28	0·3	4·5	4·4

  * Figures supplied by Inspector-General of Police.
  † Figures recomputed on basis of author's estimates of population of each colony.
  ‡ Unpoliced colonies.
  § Old *and* New Colonies.
  ‖ Including Kopakulama middle-class Colony.

Sources: Data kindly supplied by the Inspector-General of Police, Ceylon, except for populations used as a basis of column headed† (see above).

The view that, whatever may be wrong with society in the colonies it is not chronically out of joint is further supported if one surveys the state of politics in the colonies. There is but little violent discontent or other symptom of malaise; in fact, in most colonies there is very little political activity at all. There is the occasional 'Leftist' agitator, or petition-writer, or 'political *bhikku*', or discontented squatter who stirs up trouble for the authorities in the shape of a hunger strike outside the Colonization Officer's office (this happened at Minipe), or an appeal to a Minister over the heads of the local authorities. Minneriya alone is reported to be 'a hot-bed of political activity'. In any case, not all of the agitation which is reported to the inquirer is necessarily reprehensible or a symptom of deep-seated trouble; ex-colonial authority is only too ready to condemn these things. Similarly, the 'tendency to mob' which was reported of the ex-servicemen at Parakrama Samudra is at least a sign of cohesion.

Conclusion

It is, in fact, important not to paint too black a picture of society in the colonies. On a pessimistic view, they emerge as yet another example of economic development which has divorced the peasant from his traditional way of life and sundered the customary bonds of his society; an example, in fact, of what Kenneth Little had in mind when he wrote:

if the change made is too drastic—if, for example, it brings about wide neglect of the obligations customary among kinsfolk—the whole social fabric may be shattered, because this type of society rests very largely on the performance of reciprocal duties and services between blood and affinal relatives.[1]

But a less pessimistic view is possible. Even in the colonies with least social cohesion and least leadership there are many sources of strength which are not present in an uprooted African group. The family unit of man, wife, and children is intact, even if other bonds of kinship are weakened or broken; ancient religious values are preserved and can be a great source of strength (in some colonies, the one thing which colonists will do for themselves is to build a temple); ancient social values are also often cherished, and work is far from being devoid of social purpose. The poverty, the overcrowded housing, the ambiguous values and depressing contact with another society which characterize so many African groups are lacking.

On the other hand, there is no room for complacency or for *Rāja Rata* sentimentalism. The Dry Zone colonies started and have continued with mixed motives, which have included on the one hand the need for food production in the face of economic and demographic instability, and on the other the settlement of peasants in order to relieve landlessness and agrarian pressure.

---

[1] In Ruopp, *Approaches to Community Development*, p. 87.

These chapters have, it is hoped, shown that the use of peasant colonists as instruments of food production, at least at levels of maximum production, faces formidable social resistances, on the detailed causes of which one still needs information. A great deal might be achieved on the technical and economic planes by harnessing energies at present lying dormant, but there will be many who will maintain that more drastic social changes are required. Changes *have* taken place and are taking place as a result of the conditions under which colonization has gone on, but some of them have been shown to hinder rather than to foster productivity, while some of them create various kinds of difficulty for the authorities; other changes make for a less cohesive and, probably, a less happy society, and more attention needs to be paid to social consequences of economic and administrative action.

Are there here, however, two irreconcilable objectives? Is it possible to agree with the Kandyan Peasantry Commission that 'the strengthening of . . . communal effort is a matter of the first importance', and at the same time to hope for maximum production?[1] Would the creation of a peasant society with stronger cohesion mean a society with stronger or weaker resistances to the technical changes which are considered so essential? Is the need for maximum food production so urgent that an alternative to peasant colonization, however purposeless socially, must be sought? These questions form themselves in the mind as one considers the facts and arguments of this chapter, but further discussion of them will be more profitable after a number of other aspects of colonization, set in a broader context, have been considered.

Meanwhile, one last point must be stressed. Whatever the answer to these questions, there is no doubt that more information about society in Ceylon in village, town, and colony is needed. The answers to such social questions largely lie in further research. It is good to note, then, that the work, including research, which was started by Unesco at the Fundamental Education Centre at Minneriya is to be continued by the Ceylon Ministry of Home Affairs;[2] and that Unesco is also to provide a sociologist and statistician to 'evaluate rural development plans of the Government'.[3] Ceylon might also follow examples set elsewhere; thus the Uttar Pradesh Government has set up a 'Planning and Action Research

---

[1] See *KPC*, p. 37.
[2] See *Ceylon News Letter*, 19 June 1954.   [3] Ibid. 26 Dec. 1953.

Institute' at Lucknow which will *inter alia* 'study the effect of community development on the life of villagers', and 'the basic background elements in the village that tend to help, limit, or retard the co-operative effort';[1] and much might also be learnt from the 'social development' work of the Sudan Gezira Board, with its emphasis on research into individual and social response to technical and economic change.[2]

[1] See *Ind. Trade and Industry*, vol. iv (1954), p. 76.
[2] See Sudan Gezira Board, *First Annual Report* (Khartoum, 1951), pp. 3–4 and 13–18.

16

The Cost and the Return

The Cost of Peasant Colonization

IT has not until recently been easy for the unofficial research worker to arrive at the capital cost of establishing a colonist in each scheme, for published data have been few and confusing.[1] It is now possible, however, to make an estimate, though not an accurate assessment, of the cost per colonist of irrigation and of land development, while subsidies, being on a standard basis, may be accurately determined. Strictly the colonist should also be debited with the cost of certain other goods and services which he receives in ampler share than the average citizen (for instance, with the cost of special surveys and of the extra attention given him by a number of administrative and technical departments). These costs, however, lie heavily concealed in the annual estimates;[2] they form a relatively small proportion of the total capital cost of establishing a colonist, and will be neglected in the discussion which follows. On the other side of the account, the discussion will necessarily omit the proportion of the cost of colonization which provides roads, schools, and so on, which benefit others besides the colonist.

Taking first the capital cost of irrigation, the World Bank Report included estimates of the cost of works which were to form the basis for peasant colonization, and to be undertaken during the period 1947–53.[3] Since the area to be irrigated was also quoted in each case, it is possible to evaluate very simply the estimated cost of providing irrigation works for a 5-acre, 4-acre, or 3-acre paddy allotment in each scheme. (A 5-acre allotment was, it will be remembered, generally standard until 1953; a 4-acre allotment was standard at Gal Oya until that year; and a 3-acre allotment became

---

[1] See, for example, *ARLC*, 1939–47, Schedule D, p. 19; see also Jennings, *Economy of Ceylon*, p. 65.

[2] See the *Annual Estimates of the Revenue and Expenditure of the Government of Ceylon*, which also show *actual* expenditure for the year previous to that to which the estimates refer.

[3] See *WBR*, pp. 418–19 (ii. 194).

standard almost everywhere in 1953.[1]) The results are shown in
Table 26. It is possible, of course, to object to these results on a
number of grounds. The basic figures are only estimates of the
total cost of each scheme, not actual costs; but at least the estimates

TABLE 26

*Estimated Cost of Colony Irrigation Works to be Constructed,
1947–53*

Work	Cost per irrigated acre (rupees)	Cost per colonist given paddy lot of		
		5 acres (rupees)	4 acres (rupees)	3 acres (rupees)
Allai extn.	760	3,800	..	2,280
Attaragalla	660	3,300	..	1,980
Bathmedilla	930	4,650	..	2,790
Dewahuwa	1,500	7,500	..	4,500
Elahera	770	3,850	..	2,310
Gal Oya	1,100*	..	4,400*	3,300*
Giritale	650	3,250	..	1,950
Huruluwewa	1,000	5,000	..	3,000
Iranamadu extn.	700	3,500	..	2,100
Kagama extn.	580	2,900	..	1,740
Kandalama	1,450	7,250	..	4,350
Kantalai extn.	810	4,050	..	2,430
Kottu Kachchiya	210	1,050	..	630
Minipe	260	1,300	..	780
Minneriya	450	2,250	..	1,350
Okkampitiya	160	800	..	480
Parakrama Sam.	530	2,650	..	1,590
Ridibendi Ela	600	3,000	..	1,800
Unnichchai extn.	104	520	..	312
Average	920	4,600	3,680	2,760

* Also includes relatively small proportion of cost which ought strictly to be
debited to hydro-electric power station.

Source: WBR, pp. 418–19 (ii. 194).

are based on a single real value of the rupee and, in point of fact, in
most cases probably do not differ greatly from the ultimate actual
cost, a figure which it is not easy for the unofficial research worker
to arrive at. A more serious objection is that whereas some works,
like Gal Oya, involved completely new construction of *bunds* and
major channels and mainly new construction of all other associated

[1] See above, pp. 263–4.

works, others, like Dewahuwa, started with an ancient *bund* only partly destroyed or even, as in the case of Stages II and III of Minneriya, with a completely restored *bund* and partially constructed major channel system. Strictly, it might be argued, the colonist in these latter schemes should be debited with his share of the capital cost of the initial work; but the amount is not readily determinable for modern construction and restoration, and, if determinable, is in terms of rupees of different value from that which prevails today; while in the case of ancient works there is, of course, no available figure for cost at all. In the circumstances, it seems best to accept the figures as quoted in the World Bank Report, and to recognize that the differences between the cost per acre in different schemes largely reflects the extent to which they have inherited basic works from the recent or ancient past. These differences are in fact wide, as the table shows. The estimated cost per acre varies from only Rs. 104 (£8) in the case of the relatively small and simple extension of an existing work at Unnichchai, to Rs. 1,100 (£85) at Gal Oya (this figure, however, including part of the cost of the power station) and to Rs. 1,500 (£115) at Dewahuwa. The high cost of Dewahuwa and of Kandalama, also in the Kala Wewa catchment, strengthens the doubts of the wisdom of these schemes which were raised, on hydrological grounds, in an earlier chapter.[1]

The average cost per acre lies, however, nearer the top of the range of figures than the bottom, for it is very heavily weighted by the high cost of the larger schemes such as Gal Oya; it is, in fact, Rs. 920 (£71), so that the estimated average cost of providing irrigation for a single colonist is in the region of Rs. 4,600 (£354) if he is to have a 5-acre paddy lot, or Rs. 2,760 (£212) if he is to have the 3-acre lot which became standard in 1953.[2]

Quite apart from the possible effects of inflation, these costs are likely to rise as the simpler and less damaged major works are restored and as effort turns more and more to costly restorations or to completely new schemes, based on major barrages, like Gal Oya and Walawe Ganga. The latter, in fact, is likely to be very expensive indeed. It has been officially estimated that it would cost Rs. 117 million to irrigate 40,000 new acres on the Walawe, so that the cost per irrigable acre would be Rs. 2,925 (£225); but

---

[1] See above, pp. 188–90.
[2] Cf. the figure of Rs. 4,000 quoted for a 5-acre lot in *WBR*, p. 425 (ii. 198).

the World Bank mission thought that the cost would be even higher, Rs. 200 million or Rs. 5,000 (£384) per irrigable acre.[1] Walawe, however, is likely to be an extreme case, and its very expensive nature, combined with the poor soil under its command and the very grave danger of siltation, makes it a singularly doubtful proposition.[2]

To the capital cost of irrigating a colonist's holding there must be added the capital cost of actual colonization, that is, of the measures over and above the provision of irrigation which were introduced on a mounting scale after 1932 and especially after the promulgation of the 'New Policy' in 1939.[3] Recent official reports, supplemented by inquiries in Ceylon and by the fruits of correspondence, render it possible to make a fairly accurate assessment of this cost as it was in 1951, and as it was in 1953 immediately after the economy measures.[4] This assessment is given in Table 27. The average cost per colonist of Rs. 8,150 (£627) is very near the figure of Rs. 8,000 given by the World Bank mission;[5] and adding Rs. 4,600 for irrigation costs, the total capital cost of irrigation and colonization may be estimated to have been Rs. 12,750 (£980) per colonist in 1951. This is slightly less than the estimate of Rs. 14,000 made by the Committee on the Utilization of Crown Lands.[6]

There are no comparable checks on the totals for 1953, but the estimate of Rs. 3,775 (£290) as the average cost of colonization is probably not far wrong; the total cost of irrigation and colonization in 1953 would then be Rs. 6,535 (£502) per colonist.

The provision of irrigation and of facilities for colonization had thus by 1951 become a very costly affair. The cuts made by 1953 nearly halved the total capital cost per colonist; but since they were mainly achieved by reducing the size of the allotment, and since the reduction in the cost of the type-plan house is almost offset by the cost of providing more houses per scheme, there was a much smaller reduction in the cost per irrigated acre and per scheme. The former cost, for example, was about Rs. 2,550 in 1951 and about Rs. 2,178 in 1953, a reduction of only about 14 per cent.

And it is clearly still a very costly matter to settle a family in the

[1] See *WBR*, p. 431 (ii. 202).
[2] Cf. above, p. 193; also ibid., pp. 431–2 (ii. 202).
[3] See above, pp. 151–6.
[4] Especially *ARDLD*, 1951, and *ARLC*, 1953.
[5] See *WBR*, p. 425 (ii. 198).　　　　　[6] See *CUCL*, p. 26.

Dry Zone of Ceylon. Is anything to be learnt from a study of costs in other South Asian schemes? Unfortunately, as Pelzer found when studying Dutch efforts in the Indies, it is very hard to arrive at satisfactory assessments because of confused or missing data and

TABLE 27

Approximate Average Costs of Colonization

Head	1951 (rupees)	1953 (rupees)
Land Development:		
Clearing	2,605	1,000
House	2,700	1,500
Latrine, wells, &c.	455	245
Share of general buildings . . .	1,000	290
Fencing	150	90
	—— 6,910	—— 3,125
Subsidies:		
Stumping	600*	200
Subsistence	90	180
High land	200	—
Seeds, buffalo, &c.	150	120
	—— 1,040	—— 500
Overheads	200	150
Totals	Rs. 8,150 (£627)	Rs. 3,775 (£290)

* Maximum.

Sources: ARDLD, 1951, p. 20; ARLC, 1953, pp. 7–8; Joint United Kingdom and Australian Mission on Rice Production in Ceylon, *Report*, S.P. 2 of 1955; author's inquiries (cf. above, pp. 167–8) and estimates.

because of the changing value of money;[1] moreover, the physical setting of any two schemes in different countries is scarcely ever comparable. One or two figures may, however, be quoted for what they are worth. Boeke estimated that the pre-1929 Indonesian colonists had cost the Government some 800 guilders per family; this would amount to about Rs. 860 (£66) at 1929 values of money, so that the same scale of aid would have cost something over Rs. 2,000 (or about £155) in 1951.[2] Only about 30 per cent. of the 800 guilders went in irrigation works, a result presumably of the generally easier physical conditions in a region of perennial

[1] See Pelzer, *Pioneer Settlement*, pp. 199 and 214.
[2] See Boeke, *Evolution of the Netherlands Indies Economy*, pp. 144–5.

rainfall like Sumatra. Costs other than irrigation might thus have amounted to something over Rs. 1,400 per family if incurred in 1951, compared with Rs. 8,150 and Rs. 3,775 in Ceylon in 1951 and 1953 respectively. The differences are, of course, due to the much lower scale of aid operated by the Dutch.[1]

The first stage of the Indian Terai scheme, to take another example, was estimated in 1947 to cost *in toto* Rs. 4,546 per colonist;[2] but of this only some Rs. 823 per colonist was for irrigation, roads, and related works, leaving Rs. 3,723 per colonist for other provision, a figure which is very near the comparable figure for Ceylon in 1953, viz. Rs. 3,775. The basis was, however, different, for much expenditure was to be on equipment for co-operative farms; moreover, expenditure on houses and other items was, technically at any rate, recoverable.

The Thal scheme in Pakistan may be chosen as a final comparative example. There, estimates show that the total cost per colonist may be in the region of Rs. 7,000, made up of Rs. 3,400 for irrigation and Rs. 3,600 for other provision.[3] Here at last are figures which exceed the 1953 Ceylon total (Rs. 6,535); for here is a scheme in an arid region which is utterly dependent on irrigation and for which a high scale of aid was judged appropriate in order to hasten development, and for other reasons. But, once again, a part of the cost was to be recoverable.

One is, in fact, brought back in the end to conclude that the Ceylon schemes *are* very expensive, and to consider possible grounds for still further economies. It must at once be conceded that, although in the postwar 'spending spree' optimism about Ceylon's finances engendered a certain amount of extravagance, there have also been constant efforts to achieve economy. An examination of the detailed story of a scheme such as Parakrama Samudra shows how frequently estimates of cost have been evaluated and then pruned. But in any attempt to prune costs, one inevitably comes up against the high figure for irrigation, which it will be remembered, constituted over a third of the estimated total cost of installing a colonist in 1951, and a rather higher proportion of the comparable cost in 1953. It will be realized that

[1] See above, p. 280.
[2] See the *Tarai and Bhabar Report*, pp. 333–4.
[3] Data derived from Khan, in *Pakistan Q.*, vol. ii, no. 3, pp. 20–26, and from information kindly supplied by the High Commissioner for Pakistan in London.

the provision of irrigation is essential to the growing of paddy in
the Dry Zone; and it will further be realized that the growing of
paddy is no mere craven concession to dietetic prejudice, but is,
with *gangoda* cultivation also made possible by irrigation, the only
method of land use which at present seems capable of ensuring
long-term fertility. Even if unirrigated or 'dry' farming should
eventually prove a success,[1] it is by no means certain that it will be
much less expensive in capital cost. The total cost of installing
a colonist in the two experimental dry farming schemes at Kurundankulama and Relapanawa has been quoted as Rs. 13,500.[2] Now
it will be remembered that the estimate of the total cots of a
colonist in the orthodox, pre-1953 schemes was Rs. 14,000. There
seems thus little to choose between the two methods of colonization
on the basis operative in 1951. It is true that 'the extent of
each dry-farming unit is nearly double that in a major colonization
scheme, while the standard of land developed and the amount of
assistance . . . are higher'.[3] But these, as will shortly be seen, are
conditions imposed by the nature, technical uncertainty, and un-
familiarity of dry farming; and it seems unlikely that for the foreseeable future any major economies can be effected within the
present general framework apart from measures (e.g. a reduction
in the scale of aid) which can also be applied on a comparable scale
in the orthodox irrigated colonies.

The cost of providing irrigation or an equally expensive alternative has thus to be faced if the Dry Zone is to be developed at all,
at least in terms of current techniques. No doubt economies in the
capital cost of normal, irrigated colonies can be achieved by wise
choice of site and by careful planning of irrigation work, but heavy
expenditure is bound to remain. There seems to be more scope
for reducing the cost of aid to the colonist, including preparatory
land development. A case has, in fact, already been made out for
a thorough inquiry into the whole question of aid to the colonist
because of the apparently undesirable effects of recent high scales
of aid.[4] There is clearly every reason for such an inquiry on financial grounds as well; indeed, it is fortunate that a lower level of aid
seems desirable on each of a number of different lines of argument.
The case for economy becomes all the more striking if it is

---

[1] See below, pp. 342–8.   [2] See *CUCL*, p. 26.   [3] Ibid.
[4] See above, pp. 279–80. Further economies have been made since 1953,
but costs have also risen.

remembered that it is not only capital expenditure which the Ceylon Government incurs on the colonist's account; there is also recurrent expenditure on the maintenance of irrigation works and of special roads, and on administrative arrangements peculiar to the colonies. Some items of recurrent expenditure, notably the share of the colonists in the cost of administration by the *kach-cheries*, cannot be separately accounted for. But some idea of the recurrent cost of colonization can be formed from consideration of expenses borne on the annual votes of the Irrigation Department and of the Land Commissioner.

Table 28 is an attempt to show the estimated costs to be borne on the first of these departmental votes for five reasonably representative schemes which include colonies and which are allotted specific sums for the maintenance of irrigation works and of Irrigation Department roads in the official Estimates for 1951–2.[1] These specific sums are shown in the first two of the columns under the general heading of 'Estimated Costs'. The figures in the third column, headed 'General', represent an attempt to allot to each of the schemes tabulated some share of the burden carried by Vote 1 in the Irrigation Department Estimates, which covers salaries, and expenditure on plant, offices, transport, research, and so on, the other two departmental votes, Votes 2 and 3, covering maintenance and new works respectively. In order to arrive at the figures in the 'General' column, the total amount in Vote 1 which might reasonably be charged to maintenance was first computed; it was taken to be that proportion of Vote 1 which Vote 2 is of the sum of Votes 2 and 3. The total irrigable area in Ceylon being known, the amount of this part of Vote 1 chargeable to one acre of irrigable land was calculated, and this quantity, multiplied by the irrigable acreage of each scheme in the table, gave the rough measure shown in the column headed 'General' of the amount chargeable to each scheme.[2] The rest of the table is self-explanatory.

The final result, the figure at the foot of the last column, suggests that each irrigable acre in the colonies concerned costs, on an average, Rs. 17 per annum to maintain, so that a 5-acre paddy lot costs Rs. 85 (£8–9) and a 3-acre lot Rs. 51 (£4). To these recurrent

[1] See *Estimates of the Revenue and Expenditure of the Government of Ceylon for the Financial Year 1st October 1951–30th September 1952*, pp. 286–95.
[2] Total irrigable area from *Admin. Report: Irrigation*, 1951, p. 6. For note on basis for irrigable acreage for each scheme, and reason for choice of *schemes* rather than colonies, see Table 28.

costs must be added the cost of Colonization Officers and of their clerks and messengers, which is borne on the Land Commissioner's vote.[1] This cost was estimated at Rs. 95,153 for 1951–2, and as there were some 9,315 colonists at the end of 1951, the annual cost per colonist may be reckoned at about Rs. 10.[2] It is unlikely that this figure has been reduced subsequently.

TABLE 28

Estimated Cost of Irrigation Maintenance, 1951–2

| Colony | Irrigable acreage* | Estimated costs (000 Rs.): | | | | Estimated total per irrigable acre (Rs.) |
		Irriga-tion works	Roads	General†	Total	
Dewahuwa .	2,337	34	52	7	93	39
Minneriya .	10,000	108	32	30	170	17
Nachchaduwa .	7,332	70	30	22	122	17
Parakrama Samudra .	18,200	145	37	55	237	13
Unnichchai .	6,400	70	30	19	119	19

Average total for schemes tabulated .   .   .   . Rs. 17 per acre

* Irrigable acreage for whole major work which feeds colony (i.e. including some private lands) since costs are given in terms of major works rather than colonies.

† For basis, see text.

Sources: Acreage from *Admin. Report: Irrigation*, 1951; costs from *Estimates . . . for Financial Year 1st October 1951–30th September 1952.*

Adding together the costs borne on the votes of the Irrigation Department and of the Land Commissioner, and remembering that a number of smaller items are not accounted for, it seems likely that the recurrent cost to the Government of average colonists settled in 1951 and 1953 respectively was not less than Rs. 95 and Rs. 60 per colonist per annum.

The Financial Return from Colonization

What financial return, if any, may the Ceylon Government reasonably expect from its peasant colonization schemes? How does the actual return compare with this reasonable expectation,

[1] See *Estimates . . . for Financial Year 1st October 1951–30th September 1952*, pp. 256–9.

[2] Figure for number of colonists from *ARLC*, 1951, p. 14, supplemented by field investigations.

and does the comparison reveal the need for a change in the charges levied on colonists? These questions must now be briefly considered. The first of them, of course, raises the whole problem of assessing a 'reasonable return' from public works in general and from irrigation and land-development projects in particular.[1] The return may be measured in many ways; for example, in terms of the net direct revenue (e.g. water charges, in the case of an irrigation work), or in terms of estimated total revenue (i.e. direct revenue plus other forms of revenue resulting from increased prosperity occasioned by the scheme); or a scheme which is uneconomic when judged by these criteria may be adjudged socially desirable because of the 'indirect and largely immeasurable benefits to society as a whole'.[2]

The historical chapters of this book have shown that the criterion of direct net revenue, usually called 'a fair return on the capital invested', was long the dominant one in the story of irrigation and settlement in the Dry Zone of Ceylon.[3] And the Gal Oya Development Board is today enjoined by the Minister of Agriculture and Lands

so to order its affairs that, as soon as practicable, all its recurrent expenditure ... should be met from its own revenue, and that it should show a surplus which, after due allowance is made for depreciation, would represent a reasonable return on the capital expended on the Scheme.[4]

Let us first, then, inquire whether any direct net revenue is left after the recurrent expenditure summarized at the end of the preceding section has been met.

The gross financial return which the Government receives from the colonist by way of water and land charges has already been tabulated. It was there made clear that the *maximum* annual charges levied on the colonists at the time of the author's inquiries in 1951 were Rs. 5 per acre for water and Rs. 10 per acre for land, but that in many colonies lower rates were in force. There are a number of cases to consider, for instance:

(*a*) Given an 8-acre allotment of which 5 acres are irrigable and

[1] See, for example, D. R. Gadgil, *Economic Effects of Irrigation* (Poona, Gokhale Inst. of Pol. and Econ., 1948).

[2] Quoted from A. E. Kahn, 'Investment Criteria in Development Programmes', *Q.J. Econ.*, vol. lxv (1951), p. 57.

[3] See, for example, above, pp. 104–5.

[4] See GODB, *Ann. Report*, 1949–50, p. 5. (The Minister's directions were issued under Section 30 of the Gal Oya Development Board Act, No. 51 of 1949.)

given the maximum charges, the gross revenue is Rs. 105 per annum, so that if the colonists settled in 1951 are ultimately charged at maximum rates there will only be an estimated net return of Rs. 10, which is so small as to be insignificant in view of the likely errors in the calculation.

(*b*) Given a 4½-acre allotment of which 3 acres are irrigable, the total charges at the maximum rates would be Rs. 60, which just equals the estimated recurrent costs.[1]

(*c*) Some of the colonists charged the maximum rates were settled some years ago when costs and scales of aid were lower. (This applies, for example, to Minneriya Stage I.) In such cases, there would appear to be a small net revenue.

(*d*) Gal Oya merits separate consideration. Since October 1953, colonists there have been subject to an inclusive charge of Rs. 180 per annum.[2] This is, clearly, higher than the maximum so far charged elsewhere, and should easily cover recurrent costs in spite of such measures as the provision of 'Village Officers' as well as Colonization Officers. It may, in fact, leave something under Rs. 100 net revenue per colonist per annum. This is, however, probably under 1 per cent. of the capital invested, and it is not easy to see how the Gal Oya Board will fulfil its obligation to earn a 'reasonable return' unless this phrase is very liberally interpreted or unless the Board leans heavily on proceeds from enterprises other than peasant colonization.

On the whole, then, it would appear that, quite apart from colonies in which charges have been waived, colonization in Ceylon yields little or no direct return on capital invested in it. This is, however, no new phenomenon in the island, for 'the direct revenue derived from irrigation in Ceylon was never appreciable . . . and even when full rates were levied only amounted to Rs. 100,000 or 30 per cent. of the costs of maintenance and operation'.[3] There are colonies, clearly, which can do better than this. On the other hand, there have been irrigated colonization schemes elsewhere which have done better still. The irrigation works of the Punjab Canal Colonies, for example, earned 12·6 per cent. net in 1945–6,

[1] In certain new colonies the annual payment for land is now (1956) Rs. 20 per acre, giving a net annual revenue per colonist in case (*b*) of about Rs. 45.

[2] GODB, *Ann. Report*, 1951–2, p. 58 and 1952–3, p. 65. This is for the pre-1953 allotment. For the smaller post-1953 allotment the inclusive annual charge is Rs. 135, giving a probable net revenue of Rs. 75 per colonist per annum.

[3] See *Admin. Report: Irrigation*, 1946, p. 5.

and in 1938–9 over 30 per cent. net profit was made on the three main colonies of Lyallpur, Shahpur, and Montgomery.[1] It may be asked, then, whether in view of these facts, in view of the evident prosperity of the colonist, and in view of the strained financial resources of the Ceylon Government, there is not a case for increasing the charges on land and water in the Dry Zone colonies.

It must be admitted at once, however, that conditions in regions like the Punjab are exceptional, because of the ease with which works may be constructed in its flat plains and because of the fertility of its soil. Other Indian irrigation works, notably those in the Deccan, 'hardly yield 1 to 2 per cent.'[2] Again, while the annual value of the crops produced in the Punjab colonies was usually over 100 per cent. of the capital invested in irrigation works, it seems likely that the annual production in the average Dry Zone colony is under 50 per cent. of the capital invested in irrigation and only about 16 per cent. of the *total* capital invested.[3] The difference is due to many factors, including the higher scale of aid and the lower level of agricultural technology in Ceylon; but the effect of physical conditions on construction costs and on yields is also operative. In other words, one cannot expect the Ceylon colonies to yield the same return in either crops or revenue as their Punjab counterparts.

But the general prosperity of the colonist and the relatively poor financial resources of the country[4] cannot be in doubt, and there is, to say the least, a case for the collection of accurate data to replace the estimates here made, and for an inquiry into the whole question of a possible increase in charges and of repayment of aid.

It seems generally undesirable, however, that the return on capital which might be considered by such an inquiry should be fixed on a commercial basis, that is, at 3 per cent. or some such figure. Other criteria of what is profitable are relevant. A wise Revenue Officer of the North-Central Province, a man who was as keen as any of his kind to safeguard the colony's revenues, wrote

[1] See Darling, *Punjab Peasant*, p. 114, and G. B. Jathar and S. G. Beri, *Indian Economics*, 9th ed. (Madras, OUP, 1949), i. 196–202.

[2] See Jathar and Beri, *Indian Economics*, i. 196.

[3] Punjab figures from Darling, *Punjab Peasant*, p. 114. Dry Zone figures based on gross incomes discussed in Chapter 13 (pp. 260–2) and on estimates of capital invested in irrigation and *in toto* (pp. 316–21).

[4] See below, pp. 328–34.

fifty years ago in reply to those who were sceptical of the wisdom of restoring irrigation works because of their doubtful direct return:

> Even were it not the first duty of every Government—a duty long lost sight of in this Province—to promote the health and well-being of the people, it may be demonstrated that regarding purely financial interests the investment is remunerative, and that a prosperous population is the source of an abundant revenue.[1]

And a short time in the Dry Zone colonies soon demonstrates qualitatively, at any rate, how additional revenue flows in through customs and excise, the railways, the post office, and even through income tax.[2] If quantification were possible it might well be that some established colonies at least would earn their 3 per cent. net revenue, especially with economies in scale of aid and with judicious increases in charges.

And, using wider criteria still, the colonies undoubtedly make their contribution to the solution of problems of landlessness, agrarian unrest, food shortage, population pressure, and shortage of foreign exchange wherewith to import foodstuffs. But there still remains the possibility, of course, that some other system of Dry Zone land use would be more economical or more profitable as judged by one or more of the possible criteria; or that alternative channels of investment, say in industry or in Wet Zone agriculture, would use scarce capital more wisely. These are problems which must be taken up in the Conclusion.

Funds for Colonization

Meanwhile, this chapter will end with a short review of the sources of funds for peasant colonization; it will, *inter alia*, drive home the point about the relative scarcity of financial resources which has already been made.

During the period 1939–53, when almost all of the colonization schemes which form the subject of this book were in the making, it was the general custom of the Government of Ceylon to finance most irrigation and land-development works out of loan funds, leaving current revenue to cover aid to colonists, recurrent expenditure, and the service of the loans. Operations connected with colonization in fact took up a fair proportion of annual loan-fund expenditure, especially towards the end of the period under review.

---

[1] See Ievers, p. 162.   [2] Cf. *Admin. Report: Irrigation*, 1946, p. 5.

It is not possible to be precise, but some idea of the figures involved may be gathered from the fact that of an estimated total loan-fund expenditure of Rs. 128,318,368 (about £9·9 million) for 1951–2, approximately Rs. 25 million (19 per cent.) went on land development, Rs. 45 million (35 per cent.) in a grant to the Gal Oya Development Board, and Rs. 30 million (23 per cent.) on irrigation works serving colonies or future colonies.[1] Not all of the land-development vote or of the Gal Oya grant went on peasant colonization, of course, though a high proportion of each must have been so spent; but expenditure on land acquisition in connexion with colonies was, in addition to the items mentioned, met out of loan funds. Altogether, it seems reasonable to estimate that between half and three-quarters of the loan-fund expenditure for 1951–2 was on peasant colonization.

The proportion of expenditure from current revenue which was so spent was much smaller. For example, of a total estimated expenditure from revenue of Rs. 135,544,841 for 1951–2, only Rs. 5·4 million (4 per cent.) was on the Land Commissioner's votes connected with peasant colonization (and even this includes some expenditure on village expansion); about Rs. 0·8 million (0·6 per cent.) was on recurrent Irrigation Department expenditure in colonies, if the cost per colonist reached on p. 323 above is accepted; and there was Rs. 1·1 million (or 0·8 per cent.) on new irrigation works in connexion with existing or future colonies. The total under these heads is therefore only about 13 per cent. of the grand total, plus, of course, an indeterminable part of a number of departmental expenses.

The loan funds which have just been mentioned, and which have borne the brunt of the cost of colonization, were almost entirely raised by the floating of a number of internal loans, notably towards the end of the period 1939–53, under the National Development Loan Act, No. 3 of 1950, which authorized the Minister of Finance to raise a loan not exceeding Rs. 400 million for development purposes. The amount which can be borrowed from the Ceylonese public and from the banks in this way depends very largely on the prosperity of the tea, rubber, and coconut industries, the main contributors to the country's money economy; so that, whatever be the damage done by the estates to the

---

[1] See *Estimates . . . for the Financial Year 1st October 1951–30th September 1952*, pp. 745–54.

peasantry,[1] it is money earned through the existence of the estates which made possible the peasant colonization schemes of 1939–53. The amount which the Government can borrow internally is, however, not as large as it might be because of the financial habits of the moneyed classes in Ceylon, notably the habit of acquiring landed property for prestige or as a speculation.[2]

The revenue of the Government, and therefore the volume of expenditure which can be met out of revenue without recourse to deficit financing, is also very strongly tied to the prosperity of the three great plantation industries, as became clear once again in the slump of 1952 and 1953. The tie is direct in the case of export duties, which were estimated to provide 47 per cent. of the revenue in 1952–3 and which are derived almost entirely from the export of tea, rubber, and coconuts;[3] it is less direct, but nevertheless real, in the case of other categories of revenue, such as income tax and post office earnings, which depend on the general prosperity of the money sector of the national economy. Clearly, too, this source of funds for expenditure on colonization is limited by the size and wealth of that sector.

Up to the end of 1953 there had been but little external financial assistance to help forward the work of peasant colonization. Experts had been provided by F.A.O. and under the Colombo Plan; Australia had sent tractors, lorries, and agricultural equipment which were used in colonies and in other places; and New Zealand had provided funds to develop the dry-farming research station at Maha Illuppallama which may help to shape the future course of colonization.[4] But it is worth stressing that the colonies mainly discussed in this book, that is, those established by the end of 1953, were almost entirely financed from internal resources, no mean feat for a country of the size and character of Ceylon and a point to be borne in mind by those who imagine that help for Asia arose because Asia would not help herself.

Since the beginning of 1953 the Government of Ceylon has, on

---

[1] See above, pp. 90–91.

[2] See in this connexion *WBR*, p. 90 (i. 56); and *CUCL*, pp. 10–12; and cf. I. G. Patel, 'Mobilization of Domestic Resources for Economic Development', *Civilisations*, vol. ii (1952), pp. 487–97, and W. A. Lewis, 'Economic Development with Unlimited Supplies of Labour', *Manchester School of Soc. and Econ. Studies*, vol. xxii (1954), pp. 139–91, espec. pp. 159–60.

[3] From figures in report of budget speech, *Ceylon News Letter*, 11 July 1952.

[4] See below, pp. 344–8.

the one hand, been faced with financial stringency in terms of internal resources, because of the difficulties of the export trade, but has, on the other, been able to draw to an increasing extent on external resources. A £5 million loan was successfully floated on the London market in March 1954; its proceeds will be used for the general long-term development programme, including peasant colonization. A loan has been obtained from the World Bank to cover the foreign-exchange costs of Stage II of the Laxapana hydro-electric scheme, and, although this will not directly help colonization, it will help indirectly by removing one competitor for funds in general and for foreign exchange in particular. It seems possible that a loan of more immediate utility to colonization will come from Commonwealth countries as a result of discussions at the Commonwealth Finance Ministers Conference at Sydney in January 1954, and of the subsequent visit to Ceylon of an Anglo-Australian mission to advise on means of increasing rice production:[1] the mission were concerned with such measures as village expansion and the improvement of yields on existing lands as well as with colonization, but it is clear that a substantial part of the loan of Rs. 1,500 million for which the Ceylon Government is said to be negotiating would in fact go into colonization schemes of one sort or another.[2] Finally, under the Colombo Plan, a steady stream of aid has flowed into Ceylon, notably a gift of flour from Australia which was worth Rs. 22 million (about £1·7 million) and from the proceeds of the sale of which land development work is to be done on three new colonization schemes (Padawiya, Pavatkulam, and Vavunikulam).[3]

In thinking of the future financing of peasant colonization in Ceylon, it is important to see these recent flows of capital from outside in proper perspective. The London loan of £5 million (Rs. 65 million) only represents about half the total estimated loan fund expenditure for 1952–3, and, on the argument of p. 329, would probably cover under one year's expenditure on peasant colonization at the rate prevalent in that year. The Australian aid, welcome as it is, represents under one-third of the annual cost of colonization at the 1952–3 rate. The Rs. 1,500 million

[1] See Joint United Kingdom and Australian Mission on Rice Production in Ceylon, 1954, *Report*.
[2] See *The Times*, 14 Jan. 1954 and *Ceylon News Letter*, 26 June and 20 Dec. 1954.
[3] See *Ceylon News Letter*, 14 Aug. 1954.

Commonwealth loan, if it is forthcoming, will represent some 14–20 years' capital investment in colonization at the 1952–3 rate: such a loan would, however, certainly not all be available for colonization alone; many other government fields of investment also have a claim, and funds may be needed for the redemption of earlier loans. It should also be noted that among the recent accessions of capital, only aid under the Colombo Plan is in the nature of a free gift; the loans have to be serviced and amortised, and this must be done out of revenue. This fact lends point to all that has been said about the importance of securing an increased revenue from the colonization schemes.

It is clearly impossible to forecast the amount of capital which will be available for colonization in future years, assuming that colonization is to go on. Capital raised internally, whether by loans or by revenue, will depend on unpredictable fluctuations in international trade, and capital raised externally will depend on internal and international politics and on many other factors. Neither is there any need to attempt an estimate even for the next few years, for the World Bank mission have admirably summed up the situation in their report (it is possible, however, to accuse them of over-optimism, for they wrote before the 1952 slump).[1] But it would be as well to conclude with a summary of the ways in which Ceylon is more or less fortunate than her Asian neighbours in terms of likely availability of capital.

Considering favourable conditions first, there is the fact that internal capital accumulation is apparently higher in Ceylon than in India and many other Asian countries,[2] though lower than in Japan; gross savings (capital formation plus accumulation of foreign assets) have been estimated as 14 per cent. and 9 per cent. of national income in 1951 and 1952 respectively, though it should be noted that net savings after allowing for depreciation of existing assets were probably not above 5 per cent.[3] It is possible, too, that private capital now wasted or squandered will be mopped up by the Development Finance Corporation which is to be set up on the advice of the World Bank mission;[4] by the various efforts that

---

[1] See *WBR*, pp. 88–105 (i. 55–65).

[2] According to a statement by Mr. N. U. Jayawardena, formerly Governor of the Central Bank of Ceylon, reported in *Ceylon News Letter*, 5 Sept. 1953.

[3] See B. B. Das Gupta, 'The Ceylon Economy in 1953', *Civilisations*, vol. iv (1954), pp. 337–47, espec. p. 345.

[4] See *WBR*, pp. 84–87 (i. 52–54), and *Ceylon News Letter*, 20 Feb. 1954.

are being made to interest capitalists directly in the work of land development;[1] and by proposals which may emanate from the Taxation Commission which has been appointed, *inter alia*, 'to find the necessary capital to finance the development projects of the Ceylon Government' and 'to suggest adequate incentives for private investment and effort'.[2]

Turning to the advantages which Ceylon possesses when she seeks to attract external capital, there is first the very great boon of confidence generated by political stability and general administrative competence. There is also the fact that recent pronouncements of the Ceylon Government have stated that foreign capital and enterprise are welcome and that no restrictions are proposed on the repatriation of profits, dividends, or capital.[3]

In most of these things Ceylon has an advantage over many of her neighbours, notably over such disturbed and xenophobic countries as Indonesia, where the only source of money for the ambitious colonization schemes is current revenue. But there are certainly no grounds for facile optimism, or for anything but economy in spending and a sensible policy on collecting returns. The 5 per cent. net rate of capital formation which has just been quoted is a pointer to the poverty of Ceylon compared with more 'developed' countries, with their net rate of voluntary saving of 12 per cent. or 15 per cent.[4] And, quite apart from the availability of capital in the countries likely to invest in Ceylon, confidence in the country, though generally great, is not universal or unlimited. It should also not be forgotten that a programme of investment in colonization or in some similar enterprise makes demands not only on capital but also on foreign exchange because so much equipment and other capital goods has to be imported. Foreign exchange might conceivably be the limiting factor if in any future period there were heavy reliance on internal, rather than imported capital.

Altogether, then, it is clear that development projects in Ceylon,

[1] See, for example, *CUCL*, pp. 61–67; see also below, p. 368.

[2] See *Ceylon News Letter*, 24 July 1954. (This Commission has now reported; see *Report of Taxation Commission*, S.P. 17 of 1955.)

[3] See the statement by the then Finance Minister, Sir Oliver Goonetilleke, *Ceylon News Letter*, 20 Feb. 1954 and White Paper on *Government Policy in respect of Private Foreign Investment in Ceylon* (Colombo, Govt. Publications Bureau, 1955). Policy may change as a result of the elections of 1956.

[4] See, for example, W. A. Lewis, in *Manchester School of Soc. and Econ. Studies*, vol. xxii (1954), pp. 139–91, espec. p. 155.

however desirable, cannot count on unlimited financial resources. Thus any increased rate of colonization which may be held to be desirable on account of rapid population increase must be carefully considered in relation to available capital and foreign exchange; and sooner or later the question must be asked whether colonization is the best means of dealing with the current situation, if only because of its high capital cost.

17

The Colonies, the Population Problem, and the Future

IT is common knowledge that the population of Ceylon is increasing with a rapidity that is probably unprecedented and that certainly can scarcely be paralleled in the world today. Thus between the census of 1946 and that of 1953 there was an average annual increase of 2·85 per cent.;[1] and the total recorded population grew from 6,657,339 to 8,098,637.[2] As in the case of similar but generally lower rates of increase elsewhere, the phenomenon is associated with the maintenance of a high crude birth-rate (40·6 per thousand in 1921, 37·4 per thousand in 1931, 36·5 per thousand in 1941, 40·4 per thousand in 1950) at a time when the crude death-rate was falling markedly (from 31·1 per thousand in 1921 to 22·1 per thousand in 1931, 18·8 per thousand in 1941, and only 12·2 per thousand in 1950).[3] Ceylon is, in fact, confronted with what Gourou called 'une natalité du Moyen Age en face d'une mortalité moderne'.[4] On the basis of available data, it is not easy to forecast future trends with any pretence of precision. But given the present rate of increase the population of Ceylon would clearly soon reach fantastic proportions; it would be over 10 million in 1963, 14 million in 1973, 18 million in 1983, 24 million in 1993, and well over 30 million at the beginning of the next century.[5]

Clearly, no discussion of the peasant colonization schemes in the Dry Zone of Ceylon would be complete if it were not at some point set in the context of the pressing demographic problem that faces Ceylon today. Since an adequate food supply is basic to a solution of this problem, and since also it is by supplying food, especially rice, that the colonies can most readily and most directly made

---

[1] See report of broadcast by the Director of Census and Statistics, *Ceylon News Letter*, 28 Mar. 1953.

[2] See *Census of Ceylon*, 1946, vol. i, pt. 1, p. 57 and ibid. 1943 (Preliminary Abstract), p. 1.

[3] See ibid. 1946, vol. i, pt. 1, pp. 61–62 and *Ceylon News Letter*, 25 July 1952.

[4] See Gourou, *Les Pays tropicaux* (Paris, Presses Universitaries, 1948), p. 134.

[5] See *Ceylon News Letter*, 28 Mar. 1953.

their contribution, the relation between colonization and population may be considered mainly in terms of food supply. This
chapter will, then, examine the contribution to food supply which
peasant colonization seems so far to have made, and go on to discuss its likely contribution in the years that lie immediately ahead
and in the more distant future.

Colonization and Population, 1948–53

From what has been said earlier, it will be clear that no exact
assessment can be made of the foodstuffs produced in the peasant
colonies. We can, however, arrive at a rough figure for the number
of people that can be fed at current nutritional standards from the
rice produced in the colonies (and rice is, after all, both the staple
article of Ceylonese diet and the main product of the colonies
in the present state of high land cultivation). Table 22 (p. 261)
enables us to make the rough assumption that the established
colonist with a 5-acre paddy lot sells about two-thirds of his paddy.
If the one-third that he keeps feeds a family of seven, then clearly
his paddy lot is feeding about twenty people with the same average
consumption as his family or, perhaps, fifteen adults. On this
assumption, which appears reasonable, the figure for each of the
years 1948–52 in column (b) of Table 29 is fifteen times the
corresponding figure in column (a); for, apart from a few allotments in Bathmedilla, in the early stages of Gal Oya, and elsewhere, all of the colonists recorded in the table for those years
occupied 5-acre paddy lots (cf. Table 23, p. 264).

In 1953, on the other hand, the 3-acre paddy lot was standard
and a new basis is necessary. Given the same average yield per
acre as before and a similar correction for the proportion of heavy
eaters, it is reasonable to assume that the 1953 colonist fed nine
people altogether on the produce of his paddy lot; accordingly the
figure for 1953 in column (b) is nine times that for the same year in
column (a).

The only figure that can be used in column (c) is an average
based on the increase between the 1946 and 1953 censuses. It can
safely be assumed that the annual increase was larger at the end of
the period than at the beginning of it, but it would be unwise to
attempt to express the difference quantitatively.

Table 29 is, then, based on a series of estimates and approxima-
tions; but it does at least give some measure of the contribution

which the colonies have made to the problem of feeding a rapidly increasing population. The final column of the table suggests that since the postwar programme settled down to its stride in 1948, a proportion of the annual increase in population which has varied

TABLE 29

Estimated Contribution of Colonization to Feeding of Population Increase, 1948–53

Year	(a) Colonists settled	(b) Population which can be fed by (a) (estimated)	(c) Average annual population increase	(d) (b) as a percentage of (c)
1948 . . .	713	10,700		5
1949 . . .	2,304	34,700		17
1950 . . .	2,110	31,500	205,900	15
1951 . . .	1,218	18,300		9
1952 . . .	2,683	40,000		19
1953 . . .	4,534	40,800		20
Total, 1948–53 .	13,562	176,000	1,235,400*	14

* Total for six years at average annual rate.

Sources: (a) See Table 17, p. 167; (b) see text; (c) from *Census of Ceylon,* 1946 and 1953.

from one-twentieth to one-fifth will be fed by the corresponding annual accession of colonists by the time that the colonists are established and that the new-born have adult appetites. The highest proportion was achieved in the last year of the period, by which time Gal Oya had begun to absorb its full quota. The average proportion was about one-seventh, and this is, if one reflects, no mean achievement. There can, one imagines, be few Asian countries which have recently been able to feed such a proportion of their new citizens from newly settled lands. There are certainly no grounds for endorsing the view of the Kandyan Peasantry Commission that 'The numbers provided with land under the various colonization schemes . . . are too small to make an impression upon the problem of over-population';[1] unless, of course, one measures successful impact on the population problem solely in terms of the number of landless settled, a method which seems

[1] See *KPC,* p. 103.

to be implicit in some of the statements of the Commissioners, and a method which is singularly short-sighted.[1] For the ability of the colonies to produce a surplus, even with present technology and the smaller allotment now standard, implies that a proportion of the increase in population can be employed in occupations other than the growing of paddy, to the encouragement of that diversification of the economy which is itself desirable. An estimate of the number eventually fed by new colonists is a better measure of their contribution to the solution of the population problem than a mere statement of their own numbers; and it shows that the colonization schemes must certainly be taken into account in any assessment of the provision that is being made for the increase in population.

But, on the other hand, there are no grounds for facile optimism. If one-seventh of the rice for the increase of population between 1948 and 1953 is to come from contemporary development in the colonies, six-sevenths must still come from elsewhere, unless the standard of nutrition is to decline or unless rice is to be partially replaced by other foodstuffs; and the proportion to be met from other sources was still over four-fifths in respect of the last and best year in the period. If nutritional standards are to be safeguarded, much is clearly left to be done by such means as the improvement of yields on existing land and the importation of food to be paid for by increased exports; and none of these means is easy of application.

Colonization and Population in the Near Future

If peasant colonization continues on the same general basis as in 1953, but at the fastest rate practicable, are there any indications that it will improve on the contribution which it seems to have made during the recent past? Some slight grounds for optimism may be found in the fact that the best performance in the years 1948–53 was in the last year of the period; as has already been stated, this state of affairs owed much to the development of the Gal Oya scheme, which may be expected to continue its influence for some years to come (it absorbed only 600 colonists in 1953–4, however).[2] It is also to be hoped that more intensive methods and higher yields will follow from the introduction of the smaller allotment and from other measures. But, on the other hand, it is

---

[1] e.g. *KPC*.   [2] See GODB, *Ann. Report*, 1953–4, p. 7.

always possible that the trends towards *lower* yields in older colonies[1] will not be interrupted by the application of improved methods of husbandry, and that there will be low *initial* yields in some new colonies. Moreover, severe restrictions on the rate of colonization are clearly imposed by lack of capital, plant, and technicians, and by administrative difficulties; and the rate is tending to be slowed down by the increasing difficulty of providing irrigation as the more easily restored works are completed. All things considered, it would be very surprising if in the foreseeable future more than 8,000 colonists were settled annually on 3-acre paddy lots, or if this number of colonists eventually fed more than 80,000 or 90,000 adults. This would clearly still be less than half the average annual increment in the population at 1946–53 rates. But the annual increment is itself increasing, and in ten years' time may well be in the region of 300,000, so that only a third of it would then be catered for by a colonization programme capable of feeding an eventual 90,000 adults. The conclusion seems inescapable: even though some temporary success may be achieved by an accelerated colonization programme and by improved yields within the colonies, it is a losing battle that is being fought. Before very long, if present conditions are maintained, a decreasing proportion of the annual increment in population will be fed from the produce of colonization.

Colonization and Population in the More Distant Future

If one looks a little farther ahead still, the prospect for peasant colonization becomes at once more gloomy and more unsure.

It becomes more gloomy because of the absolute certainty that there is a definite physical limit to the area of the Dry Zone which can support the present type of partly irrigated colony. In the Dry Zone as a whole, as in most of its separate catchments, it is scarcity of water rather than scarcity of land capable of growing paddy which sets this ultimate limit. In the absence of long-period hydrological data and of a comprehensive land-use and land-potential survey it is not possible to estimate with any precision where this limit lies; but two recent estimates may be quoted with profit. The departmental Committee on the Utilization of Crown Lands quoted a computation made by the Surveyor-General which suggested that 'with the maximum development of our irrigation

---

[1] See above, pp. 242–3.

potentialities, only about 930,000 acres [of the Dry Zone] could be rendered irrigable'; and that this would leave nearly 2,650,000 acres of cultivable but uncultivated land without possibility of irrigation.[1] The World Bank mission were slightly less conservative and estimated that 'on balance, assuming no reduction of the irrigation duty, the development of new irrigation might reasonably be expected to double the present irrigated area [in the Dry Zone]— i.e. provide about another 600,000 acres of paddy land'.[2] On this basis there would clearly be water to irrigate 1,200,000 acres of the Dry Zone altogether.

Both estimates are probably over-optimistic and nearer to a theoretical than to a practicable maximum. They assume a measure of flood-water storage which is so far rarely achieved and which may raise great practical difficulties.[3] They take no account of the fact that in some catchments and schemes there is not enough land, or not enough land of the right quality, to take all of the potentially available water. It is always possible, of course, that the actual limit will be pushed nearer to the potential limit by technical advance: water resources may in the future be more efficiently used because of avoidance of waste, because of flood-water storage, and because of better planning;[4] and land hitherto beyond the reach of irrigation water may be made available by pumping, or by such schemes as those for reclaiming land around the lagoons of the Jaffna Peninsula or in Periya Kalapuwa, a lagoon under the command of the Gal Oya Right Bank channel.[5] But it does not seem likely that any such triumphs of technology over natural difficulties will make much impression on the limit to the extension of the irrigated area.

And, even assuming that the whole of the 600,000 acres estimated by the World Bank mission can eventually be irrigated, the scope for peasant colonization on the present basis will obviously be severely restricted. For 600,000 acres would provide only 3-acre paddy lots for 200,000 colonists; so that there would be irrigable land for only about forty-five years' colonization at the 1953 rate, or for twenty-five years' colonization at the rate which

[1] See *CUCL*, pp. 17–18.
[2] See *WBR*, p. 427 (ii. 200).
[3] See above, pp. 184–6.   [4] Cf. Chapter 9, pp. 184–94.
[5] See F. R. G. Webb, *Report on the Jaffna Peninsula Lagoon Scheme* (Colombo, Govt. Press, 1945); proposals for Periya Kalapuwa from a memorandum of the Gal Oya Development Board kindly made available by its Chairman.

seems to be the likely maximum in the near future, even if no provision is made for other ways of using irrigable land.

What is to happen when all land irrigable by all possible means has been developed, and, one should add, when all land capable of transformation into *gangoda* by proximity to irrigation works has been converted into village gardens? There will remain the intractable 'high land' of the Dry Zone, of which there may well be close on 2 million acres. Earlier chapters have shown how this land is burdened not only with the general problem of soil erosion and degradation so characteristic of tropical regions, but also with a seasonal lack of ground water that inhibits the cultivation of many useful tree crops and makes for great difficulties in domestic water-supply.[1] It has been explained in Chapter 3 that the traditional method of using high land was by *chena* cultivation, and that, contrary to an often expressed belief, this method is neither backward nor pernicious in most parts of the Dry Zone provided that population density does not exceed a certain critical figure.[2] But it may with reason be argued that in planning for the future it is patently absurd to visualize a density below the critical mark, and that no policy for the eventual colonization of high land can be based on traditional *chena* methods.

It has been shown in Chapter 12 that many serious problems attend the permanent cultivation of high land in the Dry Zone colonies. Some of these problems concern the establishment of tree crops, some the cultivation of cereals, some the provision of improved pasture, but all are deeply rooted in the physical geography of the Dry Zone; and all strongly suggest that it is not only extremely difficult to grow crops on, and to reap an economic return from high land, but that it is also extremely dangerous to do so if soil fertility is to be preserved. It may also be noted here that the same conclusion follows from study of V.E. schemes, of spontaneous settlement, and of squatting, where these have involved permanent or semi-permanent high land cultivation.

These difficulties have not, however, discouraged the Ceylon Government from establishing 'dry farming' research stations and pilot 'dry farming' colonies, based on unirrigated permanent cultivation of high land. Given on the one hand the physical limit to irrigated development and the relative abundance of high land, and given on the other hand the population problem, these

---

[1] See above, pp. 249–55.   [2] See above, pp. 47–50.

experiments are *a priori* sensible; but failures and difficulties must be taken to heart and not glossed over in the interests of speed or of mere political expediency. Since so much hinges on the outcome of these experiments, they will be considered briefly here (though it would be out of place to treat them in the detail which has been accorded to normal, irrigated peasant colonization).

The Problems of Dry Farming

For more than fifty years experiments and discussions have been going on with the object of replacing *chena* cultivation by something more permanent.[1] As long ago as 1903 an experimental station was established at Maha Illuppallama, in the North-Central Province; and, although this was abandoned in 1919, work continued in other places. By 1926 it was possible for F. A. (later Sir Frank) Stockdale to claim that systematic high land cultivation was possible; and the Land Commission of 1927–9 expressed agreement with his view.[2]

But until 1938 dry farming research was entirely a matter of experiments in government agricultural stations, and there were no attempts to set up colonies worked by peasants and devoted entirely to the permanent cultivation of high land. In 1938, however, an important scheme was inaugurated at Kurandankulama, four miles east of Anuradhapura.[3] This scheme was manned from the outset by peasants, and the objects were to determine (*a*) the area of unirrigable land which a peasant could farm efficiently with simple implements; (*b*) the income which a farm of such a size was likely to yield; (*c*) the likelihood of maintaining soil fertility; and (*d*) the possibility of training the villager to substitute rotational farming for *chena*. Ten colonists were selected and given 10 acres each. One acre of the holding was to be a homestead lot on which the peasant was meant to grow tree crops; a 6-acre block was designed to grow arable crops (chillies, pulses, cereals, gingelly, and cotton) in rotation; a 2-acre block was to grow plantains on 1 acre and fodder grass on the other, the two crops being interchanged every five years; and 1 acre was to

[1] For the history of these, see *CUCL*, pp. 20–26, and *ARDLD*, 1952, pp. 18–19.

[2] See F. A. Stockdale, 'The Chena Problem and Some Suggestions for its Solution', *Trop. Agriculturist*, vol. lxvi (1926), pp. 199–208; and *LC*, p. 31.

[3] See G. Harbord, 'Rotational Farming Scheme, Kurundankulama', ibid., vol. xcvii (1941), pp. 28–34; and editorial, ibid., vol. xcix (1943), pp. 131–3.

be a permanent paddock. It was soon discovered that to clear the holding was beyond the capacity of the colonist, and after 1939 the Government took on the work of land development; it also provided wells, animals, and tools.

A fair measure of success has been claimed for these schemes, and it has been stated that the average income of a good allotment was Rs. 1,150 per annum.[1] But two problems early came to the fore. One was the tendency for low-lying holdings to become waterlogged in *Maha*, partly because the soil conservation works had been planned for each holding separately so that one holding was liable to discharge its whole run-off on to its neighbour. The other problem was the difficulty of maintaining soil structure and fertility.

In an attempt to overcome these difficulties, a new order of things was initiated at Kurandankulama in 1948. Soil and water conservation were planned for the scheme as a whole, all the run-off being diverted into an abandoned tank and a pond; and low-lying areas were converted for use as rain-fed paddy or *elvi* (hill paddy) fields. The rotation area was designed to be farmed co-operatively so that colonists with waterlogged or otherwise difficult land would not be placed at a disadvantage. And a new rotation was planned involving the alternate use of each block of co-operatively farmed land for four years under arable crops and four years under stocked pasture. The allotment was increased in size to 14 acres, made up of 2 acres homestead and 12 acres to be farmed co-operatively.

This series of experiments was taken a stage farther in 1950 when steps were taken to lay out an additional forty allotments at Kurandankulama on the same basis as in 1948, and also to lay out an entirely new dry farming colony, again on the same basis, at Relapanawa, ten miles south-west of Anuradhapura. In both of these land-development work and building were undertaken by the Land Development Department while soil-conservation work, such as the construction of contour *bunds*, was entrusted to the Department of Agriculture. In order to supply domestic water and at the same time to help cultivation by raising the water-table,

[1] Cf. above, pp. 260–2 and see *CUCL*, p. 23; see also P. T. Jinendradasa, 'Rotational Farming Scheme, Kurundankulama', *Trop. Agriculturist*, vol. civ (1948), pp. 27–37. The author is indebted to Mr. C. R. Karunaratne for help and information at Kurundankulama and Relapanawa.

all old tanks were restored and new ones constructed in suitable
hollows; and cottages were built in groups in high land near to
these tanks, a well being provided for each group. (It will be
noted that these are sensible reactions to Dry Zone hydrology
which might well have been carried out in high lands in normal
irrigated colonies.[1]) It may also be noted that other wise measures
of conservation are included in the planning of dry farming colonies, notably wind-belts 300–500 feet wide every 1,500–2,500 feet
(using ridges where possible), and the harnessing of all run-off to
feed the tanks.

When the author visited Kurundankulama and Relapanawa in
1951, land-development work and initial soil-conservation measures
were nearly complete and the process of selecting colonists had
been set in motion. It was at the outset intended to restrict to
married and landless peasants who had successfully completed a
course of training at a Practical Farm School; and it was announced
that a successful applicant would be required *inter alia* to become
a member of a Co-operative Society, to work 12 acres of his allotment Co-operatively with 3–9 other colonists, and to give up his
allotment if reported by three-quarters of his group to be a non-
Co-operator or an indifferent farmer. Other requirements, and
the general scale of aid, followed the lines usual in contemporary
irrigated colonies.

While all this was going on at Kurundankulama and at Relapanawa there were proposals for dry farming colonies elsewhere,
and continuing research on government agricultural stations. In
particular, the historic station at Maha Illuppallama had been
reopened in 1943, partly as a 'state *chena*' in connexion with the
war-time food drive, but also as the future main centre for Dry
Zone agricultural research.[2] During the author's work there in
1951 the station was in full swing under the keen and perceptive
eye of a young Research Officer, E. F. L. Abeyaratne. Interesting
and fundamental work was being done on such things as the
behaviour of the water-table, the recognition of different categories
of high land which demand separate agronomic treatment because
of differences in soil and ground water, and the all-important
problem of the maintenance of fertility.[3] One of the most useful

[1] Cf. above, pp. 229 and 252.
[2] See *Admin. Report: Agriculture*, 1944, p. 22.
[3] See ibid. 1952, pp. 37–42.

grants which Ceylon has received under the Colombo Plan has been one from New Zealand for the extension and development of the work being done at Maha Illuppallama.[1]

It is clear to the author from work in the field and from study of official reports that the problem of farming the high land of the Dry Zone of Ceylon is nowhere near a solution as yet. There are, in the first place, a whole host of problems of husbandry rooted in the physical geography of the land concerned, and not unnaturally reminiscent of those discussed in connexion with high land allotments in irrigated peasant colonies.[2] Thus at Kurundankulama it was clear that there was no hope of growing coconut and other economic tree crops or of obtaining perennial well water on a number of homesteads because of their hill-top situation. The answer to this problem is, however, plain: to place all homesteads in *gangoda*-like situations beside tanks, as was indeed being done in the 1951 development at Kurundankulama and at Relapanawa; or, alternatively, to grow trees like the palmyra which can stand drought.

But the answer to another group of problems is far from plain; these problems are all concerned with the field cultivation of crops like maize, millets, cotton, and chillies. One source of great difficulty is the fact that the wet season is bound to be the period of cropping, but the high intensity of the rain makes it almost impossible to prevent serious erosion. Abeyaratne has drawn attention to the high incidence of splash erosion resulting from the destruction of soil aggregates by the impact of large rain drops on bare land.[3] There is also the point that purely mechanical methods of conservation, such as *bund*ing, are quite inadequate; what is needed is some protection for the soil between the rows or clumps of the growing crop—yet leguminous cover crops in this position reduce yields appreciably or even disastrously.[4] Chillies, in fact, will not tolerate any kind of associated crop. The answer may be a cover of trash between the rows.

Another source of trouble, which has already been mentioned in connexion with high land allotments in the colonies, is the difficulty of finding a cover crop which will not only protect the soil

[1] See *The Colombo Plan: The Annual Reports of the Consultative Committee on Economic Development in South and South-East Asia: 1952*, Cmd. 8529, p. 17; *1953*, Cmd. 9016, p. 21; and *1954*, Cmd. 9336, p. 23.

[2] See above, pp. 249–55.

[3] See *Admin. Report: Agriculture*, 1952, p. 39.   [4] Ibid.

during the dry season but still be able to give protection during the critical phase at the beginning of the *Maha* rains, before the main crop and any associated cover crop are sown. Most leguminous plants tried at Maha Illuppallama died before the end of the dry season; and even the most promising, dhall (*Cajanus cajan*), may well fail to survive the driest years.

There is also the problem, common to most tropical regions, of conducting mechanized cultivation without ruining soil fertility and structure; and the problem of finding pasture and water for cattle throughout the dry season if, as the current orthodoxy has it, a fallow under-grazed pasture is vital to the maintenance of fertility.

The problem of maintaining fertility, and even of keeping any soil on the holding at all, is so great that one cannot with confidence say that any device so far exploited can guarantee dry, rotational cultivation of Dry Zone high land in perpetuity. A similar conclusion has been reached in other tropical regions. In the interior of Sierra Leone, for example, where climatic conditions appear to be similar to those in the Dry Zone, a solution to the problem has long been sought, but 'no sure rotation has been found that would dispense with the need to let cropped land go back to bush for regeneration.'[1] In consequence, a recent report has found it necessary to state that 'until a means other than a bush fallow has been found to restore soil fertility on the uplands, full use must be made of the regenerative powers of the natural vegetation'.[2] In the Belgian Congo a further step has been taken, and a system of 'rationalized' bush fallow, by which a series of demarcated blocks is farmed in successive years, is in force;[3] while in the eastern region of Nigeria peasants have developed planted bush fallow systems based on two hardy, deep-rooted shrubs, *Acion barterii* and *Macrolobium macrophyllum*, and their systems have been officially encouraged as providing a sounder basis for short-term regeneration than natural forest regrowth.[4]

It may well be that in the Dry Zone of Ceylon also the despised *chena* cultivator is at present a sounder guide than the European or

[1] See Roy Lewis, *Sierra Leone* (London, 1954), p. 82.
[2] See *Soil Conservation and Land Use in Sierra Leone*, Sierra Leone Sessional Paper No. 1 of 1951 (Freetown, Govt. Printer, 1951), pp. 26–28.
[3] Ibid., p. 27.
[4] See *The Nigeria Handbook* (London, Crown Agents for the Colonies, 1953), pp. 129–30.

American farmer; and that it would be better, until Maha Illuppallama and its aides discover a foolproof technique of dry farming, to base experiments and plans for high land colonization on accelerated regeneration under trees. Certainly research must continue, and it would be as well not to confine it to field work in Ceylon but also to institute comparisons with conditions and experiments in areas with apparently similar physical problems. Some African examples of such areas have just been mentioned; and so far there does not seem to have been sufficient contact with dry farming research in India.[1] There is, in fact, a pressing need for a thorough study of those tropical regions which suffer an alternation of drought and flood. It might well emerge from such a study that these regions throw out a stronger challenge than tropical regions of perennial rainfall, where economic tree crops at least can normally be successfully established without ruining the soil.

There must be work, too, on the systematic classification of Ceylon's high land into land-potential categories; for, clearly, even from top to bottom of a single slope there are differences in soil and hydrology which demand separate agronomic treatment. The need for a land-potential survey has been stressed by a number of authorities;[2] Abeyaratne has devised a scheme 'intended to serve as a starting point for the development of a system of land classification in the dry zone', but much work remains to be done before the potentialities and weaknesses of each of the many categories of Dry Zone land have been fully explored.[3]

But the problem of devising a system for the colonization of high land is not merely a matter of experiments in husbandry and in the physical aspects of land use. Any attempt to teach new methods, whether of dry farming or of systematized bush fallow, necessarily involves a whole range of human problems such as resistance to technical change and the social consequences of new procedures; and it involves them in an even more acute form than in the orthodox, irrigated colonies. Initially, resistance to new

---

[1] See, for example, A. Subba Rao, S. V. Kuppaswami, and A. Abdul Samad, 'Soil and Water Losses by Run-Off', *Madras Agric. J.*, vol. xxvii (1939), pp. 244–6; Kanitkar, *Dry Farming in India*; John Russell, 'India's People and their Food', *Geography*, vol. xxxvii (1952), pp. 127–8; and C. Mayadas, *Between Us and Hunger* (Bombay, OUP, 1954), pp. 59–76. See also above, p. 55.

[2] See, for example, *KPC*, p. 103, *WBR*, pp. 365–6 (ii. 157–8), and *CUCL*, pp. 12–16.   [3] See *Admin. Report: Agriculture*, 1952, p. 38.

methods may be so strong that, in spite of poverty and pressure on the land in existing villages, no colonists willing to try them may be found. In fact, the notices of the 1951 vacancies in Kurundan-kulama and Relapanawa which have already been mentioned[1] produced only two applicants from the whole, greatly overcrowded area of Western Province; and both were ineligible, one being a bachelor and the other a woman. Again, any system of husbandry which, like current dry farming methods, depends on co-operation among colonists chosen without respect to their mutual social relationships is bound to run headlong into an intensified form of the individualism that, as has been seen, characterizes all too many of the orthodox, irrigated colonies.[2]

There are also likely to be grave economic problems. For the state, under present arrangements, there is the high cost of preparation for dry farming and the danger of heavy over-capitalization. For the colonist there is the risk of failure and, even, in good years, the risks attached to marketing high land produce which is rarely a staple foodstuff with a large and assured market. Perhaps the only answer is the state farm.

In fine, it is hard to speak with approval of currently proposed methods of using high land, and harder still to envisage what the Dry Zone landscape will look like if and when a safe system of unirrigated farming is evolved. One thing, however, appears absolutely certain: if the time ever comes when the people of Ceylon have obeyed the injunction of their great king, Parakrama Bahu, who said 'Let there not be left anywhere in my kingdom a piece of land, even though it were the least of the yards of a house, which does not yield any benefit to man', then those pieces of land which form the high land of the Dry Zone are bound to yield less benefit to man than pieces of comparable size which are under paddy in the Dry Zone, or under almost any crop in the Wet Zone.[3]

Conclusion

There is clearly a limit to the agricultural colonization of the Dry Zone by any foreseeable technique. And, because it seems inevitable that far fewer peasants will be settled on each acre of high land than on each acre of paddy land, the limit is nothing like as far away as is often fondly imagined in Ceylon. There are certainly

---

[1] See above, p. 344.   [2] See above, pp. 295-9.
[3] See *The Mahávaṃsa*, p. 2 (trans. L. C. Wijesinha), p. 149.

no grounds for the optimistic belief that future population increase can safely be taken care of by the emptiness of the Dry Zone. A few decades of irrigated colonization, then a few more decades of dubiously practicable high land colonization, are all that remain, and in them a decreasing proportion of the increment in population will be fed by the colonies. But even this respite is more than is given to some other Asian countries; and it behoves those in authority in Ceylon to use this respite by showing true statesmanship, by eschewing short-term expediency, and by considering the future of their country with great care. This is not the place to review what, apart from colonization, might be done to solve the population problem; but it may well be that the only answer is a deliberate and carefully applied policy of reducing the birth-rate.[1]

[1] Cf. *KPC*, p. 37, and *WBR*, p. 710–11 (ii. 387).

18

Conclusion

THIS conclusion will try to do three things: first, briefly to review the argument of the book as a whole; second, to sum up the conclusions which have been reached on the present state of peasant colonization in the Dry Zone of Ceylon and on possible improvements within the general framework of existing policy; third, to consider certain alternatives to the present general framework.

The Argument of this Book

This book has set out the ancient glory and recent decay of the Dry Zone of Ceylon, and has described the forces which appear to have made it a region of difficulty in modern times. It has also described the techniques by which the contemporary Dry Zone peasant attempts to wrest a living from a refractory soil, and has shown that although superficially the Dry Zone is a region of generally sparse human settlement there is nevertheless widespread pressure of people on irrigable land. It has, further, shown how a very different dual settlement pattern has grown up in the Wet Zone and Up-country, and how there are serious agrarian pressures in the peasant sector and, in the plantation sector, the dangers associated with a narrow-based export economy. It has then gone on to discuss the stages by which there has evolved a policy of government-sponsored and highly organized peasant colonization of the wastes of the Dry Zone, with such mixed motives as the relief of food shortage (whether due to lack of production at home or the difficulty of importing from abroad), the relief of agrarian pressures, and the preservation of a peasant society (conceived, by some of its protagonists at any rate, as a society of individual peasant proprietors on the European model).

The modern peasant colonies have then been reviewed in order to discover, if possible, what factors in them create their successes and their failures as instruments of government policy. It has been seen that, from a number of points of view, notable successes have indeed been achieved: a considerable number of peasants has been settled, and their establishment as colonists has made an appreciable though necessarily limited contribution to the relief of landlessness and of agrarian pressures; a noteworthy contribution has been made to the solution of problems associated with the feeding of a rapidly growing population; many colonists have experienced a prosperity which could never have been theirs in a *purāna* village; large expanses of jungle and waste have been transformed; extremely useful experience has been gained in the utilization of the resources of the Dry Zone; and the colonies have helped to dispel popular fear of the Dry Zone.

But, for all this, many grave problems face the Government of Ceylon as it tries to carry out its established method of Dry Zone peasant colonization. The chief of these have been elicited by the discussion in Part III of this book, and will now be summarized, together with the suggestions which have been made for their solution; for some problems (e.g. those concerning physical planning) the solution seems fairly clear, but, in the case of many others, only tentative suggestions can be put forward in the hope of stimulating further research and further discussion.[1]

The Main Problems incurred by Current Policy and Some Suggestions for their Solution

A. *The physical planning of colonies*

1. Many problems of land use arise because insufficient attention has been paid in the planning of colonies to local variations in physical conditions; standardization has in fact gone much too far since 1939 (see pp. 166–7).

2. A number of problems of land use, of communications, and of social conditions arise because considerations of irrigation are uppermost when a colony is planned; to some extent this is inevitable so long as colonization is based on irrigated rice cultivation, but there is much to be said for a system in which the planning of colonies is in the hands of a body separate from the Irrigation Department and able to pay due attention to all relevant factors (see pp. 170–1, 252, 269–70, and 297–8).

[1] It should also be stressed that these suggestions were made before the author became a member of the new Land Commission appointed in 1955 and before new evidence and new ideas for reform were thus brought to bear on him.

3. Land-use difficulties have arisen because insufficient attention has been paid to soil surveys (see p. 171).

4. While small colonies necessarily have to be run by normal government departments, there is much to be said for the greater degree of independence and for other advantages associated with a separate statutory authority like the Gal Oya Development Board (see pp. 173-4).

B. *Irrigation planning*

1. The highest possible degree of utilization of water resources being desirable, more attention should be paid to over-year flood storage in order to utilize water now running to waste in years of high rainfall (see pp. 184-6).

2. Difficulties have arisen, notably in the Kala Oya and Malwatu Oya catchments, because of the piecemeal restoration of ancient works; the planning of catchments as a whole is highly desirable and is in fact now attempted; but it is often a counsel of perfection (see pp. 190-1).

3. Siltation has caused difficulty in some tanks and threatens difficulty in others. Much more information is needed about this phenomenon, especially in the Gal Oya catchment; but it seems certain that it will eventually cause trouble if the Walawe Ganga scheme is completed (this scheme also appears to be undesirable because of high cost and because of poor soil under command; see pp. 191-4 and 318-19).

C. *The selection of colonists*

1. So long as the relief of agrarian pressures is a primary aim of colonization, it is clear that some attempt ought to be made to match the number of colonists selected from an area with the agrarian needs of that area; this is all the more important in view of the new mobility of the peasantry and of public interest in colonization. It is clear that an attempt *has* been made to obey this principle, but (a) it would appear that too many places have gone to peasants hailing from villages in the vicinity of colonies; and (b) some districts appear to have sent too few peasants to the colonies (see pp. 211-14 and 217-18).

2. A fairer distribution would result if (a) the Land Commissioner were freed from political control in the choice of source areas for colonists; and (b) if he were to apply some objective and

publicized formula in determining the number of colonists to be drawn from each area (see pp. 210 and 218).

3. Such an objective formula demands, however, far more knowledge of the incidence of agrarian pressures than is at present available; the need for research into conditions in the villages of Ceylon is evident (see p. 218).

4. Selection of groups of kinsfolk is desirable in order to overcome problems of economic co-operation and of caste friction in the colonies; but this would complicate the application of an objective selection formula (see pp. 298–9).

5. If efficient cultivation in the colonies is to be a criterion as well as the relief of agrarian pressures, then more attention must be directed to the selection of good cultivators and, somehow, the problem of inaccurate reports on candidates from Village Headmen must be overcome (see pp. 219–20).

6. Present methods at Land Kachcheries seem, other things being equal, to put a premium on the possession of a large family; this may eventually have undesirable effects (see p. 219).

D. *Diseases in the colonies*

1. Thanks to DDT the old Dry Zone bogey of malaria has been largely conquered, though there is no room for complacency, especially about conditions during the preparatory work on colonies (see pp. 221–3).

2. The provision of hospitals seems to be lagging behind the work of colonization (see p. 225).

3. Much work on malnutrition still remains to be done (see p. 226).

4. One of the greatest remaining medical problems concerns 'stomach troubles', many of them due, in part at least, to poor supplies of domestic water in the colonies (see pp. 226–7).

E. *Domestic water-supplies*

1. Piped water being in general out of the question on grounds of cost, recourse must be had to other sources and, in particular, to wells; these usually fail in the dry season unless they are so situated that the water-table which feeds them is preserved by proximity to an irrigation work or to a perennial river. The number of perennial wells could be increased (*a*) by siting wells according

to sound hydro-geological principles and, in particular, by siting them near perennial surface water, natural or artificial; (*b*) by building houses around wells so sited, rather than by sinking wells merely by reference to houses located with other considerations in mind; (*c*) by taking all possible steps to preserve the water-table in high lands, thus reproducing *gangoda* conditions and helping tree crops as well as domestic water-supplies (see pp. 227–31 and 252). But in true high lands, where *gangoda* conditions are unattainable, nothing can be done to improve supplies of well-water.

2. Research is needed, not only into the general seasonal régime of the water-table under different conditions in the Dry Zone, but also into the apparently capricious occurrence of brackish water underground (see pp. 231–2).

F. *Land use*

Some problems of land use have already been mentioned, but others remain.

1. Paddy cultivation is undoubtedly an ecologically sound use of Dry Zone land wherever it can be practised, but higher yields would be obtained in older colonies, and pristine yields maintained, if not augmented, in new colonies, if cultivation techniques were improved; in particular, there would seem to be scope for the extension of manuring, transplanting, weeding, and improved ploughing. But the caution with which the colonist, like the villager, views these things has often in it a perfectly rational objection to methods which he knows to be of doubtful utility (see pp. 242–7).

2. Mechanization has as yet made but little headway in the colonization schemes; and for many reasons plans for its extension must be greeted with reserve (see pp. 247–9).

3. If paddy cultivation in the colonies is ecologically sound, high land cultivation is rarely so, except where *gangoda* conditions are reproduced; the problem of a sound method of land use where such conditions cannot be reproduced and where the traditional answer, *chena* cultivation, is no longer practicable, is one of the most baffling problems which faces Ceylon today (see pp. 249–50).

4. One solution is certainly to grow tree crops wherever possible, and to increase the area where these *are* possible by preservation of the surface water-table and, if practicable, by lift irrigation.

Adaptation to local conditions is essential, and in some places, it may be necessary to fall back on trees like the palmyra which are adapted to drought (see pp. 250–3).

5. The growing of field crops in perpetuity raises greater problems and may even over wide areas be impossible. Something might be done to check gross erosion if preparatory land-development work included the construction of contour *bunds*, if the planning of high land lots conformed to the contours and not to geometrical patterns or to irrigation requirements (cf. A. 2 above), and if cover crops could be found which would weather the dry season (see pp. 253–5).

6. The problem of the modernization of pasture provision raises most of the problems of growing high land field crops, and is not made simpler by the difficulty of encouraging the Co-operative use of pasture favoured by current orthodoxy (see pp. 255–8).

7. The reservation of forest for use by colonists raises many problems but needs attention (see p. 258).

8. Much more information is required about the potentialities of the many categories of land to be found in the Dry Zone, and sound land-use practice depends on the collection and application of this information (see p. 347).

G. *The economy of the colonist*

1. The income earned by the average well-established colonist under the conditions prevailing in 1951 was certainly higher than that earned by the average villager; the colonist was, in fact, prosperous, and able to grow a surplus for sale. His prosperity and his surplus would, however, in many cases have been greater if there were improvements in communications, in marketing, in the efficiency of Co-operatives and, of course, in the productivity of high land lots (see pp. 260–71).

2. Colonists installed in 1953 and thereafter received a smaller allotment and, in consequence, earned a lower income and produced a smaller surplus than their forerunners (see p. 168).

3. There has been considerable confusion almost throughout the history of peasant colonization in Ceylon over the definition of an 'economic holding'. Clarification of the issue is desirable, as is the determination of an ideal initial allotment size, but local variation appears to be essential and consideration might be given to

the provision of a larger allotment to specially efficient colonists, at least if the maximization of production is one of the ends in view (see pp. 276–9).

4. If the same criterion is relevant, a smaller allotment than that standard in 1951 might be considered a stimulus to intensive cultivation, so that the change made in 1953 may be considered a step in the right direction (see pp. 276–7).

5. There is room for a thorough-going review of the whole question of the aid given to a colonist; a lower scale than that prevalent in 1951, or even than the reduced scale of 1953, may be thought necessary, not only as an economic stimulus to the colonist but as an economy to the Government and as a means to certain social ends that may be thought desirable (see pp. 279–80).

6. At the same time, there should be a review of the charges made to the colonist for his land and water (see pp. 280 and 327).

H. *The social factor*

1. In general, it seems true to say that the various aspects of current colonization policy have been imposed on the colonist without sufficient regard for the attitudes, values, and technical notions of his own society in its many regional variations (see p. 283).

2. In particular, the Land Development Ordinance, though well-intentioned, has brought the colonies into difficulties in a number of ways, most of them due to the fact that the form of tenure enshrined in the Ordinance is contrary to local custom; the difficulties concerning concealed *ande* tenancy and concerning succession are among the most evident; it might even be argued that the rules of succession are such that an Ordinance designed to cure landlessness has in fact caused it. It is also possible that the failure of the Ordinance to provide a title to land understandable in traditional terms is a disincentive to maximum effort on the holding. The remedy, short of sheer compulsion, is by no means clear; but it may be said that experiments with ways in which the law might harness, rather than oppose, local custom would be useful as are proposals for outright alienation (see pp. 289–92).

3. In many other ways too (e.g. in agricultural education) the value of basing effort on indigenous cultural motives should be explored (see pp. 292–3).

I. *The social results of policy*

1. It is evident that few colonies are worked by the co-operative practices that characterize at least some Ceylon villages (those of Nuwarakalawiya appear, further, to be useful adaptations to the Dry Zone environment). Work is needed on possible incentives to co-operation but it is possible (*a*) to commend the Gal Oya Development Board's practice of grouping colonists in 'village units'; (*b*) to suggest a reduced scale of government provision of meeting-halls and so on, in order to encourage colonists to work together;[1] (*c*) to recommend the selection of a number of kinsfolk from the same village as colonists on adjacent holdings (cf. C. 4 above); and (*d*) to suggest the harnessing of the cohesive properties of indigenous religion (see pp. 295–9).

2. Caste is apt to cause friction in colonies; the suggestion just made for the grouping of kinsfolk would minimize such friction (see pp. 301–3).

3. The problem of Colonization Officers of lower caste than their colonists is a more difficult problem and involves the ambivalence of Ceylonese society concerning the whole question of caste (see p. 303).

4. For reasons that are largely rooted in contemporary Ceylonese social conditions, some Colonization Officers give poor leadership to their colonists; there is no easy remedy, but a trial might be made in due course of the selection of Colonization Officers from the ranks of the colonists (see pp. 305–6).

5. Middle-class colonists have also proved unsatisfactory leaders in the colonies; there seems no answer but to encourage the colonies to throw up their own leaders; here again the selection of groups of kinsfolk would have advantages (see pp. 306–8).

6. Relations between colony and *purāna* village often cause trouble, in spite of the tenderness for *purāna* interests which the Government of Ceylon has shown in its colonization policy. The tidiest solution, that of giving all affected villagers the rights of colonists in the scheme, is too uniform to be wise and too thorough-going to be practicable; the problem remains (see pp. 308-10).

7. The last-named problem is made worse if colonization takes place before Crown title to the land to be colonized has been

---

[1] Meeting-halls are not now (1956) provided.

established; or if colony and village contain different communities (see pp. 309–10).

8. For all the social problems which result from current policy, society in the colonies is not to be viewed as a chronically diseased society like those that have been brought about in Africa and elsewhere by the impact of the West; but there is no room for thoughtless optimism, and careful attention should be given to the social effects of colonization policy. Here again research and experiment are needed (see pp. 310–13).

J. *The cost and the return*

1. The capital costs of colonization are high and there are good grounds, from the point of view of the Treasury, for economy (see pp. 321–3). It is fortunate that a lower scale of aid appears desirable on other grounds (see G. 5 and I. 1).

2. Recurrent costs are likewise high and there is a similar need for economy (see pp. 323–5).

3. The financial return made by the colonies to the Treasury is low, and should be inquired into (see pp. 326–8).

4. Economy in expenditure is all the more desirable because expenditure on colonization affects the country's external balance of payments (see p. 333).

5. Economy in expenditure would enable the same outlay as at present to make a more effective contribution to the solution of agrarian and other problems (see p. 334).

K. *The contribution of colonization*

1. Colonization is making a significant contribution to the feeding of Ceylon's increasing population, but a losing battle is being fought and there appears to be a not far distant limit to irrigated colonization (see pp. 339–41).

2. The problem of using unirrigable high land therefore becomes urgent; it raises all the problems of high land cultivation in the colonies (see A. 3–6) and one cannot be confident that a satisfactory technique has yet been developed (see p. 346).

3. A possible answer lies in a system developed from, rather than departing from, *chena* (see pp. 346–7).

4. Even if the technical problems are solved, there remain the human problem of teaching new techniques and the economic

Conclusion

necessary (see pp. 347–8).

5. The Dry Zone must not therefore be viewed as a field for
indefinite future colonization, and other solutions of the population
problem will have to be found (see p. 349).

Possible Alternatives to Peasant Colonization as it is at present understood in Ceylon

The government-controlled agricultural resettlement of the
long-neglected Dry Zone of Ceylon is at present being carried out
by means of peasant-colonization schemes, middle-class Ceylonese
schemes, and village-expansion schemes, and to a lesser extent by
other means (e.g. by the leasing or alienation of land for large-scale
cultivation). Taken together, these may be seen as the pattern of
Dry Zone development which took shape as the result of the work
of the Land Commission of 1927–9, and of the promulgation of
the Land Development Ordinance;[1] it is a pattern which has only
been slightly modified by the tentative essays at large-scale and
'capitalist' development which were recommended by the departmental Committee on the Utilization of Crown Lands and which
have been put into practice, to some extent, in the Gal Oya scheme
(where 1,250 acres, nearly 1,000 of them irrigable, have been
leased to the Gal Oya Valley Food Production Company, a creation
of a number of estate-owning companies).[2]

Now discussion of peasant colonization in this book has hitherto
tended to rest on the tacit assumption that all that is necessary is
a series of changes within the general framework of established
colonization policy, rather than a new framework altogether; and
the conclusions which have recently been summarized clearly rest
on the same assumption. At several points in the book, however,
the argument has drawn near to a challenge to this assumption
(e.g. on p. 220). It is now proposed to consider some possible
alternatives to peasant colonization as it is at present understood
in Ceylon. But only a system whereby nobody at all is to farm in
the Dry Zone completely destroys the conclusions which have
just been summarized; most of them clearly apply, *mutatis mutandis*, within all other possible frameworks of Dry Zone agricultural
development.

[1] See above, pp. 126–8, 137–9, and 158–60.
[2] See *CUCL*, especially pp. 63–67, and GODB, *Ann. Report*, 1953–4, p. 8.

There are, of course, very many possible methods of envisaging the reoccupation of the Dry Zone by agriculturalists. Discussion will be confined to those which appear most practicable, or most likely to be tried out in the near future, together with those which are not so practicable or so likely, but are nevertheless apt to be canvassed in discussions in Ceylon and elsewhere.

The proposals which will in fact be discussed in the following pages are these:

1. That government-controlled opening up of new lands in the Dry Zone should cease.
2. That the opening up of new lands should include the other methods now current, but *not* peasant colonization.
3. That a more revolutionary approach to Dry Zone development is required in terms of capitalist farming, or collective farming, or Co-operative farming.
4. The eclectic solution that peasant colonization should continue, but with clarified aims, on a modified basis, and in conjunction with other methods of opening up the Dry Zone.

1. *The suggestion that government-controlled opening up of new lands in the Dry Zone should cease.*

There appear to be two distinct schools of thought which support this suggestion. The first considers that there is no need to open up new lands in the Dry Zone at all; the second is willing to see new lands opened up, but wishes this to be the spontaneous work of individual citizens virtually uncontrolled by Government.

Throughout the history of Dry Zone colonization there have been members of the first school, notably those who have considered colonization to be an uneconomic proposition. The view has recently been restated by E. B. Tisseverasinghe in a paper which is of value because it is provocative and unorthodox; Ceylon needs more students of her problems to emulate Tisseverasinghe in these respects. If one understands him aright, he argues that there is no need to open up new lands for paddy cultivation because there is plenty of paddy land already, land-hunger being illusory and a politician's ramp, and because yields on existing lands are capable of very substantial improvement.[1]

It is, of course, unfortunately true that the unscrupulous

[1] See E. B. Tisseverasinghe, 'The Pattern of Occupation in Idealised Ceylon', *New Lanka*, vol. vi (1955), pp. 47–59, espec. pp. 52–53.

politician is always willing to exploit landlessness, but for all that Tisseverasinghe's conclusions on the subject seem to be based on a false reading of statistics. He divides the 913,000 acres of paddy recorded by the 1946 Census by the 289,000 persons shown as paddy cultivators by the same census, and concludes that the average cultivator therefore has more than the maximum of 3 acres which, it is said, he can cultivate under intensive techniques. Even assuming that 3 acres is the right size for a maximum unit of paddy cultivation, Tisseverasinghe has forgotten that, in addition to the class of 'paddy cultivators', the Census records 182,000 cultivators the precise nature of whose land was unspecified but some of whom certainly tilled paddy fields.[1] If one includes these or even only some of these, the answer for the average unit of cultivation clearly becomes smaller. And there are also those who would be cultivators if they could find land. In fact, one cannot seriously doubt that there is indeed grave pressure on land in many, though not all, parts of Ceylon.

As for the argument that the nation's need for food can be met by increasing yields on existing holdings, this rests on the assumption that average net yields can be stepped up to 100 bushels per acre. Now it is important not to overemphasize either the relative infertility of many of Ceylon's paddy soils, or the resistance of the peasant to improved methods; but nevertheless one must assuredly recognize that to treble the average net yield is no more than a pipe-dream at present.[2] Moreover, Tisseverasinghe is thinking in terms of the present population, both in denying the existence of landlessness and in dreaming of an ideal Ceylon in which actual yields are equal to maximum possible yields; even if one concedes that his arguments are correctly based at present, what of future trends in landlessness and food consumption?

In fact, as long as one accepts the relief of agrarian pressure as essential for social or political reasons, or as long as one agrees that Ceylon should seek to grow more food at home because of the mounting difficulty of finding and paying for imported supplies, so long will it be necessary to open up new lands for cultivation. Even if one considers the first aim as irrelevant, the second remains. If a growing population is to be fed *without* increasing home production, food imports must be increased, and these must

[1] See *Census of Ceylon*, 1946, pt. 2, p. 210.
[2] Cf. above, pp. 338–9.

be paid for by an expansion of exports, agricultural, industrial, or invisible, and with foreign exchange saved by reduction in imports of manufactured goods made possible by industrialization and other measures at home. He would be an optimist indeed who could envisage changes in the economy of Ceylon which would bring these things about quickly enough to feed the growing population. Increased home food and production of food is there-fore essential; and unless unbelievably rapid strides are made in existing paddy fields, this means some attention to the opening up of new lands, at least as an insurance policy.

There is also the point that in a country like Ceylon there is much to be said for attacking the hard core of economic problems at as many points on its periphery as possible; by this criterion, it is foolish to attack the food problem only by increasing yields on existing lands and by seeking to obtain increased imports, ignoring the opening up of new land. It is indeed significant that, as a recent report has emphasized, none of the many authorities who have studied economic problems in Ceylon 'have reached the con-clusion that the agriculture of the Dry Zone must remain un-developed on the ground that the gain to the national economy is incommensurate with the cost involved'.[1]

But most of these same authorities have insisted that a heavy cost *is* involved in Dry Zone development; and this book has shown that, whatever economies may be achieved (and many ought to be achieved), heavy the cost is bound to remain if the present frame-work is preserved. In fact, it may well be argued that, because of the physical difficulties which abound even after the conquest of malaria, the Dry Zone is an example of 'marginal land' in the economists' sense of the term; and that the real cost of Dry Zone development is such that it will bring decreasing returns and hence run counter to attempts to improve *per capita* income. But, if the argument of the preceding paragraphs is correct, this is an un-avoidable consequence of the present state of the national economy and of the associated population pressure. The people of Ceylon, like many people before them, must expect levels of living to be affected if their inability or unwillingness to live in the more tractable parts of their country forces them into the less tractable parts. But whereas the contrast between tractable and intractable

[1] See Joint United Kingdom and Australian Mission on Rice Production in Ceylon, *Report*, p. 24.

regions has usually been reflected in a contrast between a higher and a lower level of living (like that, for example, between lowland England and highland Scotland in the eighteenth century), the economic contrast in present-day Ceylon is reduced and in many cases actually reversed because of the part which the state plays in Dry Zone development.

This point leads us on to consider the views of the second of the two schools of thought which suggest that government-controlled development of Dry Zone lands should cease; this school wishes to see a continuance of Dry Zone settlement, but wishes it to be the spontaneous work of individuals. On this view, there is plenty of land in the Dry Zone, and manifestly, now that the conquest of malaria and other factors have induced mobility, there are people willing and able to settle on that land; why, then, is all this expensive and complicated land administration necessary? Why all this preparation to attract colonists who would now come anyway? This view receives some support on economic grounds, for clearly capital investment by the personal labour of settlers would revolutionize the economics of Dry Zone development (and, incidentally, it would bring into the open the reduced or reversed economic differential discussed at the end of the preceding paragraphs). And variants of the view are held by those nationalists who see government action as a continuance of colonialism, and spontaneous settlement as a welcome return to custom and a stage in the reoccupation of *Rāja Rata*.

Now there is a good deal to be said for harnessing the new mobility of the peasant and his potential ability to save scarce funds by investing his labour in the land. But there is less to be said for the arguments of the nationalists, who conveniently forget that even in their Golden Age, during the empire of the Sinhalese kings, it is tolerably certain that 'the king was *bhūpati* or *bhūpāla*, lord of the earth', and that he and his *disāvas* controlled grants of rights in land.[1]

But there are further and perhaps more cogent objections to a policy of 'free-for-all' in the Dry Zone. Thus there is, in the first place, the point that because cultivation in paddy is at present the wisest use for as much of the Dry Zone as can be irrigated, irrigation must be provided on a large scale; and, apart perhaps from the restoration of a few minor tanks, the planning and execution of

---

[1] See Codrington, *Ancient Land Tenure*, pp. 5–7.

irrigation works must remain a government commitment, as must the provision of major lines of communication. Further, whatever the rights and wrongs of the original enactment of the Crown Lands Encroachments Ordinance,[1] the Crown estate is now envisaged as a trust held on behalf of the people. This concept may, it is true, owe much to the West, and it certainly raises problems of conflicts between the law on the one hand, and between peasant custom, or what is alleged to be peasant custom, on the other. But, for all that, land is almost the only resource which Ceylon possesses in any quantity, and it is criminal folly to squander it by allowing a scramble for it, and by making no effort to ensure that it is cultivated by methods which will secure its use for posterity. Moreover, a 'free-for-all' would inevitably result in the concentration of Dry Zone land in the hands of an unholy legion of land-grabbers and land-speculators whose operations would neither help to ameliorate landlessness where help is most needed nor foster maximum food production.

For many reasons, then, it seems inevitable not only that the Dry Zone of Ceylon must be developed, but that the Ceylon Government must be very much concerned in its development. It also seems that the government commitment should not be limited to the provision of irrigation and of communications, but that there must also be some sort of control over the general planning of land use, and over the alienation of Crown land. How should this control be exerted?

2. *The possibility of opening up new lands in the Dry Zone by government-controlled methods now current, particularly by village expansion, but* excluding *colonization*

There is something to be said for the view that the settlement of peasants in the Dry Zone should be mainly or entirely through village-expansion schemes; that is, the Government would maintain control as at present, but settlers would be chosen entirely from *purāna* villages near to the area to be developed, and not, as in colonization schemes, brought in wholly or partly from distant areas. There are a number of possible advantages in such a scheme. For instance, costs could be substantially reduced, for a much lower scale of aid is justified if the peasant settler is operating from his *purāna* village as a base. Again, it may be argued that peasants

[1] See above, p. 65.

used to the difficulties and hazards of the Dry Zone environment can be relied on to use land more wisely and to produce more food per acre than immigrants used to very different conditions; that the social problem of relations between immigrant colonists and *purāna* villagers is avoided, as is the political issue of the introduction of colonists of one community into an area which is traditionally the home of another; and that internal social cohesion is more likely to be assured.

Even if one accepts these arguments, however, there are still very good reasons for rejecting a total reliance on village expansion as the means of settling peasants. Dry Zone village-expansion schemes have not for the most part been a conspicuous success by any criteria; they offer no solution at all to the problem of landlessness Up-country and in the Wet Zone lowlands (and concentration on them is therefore likely to be politically unacceptable); and they provide no means of settling those wide areas which are almost devoid of *purāna* villages. There remains, however, the possibility that where areas for development are relatively small, and are rich in existing village nuclei, then village expansion of some sort may be a more economical and generally satisfactory method of opening up land than present methods of peasant colonization.

Is there, then, no possibility of extending village expansion to all areas in which it is practicable (in spite of the objections just made), and of avoiding the expense and the difficulty of peasant colonization by throwing open all areas outside the reach of existing village nuclei to the third main current method of land development, namely middle-class colonization? This would, of course, enormously reduce cost to the Government. But there is no doubt that such a method would be impracticable. It seems certain that insufficient middle-class persons with adequate capital would come forward. In any case, existing middle-class schemes have not for the most part proved very satisfactory; much land in them remains undeveloped, and production is low.[1] And, of course, while middle-class colonization, where successful, absorbs labour, it does not help to solve the problem of peasant land hunger.

Is one, then, forced back to the conclusion that some sort of peasant colonization is inevitable? To accept this conclusion at this stage in the argument is to assume that the only methods of development open to the Government are those which it has mainly

[1] Cf. above, pp. 306–7.

used since the changes in land policy which followed the work of the Land Commission of 1926–9. This assumption is frequently made in Ceylon; but there are, of course, many possible methods of Dry Zone development in addition to peasant colonization, village expansion, and middle-class colonization. It is particularly important to consider three possibilities: capitalist farming, Co-operative farming, and collective farming.

3. *A more revolutionary approach to Dry Zone development: capitalist, collective, and Co-operative farming*

'Capitalist' land development in Ceylon is usually taken to mean development by a company, or by an individual too wealthy to be classed as a peasant or as a middle-class Ceylonese. Capitalist land is nearly always worked in large units—the plantations or estates which are so often set in contrast to peasant holdings in works on the tropics. Capitalist development was, of course, the method by which most of Ceylon's tea, rubber, and coconut estates were opened up. Some thinkers in Ceylon are now pointing out that great acreages of commercial crops were planted by capitalists before the era of the Land Development Ordinance with hardly any cost to the Government but to the enormous enrichment of the country's economy; and they are asking whether the volte-face of the Land Commission was not too violent, and whether, instead of the heavy concentration on the peasant, large blocks of the Dry Zone should not be alienated to capitalists to be worked in large units, possibly by machinery.

It must be emphasized that concentration on the peasant has not been absolute; but it has been very heavy, and there are very few examples of capitalist Dry Zone development in the Dry Zone proper (one example, the mechanized paddy farm of the Gal Oya Valley Food Production Company, has already been mentioned;[1] another is the large-scale venture in paddy cultivation run by Mr. Jayakoddy near Chilaw).[2] Any general change-over to capitalist methods of Dry Zone development would therefore be truly revolutionary, and may suitably be considered at this stage of the discussion.

The pros and cons of large-scale, as distinct from peasant,

[1] See above, p. 359.
[2] See Joint United Kingdom and Australian Mission on Rice Production in Ceylon, *Report*, pp. 5–6.

agriculture constitute a familiar argument and need not be re-capitulated, but a few points of particular relevance to Ceylon conditions may be made here. To consider the advantages first, there is the obvious point that Government would be spared much of the heavy burden of capital expenditure now poured out in colonization schemes (though it would still, presumably, have to install irrigation and communications). Further, capitalist development would provide the economic stimulus to efficiency which is lacking in the case of peasant colonization; a man who, through enterprise, thrift, and efficient cultivation of his village or colony holding, acquires wealth which he wishes to invest in land development cannot do so in a colonization scheme or, if his income exceeds the limit, in a middle-class scheme; but an outlet for his capital, and a further stimulus to economic efficiency, would be provided by a system of alienation to 'capitalists' in the Ceylon sense; and this may be held to be important as a means of achieving maximum food production. It is again sometimes argued that the presence near a conventional colony of blocks alienated to large-scale farmers would help to provide employment for sons of colonists unable to inherit because of the rules of succession under the Land Development Ordinance; and that under the same scheme of things the large farmers would be an example to the peasants.[1] There is also the fact that capitalist agriculture is able to absorb some members of the urban unemployed, who cannot normally become colonists (unless they have served as labourers on a scheme) and who, with some villagers, are apt to work better as employees than as peasant proprietors. The impossibility of making everybody into a peasant colonist was, in fact, recognized by D. S. Senanayake.[2]

But there are also disadvantages in the development of the Dry Zone by capitalist methods. The mechanized techniques which, it is usually assumed, would be employed are virtually untried both as agronomic methods and as business propositions. Although wage labour would be absorbed, this is no solution to the problem of land hunger among many of the peasantry, and hence, and because of its counter-egalitarian tendency, capitalist development would be politically impossible as a thorough-going measure of reform. The social implications (notably the tendency to replace a peasantry by a class of landless labourers) give one pause to think.

[1] See ibid., p. 30.   [2] See *Agriculture and Patriotism*, pp. 95–97.

And, finally, there is the severe practical limitation that risk capital is so scarce in Ceylon and that, in particular, persons of substance are so unwilling to invest in land development or food farming in the Dry Zone; recent attempts to attract them have proved somewhat disappointing.[1] There are many reasons for this state of affairs, notably the failure of earlier capitalist ventures in the Dry Zone[2] and the general habits of Ceylonese capital,[3] and for the foreseeable future they are likely to prevail unless some sort of Development Corporation can take on the risk. Such a Corporation, or the state itself, might be a better means of undertaking the large-scale planning and novel technology involved in dry farming than the peasant or the Co-operative.

The virtual replacement of peasant colonization by capitalist agriculture is therefore likely to be impossible and, even if it were possible, undesirable. But one must bear capitalist development in mind as one way of dealing with the problem, a way which may suit some types of land (especially flat land suitable for mechanized cultivation) and some types of people (notably the capitalist who *is* willing to invest and whose enterprise is worth encouraging for economic reasons, and the labourer who is already landless and detached from his society and therefore not a case for preservation as a peasant).

Any widespread application of collective farming as a solution to Dry Zone development problems would, of course, be even more revolutionary than the widespread application of 'capitalist' farming. The latter has at least been the conventional solution at some periods and for some purposes in Ceylon; the former has never been applied at all (the war-time 'state farms' were merely farms operated by the Government, but employing wage labour and in all major respects behaving as 'capitalist' concerns). It is not surprising nevertheless that collective farming is sometimes suggested, not only by doctrinaire Marxists but also by others who have read of its working in the Russian *kolkhoz* or the Jewish *kibbutz*.

Dry Zone development by collectives might, of course, come about if Ceylon came under a Communist Government, whether by electoral victory, or by a revolution starting in the urban and coastal areas, or by a Communist triumph in South India, or in other circumstances which it is possible to envisage. In that case,

---

[1] See *ARLC.* 1954, p. 5 and Schedule C.
[2] See above, pp. 129–30.   [3] See above, p. 330.

there might eventually come about the collectivization of land at present held privately or from the Crown, and the establishment of new collectives as a means of Dry Zone colonization. There can be no doubt, however, that collectives would be extremely unpopular amongst the mass of the peasantry and of colonists, and would extend to Ceylon that war of 'Marx against the peasant' which has come about in most countries that have already fallen under Communist domination.[1] Collective farming could, in fact only be imposed by downright compulsion, and it might well be that even a Communist régime would at first not adopt the stock Marxist solution of agrarian problems.

Under other régimes wholesale collectivization and wholesale development by collectives is unthinkable. Ministers have, it is true, been known to talk of compulsion when particularly exasperated by large-scale squatting, or by some particularly irritating example of peasant resistance to the agronomic fad of the moment; and Ceylon, unfortunately, has lacked neither native-born administrators nor visiting 'experts' who have concluded that the peasant is so stupid and so backward that he must be made to mend his ways by rigorous compulsion. But for the most part the degree of compulsion which would be involved in collectivization is repugnant to the present régime in Ceylon; and any attempt to impose it would bring it short shrift at the polls in the countryside. Even if collectivization were imposed, experience elsewhere suggests that it is very unlikely that it would lead to increased efficiency of agriculture.

But there may be groups of young Marxists in urban and other areas who would like to try collective colonization. The author, as an empiricist, would certainly be willing to let them try out their method, given the essential prerequisite that they are at present likely to use their land wisely and efficiently. The example of groups in Israel who have been fired by the collective ideology would be before them.[2]

There is but a thin line of partition between voluntary collective farming of the sort just mentioned and Co-operative agriculture; if, indeed, there is a line at all. Co-operative agriculture is, of course, nowadays often recommended by agrarian experts, so much

---

[1] See David Mitrany, *Marx against the Peasant* (London, Weidenfeld & Nicolson, 1951).

[2] See, for example, Warriner, *Land and Poverty in the Middle East*, pp. 67–73.

so that it is part of current orthodoxy; some of its supporters draw their inspiration from Western socialism, some from the real or imagined communal village of their ancestors, some, notably in India, from both; others, the pragmatic school, see Co-operative cultivation as a means to the introduction of mechanization.[1] Is there any hope of introducing Co-operative colonies, peasant or otherwise, as an alternative to current methods of peasant colonization? There would be after all, a number of precedents: for example, Ceylon's own dry-farming colonies at Kurundankulama and Relapanawa, and the Co-operative colonies in Burma.[2]

It has, in fact, quite often been suggested that the solution to the problem of colonization lies along Co-operative lines, or at least that Co-operative colonization should be tried. Thus, as has already been mentioned, the original proposal for the ex-servicemen's colony in Parakrama Samudra scheme was on Co-operative lines. More recently, the Joint United Kingdom and Australian Rice Mission saw Co-operative farming as an alternative to large-scale farming which would also enable power cultivation to take place, and recommended that it should be tried in major schemes.[3]

But, as this book has suggested in other discussions of Co-operative methods, Co-operation demands a degree of spontaneity and of social cohesion; otherwise it is purely an imposed solution, in its way as much a measure of compulsion as collectivization. The failure of Co-operation where it is merely imposed, where there is no social group which naturally co-operates, and where 'everybody's property is nobody's concern' is borne out by the state of affairs in some sections at least of Ceylon's Co-operative dry-farming colonies.

In fact, the wholesale application of Co-operative tenure and Co-operative cultivation to land development in Ceylon would almost certainly be unsuccessful in the vast majority of cases. It would, moreover, neither satisfy the landless peasant, who wants individual title to a plot of land; nor would it tend to maximize production, for, in the absence of the right social basis, it would almost certainly be grossly inefficient. But, as in the case of collective farming, Co-operative methods should certainly be borne in

[1] See, for example, *Land Reform*, pp. 80–82.
[2] For the Burma colonies see *Co-operative Societies in Burma*, 1915–16 to 1920–1.
[3] See Joint United Kingdom and Australian Mission on Rice Production in Ceylon, *Report*, p. 29.

mind as one possibility, to be tried where a suitably cohesive and skilful group presents itself and where the mechanized cultivation made possible by Co-operative methods seems to offer advantages; the Co-operative group need not, of course, be confined to peasants. (It will be of interest to watch the progress of the Co-operative society which has very recently been formed among *landed* persons from Kotmale in order to farm some 500 acres in Gal Oya.)

One may conclude, then, that neither the large-scale capitalist method, nor the compulsory collective method, nor the Co-operative method, is likely to be a generally applicable solution to the problem of Dry Zone colonization. Each, on the other hand, offers possibilities under certain restricted conditions, as does large-scale development by the state or by public corporations.

4. *An eclectic solution*

Now earlier passages in this conclusion have suggested that what is true of capitalist, collective, Co-operative and 'state farm' methods is also true of modified village expansion and of middle-class colonization: all have potentialities in certain circumstances, none promise a universally applicable solution. In other words, if the Dry Zone is to be developed at all (and the argument of this conclusion suggests that it must be developed), then the answer may well lie in an eclectic solution, in which several different methods of agricultural development are tried. Several authorities have, in fact, suggested a diversified attack of one sort or another on Dry Zone development;[1] and, writing in more general terms, Sir Bernard Binns has said:

Perhaps the best foundation for rural progress may be an eclectic system of land tenure, in which there is something of everything: some small holdings, some medium-sized farms, some large farms, some really large estates, some co-operative farms; some landlords, some owner-cultivators, some tenants; some state-owned land, some common land and some private land. At least it is quite certain that no system of land tenure will support a sound and progressive agriculture which does not recognize the great variety that exists both in the land itself and in the capabilities of individual men to develop its resources.[1]

If such an eclectic solution to Dry Zone problems is adopted,

[1] See, for example, *WBR*, pp. 33–34 (i. 21), and Joint United Kingdom and Australian Mission on Rice Production in Ceylon, *Report*, pp. 29–30.
[2] INCIDI, *Rural Development*, p. 75.

should peasant colonization have a place alongside the other methods listed at the beginning of the previous paragraph? There are many reasons why it should; two of them are particularly cogent. In the first place, whatever future there may be for wage labour under other methods, peasant colonization alone is likely to make much impact on land hunger in those strongly peasant areas which are subject to agrarian pressures; it is therefore the only method which is politically realistic for such areas. In the second place, some peasant colonists at least are able to grow paddy efficiently on a sustained yield basis, and to earn a living by doing so; but it has yet to be proved that the same can be said of most alternative methods.

Future peasant colonization of the Dry Zone therefore appears to be necessary both for the relief of land hunger and for the production of staple foodstuffs. But, as has already been mentioned, these two aims are often, though not always incompatible. The landless are not necessarily inefficient;[1] but they are also not necessarily efficient. There has, in fact, been growing recognition of the possible incompatibility of the two aims, and any new formulation of colonization policy must attempt to remove the confusion of aims which has existed. There is also a further confusion, between the egalitarianism enforced by the Land Development Ordinance and the economic individualism which appears to be necessary if colonists are to become highly efficient producers.

The two categories of confusion would be removed if there were two distinct types of peasant colony. In one type the aim would be primarily the relief of landlessness and of land hunger in such undoubted black spots as Kotmale and other Kandyan valleys. Relatively small lots would be issued, and there would be no great expectation of high productivity; since, however, a proportion of landless colonists would undoubtedly turn out to be efficient, there should be an incentive to efficiency in the shape of a promise of extra land. The aim of the second type of colony would be frankly economic. The best cultivators would be chosen, and they would not necessarily be landless. They would be given economic incentives, particularly individual freehold tenure of part at least of their allotment, and the possibility of buying more land as they proved their efficiency and formed capital. In this way one would hope to encourage a dynamic element in rural society, an element

[1] Cf. *WBR*, p. 391 (ii. 175).

which, as Boeke complained and as this book has demonstrated, is lacking in conventional peasant colonies.[1] There are, of course, objections to the encouragement of economic individualism. Some peasants will rise, but others will fall. And those who rise will include the *boutique*-keeper and the *mudalāli*, those ogres of contemporary agrarian literature. But it is difficult to see how, in present circumstances, productivity can be sufficiently increased without encouraging individual enterprise. And the *boutique*-keeper and *mudalāli* are not entirely the parasites they are often made out to be. They provide credit and supplies for the peasant in circumstances unfavourable to Co-operation and other fashionable remedies; and they often appear as the only members of rural society who are capital-formers (it would be interesting in this connexion to know how much capital they have invested in Ceylon in rural bus and lorry services).

It is worth noting at this point that the recent East Africa Royal Commission has also proposed a solution to agrarian and economic problems in terms of economic individualism coupled with individual land tenure.[2] The Commission, however, recommended a high degree of fluidity in the application of this policy, local solutions being adapted to social needs even if not economically perfect.[3] For much the same reason, the author advocates two distinct types of peasant colony, each varied according to the land to be cultivated and the people to be settled.

Most of the conclusions of this book on peasant colonization within the existing framework can of course be applied, *mutatis mutandis*, to the proposed new dual framework. The author regards as particularly important his conclusions on land-potential survey, on the adaptation of colonization to local physical conditions, on water conservation both for irrigation and for high land development, on the need for a lower scale of aid and higher direct return to Government, on the grouping together of kinsfolk and neighbours, and on a reformed system of tenure which would give a greater incentive and be more practicable for the administrator.

It is not easy to decide how effort should be divided between the two proposed types of colony, for the decision is clearly not one that can be based solely on the likely economic return from two

[1] See Boeke, in *Amer. J. Soc.*, vol. lvii (1952), pp. 315–24, espec. p. 321.
[2] See *Report of the East Africa Royal Commission*, 1953–55, espec. pp. 290–3 and 346. [3] Ibid., p. 292.

alternative avenues for investment. At any one time the balance would depend on the Government's view of the relative importance of the relief of land hunger *per se*, and of sheer food production. On purely economic grounds, of course, it might be decided to concentrate entirely on the food-production colony; on social and political grounds, entirely on the maximum relief of land hunger— though in this connexion it must be remembered that because political stability depends partly on living standards, and because living standards depend mainly on productivity, the food-production colony also contributes to political stability.

Whatever the future framework of peasant colonization, and whatever other methods of opening up the Dry Zone are combined with peasant colonization, one thing is clear: the keynotes of Dry Zone agrarian policy should now be experiment and flexibility; experiment because, in spite of all the experience of the last few decades in Ceylon and in spite of all that has been done elsewhere, one cannot be sure of the results of any one line of action; flexibility because note must be taken of the results of experiments and because Ceylon is a country of marked regional differences in its physical conditions and in its societies, so that different solutions are necessary in different situations. One would, in fact, like to see an era of experiment with the eclectic solution just suggested. Ceylon has here a great potential contribution to make to Asian agrarian development.

GLOSSARY

akkarai-karaya (Sinh.): one who cultivates land bought from the Crown (*akkarai* is a corruption of the unfamiliar 'acres' in which the land is measured).

akkarai-vel (Sinh.): the field so bought.

amuna (Sinh.): (1) a measure of rice; (2) an irrigation dam.

ande (Sinh.): share-cropping system of land tenure.

anicut: a dam or weir to direct water into a channel.

bethma (Sinh.): custom whereby only part of the village paddy fields are cultivated in drought; see text, p. 45.

bhikkhu (Sinh.): a Buddhist priest.

bissa (Sinh.): basket, erected on poles, for storage of paddy.

bund: the dam of a tank or reservoir, or the earthen ridge between paddy fields.

cadjan: material woven from coconut fronds and used for building purposes, &c.

chena: patch cultivated by shifting cultivation (from Sinhalese *hēna*).

damana (Sinh.): dry park country of grass and stunted trees.

deniya (Sinh.): valley suitable for paddy cultivation.

dissawe (*disāva*) (Sinh.): provincial governor under Sinhalese kings; now honorific title.

ela (*äla*) (Sinh.): irrigation channel, brook.

elvī (Sinh.): hill or 'dry' (rain-fed) rice.

gama (Sinh.): village (roughly speaking).

gamarāla (Sinh.): person of status in a village.

gangoda (*gamgoda*) (Sinh.): site of village, especially in Dry Zone; see text, pp. 46–47.

gansabhā (*gamsabāya*): traditional village council.

goigama (*goyigama*) (Sinh.): cultivator caste.

goya (*goyiya*) (Sinh.): cultivator caste.

hēna (Sinh.): see *chena*.

high land: dry or unirrigable land, as distinct from paddy, wet or mud land.

illuk (Sinh.): the grass *Imperata cylindrica*; see text, p. 32.

isohyet: line joining places with equal rainfall (mean annual, &c.).

isopleth: line joining places with equal quantities of something.

kāchchān (Tam.): literally 'south-west wind'; used in Batticaloa District especially of dry, searing wind during south-west monsoon.

kachcheri: offices of Revenue Officers.

kampong (Malay): village.

katurumurungā (Sinh.): variety of *murungā*, q.v.

kōralé (Sinh.): an administrative division.

kulam(a) (Tam.): an irrigation tank.

kumbura (Sinh.): a paddy field.

Land Kachcheri: court or board assembled to allot parcels of Crown land, &c.

Lankā (Sinh.): Ceylon.

little monsoon: period of variable rains between north-east and south-west monsoons.

maha (Sinh.): great, the period of paddy cultivation during the north-east monsoon.

meda (*mäda*) (Sinh.): middle; the period of paddy cultivation between *maha* and *yala* (q.v.).

mudalāli (Sinh.): a merchant.

murungā (Sinh.): tree (*Moringa pterygosperma*) yielding edible pods known to Europeans as 'drum-sticks'.

oya (Sinh.): a river.

palāta (Sinh.): an administrative division.

patana (Sinh.): Up-country grassland, especially characteristic of Uva.

perahera (Sinh.): a procession.

pirith (Sinh.): chanting of Buddhist texts in Pali.

pōya (Sinh.): full moon day.

purāna (Sinh.): old, ancient, often with overtones associated with 'ancestral'; 'old' village as distinct from new village, road-side bazaar or colony.

rājakāriya (Sinh.): services to the king; services due on account of tenure of land.

rata (Sinh.): country, district, as in *Rāja Rata* (the king's country, Nuwarakalawiya) and *Uda Rata* (of which 'Up-country' is a literal translation).

ratamahatmaya (Sinh.): chief headman, official formerly in charge of administrative areas now under Divisional Revenue Officers.

ryot: Indian peasant.

samudra(ya) (Sinh.): sea, ocean.

talāwa (Sinh.): grassland intermixed with trees, savana.

tattumāru (Sinh.): tenure in undivided shares (see text, p. 57).

ukas (Sinh.): traditional form of mortgage.

vel vidāne (Sinh.): elected irrigation headman.

villu (*vila*) (Sinh.): pond, swamp (especially marginal to the Mahaweli Ganga in Tamankaduwa).

wadiya (Sinh.): temporary hut of *cadjan* (q.v.).

watte (Sinh.): garden.

wet land: irrigable land suitable for paddy.

wewa, wawe, wiya (*väva*) (Sinh.): an irrigation tank.

yal hulunga (Sinh.): the wind that blows during *yala*, q.v.

yala: little, the period of paddy cultivation during the south-west monsoon.

yāya (Sinh.): tract of paddy land.

yoda, yodi (*yōdhha*) *ela* (*äla*) (Sinh.): major irrigation channel.

INDEX

Abdul Samad, A., 347 n. 1.
Abeyaratne, E. F. L., 26 n. 1, 34 n. 4, 344–5, 347.
Abeyawardena, D. F., 172 n. 2.
Abraham, M. C., 191 n. 2.
Africa, 47, 58, 110, 236, 313; East, 33–34, 373; South-east, 236.
Agrarian pressure, see Landlessness; Population pressure.
Agriculture: census of, 41; Department of, 144, 158, 343; extension work in, 139, 158; in colonization schemes, 241–59; plantation, see Estates; Royal Commission on (India), 37 n. 4, 52–55, 273; shifting, see Chena; techniques of, 38, 39, 40–41, 45–56, 81, 243–6. See also Irrigation works; Land; Paddy; Soil: erosion and fertility.
— and lands, Ministry of, 144–5, 147, 156, 229.
Ahmed, Kazi, 178 n. 4.
Alkalinity, 231, 234–5.
Allai: Colony, 147, 165, 208, 221, 224, 309, 317; Tank, 121.
Allotment, size of, 129.
Alluvium, 33–34, 35, 38, 39, 44, 50–51, 60, 186, 224.
Aluwihare, Sir Richard, 311–12.
Amban Ganga, 30, 186, 190.
Amparai, 227; Tank, 103, 105, 227.
Anacardium occidentale, see Cashew.
Ancient civilization of Ceylon, 10, 14–17, 20–21, 26, 43; its decay, 12, 13, 16–17, 21–22.
Andaman Islands, 179, 201, 280.
Andropogon sorghum, see Sorghum.
Animism, 31, 74.
Anopheles culicifacies, 20, 22.
Anthropologists, anthropology, 42, 284.
Anuradhapura, 10, 11, 15, 16, 25, 44, 49, 106, 107, 188, 190, 269, 283, 342, 343; District, 57–62 passim, 76, 209, 214, 217, 247.
Arabs, 8, 9, 308.
Aristocracy, Kandyan, see Bandāras.
Artocarpus integrifolia, see Jak.
Asia, 45, 46, 47, 92, 330, 337; Monsoon or South, 47, 49, 54, 236, 278, 280.
Attaragalla Colony, 147, 165, 208, 317.
Atukorala, S. W., 172 n. 2.
Australia, 236, 249 n. 1, 330, 331.

Badulla, 3, 107; District, 83–98 passim, 208–9.
Bailey, John, 104 n. 6.
Bailey, S. D., 46 n. 1, 104 n. 5.
Balasingham, K., 119 n. 3.
Balfour, J. A., 185 nn. 1 & 4.
Bandaranaike, S. W. R. D., 210 n. 2.
Bandāras, 73, 86, 304.
Banks, M. Y., 71 n. 1, 245 n. 3, 295, 296.
Bathmedilla Colony, 147, 165, 208, 226, 236, 248, 255, 256, 263, 264, 309, 312, 317, 336.
Batticaloa, 8, 9, 106, 122, 124, 270; District, 8, 60–66, 76, 89, 105, 202, 209, 215; Lagoon, 33, 224; Region, 8–10, 18, 33, 35, 44, 50–52, 60, 64, 66, 105, 113.
Belgian Congo, 346.
Bell, H. C. P., 75 n. 1.
Beragama, 134, 146; Colony, 147, 156, 164–5, 208–9, 246, 251, 256, 261, 264, 265, 274, 300, 302–3; Malay Colony, 125, 134–5, 147, 148, 164–6, 208–9, 224, 245, 246, 251, 256, 261, 263, 264, 265, 268, 296, 310.
Beri, S. G., 327 nn. 1 & 2.
Bethma, 45–46, 71, 185, 232.
Bhakra-Nangal project, 186.
Bibile, 51, 251.
Binns, Sir B. O., 371.
Bintenne: Division, 66 n. 1; region, 12–13, 22, 43, 44, 51, 56, 96, 164, 216, 236.
Birch, J. W., 103 n. 2.
Blunt, Sir Edward, 69 n. 4.
Bocks, S. J., 28 n. 4.
Boeke, J. H., 180 n. 5, 282 n. 1, 293 n. 4, 320, 373.
Bombay Deccan, 55.
Bonné, A., 272 n. 2.
Borassus flabellifer, see Palmyra.
Borneo, North, 181.
Bowman, Isaiah, 177 n. 2.
Brayne, C. V., 124–5, 130, 137, 145, 148.
Brayne, F. L., 123–4, 282 n. 1.
Bribery and corruption, 305, 310.
British Overseas Food Corporation, 238.
British, the, 6, 8, 9, 17, 95, 101; and evolution of colonization policy, 101–39, 284.

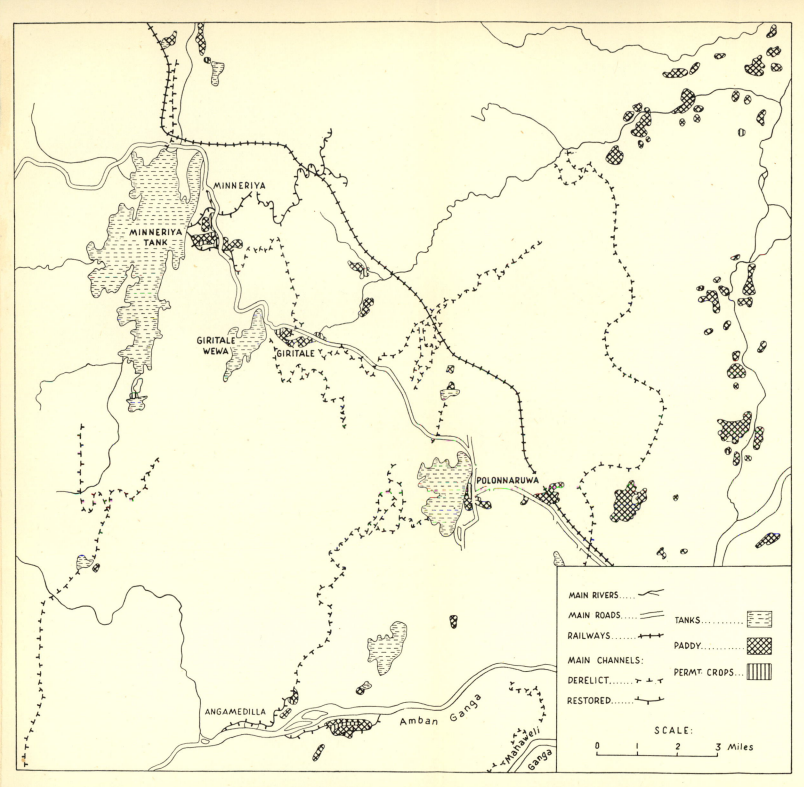

MAP 7. THE MINNERIYA-
POLONNARUWA   AREA
BEFORE COLONIZATION
(c. 1930).

MINNERIYA

MINNERIYA
TANK

GIRITALE
WEWA

GIRITALE

POLONNARUWA

ANGAMEDILLA

Amban Ganga

Mahaweli
Ganga

MAIN RIVERS.....

MAIN ROADS.....   TANKS...........

RAILWAYS.......   PADDY...........

MAIN CHANNELS:

DERELICT.......   PERMᵗ CROPS...

RESTORED.......

SCALE:

0   1   2   3 Miles

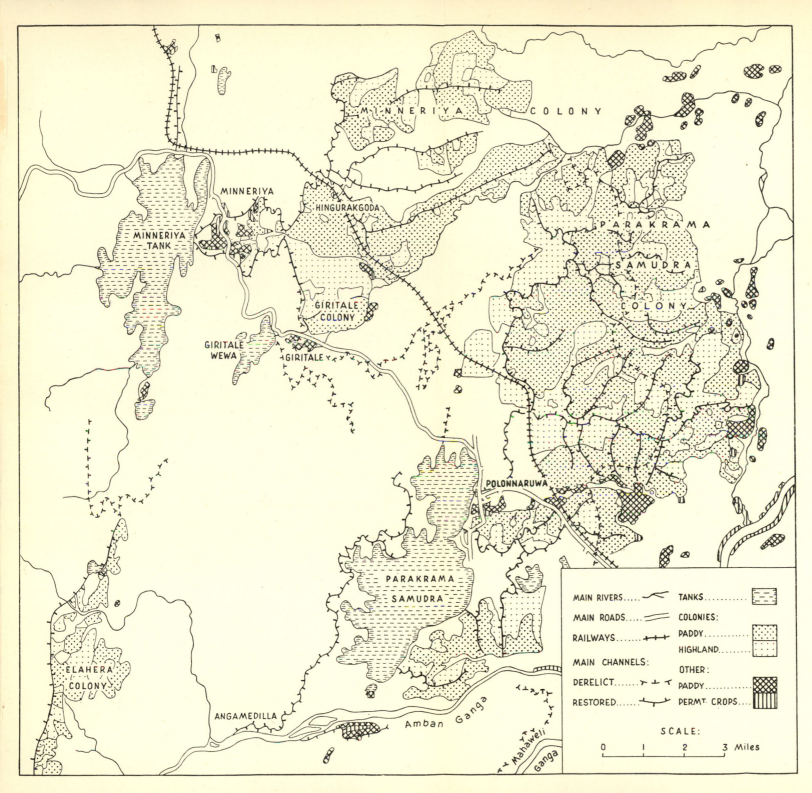

MAP 8. THE MINNERIYA-
POLONNARUWA AREA
AFTER COLONIZATION
(1951).

An area to the north-east of Parakrama Samudra Colony remained to be
colonized, and there was a possibility
of further development between Giritale and Polonnaruwa, and north of
Minneriya Colony.

MINNERIYA COLONY

MINNERIYA

HINGURAKGODA

PARAKRAMA

MINNERIYA
TANK

SAMUDRA

GIRITALE
COLONY

COLONY

GIRITALE
WEWA

GIRITALE

POLONNARUWA

PARAKRAMA
SAMUDRA

ELAHERA
COLONY

ANGAMEDILLA

Amban Ganga

Mahaweli
Ganga

MAIN RIVERS.....	TANKS...........	
MAIN ROADS.....	COLONIES:	
RAILWAYS........	PADDY...........	
	HIGHLAND........	
MAIN CHANNELS:	OTHER:	
DERELICT........	PADDY...........	
RESTORED.......	PERMT. CROPS....	

SCALE:

0   1   2   3 Miles